Taking On the World

TAKING ON THE WORLD

A Sailor's Extraordinary Solo

Race Around the Globe

✦ELLEN MacARTHUR ✦

International Marine / McGraw-Hill
Camden, Maine • New York • Chicago • San Francisco • Lisbon
London • Madrid • Mexico City • Milan • New Delhi • San Juan
Seoul • Singapore • Sydney • Toronto

The *McGraw-Hill* Companies

1 2 3 4 5 6 7 8 9 0 DOC DOC 0 9 8 7 6 5 4 3

LIBRARY OF CONGRESS CATALOGING-IN-PUBLICATION DATA
MacArthur, Ellen.
    Taking on the world : a sailor's extraordinary solo race around the globe / Ellen MacArthur.
        p.   cm.
    ISBN 0-07-138227-5 (pbk. : alk. paper)
    1. MacArthur, Ellen. 2. Women sailors—Great Britain—Biography.
3. Vendee Globe (Yacht race). 4. Sailing, Single-handed. 5. Voyages around the world. I. Title.
    GV810.92.M33 A3 2003
    796.1'24'092—dc21   2002152866

Drawings on chapter-opening pages and photo on page ii by Ellen MacArthur. Maps copyright © 2000 by John Gilkes. The publisher would like to thank the following photographers, organizations, and collections for their permission to reproduce images in this book: MacArthur Archive 1, 2, 3, 4, 6, 7, 8, 10, 11, 42; Ken MacArthur 5, 76; Auntie Thea (Lewis) 9; Maureen King 12, 13; News International 14; Ellen MacArthur 15, 16, 20, 21, 22, 24, 25, 26, 28, 30, 36, 58, 59, 60, 61, 62, 63, 64, 65, 66, 67; Graham Percy 17, 18, 23; Carol & Derek Jones 19; Alan Wynne-Thomas 27; Peter Bentley 32; Thierry Martinez 33, 43, 44, 50, 52, 54, 77, 79, 80, 87; Liam Dryden 35; Marie-Pierre Tricart 37, 38, 74; Jon Nash 39; Marten Yachts 40; Rick Tomlinson 45, 56; Jason Kerr Yacht Design 48; Jacques Vapillion 49, 55, 81; Kingfisher Challenges 51; Pat Ashworth 73; Marie Cairo 53; Offshore Challenges 57; Michael Birot 72; Conseil General de la Vendée 75; Yvan Zedda 82; BBC Picture Archives 83; CEDM Visual Media, University of Derby 84; Penquin U.K. 86. Every attempt has been made to contact permission holders for the following images: 29, 31, 34, 41, 46, 47, 68, 69, 70, 71, 78, 85

Contents

Photographs appear following page 210

PREFACE

I HAVE WANTED to write a book for as long as I can remember, although when the time appeared right, the process was far harder than I could ever have imagined. As a shy six-year-old, I won a writing competition on *Jackanory*, and when interviewed by the local paper, I apparently said, "Don't make it too long, just a few pages of your exercise book will do!"

If only I had taken my own advice!

The reality of a naturally active person locking herself in a room to make a deadline has been a massive test in itself—never did I think that I would be able to spend three days in a house without leaving its walls.

I can only apologize for the fact that the book did not come out last year, the winter after the finish of the Vendée Globe, but I can't help but feel that it is a more complete story as a result of the extra year. In 2001, my life went upside down—with pressures from many directions—and it's been important for me to look back on it and reflect. Writing this account as seen through my eyes has been tough, but it has forced me to take time to try to understand everything that happened.

This book has been written and edited in the oddest of places—from the back of a car to departure lounges, at home and in hotel rooms. The long-lost depths of the loft have been explored for photos, and I think I may have visited some of the darkest recesses of my soul to transfer my experiences and memories as clearly as possible onto these pages. On the subject of pages, I must thank from the bottom of my heart Rowland White, who must be the most patient and tolerant editor in the world.

Without him, this book would have needed to be published in at least two volumes!

I have included some early transcribed logs, correspondence, and more recent e-mails sent from the ocean in their original form, so you will find spelling mistakes or typing errors which are often a measure of the degree of roughness at sea at the time! *(In a few such instances we have added clarifying words in brackets.——Editor)* I have assumed basic sailing knowledge in the text, but for those of you who have not yet experienced the feeling of the water beneath you, there is a glossary at the back.

The hardest part of writing has been the sheer number of people and experiences that we have had to leave out. The original text has been reduced by half, which has made it difficult to thank all those who have played such important roles in my life—from the time I began sailing up to our present projects. That is why there is such a mammoth set of acknowledgments at the end of the book!

But this book would not have been possible without the belief of lots of people over the years. So many have made such a big difference to our projects and have made them what they are so far—from Jim in Hamble, Lindsey who made *Kingfisher's* beautiful tillers, BT for sponsoring years of communication, allowing us to share our races with millions, to the French boy with his "THANK YOU ELLEN" banner at my Vendée arrival—though much of the sailing I have done so far has been single-handed, I have not been alone. Mark Turner, in particular, and the extraordinary team around me really have made that difference: from those who prepared the boats for their voyages to those who, hidden away in the office, communicated the story, and without whom this would have been a *much* shorter story—if it could have been written at all.

I cannot finish this introduction, though, without thanking Kingfisher PLC. People often say ". . . and I would like to thank my sponsors," but I really mean it. Offshore racing as we know it simply would not exist without sponsorship. Kingfisher believed in us back in 1998 when we walked into their boardroom with a plan and more passion and energy than you could imagine. In a pivotal year, when for us it was make or break, they made it!

When I was a kid, I was inspired by books, and I would lose myself in a world of my own, huddled in a corner of the school library. One of my favourites was *Gipsy Moth Circles the World* by Sir Francis Chichester, published in 1967. When I visited my old school library just a couple of years ago, I found that same book. The library card tucked in its cover still bore the name Ellen MacArthur several times—but there were no other names after mine, and only one before!

I always try to give my all to any project that I undertake, and this book has been no exception. I have not tried to write a sailing book, nor a book about the Vendée Globe,* but more simply a book about my life. I just hope that you enjoy it.

---

* In chapter 16, which covers the Vendée Globe, the e-mail logs sent back by Ellen start with the log code of "ellenmacarthur.com/dayX." If you look up these links (e.g., www.ellenmacarthur.com/day4) on the web, you will find a complete day-by-day account of the Vendée Globe, including weather charts, positions of the race boats, full accounts of the race situation, photos taken during the race, and a complete collection of Ellen's logs, impossible to print in their entirety in this book.

Round Britain 1995

Pacific
Ocean

Indian
Ocean

Southern   Ocean

Day 32

Day 50

International Date Line

80°N

60°N

40°N

20°N

0°

20°S

40°S

60°S

30°E   60°E   90°E   120°E   165°E   180°E

1 August 1995

Dearest Ellen,

Mum told me you had read recently a book by another young girl about sailing, and were overawed and convinced you could never write one as good. Of course you could.

Nobody wants to read a book which is almost a replica of someone else's. What they would be interested in, is how it feels to a young teenager in a very tiny home-worked-on boat, to venture out around a coast she's never touched before, having to make friends as she goes. Don't use sentences everyone else has always used. Surely at your age, spurred only by your own ambition, everything is different to you from the norm. Recapture the feeling—of loneliness—of occasional panic—of irritation.

The thing to do is GET WRITING. Concentrate on that, and not on producing perfection. Get it written, then leave it to mature in a desk or drawer. Get it out and read it again in a month's or two months' time. You will see its faults then, its badly written bits, its boredoms. GET WRITING. . . .

Best of luck,
Love,
Nan

PROLOGUE

"I'M NOT THERE YET, we haven't crossed the line yet."

I spoke in French into the satellite phone as I struggled to answer too many questions. "It's not over till it's over" went through my mind. I was acutely aware that *Kingfisher* and I had not finished the race. Please, I thought, please leave us alone to concentrate on getting over that line.

Outside, the fog was closing in, though the sea had remained calm. I was worried that I would hit someone or something over the last few hectic miles of the race. We simply had to finish safely; I had already seen what a fragile existence we were living out there. More often than not the land is a boat's greatest threat, and it was land we were approaching. The first support boat that had come out to meet us was already almost out of sight, though only a few yards ahead, disappearing in the thickening fog.

I had felt torn over the last days of the race. Problems with the forestay had posed a constant risk of losing the mast—a massively stressful development. But despite this, I wasn't sure I wanted to finish. Part of me quite definitely wanted to stay out there forever.

The fog rolling in as the light faded felt like a sign, as if we weren't meant ever to see the finish. It was as if the end were never meant to come, or as if we might be able to pop across the line and slip back out again silently under cover of the blanket of mist. I thought back to my very first transatlantic crossing, in which our first landfall after leaving America was Les Sables d'Olonne. Alone on deck then, seeing the

1

shoreline for the first time, I'd wanted to turn back, imagining that the other side of the ocean would never come.

Five years later, I had that same feeling.

Within the fog it was eerie. I could hear other boats around me, but all I could see through the grey density were the few square metres of dull water around us. The suspense gripped me. Small waves began to build as the wind increased, bringing a damp chill into the late evening air. My heart beat faster as, with our growing motion, my fears for the mast returned. I set about reefing the sail, reducing its area to lessen the strain. Moving through the darkness, I worried about a collision while I was busy concentrating on the sail. The support boat was out of sight now, blanketed in the fog, and I was worried she would lose me completely. With the reef in, I was happier; although we were slower, at least we were safer. The ends of races are never easy, so why should the Vendée Globe be any different?

I popped below to the cabin to check our distance from the coastline; we were heading right for the shore, and it was time to tack. Back on deck, I looked up and could begin to pick out a few lights around me. As the seconds passed, the fog began to lift, and I could see lights distinctly for the first time. My little world evaporated. I suddenly felt I'd been dropped into a Hollywood film set—there couldn't have been a greater contrast between the silence of the fog and the thousands of lights now surrounding me. Boats of all sizes were heading towards us, and helicopters hovered above with searchlights sweeping as if looking to pinpoint an escaping prisoner. The noise dominated the moment—whenever the sound of the rotors drifted away on the wind, it was replaced by the radio chattering out information on our position and speed. I stood in the cockpit, took a few long, deep, and calming breaths and looked up and around to try to take in the situation. It was breathtaking.

As the boats moved close around us, the water felt confused—a choppy, fidgety motion I hadn't felt in months. I could hear voices coming from the radio—some in English, some in French, some of strangers, some of people I knew. I thought I heard the name of the boat that my parents had come out on at the start of the race. I knew they were near, I could sense it, but my world was blinded by the blazing searchlights. I had my own floodlight ready on board and tried pointing it at several of the large motor cruisers to see if I could spot Mum and Dad. No luck, just many waving figures and rolling cameras.

I had the photocopy of the finish line configuration that was given to all the skippers at the briefing before the race. I had put it in the waterproof folder, hoping then that the day would come when we could use it to find our way in. Everything seemed so different from our departure—even the lighthouses on the harbour breakwaters were lost in this artificial brightness.

I ran up and down *Kingfisher*'s deck, making final checks as we glided towards the finish line. I could see every part of the boat, so there was no need for a head torch. I stood by the shrouds, squinting to catch sight of the *Nouch Sud* buoy that helped signal the finish, but it was impossible. I returned to the chart table to study the chart. We needed to tack again.

I talked on the radio to the support boats, asking them to warn others that we were about to turn. I had to make sure of enough space in the crowds so I could turn *Kingfisher* safely. I dashed below a couple of times to use the main VHF radio when the hand-held's battery had gone flat. Although we were clearly not alone, it seemed so much quieter inside the boat. I tried to believe that the finish was not imminent, that I was just sheltering inside from a rough sea—still in the same world I'd been in for so long—but I couldn't. Our sole objective for more than ninety days had been to cross the line as quickly as possible, and now it was less than a mile away. We'd sailed 26,000 miles, but I wished we still had 26,000 more to go.

As I peered into the cockpit of each boat, I could see people—people I knew, faces I had not seen for more than three months, tearful but smiling. Everyone hung on every second of every minute as we neared the finish.

Although I still wasn't ready for the race to end, I was desperate to see everyone again and to cross the line before we had more problems. Our focus on getting here had been so intense that it was hard to see to the other side of it. I had been through the experiences in my head a million times, but at the end of it all, something somewhere inside me knew that everything was going to change.

Things began to happen more quickly. The RIB carrying our support team was now almost alongside us. The flashing white light of the buoy marking one end of the finish line was getting closer, and its enormous black-and-yellow superstructure materialized ahead of me. For a brief moment there seemed to be complete silence. I looked around *Kingfisher* for one final check that everything was still OK. As my eyes refocused on the buoy, there was a deafening crack . . . the gun had fired. At 1936 and 40 seconds on 11 February 2001, we had crossed the finish line.

Adrenalin surged through me. The RIB pulled alongside us, its passengers jumping aboard like a raiding party, and as the horns blew and the voices screamed, I was embraced and wrapped up in loving arms—my first human contact for more than three months.

Strangely, there were no tears—just the most incredible feeling of relief. As if a plug had been pulled, my concentration ebbed away in the time it takes for a gun to fire. No longer did I need to sleep for just ten minutes to recover, no longer did I need to look at the instruments each time I blinked. It was over, the race was over, and if it weren't for the adrenalin I'm sure I would have collapsed. We had made it. Together, *Kingfisher* and I had made it.

The whole team was soon on board and getting to work. As we pointed towards the harbour entrance, I tried to say that the course was 055, but my voice was drowned out by the noise. Alain Gautier, a member of the *Kingfisher* team and himself a veteran of the Vendée Globe, came on board. Placing his hands on my shoulders, he looked straight into my eyes—he understood. Then he handed me a rucksack like a radio pack connected to a pair of headphones. For the next hour I was interviewed live on at least two TV stations, but I found it difficult to concentrate, my first priority still being to get *Kingfisher* into the harbour. Alain asked what I had learnt about myself and how I had changed during the race. I tried to explain. But he knew, he had already been through this. We had lived through extraordinary and dangerous situations out there, and I reflected on how much people can endure. But while it's tough, it's still our choice, and in that way we are very, very lucky.

Without warning, the mainsail dropped as we approached the entrance to the harbour channel. I reacted without thinking, before checking myself—for the first time in months, *Kingfisher* was out of my hands. I wanted to talk to the guys sailing her in, I wanted to be with them, but as we neared the breakwater more and more boats closed in. Once in the channel, I could have walked from one side of the harbour to the other across the boats. It was euphoric mayhem.

People were cheering, waving, and calling my name. Through the smoke from the flares I could see whole families, people old and young on the edge of the harbour walls and along the water's edge. In the distance I could see thousands of people hanging over their balconies. I'd never seen so many smiles at one time. Overwhelmed by the welcome, I could only smile back, from ear to ear. I tried to smile for every single face in that crowd as we slowly crept up the channel.

I was handed a pair of distress flares, which I banged on the deck to light. The heat was intense and the fumes filled the air. Through the red light of the flares I could see even more, and I made out individual figures. "THANK YOU ELLEN" was written on a piece of wallpaper held up by a boy and his mother—he was standing on tiptoe, trying to lift his message high in the hope that we would see it. People were waving flags and flares, scarves and torches. I felt every person in that crowd had been with us and that everyone was sharing in the moment. It seemed as if I was enjoying a party, not a celebration laid on especially for *Kingfisher* and me. I was smiling and cheering *with* the people.

The contrast from being completely alone to being surrounded by 250,000 people within a matter of hours could not have been greater. It was such an intense situation that it was almost too much to bear. I wanted to jump high in the air to thank everyone. The last time I had passed these harbour walls was when we set off for the start. I remembered the nerves, the reality of the situation, and the concentration of trying to focus on the race that was about to start. Although I had to believe we would finish the race, I was aware of the dangers to come. Every one of the twenty-four boats crossed that start line with the hope of finishing. I found it difficult to comprehend that of all of those, I was just the *second* to make it. As I thought of what we'd been through together, I dropped to my knees and kissed *Kingfisher*'s cold deck, the two flares still burning bright and hot in my hands.

As the flares burnt themselves out, I began to see the faces around the boat more clearly. Through the constant barrage of camera flashes I looked ahead, and there, in a small RIB, was Michel Desjoyeaux, the Frenchman who had crossed the same line just over twenty-four hours earlier to win the race. I walked to *Kingfisher*'s bow and swung over her pulpit to climb below her bowsprit. In the shadow of the bow I could only see Mich's eyes as he approached; not a single communication had passed between our two boats while we'd been out there, but we had shared so much. Mich knew that too. We hugged briefly, then he was gone.

There was still another surprise awaiting me in the channel: Friends had brought *Iduna* to Les Sables d'Olonne. She was my first "real" boat, bought with school dinner money saved over eight years. She had been laid up in Mum and Dad's garden for the last three years, and I was stunned by the thoughtfulness of the gesture. At a little over 20 feet long, she was tiny, and as I looked down into her cockpit from *Kingfisher*'s enormous bow, it just emphasized how much life had changed over the last three years.

Seconds out from the pontoon we had left on the start day, Mum and Dad came on board for the first time, their faces showing sheer happiness and relief. Dad walked across and held out his arms, and as they closed around me, the length of time I'd been away was suddenly apparent. Mum hugged me too, and as I wrapped my arms around both of them, she kissed me on my forehead . . . now I was home.

As *Kingfisher* finally approached the pontoon, I felt like a child awaiting an exam. All I could see were the hundreds of journalists, their lenses and microphones pointing directly at me. When we touched the dock moments later, I was standing completely alone.

I talked, but I couldn't concentrate. The situation felt unreal. How could it be me talking to these people? Questions were asked, and I remember saying that it felt "too much, both doing the race and being here right now." Someone passed me an enormous champagne bottle, and I stood there with my knees shaking. If ever there was a time when I had to look like I could open one, it was now! The whole world must have been watching us . . . I shook the bottle and the cork exploded out above the heads of the crowd. As champagne sprayed into the air, it sank in: we'd done it, we'd finished second in the Vendée Globe! *Kingfisher* and I had been out there for ninety-four days and we had done it together. I simply felt like her pilot—we had worked together but she, and she alone, had, at the end of the day, carried me home.

I was asked what had been the best and worst moments of the race. I replied, "The best moment is right now, and the worst moment will be in five minutes' time when I have to leave and I don't want to get off." I was dreading it.

Mark Turner, without whom we'd never have come this far, walked towards me, and I saw by the look on his face that it was time to leave *Kingfisher*. I felt a knot in my stomach and wanted to run away, I wanted to turn back time, somehow to pinch myself to wake up and be back out there again. But I knew that was not possible—my time was up now.

Tears welled uncontrollably in my eyes, and I could feel a pain burning inside me. I felt numb as Mark's arm touched my shoulder, and involuntarily my feet began to walk me to her bow to climb off. Like in a nightmare, my feet wouldn't do as they were told. I wanted to stop and stay put. I knew I wasn't ready to go.

I turned away from Mark and slipped out from beneath his arm, the tears blurring my vision. I was oblivious to the noise and the hundreds of flashing cameras. How could I leave *Kingfisher*? How could I walk away? Our trip was over, and I knew deep down inside that things never could or would be the same again.

I walked blindly to the cockpit. Never before in my life had I wanted to disappear like this. I stood facing *Kingfisher*'s bow and closed my eyes, my forehead pushing hard against her coach-roof. We needed time alone. I wanted to say thank you, I wanted her to know how sorry I was that it was all over, that I would have to leave her. Those few minutes felt like hours as I thought harder about one single thing than ever before in my life. Sadness felt so different from exhaustion. This was a pain in my heart, whereas before pain had only run through every bone in my body.

The last three months felt like forever, and I could not remember what life had been like before the race. My feelings were coming out, their rawness impossible to hide. I was about to leave my friend, and it was breaking my heart.

Deep down, I knew that I could not have done more to look after her. As I stood with my head bowed, I could only say my last thank-you as I heard the noise of the crowds once again. Just the fact that I was alive and standing with her was evidence enough to me that she had done her level best to look after me too.

Until this moment, the finish had felt like a dream—the thousands of people, the yells from the crowds, and the bright lights continuously shining. But now those images were blurred and distorted by the pain. I clenched my teeth and tore myself away.

I cannot remember those final steps to *Kingfisher*'s side, but as I climbed over her guard wires for the first time in more than three months, I felt as if I was leaving a very large part of me behind. As I jumped onto the pontoon, I held her wires tightly, then laid my head against her. My eyes were closed as I reached out to stroke her hull. Her rounded gunwale felt cool and calming, and for one last moment, the world closed off.

Then I heard the gentle words, "Come on, Ellen," as an arm slipped around me, and as I turned to leave, my hand slid silently away from *Kingfisher*. Our Vendée Globe was over.

CHAPTER ONE

I WAS CLEARLY a stubborn child from the word go. I was not in the mood to come out, so Mum had to be induced three weeks after my expected arrival date.

I was very lucky with where I was brought up. Our house near Whatstandwell was in the heart of rural Derbyshire. We lived on a smallholding which had been growing slowly over the years, shed by shed and fence by fence, as Dad worked in his spare time filling our small field. The house was away from main roads, surrounded by farm tracks, fields, and footpaths which scattered across the hills and woods as they disappeared into the distance.

The rattle of tractors and the mooing of cattle were more common than the sounds of cars and people, and we were always surrounded with things to do, whether it was converting an old motorized lawn-mower into a ride-behind, or building a flying fox from the massive sycamore tree. We would generally amuse ourselves outside and were never without a project underway.

While I was young Mum was at home most of the time. She had left her job as a teacher to take maternity leave, though as I grew up she started working again as a home tutor. Dad was a teacher, as he had always wanted to be even as a small child, and taught craft design and technology.

Dad is a bit of a collector of tools and old machinery. What most people would consider junk, he treasured—but junk or not, it needed to be housed somewhere. In and around the duck yard were sheds of varying shapes and sizes, which sprang up year by year as I grew older. We had a small field next to the yard, and once the bull had been removed by a local farmer, the field became an outlet for our energy—an amazing playground.

I was fascinated by spy and survival books, and I spent hours crawling around like a commando in the long grass, which came well above my waist as a small child. I can still vividly remember seeing the stalks waving gently above my head, dancing in the breeze as I lay on my back staring up at the sky and dreaming of being marooned on a faraway, hidden island.

As a kid I was full of imagination. I would play for hours with a few bits of cardboard, a pair of scissors, and cellophane tape, happily muttering away to myself as I worked alone on the kitchen floor. Failing that, I could spend happy hours swinging from the table edge, hanging on by my fingertips—just because it was there. I could not sit still.

I was always headstrong. From the age of three, I was sent to ballet classes in an attempt to straighten my pigeon-toed feet. I hated it. Dancing round a room in a leotard just wasn't my idea of fun. It got to the point where I was so frustrated that one day I lay back in the car seat and simply said, "Mum, I'd rather be dead than go to ballet." Although I was only four years old, I think Mum understood that I really did hate it and had made my mind up, though I suppose I should grudgingly thank her for making me stay long enough to straighten out my feet!

When I was four, my younger brother Fergus was born. Mum was worried at my initial lack of interest in him, so when I asked if I could carry him into the house when they came back from hospital, she let me. Unfortunately, I tripped and fell at the doorstep with the tiny Fergus in my arms. I immediately burst out crying, joined by Ferg once he'd bounced on the floor. Then Mum came rushing in, crying too. I was clearly lacking doll skills! And I'm not sure Ferg has ever really forgiven me.

The extended MacArthur family all lived within walking distance of each other and therefore spent a good deal of time together. The villages in Derbyshire tend to be quite insular, so for most of the years of my childhood, our life revolved around the local area.

Nan was Mum's mother and lived alone. Gran and Grandpa were Dad's parents and lived with Great-Granddad, Gran's father. Gran still lives in the house where she brought up my dad and his brother, Glyn. There were sheds and fields there, too, and a big orange Jersey cow that we kept for the family's milk. I remember sitting on Grandpa's knee on the old wooden three-legged stool, milking the cow, and then riding her in the field afterwards. Grandpa was a gentle, patient man who was very fond of his family. He was a stonemason by trade, working from home in his workshop down the yard behind the house, which was bristling with tools, saws, and machinery. While he worked I would spend hours in there, amusing myself by cutting and fiddling around with small chunks of local grit stone. Afterwards, he would head inside to the cozy kitchen for orange squash and biscuits. If we were lucky, we'd also get a slice of Gran's fantastic sausage and egg pie, before settling down to listen to the football results with Great-Granddad.

We'd often play hide-and-seek in the yard, go climbing and build dens in the hay barn, or go on "expeditions" in the attic. Grandpa was very keen on cricket, and on a fine day we'd play a game together on the long, flat lawn which had been hand-laid years earlier by Great-Granddad. He loved being outdoors and was an enthusiastic gardener, tending his vegetables with great care and joy and delighting in his brightly coloured sweet peas. He had an incredible affinity for nature, and as a child I was immensely impressed that he had a pet robin that often came and sat on his spade. I would spend hours sitting with him and talking about his life in the coal mines, not realizing what danger he'd been in back then. He talked of the canaries they took down with them to warn of gas, and he told me the names of every single one of his pit ponies, which he continued to reel off faultlessly at the age of ninety-three. There was a strange connection between Great-Granddad and me; somehow, even with a good eighty-five years between us, we were soulmates.

He had always maintained that he did not want us children to see him if he became very ill in his old age, and suddenly after he had a stroke, we just did not see him any more. Mum told me that he was very ill, but I didn't understand what a stroke was, and when she told me that he wasn't eating, I felt sure that if I went over to their house I could make him eat. When he died I was sure my heart was broken.

Nan lived across the valley in a small cottage which was also where Mum and Dad first lived together. Lewis, my elder brother, spent the first few years of his life there too, before they moved across the valley to the family house where Fergus and I were also brought up.

I will always have the fondest memories of Nan—especially of going for long walks in the Dales with her wearing her woolly marmalade-

coloured hat. From childhood she had a passion for learning, and her enthusiasm was rewarded when she won a scholarship to go to university.
Tragically, her father forbade her to study further and forced her to go
out to work as soon as she was old enough. She dutifully followed his
wishes and worked as a secretary after taking evening classes in short-
hand and typing. By the age of sixteen she was providing for the family.
But fate intervened again when her husband died young. She was forced
to stop pursuing her dream and worked ridiculously long hours to support Mum and her sisters, determined that each of them would have the
chance to go to university.

We were lucky that Mum and Dad were at home with us during the
school holidays, which we generally spent as a family. In this close environment we did most things for ourselves. A great deal of our food was
grown in the garden after Dad had fenced off and cultivated an area of
the field. He would always try to do all the car repairs and services himself, and our early holidays were generally in the caravan, bought when
Mum and Dad sold the little Fiat car which Mum won in a competition.

Family walks would last for hours and hours in any weather. We'd pick
bilberries in the summer on the moors, have snowball fights in the winter down the farm tracks, play hide-and-seek in the enormous rhodo-
dendrons, and learn from Dad how to sharpen our penknives on loose
bits of stone.

As a result of our father's love of machinery and antique engines, we
frequented the Crich Extravaganza each summer, taking along our
Wolseley stationary engine and the little caravan. Dad loved these
events, and as children we revelled in the chance to ride on the massive
steam-powered, coal-fired traction engines, or feel the beating of the
fairground generator steam engines, which were run and looked after by
friends of Dad's. I always thoroughly enjoyed being around the engines,
getting covered in coal dust, oil, and soot. The atmosphere was fantastic,
with a real commotion when the engines moved around the grounds.
The whistles would blow, breaking out above the gentle but constant
throb of the moving pistons. Dad would spend hours chatting to his
friends about threshing machines and old tools as the smoke and steam
from the engines billowed up into the blue sky.

All of this could not have been further removed from the sea.
Nonetheless, the sea was an interest that showed itself early on.

CHAPTER TWO

In 1980, Lewis went down to the East Coast to sail on *Cabaret*, my Auntie Thea's boat. I couldn't understand why I wasn't going as well, and Mum's explanation that I was too young did nothing to console me. I was only four.

We saw Lew and Nan off on the train at Derby station and then Mum took me to the Derby Playhouse to see a puppet show called *Button Moon*. I was miserable. How could a puppet show ever take the place of an adventure of a lifetime? As I thought about what Lewis was doing, I sulked until he returned.

He came back full of his trip, having loved every second of it. I think he might even have regretted being so enthusiastic, as I would not leave him alone, bombarding him with questions to find out something new about his experience, whether it was the weather, the number of sails *Cabaret* had, or a detailed description of the interior of the boat.

My day came less than a year later. It was Easter, and for the first time I went with Nan and Lewis to see *Cabaret*. I remember nothing of the journey down to London other than intense excitement. I would not relax in any way, shape, or form till I had laid eyes on *Cabaret*. I had dreamt of this moment for more than six months.

I'd been told we were heading for Paglesham, and I had no idea what to expect. The word meant nothing to me—I was just dying to see the water. Face pressed against the cold glass of the window, I found the journey endless. Buildings turned to trees, then to miles and miles of

13

long, thick, waving grass on the flat, marshy estuary. The land seemed to
go on forever, all the time ebbing away. Was this always the way to the
sea, I wondered.

As I GAZED OUT onto the river for the first time, the water was calm and
muddy, with weed floating here and there. Lewis and I were hanging
over the edges of the dinghy, looking at the boats on the river while Auntie Thea tried to answer my stream of questions. I just couldn't take it all
in. I spotted *Cabaret* as she sat on her mooring, and she was the most
beautiful boat I had ever seen. She could, I was sure at that moment, take
us anywhere in the world.

I was ready to burst as the little dinghy pulled alongside. Before we'd
even tied on I was clambering up over *Cabaret*'s tall, white topsides, trying to get under the guard wires and on board. The thought of climbing
over the guard wire (the correct way of doing things) was beyond me.
The result was that, forgetting the size of my life jacket, I got jammed
beneath the wires. My head was on the deck and my feet were waving
out over the water!

Once on board Auntie Thea unlocked the solid-looking wooden
doors. I was right next to her, and as they opened I peered down into the
deep, dark cabin. There was a smell of engines and timber, like Dad's
garage, and the cabin seemed to smile at me. From that moment on,
Cabaret felt like our little home.

Our first night on board was like a dream. I was tremendously excited
as I lay there listening to the gentle lapping of the water on the hull. I
could hear birds calling in the distance, and I was so eager to get on with
our adventures that I could hardly sleep. My world felt alive, and tomorrow we were going out to sea.

We went completely out of sight of land, and for the first time in my
life I felt totally free. It would not have surprised me if I'd asked Auntie
Thea if we could stay out at sea all week. I was hooked.

I became completely besotted with sailing and began to save every extra
penny for a boat. Everything went into a money box which sat on my bedroom radiator for ten years. Above the radiator on a piece of graph paper
was a hand-drawn box of 100 squares, and each time I made it to a pound I
would drop it in and tick a square. Once the 100 were ticked I would
proudly ask Mum to pop the money into my savings account for me.

I would spend hours poring over *Practical Boat Owner* magazine, which Auntie Thea subscribed to, and writing letters to companies in search of their latest brochures. I filed each one in order of the size of dinghy. I also began collecting sailing books avidly. I kicked off my sailing library at a very young age with Arthur Ransome's *Swallows and Amazons* series. Mum and Nan had both been keen readers of these books and had passed them on to me.

I loved the spirit of adventure the books brought me, and I dreamed of sailing on a lake to a secret island that had long been forgotten. I would spend hours and hours imagining what the secret harbour would look like, and how the firewood could be collected for the campfire. I dreamt of exploring at night with small hurricane lanterns, and of spending nights moored in a protected bay or beneath trees at the side of the water.

FEW CHILDREN from the junior school in Wirksworth, our nearest main town, will remember me for anything other than being the girl who loved boats. I would draw a tiny Optimist dinghy on everything from pencil cases and erasers to exercise books—you name it, it had a boat on it!

I made three very good friends at junior school—Ben, Sarah, and Simon. (Simon would become my boyfriend seven years later.) I was a bit of a tomboy, I guess, preferring to play with a good sharp knife and a block of wood than with makeup and dolls.

But Sarah was a bit of a loner too. She'd moved to our school from another one in Belper, and now she lived across the valley from us and shared the same school bus. Though not as interested in the outdoors as I was, she was, and still is, incredibly patient with my love for the sea. We would spend hours "sailing" around the school playground, pretending that the circles and squares painted on the concrete were islands and secret harbours. Poor girl!

I became friends with Simon when I was eight or nine years old. He'd just moved up to Derbyshire from Felixstowe on the Suffolk coast, and he had sailed before. That was enough. On discovering we shared the same passion, we got on instantly. I can still remember the excitement of our first conversation.

Along with Simon and Ben I'd climb and rappel, play at being a commando, go on expeditions, and build dens in secluded woodland. Only more recently have I come to realize how lucky I was to be able to go out into the country and create a whole world of adventure.

I worked hard at school, though I did tend to spend every minute of my free time reading still more about boats and the sea. Or I'd sit on the bus or in a corner at break-time with nothing more than a notepad and my imagination, designing possible new fittings to put on boats. The sky was the limit, but to make these dreams real I needed a boat.

For the time being, this meant *Cabaret* for a week each summer. And she was certainly no gin palace. Thea had bought her as a wreck and done her up herself. With seven people, and later a dog, on a boat designed for four, it was snug!

Cabaret was kept in a small boatyard at the end of a long, bumpy track. The main building was made of blackened weathered boards with the words "J. W. SHUTTLEWOOD" painted in white on a battered sign. This was a long way from being a marina. There were no floating pontoons to tie alongside, no fancy shower or toilet blocks, just mooring buoys scattered along the centre of the winding river. Creeks and gulleys crept inland from along the water's edge. I used to spend time looking out at the water, mesmerized by the movement around the buoys in the river, or dreaming of the adventures to be had aboard the rows of tiny dinghies lying in the marsh grass.

At just 26 feet, *Cabaret* was a small boat. Her cabin was dark and deep, with a magnificent glow of varnished mahogany from her woodwork. She was not a beamy boat, so her cabin was narrow, and it was quite difficult for two people to pass each other below. Peering down into the cabin, you could see the tiny two-burner galley on the left and the chart table on the right. There were four adult bunks, two running underneath the cockpit and one on each side of the main cabin. Beyond that was a door leading to the triangular forepeak where, along with the anchor and sails, we three children were stowed. I took the port side, Fergus the starboard, and Lewis, being the oldest and tallest, got the longest berth down the centre, above the toilet.

Nan was always the first to rise in the morning, with a thirst for her wake-up cup of tea. She was always slightly out of her depth in the galley, as she found the kerosene stove confusing to use. We'd usually wake soon after she did—to the sound of her cries as flames billowed up against the cabin roof.

For the first few years, we cruised the local rivers around the East Coast, visiting such new places as Brightlingsea and Walton-on-the-Naze, the evocative setting for one of the Arthur Ransome stories, before becoming more adventurous and heading across the North Sea to visit Holland, France, and Belgium.

On our first crossing, Fergus and I were allowed to stay up long enough to see "the galloper," which was a buoy moored near the coast, as we approached our home waters once again. After dark, we saw phosphorescence for the first time—*Cabaret*'s bow wave churned up plankton that responded by looking like a thousand stars twinkling in the water, before disappearing into the blackness behind us. I tried to take home the phosphorescence in a jam jar, but it died, no longer shining when disturbed. I began to realize that the beauty of the water can't be taken away or captured. It can only properly be appreciated at first hand. I was also struck by the many sides of the sea's personality. An angry sea on one crossing can be as smooth as silk on another. I was fascinated by how all this was possible, and I was desperate to understand much more.

I sailed alone for the first time in the French shipping port of Dunkirk—on a sailing dinghy which Auntie Thea had bought to be towed by *Cabaret*. I felt a mixture of freedom, responsibility, and respect for the water—feelings which remain unchanged today. Each day that passed seemed to reinforce my love of the sea, and photographs from that time invariably show me in knee-length shorts with a royal blue peaked sailing hat and a little telescope, which hung around my neck for years—just like the one from *Swallows and Amazons*.

We encountered our first real storm on the way back across the North Sea. I recall that *Cabaret* was thrown around, but I also remember how solid she felt, and how much faith I had in her. I never felt scared in the storm, though I knew that something was going on in which we all had to be careful, hold on tight, and clip on with our safety harnesses.

Sailing through the night was something else that left a vivid impression on me the first time it happened. Several times we had left early in the morning and anchored as the sun set, but sailing through the sunset and then the sunrise the following day was a whole new adventure. There was a feeling of constancy and endlessness about this kind of sailing. Why should we stop, why do we need to pull into port each night, why can't we carry on farther? I had made my first open-sea passage, and I'd loved it.

Following our North Sea crossings we returned to UK waters and spent time cruising a little farther north and south from our Essex home port. The first year we headed north and sailed up the Deben and the Alde Rivers. We had the dinghy, so we children also were able to do a fair bit of sailing.

I was still desperate for my own boat, so when we headed south to sail on the Solent the following year, I decided to try to raise funds by singing in the street during Cowes Week.

While *Cabaret* sat at anchor in Chichester Harbour I perched on the deck in the evening mist, practicing sea shanties on my tin whistle. I can only apologize to everyone anchored in the same harbour, as most of the shanties were learnt through trial and error—mainly the latter! Once we made it round to Cowes I lost my nerve. I felt intimidated by the multicoloured spinnakers and matching crew shirts. Everyone there seemed so much older and seemed to belong. I couldn't see any other children with sailing hats and telescopes round their necks. Theirs was a type of sailing I really wasn't used to.

LEWIS ALSO ENJOYED sailing and started going to Ogston Reservoir with the school. I was still in the junior school and theoretically not old enough to take part, but I would go with Mum to collect him and wait in the car looking out at all the boats. Eventually I managed to talk to one of the supervisors, and I was lucky enough to be allowed to join in. I had found somewhere more local than the sea to sail.

But while I loved sailing there and learnt a great deal, I still dreamed of owning my own boat. I had in mind a tiny, varnished wooden dinghy with tan sails, though Auntie Thea was against it. She was sure that a fibreglass dinghy would hold its value better. The only problem was that a fibreglass boat was more expensive. I felt stuck, especially when I found an 8-foot fibreglass Blue Peter dinghy at a local boat sales yard a short drive from home. She cost £535, but I had saved barely £200.

It was Nan who came up trumps. She knew how much I longed for a boat, and how hard I'd been saving. At the same time, Lewis was trying to save for a BBC computer. Nan decided to give each of the three of us £300. It was a terrific amount of money, and I am still amazed at just what a generous gift this was, as it was a significant lump of her life savings.

After deep discussion I named my dinghy *Threep'ny Bit*, attaching to her hull the real thing—a coin found in the depths of one of our cupboards. I used to spend my days rigging her up in the garden, making little tents for her, and working out how I could camp on board.

My bedroom at home was tiny. If I stood in the middle and stretched out my arms I could almost reach both walls, but I was determined to keep all of *Threep'ny Bit*'s gear there. The lines, oars, and sails covered the whole floor, and I could see that the only option was to keep everything on the bed and move it when I needed to sleep. In the end, however, I came up with a simpler solution: one day when Mum and Dad went out, I took the bed apart and moved it to the barn. I slept in a sleeping-bag that I could roll up every morning, making my room feel as though it had more than doubled in size.

On one wall of my room I had a 5-foot-square map of a nearby trout pond. I'd walked there several times and was dying to get afloat on it. The owners of the pond couldn't have known how many of my dreams were realized when they told me I could keep *Threep'ny Bit* there. As she slipped into the water for the first time, the little wooden oars squeaked in her rowlocks and the water flowing beneath her bow made a bubbling sound.

Over the following months I spent many happy hours playing on the pond. I took *Threep'ny Bit* into the reeds, to hide from the savages. As I looked through my tiny telescope to spy on the moorhens going slowly about their business, I pretended that not a soul in the world could see us hidden away. I would land on the island and find perfect places to moor up, and the driest place to pitch a tent. I had the place for the campfire worked out so that I could hide the flames from anyone who tried to attack the island, and I chose the tree in which to hang the lantern to show any allies the way in. Behind the island were passages which were difficult to negotiate, with thick weed pushing its way to the surface, ready to catch unwary oars and leave them stranded in the weed beds till rescue came. There were fox tracks in the woods, and enormous holly bushes which opened out into tinder-dry palaces if you were brave enough to fight through the prickles. The pond occupied my thoughts and dreams day and night.

As my tenth birthday approached, I was just old enough to attend a dinghy-racing camp at Rutland Water, a large reservoir at least ten times the size of Ogston. This was a long way from Derbyshire, but as soon as I knew that I was old enough to go, I was determined to do so. The course was a week long, and I had asked for it as a birthday present from my family.

I learned a tremendous amount during that week. At ten I was one of the youngest of the sailors and a bit too small for the boat. This wasn't helped by the weather we encountered during the week. It blew at least a Force 6 each day but one. I found it incredibly difficult to keep the boat upright and capsized eleven times during the first day. I was so frustrated when I finished last or almost last in most races; I had imagined I would be able to get better results.

It was also the first time I'd been away from home by myself, and I was homesick. I didn't have a dinghy with new sails or the latest gear, so I didn't really fit in with the crowds from the sailing clubs. Instead of sailing in a wetsuit, I wore a navy-blue anorak and a tracksuit which I would try to dry each night over the dormitory radiator. It was the first time in my life I had felt lonely. I was surrounded by people, but I might as well have been a million miles from anyone.

On the journey home I decided I would never let that happen again. I wasn't going to be last, no matter what it took.

A short while later, in a race at Ogston, I crossed the finish line first against the club sailors. It was a very satisfying feeling that made all my efforts seem worthwhile.

MY SECONDARY SCHOOLING was at an old country comprehensive school with about 600 pupils. The Anthony Gell School was very independent in spirit. Half of it had been modernized, and the other half was fairly much the same as it had been when it was built in Victorian times. The old part had high-ceilinged classrooms with worn, varnished wooden floors, the original blackboards, and two beautiful globes suspended from the ceiling in one of the rooms.

The school library, the central feature of the old part of the school, had many rows of bookshelves. The shelves containing the sailing books were in the far corner, opposite a window and beside a radiator. One of my favourite pastimes at school was to sit in the library, especially in winter, with my back to the radiator, my legs crossed, and a sailing book on my lap.

The school was in Wirksworth, about fifteen minutes by car from home. It had been a lead-mining town before switching to quarrying limestone, although that, too, was dwindling. Bare rock faces still show beneath the high conveyor-belt viaducts crossing the valley, whilst the fourteen pubs and the rows of tiny terraced cottages are also indicative of the town's history.

In the first years of secondary school I became aware that the girls and the boys were moving apart. I remember not understanding why Ben's mates were no longer keen for me to hang around with them. I had a skateboard like them, I could even hold my own in arm wrestling, but things were definitely changing. At eleven I couldn't understand the reason for it. Ben was always friendly, but I could tell that his credibility among his friends was threatened if I was around.

For the time being, life outside school continued much as it always had, and Ben and I kept on exploring. Things were about to change for good, however, and for the best of reasons, when a girl from school phoned to tell me about some puppies which would have to be put to sleep if homes were not found for them. I'd always had a love of working sheepdogs, and at the age of thirteen, I became a child with a mission. I discussed it with Mum and Dad long into the night. There were phone-calls at midnight, promises made, tears shed. But the result was that I became the proud companion to one of my very best friends: Mac, a Border Collie mix.

Every evening on returning from school I would change into my scruffs, and Mac and I would head off into the fields. At the weekends we would often disappear for the whole day, exploring every nook and cranny within miles of the house. Ben also had a dog, Ruby, who got on famously with Mac, so the four of us went on den-making expeditions and fishing trips.

At home Mac became part of the family and blended in well with the menagerie that surrounded us. I would spend hours helping Dad with the chickens and nurturing chicks, which we kept warm in a cardboard box on the back of the kitchen stove until they were strong enough to live outside. I also had a special pet in Paddy, a pure white duck, who would follow me round wherever I went. He hatched from an incubated egg and considered me his closest family. I used to take him for swimming lessons on the pond with *Threep'ny Bit*.

It wasn't long before Mac went sailing too, joining us on our summer trips on *Cabaret*—which meant there were now eight of us on board! During that first summer with Mac, Sarah also joined us for a few days' sailing around Walton-on-the-Naze. This was the first time I had the chance to navigate and try to handle things on board. I loved the responsibility, and I was thrilled that Sarah enjoyed herself so much. If nothing else, it must have helped her make sense of my unstoppable ramblings about boats and the sea.

CHAPTER THREE

WHEN I WAS ABOUT FOURTEEN, my school organized a work-experience week. We could choose where to go, and I already had an idea in my head. Earlier in the year we'd had a careers convention, and I'd chatted to Simon Reeve, a local vet. He seemed to love his job, and I found this enormously appealing. I felt I could relate to animals, having grown up around them, and I felt comfortable working with them.

I contacted his surgery, and after a short wait they were able to take me on. It was a wonderful experience. I worked at the surgery and travelled round many of the local farms with Simon and the other vets in the practice. I loved it and made up my mind that I wanted to study veterinary science when I went to university. I was no genius at school, though, so I decided to continue my experience in with the vets, which I hoped would count for something in my university application.

One day when Simon returned to the surgery he threw down a plastic glove and asked me to take a look at what was inside. It was a very strange fur ball which wasn't quite what it seemed. On closer inspection, it looked like a long-haired guinea pig with no head, legs, or tail. It turned out to be a "thing" which was born alongside a calf. My task for the morning was to dissect it, pickle it, and place it in a jar for preservation.

After work that day, Simon was going into Chesterfield to look for a new car, and I went along too, as usual. We took the bottled thing with us and without thinking left it on the seat of his old car as it was taken off to be valued.

As we waited in the garage foyer I realized where I had left the jar, but before either of us could do anything, the man returned, with a pale green tinge to his complexion. Even after we'd explained that Simon was a vet, it took him a while to get over it.

During the time I was working with him, Simon took up ultralight flying, and not long after I had moved away from home, he sold his business and flew solo from the UK to Australia. Perhaps there's something in the Derbyshire water!

My spare time was still spent reading sailing books, designing bits for boats, or getting out into the countryside with Dad, going to farm sales. The sales were always different, never dull, and Dad's bearded face was well known. He rarely let a bargain slip through his fingers, so we'd end up coming home with anything from an old hay crib to half a mile of electric cable. Often the trailer would be full and, as Lewis once pointed out, "There's a lot comes up this drive, Mum, but not a lot goes down again!"

The faces of the other bidding farmers who returned time after time also became familiar. I developed a great respect for them all. More often than not farmers were selling out, which lent an air of sadness to the sales. Watching the proceedings taught me an appreciation of time and persistence. Much of what was on sale had taken generations to accumulate. To reach a point where nearly everything which held a value could disappear so quickly reinforced my appreciation of just how hard some people work for things. There was an unspoken closeness among these people. Without words, a sentiment could be exchanged, respect shown, and condolences given. This kind of mutual understanding was something I would experience for myself when I entered the world of single-handed sailing.

I DON'T KNOW WHY I resented being a girl when I was younger. It just seemed that what boys did was more fun. I wasn't cut out to play with dolls or gossip about boyfriends. Worn boots, numerous layers of old shirts, and a large knife hanging out of my back pocket showed that fashion was not a priority, either! All I wanted was to be out filling my time with something adventurous and constructive—something I was sure was more worthwhile.

At school I never really felt I fit well into a group. I was attracted to boys now and then, but never obsessed by them, although I do remember my first kiss, when I was fifteen, beside a phone box during a party of Ben's in Matlock.

I think a lack of confidence played a big part in this. I was always quite shy about showing my feelings and about the reaction that this might prompt. On the face of it, there seemed to me little difference between being a mate and being a girlfriend. I felt I needed to share a friendship with someone in order to have a relationship, which was not a view most of the people around me seemed to share.

I remember liking a guy who moved up to school from Leicester, though I never plucked up the courage to say anything to him. Once, in art class, one of his new friends, who was in my tutor group, turned to me as I walked past them and said, "God, you're ugly." From that time on I became quieter still.

Occasionally, perhaps for some special event, I would be persuaded to go down to the pub in Matlock. I rarely enjoyed the experience and had little enthusiasm for initiating conversation. I would never buy a drink and often took a yachting magazine with me. I didn't mean to be rude or to ignore people; I did it as a defence. Bizarrely, it helped me feel more comfortable. Part of me also felt that if I took a magazine I could at least make the most of the time there and come home having learnt something, rather than feeling that I had talked about nothing very much for a whole evening.

It must all have been very difficult for others to understand. They just didn't know what made me tick. Perhaps it's easier now that sailing has become my life. At the time, though, I can only imagine how weird my behaviour must have seemed.

I WAS NEVER particularly unhappy at school; I just felt like an observer rather than a participant. My social unease, however, wasn't helped by a growing unhappiness at home.

Dad had dreamed of being a teacher since he was a child, and early in his career, I think he really did like his job. Over the years, though, things had changed, and he found himself being ground down by a job he had once loved. He was promoted to Head of Year, with all the additional burdens that brings, and as a result was continually suffering from stress.

It was a time of cutbacks. Schools were closing and merging, and Derbyshire teachers had to reapply for their own jobs. There was a very real chance that our circumstances would change. I could see the anger in Dad's eyes; he appeared close to boiling-point when he came home late in the evenings. He seemed to vent his anger on me, maybe because I was the only one who didn't hide in a bedroom upstairs. I remember once going to his school to see a production of some sort—it was rather a special occasion, as it didn't happen often. More than any recollection of the production itself, I vividly remember how happy and positive Dad was with his colleagues. It had been a long time since I had seen him so jolly, and I could not understand why he couldn't be like that at home. I felt I was to blame, so I was nervous when he came home in the evenings. Sometimes during those explosions, I would run down the field to hide, climbing into a tree and squinting through reddened eyes at the tiny glow from the kitchen window to see whether Dad would try to find me. It felt unfair, but above all it was confusing. I could never have hated Dad for it, but the times were difficult for all of us, and each year I prayed things would get better.

There were always the good times together at the farm sales, however. On these occasions it was as if Dad was able, for a while, just to be himself again. We were like mates, discussing the machinery or weighing up whether or not a tractor was a bargain.

While my strained relationship with Dad allowed room for the hope that things would one day return to normal, the death of Grandpa had no such silver lining, and it hit me hard. I remember going to Gran's before the funeral service, feeling confused. I was distressed that Grandpa was still in the house: although I felt I wanted to say a last goodbye, I could not imagine what a dead person would look like, nor understand how I should react. I found it quite painful to see the whole family so upset, too, fighting back tears. For a brief moment I looked into the front room where Grandpa was, and although I could see little of his face, I saw his closed eyes and white skin. I was overwhelmed by the stillness in the room. The air seemed motionless, as if no person had entered for years.

Suddenly I became immensely claustrophobic, as though I had to get away—I could not stay in sight of people. I ran into the kitchen, then out of the house and down to the yard, where I knew I could hide. I felt people were watching me, but as I opened the tiny gate leading from the garden into the yard, I knew that I was safe and would be more than able to disappear. Time passed very slowly from that moment on. My vision seemed to go into slow motion as I stepped down into the workshop where Grandpa's stone, tools, and half-finished projects lay around me; the floor and windows, as always, were covered in cutting dust. The machinery was all there, ready for action, and Grandpa's old black cutting apron and gloves hung ready, just waiting for him to pick them up. I was suddenly hit by the reality that Grandpa would never be within the walls of his workshop again. I felt empty, as if the breath had been drawn from my body, and tears began to stream down my cheeks. For the first time in my life I felt the awful hollowness of losing someone close, and I faced the realization that a figure who had been there for me every day of my life was no longer physically present.

IT'S IMPOSSIBLE TO SAY now whether or not events were connected, but as we struggled with our family sadness, I began to develop an intense interest in boats with tiny cabins. I think independence was what attracted me, and these boats could be more easily lived on. They promised both comfort and escape. I found myself looking at every kind of tiny boat, trying to find the perfect one. I had attempted to be pragmatic about which type of boat would be best. I was still saving, and I could afford something in the region of £900 plus the money from *Threep'ny Bit*, which I had sold for £475. She had held her value just as Thea had predicted.

When I bought *Threep'ny Bit* I had worked out that it was going to take a lot more than birthday and Christmas money to save for a boat. The only other source of income that passed through my hands was school dinner money, and once I was at secondary school, this vital source of cash came under my control rather than being paid in at the beginning of each week. I started a new regime, which lasted until I finally left school. I would take a couple of slices of bread and a tomato or banana from the cupboard when I left home in the morning, then collect apples, plums, or pears from the garden on the way to the bus. I would eat the fruit for breakfast, then save the banana and bread for lunch. My other option during the fruitless winter months was to buy mashed potato and beans, which cost just 8 pence, then smother it with gravy, which was free. A special treat would be a jacketed potato and baked beans (24 pence), though that was a fairly rare occurrence! Every night, I would religiously pile up the coins on top of the money-box, still marking off a square each time I made it to £1.

By now, despite my imminent exams, I found it hard to concentrate on schoolwork. I'd sit in my bedroom with my books open, just staring at the Crich Stand Memorial, which flashed like a lighthouse through my window from the hill opposite. And when the son of a friend of Mum's from Norway came to stay I was easily distracted. Robert was very interested in boats, so we took a family trip to Nationwide Boat Sales. As a break from my studies I decided to go along. The truth is, it would have been hard to stop me!

While walking round the boat yard we spotted a man who appeared to be looking at the same type of boats as we were. Dad wandered over to say hello and discovered that he was actually thinking of selling a boat. It turned out that *Kestrel* was exactly what I was looking for. A few days later, she came home, towed behind our old Peugeot. I covered her in a tarpaulin in the field, forcing myself to leave her completely alone until I had finished my GCSE exams.

As soon as my exams were finished, *Kestrel* and I became inseparable. I was constantly ferreting around for old bits of mahogany in the barn, then cutting and sanding them to create the perfect modification.

I worked on *Kestrel* during the two summers I had her, building everything into her from a chart table to a bilge-pump-operated sink-drain system. I learned about fibreglass work and mixing resin, and I was regularly covered in bits of polyester and glass. Almost overnight all my clothes became covered in materials, but I was happy. I had launched myself into a teach-yourself boatbuilding course, and through trial and error, it seemed to be working. Dad would often arrive home late from school to find special projects going on in the garage. I think I pushed him close to despair!

The summers spent sailing *Kestrel* were fantastic. For the first time I really was in charge of my own ship, and it inspired me to push my boundaries further. I wanted to be close to those whose everyday lives revolved around the sea. After my first week on board *Kestrel*, we packed her away and were saying our goodbyes to Auntie Thea in the dark, about to drive back home. My eyes began to fill with tears, and either to hide my emotion or try to understand it, I ran off as fast as possible along the long dyke by the side of the river. I wanted to stay there forever, never leaving the sound of the pewits and seagulls for the drone of the motorway. This was special—there was something inside me that I felt sure no one else could understand. I stood still, wiping away the tears, and watched each of the little red and green navigation buoys flash away into the distance. I took long, deep breaths, calmed myself down, and told myself that it wouldn't be long till I was back.

With *Kestrel*, Mum and Dad saw me taking real responsibility for the first time. They saw how essential sailing had become to me, and it convinced them that it would be a good idea if I went to a sailing school to get some proper qualifications and instruction. I shall always be thankful to them for suggesting this, as working on *Kestrel* had left me with no money whatsoever. At age sixteen, in my first year of A-level study, I was acutely conscious that I would have to work very hard indeed to make the grades.

I searched through the back pages of yachting magazines to find a sailing school close to home. I rang a few but found it hard to make worthwhile comparisons. I wasn't sure exactly what I should be looking for, but the decision made itself when I first spoke to David King. He obviously knew his stuff, and his friendly attitude appealed immediately.

I TRAVELLED TO HULL not knowing what to expect, and I was very nervous as I walked up to David's yacht, *Alert*, to meet him for the first time.

"Who do we have here then?" he said as we shook hands. David was a small man with strong hands, a gentle smile, and a tanned, weathered face. I didn't know it then, but we were to become great friends. Choosing the David King Nautical School completely changed my life.

David's career began with the great shipping companies of the 1970s and 1980s. He had travelled the world during his years at sea and had been the captain of a cargo vessel when he decided to concentrate on sailing. I inundated him with questions, soaking up every tiny detail he mentioned. His knowledge and his ability to share it could not have been better. And for the first time I was studying a subject that I ravenously wanted to learn. The other guys on board *Alert* were great too. Sailing in the company of such like-minded, funny, friendly people, I had a powerful feeling that I couldn't have been happier anywhere else in the world.

The week ended all too soon. I was full of it, fizzing with enthusiasm like a birthday cake candle that can't be put out. On the unpromisingly grey-brown Humber, I had found a place where I was immensely happy.

As I packed away the last of my things for the trip home, Mum and Dad chatted to David, discussing the week's activities. Strangely enough, it was only recently that Dad told me what David said.

"I don't know where your daughter is going," he said, "but wherever it is, she'll go a long way on the water."

It's nice to think that this, in even the smallest way, prepared Mum and Dad for what was to come.

CHAPTER FOUR

MY CONFIDENCE WAS SKY-HIGH as a result of meeting David King. And just hours after getting home, we'd packed up *Kestrel* and were on our way to Paglesham. Every hour I'd spent sitting on the school bus, designing each tiny feature, and every moment spent working away in the barn, was about to pay off.

After we'd launched her, the plan was to sail in convoy with *Cabaret*. I spent most of the trip with Mum, both of us sleeping on board. All space was used to a maximum, with the compartments under both bunks serving as handy food-locker space. It was wonderful to spend some time with Mum and to feel at peace, away from the pressure of exams looming at school.

It couldn't last, though. I was back at school at the end of August and, as winter drew nearer, so did the "mocks" which were crucial for successful university applications. (Bizarrely, students trying for veterinary science need higher grades than those who want to pursue medicine.) I used to sit on my bedroom floor, with folders and textbooks everywhere, trying to cram photosynthesis or molecular structures into my head—often still battling at one or two o'clock in the morning. It didn't work, though. My mind wandered and I knew I was kidding myself. I'd be constantly distracted by the sailing books on the shelves and the newspaper cuttings tacked to the walls.

My thoughts frequently drifted back to the sailing course up on the Humber. Even months afterwards I often thought about that trip. I knew it had changed me. It would creep into my daydreams and conversations and provided a sense of quiet satisfaction. The effect on me of Dave King's encouragement was dramatic.

I began to be conscious of how precious time was, and I used every spare moment for thinking and planning. I would create situations in my mind and test myself—my brain always seemed to be preparing for the next project. For some, sitting in waiting rooms or on the school bus in the morning might have seemed boring, but for me it was free time, and it started the second the school bell rang.

I knew every course on offer at the Nautical School by heart, and I was back there again by October, this time for a three-weekend theory course. Dave had decided that I was of a standard to go straight on to the Yachtmaster shore-based course, skipping intermediate courses such as Competent Crew and Coastal Skipper.

As winter approached, Hull Marina was a grey place. The Nautical School was situated in the old lock-keeper's cottage next to the lock pit. For miles east and west on either side, there were docks and oil terminals. The whole city seemed to revolve around the shipping industry. Dave had fired my interest in all that occurred on the river, and I would spend every free moment standing by the window, my forehead pressed to the glass, absorbing everything.

Everyone on the course really wanted to learn. As a result, the atmosphere was quite different from school, but despite this, I was beginning to feel the strain. I knew that every bone in my body wanted to be in Hull, learning, yet I was obliged to go back to Derbyshire to study for my A-levels. I couldn't give up on Hull, though, and I was determined to try to cope. But I couldn't.

In the early darkness of the weeks leading up to Christmas, I'd run around outside with Mac after returning home from school. I'd chase her as fast as possible while she ran rings round me before the two of us would tumble to the ground. She always brought a smile to my face, but too often this turned to tears. I was exhausted and felt pulled in opposite directions. I'd swing from happiness to misery with frightening speed. I would lie on the ground and sob, often watching the dim lights in the kitchen but feeling so far away from home that I might as well have been on the moon. I wished I knew the solution, but I couldn't even figure out the problem.

The freedom of studying in Hull during the weekends and the weight I felt from the forthcoming exams seemed like black and white. So when my weekend course ended, I jumped to fill a vacancy in a VHF radio course that came up in November.

As far as I was aware, school, exams, and university were the only way ahead, and I struggled on, knowing in my heart of hearts that it wasn't right for me. Any alternative to the sensible, correct path forward was inconceivable. Moreover, by this stage Nan had not only attended our school, following her early desire to study, but was studying at Derby University for a degree in European languages. She had clearly decided that it was never too late, and if at the age of almost eighty she could pass exams first time, then surely I should be able to do so as well!

Although I hadn't expected glowing results, I certainly hadn't thought I'd be advised not even to apply for Veterinary School—yet that is what happened. My grades had not been entirely disastrous, but I felt embarrassed by my situation. Having worked for three years with Simon in his veterinary practice, I felt that even without the very strongest grades I should have a chance, but I took my teachers' advice and did not apply. Despite what the rest of the world thought I was capable of, however, I was going to do my damnedest to get those grades, and if it meant taking a year out and applying the following year, I would. I was determined to prove the system wrong and began to work harder than ever. My bedroom light was often still on at three in the morning as I pored over the pages of biology textbooks. I was determined to give it the best shot I could.

I REMEMBER quite clearly the day in the library when I knew I was getting some kind of illness. Something felt wrong inside, and the glands in my neck were swollen.

I talked to Mum about it, sitting on the floor in the front room, realizing that although I didn't feel too ill at the time, it was on its way. I don't know why I was so sure I was going to be ill, and it was a peculiar feeling. I wasn't scared, just worried about what I would be missing.

The following day I stayed at home while my temperature began to rise and the mononucleosis I had contracted began to take hold. It was a month before I set foot outside the front door again. The next four weeks were filled with headaches and sweating. I would stick to my bed,

waking up from a fever feeling trapped. I would try to count the minutes making up the hours that would bring morning.

Just standing up was hard, and I had to cling to the banister in order to
go up and down stairs to the loo during the daytime. I had been ill before, but never like this. Mum was fantastic. She was working part-time
as a home tutor but never failed to drive home between lessons to feed
me, usually a lunch of bread and home-made soup.

When she went out to teach I would lie on the settee in the cool back
room and stare out of the window for hours, just thinking. In the garden
at the front of the house was a large eucalyptus tree, which became the
focus of my attention, the pastel-green leaves dancing against the cool,
clear blue of the sky. I don't remember any dull days, though a month
could not have passed entirely without them. I would gaze outside and
worry, tormenting myself about recovering the energy to complete
those final weeks at school before the A-levels.

While I was ill the Whitbread Race was being shown on television. The
Whitbread sailors travel around the world in high-tech 60-foot racing
boats. It's run in legs, and there are about a dozen crew aboard each boat.
I had never been excited by crewed sailing. I thought the Whitbread represented the "macho" side of sailing, and I found it difficult to identify
with the sailors. The footage from the yachts rarely seemed to show any
form of sensitivity towards the sea. Despite this, it grabbed me. Here
were boats racing at sea, and back then it was a novelty to see any kind of
sailing on television. It was also the first time I became aware of the sponsorship side of sailing. The programme came on at about 2 o'clock every
morning and we'd tape it using the video recorder we'd borrowed from
Nan—she was away in Germany on a six-month student exchange.

I practically held my breath during the opening sequence; the sharp
editing, vivid images, and dynamic sound track got me every time. I saw
those guys out there, and all I wanted was to be on the ocean too.

Perversely, contracting mono was one of the best things that ever happened to me. For the first time in my life I was stopped in my tracks and
inevitably gave a lot of thought to what would follow. And I felt a new
sense of perspective. There are so many things we take for granted, especially our health, and I understood this for the first time. I realized
that life is for living, and that I had to grab it with both hands. It's easy to
say, "I'll do that later," but the chance may never come.

It was as if I needed to burst out. With a feeling of most intense energy and clarity, I suddenly realized that there was another way. In an instant my exam pressures evaporated. The world was out there, and beyond a shadow of doubt, I was ready to take it on. I became desperate to recover, but from then on my illness was somehow different. Frustration was replaced by hope, and that sustained me and, I'm sure, hastened my recovery. The sea was waiting . . .

Just before I recovered I endured my worst night. I was virtually delirious and stumbled into the bathroom, collapsing in the empty tub at about two in the morning. It was cool there, and it helped ease the fever a little. I've no idea how long I'd been lying there before Mum found me, but she washed me in cool water and stayed with me through the night.

A day or two later I somehow knew I was on the mend. I put on a loose pair of black jeans and a sweater of Dad's I'd adopted. My boyfriend Simon came round and we headed outside. The air felt crisp and fresh as it flowed into my lungs. It was still early, and I squinted in the morning sunlight.

We walked down the drive and began to head up the adjacent farm track. I felt so vital and alive. My legs were weak, but I ran back down the track towards the house feeling brand new. The sky was the limit. I was so grateful to be better, things were going to be OK from now on—I was determined to sail for my living. Knowing where I was heading was priceless.

Just days after my recovery, Mum and Fergus left for Germany to visit Nan, and I was able to persuade Dad to visit friends in Grimsby, just the other side of the Humber from Hull. I had been thinking a lot about the Nautical School, and those thoughts had helped pull me through. Just for the day, I worked on the school's boats to help get them ready for the season.

It was a cold, northern winter's day, with a freezing breeze from the north following a snowy depression. As I gazed out over Dave's shoulder at the estuary, the massive grey silhouette of the car freighter steamed into view, and the voices around me tuned out. I was studying the dim lights on the ship as it followed its careful path between the navigational buoys. I thought I could make out the bow thrusters' markings on the hull sides, and I tried to peer up at the control bridge. There, a small figure dressed in an orange boiler-suit was wandering near the crew's accommodation. I realized I was grinning.

The need to get back to the sea had been the best medicine I could have wished for. There was a new life waiting out there, and I was desperate for it to start immediately.

WHILE I HAD BEEN laid up at home I read sailing magazines. Although I found reading hard, I could manage small amounts of text. Looking through the back of a magazine, I spotted an advertisement put in by Nationwide Boat Sales, the yard where I'd first been introduced to *Kestrel*, and was excited to see a Corribee 21 for sale. I thought the Corribee was a fantastic boat, a big yacht with tiny dimensions, but definitely a real little "sea boat." Although reasonably priced, she was more than I could afford. But I kept turning back to the page. I decided I had to go see her, as she'd been a great aid to my recovery.

After my first visit I wrote in my sporadic diary: "There she was, stern towards me like a scruffy heap. Her rudder was askew and one of her backstays hung lifelessly beside her mast . . . the word 'Poole' shadowed into her faded and battered reddish topsides."

It was love at first sight.

I think I fell in love with her because she looked unloved—but more than that, she looked as though she'd achieved something. Her windows were strong, her forestay a massive stainless-steel wire which would not have broken on a boat of twice her size. The little patchy-red Corribee was not a run-of-the-mill boat, but a tough little lady, with real character.

The second time I visited the yard was with Simon. I was desperate to return to there, and he agreed to go with me on the two-hour bus journey. I was not fully fit yet, and the snowy conditions soaked into my bones, so I had to jump around like a fool just to keep warm. The bus driver must have been aware of my excitement, because he made an unscheduled stop right outside the yard gates to allow us off.

We immediately made for the spot where I'd last seen the scruffy little red boat. I touched her hull to remind myself that she was reality. There was hardly anyone around, so we found a spare viewing ladder and scrambled on board. The snow that covered her was speckled with dirt from a railway line nearby and made her look scruffier still. With my hands I began scraping the snow from her decks, and they were soon visible.

I'd spotted it before, but her decks were suffering from osmosis, a condition in which water penetrates the resin coating. It is treatable, but only with hard, time-consuming work. Inside there was a smell of damp and rotting wood. She had water in her bilges, and the floorboards were floating. On each side immediately below the hatch were the bunks, most of which slid behind us under the cockpit. Forward of them were work surfaces: on the port side the chart area, and on the starboard the galley. There was little in the way of electronics—just a couple of strip lights and an ancient-looking switch panel made of grey-painted steel. The small brass switches should have shone through use, but they were dirty and corroded. Her cabin was tiny, but perfect.

After studying every inch of her we wandered back down to the offices. Her sale price was £1,900 without the trailer—and my only asset was *Kestrel*. The outlook seemed bleak. I certainly could not buy her there on the spot, but there was still some hard bargaining to be done!

The office was warm and our faces glowed as we asked to speak to someone. A man was sitting at a large desk beneath the far window, and it turned out he was the one we needed to speak to. I was after a direct swap with *Kestrel*, which I felt was fair—having spent hours dreaming up reasons why this was so. After all, they would *never* sell the Corribee—no one wanted a two-berth boat with an unretractable keel so far away from the sea. *Kestrel*, on the other hand, was ideal, and I knew—though the neglected Corribee was bigger—that she was worth more. I stood my ground in the office but in the end opted to quit while we were slightly ahead, saying I would be back. I think Simon was shocked by how single-minded and terrier-like I was in there. I was on a mission—and I was not going to let go.

Rather than being disheartened, I was fired up. I talked at length with Mum and Dad about her, and they were happy for me to go ahead with things. I knew Dad was concerned about launching and storage, but between us we came to sensible decisions about what was realistic. I think both of them realized that this would be more than a hobby from now on.

Knowing Auntie Thea would share my enthusiasm, I phoned her to discuss the purchase. Half an hour later, though, I walked into the front room, devastated. Thea had fairly well trodden on my plans; she thought it would be a great mistake and said so. She felt I would be far too dependent on Mum and Dad, and she had no doubt that I was too immature to handle a boat like this. I'd not seen Thea since I'd recovered, but being ill had changed my outlook on life, and perhaps she didn't realize this. It still saddens me, though, that I was unable to share my passion with her.

So Mum drove me back to the yard to try again. I was pleased that Dad had stayed at home and let me do the bargaining myself. We passed by the boat to check that she hadn't been sold, then walked down to the office. I talked to the same man again, but this time I was not going to leave without a result. Twenty minutes later we walked out with a deal. He even threw in an engine and a jib, and he had not even seen *Kestrel*.

It took me three months to think of a name for the little red boat, but I settled on *Iduna*—the Norse goddess who held the apples of eternal youth. My plan was to give her a new lease on life—and keep her young forever.

I WAS NOW RETURNING to Hull to sail most weekends. Little by little, those weekends turned into long ones. By the time I had recovered from the mono, classes at school had finished, and I was supposed to be studying at home for the upcoming exams. But the determination to sail got the better of me, even as the exams approached. Although I had decided that I would sit them, my focus now was beyond them. I'd be going through the motions.

Every now and then Dave's wife, Maureen, would call me from Hull to let me know if there was a space free on one of the courses, allowing me to fill it for just a small charge. I would leap at the chance, often packing my gear on the hoof as I ran for the door to leave, sometimes even trying to squeeze in a course between exams. On one occasion I had been sailing for a week but had an exam the following afternoon in Wirksworth. We sailed all night returning from our last anchorage, and I loved it. The overland journey home was usually a nightmare, and on this occasion the combination of trains and buses got me to the exam room just seconds before everyone sat down. Normally I was nervous before exams, but now I just felt removed from it all.

During my first months of travelling to and from Hull, I was invited to sail on board a boat called *Panic Major*. Dave knew her owner, Robert Nickerson, and had asked him whether I could sail on her. I had been told that she was a Class 1 Open 60 racing yacht, and though I didn't know what that meant, just the sound of it made my eyes roll and my heart beat faster.

When I was on her for the first time, she thrilled me. Her deck stretched out fore and aft, with purposeful-looking ropes running in every direction. She was broad and sophisticated, with a powerful-looking mast twice the height of every other mast in the marina. She also had a history. Not only had she sailed to the Azores many times, she had competed in a French single-handed non-stop race around the world called the Vendée Globe. I was in awe.

I was shy as I met the crew for the first time. Robert was the easiest to get on with initially. He was a larger-than-life character, with a sense of humour that could have you rolling in the aisles or wanting to jump overboard. Brought up on his family estate, he had no sailing background. He had learnt to sail by sitting on the dockside till someone took him along. He was a doer, not a dreamer, and he had forged his own path through building and modifying boats. He often sailed in a flat cap and overalls, and rather than buy yachting waterproofs, he wore a bright orange, one-piece, waterproof boiler-suit-type garment. He was a man who could afford to do or have anything he wanted, but he chose simply to be himself.

Soon after our first sail on *Panic Major*, Robert asked me if I wanted to work for him. I would have worked for him for nothing if he'd asked. He had designed and built *Panic Major* himself, and I loved talking to him about her. His enthusiasm made him an inspiring teacher.

The long weekends began to turn into weeks, and soon I was only returning home every fortnight or so. On those visits I would talk feverishly about all that had been going on in Hull—everything from RAF helicopter rescue drills to what we'd had for lunch when anchored off Hawkins Point. Once I'd finished enthusing, I'd go outside to where *Iduna* was laid up and make plans for her.

Every weekend, Robert would come to the marina and we'd either take *Panic Major* out sailing or work on the list of things which needed to be repaired or changed. I learnt to splice rope and use tools that I'd never even seen before. I began to learn about electronics and the use of specific custom-designed parts. I dismantled the boom with Robert, learning the best way to effect repairs, either at sea or properly in port. Whether it was a new type of joint compound or advice on sailing her fast, I was loving it all and learning a lot.

One night after a crewed race in Bridlington, we anchored outside the harbour and, after a quick pint, said goodnight to the rest of the crew. I was up early in the morning at first light, woken by the gentle lapping beneath my bunk, and wandered out on deck barefoot. I heard Robert stir. Minutes later he appeared. We grabbed some breakfast, then he announced, "I'm going back to bed. You sail her back."

I would love to have seen my face at that moment, for it must have been a picture. Why the bloody hell was the fifty-five-year-old owner of this beautiful racing machine asking a kid barely through school to take responsibility for his pride and joy? I was speechless, and I climbed outside to recover.

It took me more than fifteen minutes to get the mainsail up, but I gritted my teeth and got on with it. Her mainsail needed at least eight people to carry it, so it was no mean feat getting it up that mast. I was determined not to be beaten by what I had to do. If one man had sailed her round the world alone, I sure as hell could make it 60 miles back to Hull. I felt hyperactive, but once the anchor was up and the headsail unfurled, we were off and I settled down. I put on the autopilot as we slipped along, then wandered around making sure everything was OK. I stood in the bows, checking for fishing pots, and looked back at her cockpit. For the first time in my life, no one was there. I could as well have been alone, and I loved it.

I felt very proud gliding into the locks as the evening drew in. I was on top of the world, and anyone would have thought I'd just sailed across the Atlantic. I am so grateful to Robert for giving me that opportunity. I can see now that he knew exactly what he was up to, and I wouldn't be at all surprised if he didn't sleep a wink during the trip.

The longer I stayed in Hull the more I learnt. I was moving on, and a casualty of this, sadly, was my relationship with Simon. We agreed to call it a day.

My hunger for knowledge was insatiable. I spent an increasing amount of time with David and his students, often filling any space during courses just to gain more practical knowledge. I learnt about instructing afloat and navigating in difficult tidal waters. We might head down to Skegness or Spurn Point, where we would anchor, then row the little inflatable dinghy ashore, or sail into Grimsby and moor in the old Number Three fish docks alongside the last of the trawlers. I loved Grimsby, and occasionally we would wander around the docks in the evenings, staring up at the enormous hulls of ships and fishing boats on the slips as they were lifted out for repairs. Old photos showed the same dock filled with fishing boats. It was almost impossible to imagine the atmosphere that would have prevailed here just decades before. Now only a handful were left—a sad reminder of what had been lost.

I also sat in on a few shore courses during the early part of the season before beginning teaching in a small way myself. I had never taught before—I'd only just finished being taught! Standing in front of a class of adults at the age of seventeen was new to me, but it must have been even more of a surprise for them. I was nervous to start with, but lucky to be in an environment where everyone was eager to learn.

Along with teaching there and working on the *Alert*, I started to camp out on the radio-room floor. I would wake to the sound of the fog signals from the jetties and buoys, and smile as their low moans guided ships to their berths by the banks of the river. I felt so close to the water, living and breathing the sea.

Just a few yards behind the school was one of the largest nightclubs in Hull. It amazed me to see the clubbers as I wandered back along the cobbled docks at night. It was generally fairly cold in Hull, and the howling winter winds from the North Sea were truly bitter. I couldn't decide if I was overdressed or they were underdressed as I compared my oilskins to their miniskirts and bare midriffs. I can't say I regretted missing out on all that. The condition of the streets and doorways on the morning after was enough to put anyone off. As the evening drew in the noise would start, the back wall thumping with the music. I didn't really notice it, though; I was usually so exhausted that I collapsed into my sleeping-bag.

I continued to work and race with Robert on *Panic Major* throughout the summer, juggling this with preparation for my Yachtmaster practical exam. After a short break sailing with Thea on *Cabaret*, I headed back to Hull. I needed 2,500 miles at sea in order to qualify for the exam, which back then seemed like a massive amount. I was very nervous, but Dave told me, "Just sail the boat, Ellen, you know what to do." He was right, and once I'd relaxed the exam went well and I passed. It was a major step forward for me, but it was just step one.

Talking through the future with Dave, I decided to bring *Iduna*, still in Derbyshire, to Hull. We worked out that I would be able to afford to put her in the shed for a while, and I could then get the major jobs done under cover.

Once *Iduna* was in Hull I could tackle the most important work which needed doing. It was the first time I had seen her close to the water, and it fired my imagination, driving me to spend all my spare time working on her. As a warm-up to the massive jobs that needed to be done, I went to work on the underwater portion of her hull. Despite the major work in treating the osmosis in the hull, I was soon to discover that the problems with the deck were far more serious. There, she had extensive osmosis where rainwater had collected in puddles and had in effect rotted into the grey gelcoat. She had been very badly laid up for a number of years, and the damage was severe. I also endeavoured to make her more seaworthy by fibreglassing in a smaller hatch for her and increasing the size of the cockpit drains. David was kind enough to lend me some of his tools, and I tackled the work with great optimism—though it was gruelling, I was happy doing it. I would often teach in the school by day before hurriedly changing to spend a few hours in the evening working on *Iduna*. I always seemed to be covered in resin, paint, and skin-aggravating fibreglass dust, and with the wet weather in Hull, the dust became embedded in my jeans and sweaters. Every day I'd scrub my arms clean with special blue gritty Swarfega and pick fibres out of the sink drain. But working on her still felt like the night before you go on holiday. I knew good things were just around the corner.

When I bought *Iduna* I hadn't known what I was going to do with her, and when I started working on her, my sole objective was to try to make her as seaworthy as possible. At one point I even considered, but then abandoned, the idea of taking her to Norway. Most of all, I just wanted to make her right. She was my dream boat, and I wanted her to be perfect. But after a great deal of work I ran out of money again and couldn't afford to keep her in the boat yard any more. Dave saved the day, persuading a friend of his to let me keep her in his field near Dave's house. Whenever I was free I would stay with Dave's wife, Maureen, and work on *Iduna*.

One day Maureen pulled me to one side and said that she and Dave needed a photo of me. Under a barrage of questions, the truth eventually came out. Unbeknown to me, she had nominated me for the BT/YJA Young Sailor of the Year award. I was astounded that they had even put me in for the award, and even more astounded that I'd actually won the regional title. I learnt soon afterwards that I'd made the "final three," and that the announcement of the winner would take place at the London Boat Show. Maureen and Dave's kindness was to make a massive difference to me.

When I headed back home for Christmas, my thoughts centred on preparations for going down to London for the awards ceremony at the beginning of January. Dave, Maureen, Mum, Dad, and Auntie Thea all came to the event. Thea was in a lot of pain at the time, as just days earlier she had slipped a disc. We didn't know then that the injury would lead to years of suffering. Despite her discomfort, though, Thea soldiered on, and I was really glad she came along.

On the day of the awards we had an early start filming footage for the evening's ceremony, before heading to the Serpentine in Hyde Park for photographs. At this point I was told that I had won, and I was speechless. More than this, I was having my picture taken with Sir Robin Knox-Johnston—the first man ever to sail non-stop around the world. He finished his voyage in 1970 after 313 days at sea, and my well-thumbed copy of his book, *A World of My Own*, was one of my most treasured possessions. This year, though, he had won Yachtsman of the Year for the second time—for breaking the Jules Verne record, the non-stop circumnavigation of the world in any boat, with any number of crew. He had co-skippered his catamaran, *Enza*, with the late Sir Peter Blake, another of sailing's inspirational figures.

I was amazed at what an incredibly friendly and down-to-earth character Robin was. And yet I could not believe that I was there chatting to him. It was something I had never dreamt would happen, partly because I had never tried to win anything. We were given model sailing boats for the photos, and at one point we were asked to take off our shoes and socks and pose in the water. In January! I was finding the whole experience so overwhelming that I would have done anything I was asked, but Robin said, "No." He had calmly but firmly shown me that you must make up your own mind about what you are prepared to do and what you are not, and that you are not obliged to do whatever you're asked, however eager you may be not to disappoint anyone.

The awards themselves were a very nerve-racking experience. Over the music that signalled the announcement of the award, I could practically hear the sound of my heart beating within my chest. I saw the images of the other finalists up there on the screen, and I remember think-ing how incredibly talented they were, having achieved remarkable re-sults in dinghy racing and international competition. I felt that in com-parison with my own achievements, they seemed clear winners. The words, "And the winner of the BT/YJA Young Sailor of the Year is Ellen MacArthur," echoed through the ballroom, and I was instantly sure I would tumble and never make it to the stage. It passed in seconds as I tried to smile at the flashing cameras, and as I weaved my way back through the tables to Mum, Dad, and Thea, the award clutched firmly to my chest, the words resonating inside my head were "Thank you" . . . the biggest thank-you that an eighteen-year-old could imagine.

By February I was back in Hull when Mum telephoned to tell me that a letter had arrived from Musto, a big manufacturer of sailing gear. Standing in a draughty pay-phone box in Hull Marina, I asked her to open it and read it to me. The letter was from Keith Musto, one of the founders of the company. He said he'd like to meet me. I was so excited my feet hardly touched the ground as I ran back to the Nautical School. I needed time to think.

My only idea at that stage had been to sail *Iduna* to Norway and back. I was fascinated by the beauty of Norway, and at Robert's house I pored over maps of her coastline. I knew, though, that it would be hard to at-tempt a trip like that without a sponsor—for the safety gear if nothing else. I wrote back to Keith Musto, saying that it would be great to meet and I would go down to Essex to discuss future projects. It was an odd reply. There was no hint of what those future projects might be.

By now I seemed to be forging two distinct but parallel paths. The first was gaining Royal Yachting Association (RYA) qualifications at David's school, and the second involved my still-uncertain plans for *Iduna*. My meeting with Musto was approaching fast, and I hadn't yet come up with what I was going to present to them.

I was back at the school teaching in full force by this stage, and I had signed up for the next level of qualification, the Yachtmaster Instructor endorsement. This would allow me to teach Yachtmasters themselves out on the water. It was another water-based examination, this time of a week's duration, down on the South Coast. So I was sailing *Alert* as often as possible, as well as teaching courses in the school. I was very nervous about this course: Not only was it the most difficult practical examina-

tion in the teaching of sailing, but it also was based on the Solent—
where I had sailed only once as a child. It was going to be a tough one.

David's school was unusual because he taught commercial courses as
well as the RYA syllabus. So the people I was teaching weren't always
pleasure-craft users, but the men who worked on the river and on
coastal barges and ships. These guys were in some ways heroes to me. I
had seen the tugs and barges working the rivers in all conditions, the
men tiny in comparison with the enormous machinery and power of the
boats. I was intrigued to meet the people who worked them.

I remember shifting uneasily from foot to foot as new courses were
about to begin. Until I got to know the students I was quite shy. Someone
would ask where the teacher was, and when I found the courage to pipe
up and tell them, "Actually I'm teaching you guys," there were always
looks verging on disbelief. It was strange, though; I never felt as if I was
many years younger, nor did I feel that I had insufficient knowledge to do
the job. The biggest hurdle was just the fact that I was a quiet, unassuming
young woman and that many of the commercial guys didn't want to be
there in the first place, having been forced into it by changing regulations.

During tea breaks, after "smoko," we would talk together. I was transfixed by these men's stories. Often their fathers, and even grandfathers,
had worked the river, so the tales dated back several generations. It wasn't
an easy life; they worked long, hard hours. If the tide was right, they
went with it, night or day, winter or summer. I was very conscious that
they were already experts at what they did—skills to handle their kind
of craft came mostly from apprenticeships.

Throughout my time in Hull I was blessed by many people's generosity of time and spirit. David's calm and patience stayed with me. I respected him enormously, and we also got on famously. He was really the
first person with whom I'd ever been able truly to share my passion for
boats, the sea, and sailing. There were others, too, I met through teaching. John Duckett was studying for his Yachtmaster qualification, and his
help in reviving *Iduna* was priceless. We became great mates, and he'd
often buy me fish and chips and give me a lift with my gear in his dad's
van. More than this, though, I was inspired by him. He had been badly
injured in a serious car crash and had been expected neither to come out
of his coma nor, when he came to months later, to walk again. It took
him years to recover properly, but he never gave up. Teaching him was

immensely rewarding, and he was the embodiment of persistence, good humour, and sheer bloody-mindedness.

One other student also made an enormous impact on me. Don Hayes, a consulting engineer with his own business in the North of England, had come to study for his Day Skipper qualification. He and I got on well from the start, his sharp wit and great will to learn making the classroom an even happier place. We talked a lot about *Iduna* at that time, as I was still throwing around ideas as to what I was going to attempt next. After teaching Don for several weeks, I realized we were becoming more than friends. At the end of the weekend teaching, we walked down to his car in the rain. I had been talking about Spurn Point in class, and as he got in to leave, he suggested we drive down there.

Over the following months we spent many happy evenings together. Before meeting Don I could have counted on one hand the number of times I'd ever been into a restaurant. Choosing from a menu—just understanding it—was completely alien. Even things as straightforward as "rack of lamb" were unknowns! And I was stunned at how expensive things were. I was accustomed to scrounging food from anywhere and treating it as no more than fuel. This was a whole new world!

Don also opened my eyes to business. He talked about the agency he worked with to promote his company, and about how marketing worked. I had never before been exposed to the reality of any of this, and I began to think in a new way about how future projects could work. Don produced a massive marketing plan for me, looking at my strengths and weaknesses. It had all sorts of columns, such as Projects, Contacts, Lectures, and Speaking. I felt I poured everything I could into this chart. It became the blueprint for the future. Bearing in mind that it was put together well before my first significant sailing exploit, it turned out to be astoundingly accurate!

I was at home in Derbyshire in March when I hit on the Big Idea. I woke and rolled over in my sleeping-bag to see what the weather was doing outside. I glanced up at the collage of newspaper clippings on the wall. Among them was a British Admiralty chart catalogue, and as I looked at the map of Britain, I thought, "That's it." It was as if the feeling had always been there and all I'd done was reveal it. Sailing round Britain suddenly seemed the most natural thing to do. In that instant I was sure I knew exactly what I was going to do next.

The timing was perfect too, as the meeting with Musto was coming up. I was not sure what that would involve, but at least now I could go there with a plan. Don had introduced me to Graham Percy, his marketing agent, and the three of us decided to go to Musto together. Don had agreed to support the project through Graham, doing all he could to help raise my profile.

As we walked into Musto's offices for the first time, everything seemed so smart and organized. We waited for a few nervous minutes before being met not just by Keith Musto but by a whole group of people. One of them was Brian Pilcher, Musto's public relations manager, who took us to the meeting room. After a friendly preamble, Keith asked me what my future plans were. I answered as if I had been planning the trip for years. "To sail single-handed around Great Britain," I said, and promised to send a detailed plan to them by the end of the week.

They were genuine enthusiasts. Keith talked about his racing and proudly showed me a diagram of all the crew positions and jobs aboard his boat. I was struck by how much I had in common with these people who were clearly working with the professionals at the top of the sport. Brian was the real character, and a marked contrast to Keith, who, while fiercely competitive, was quiet and unassuming. Initially I found Brian a little overwhelming—I wasn't used to people who bubbled like this. I'd never met anyone quite as engaging as he passionately explained that the sailor on board the boat is the "engine" and has to be looked after more than anything else. To be cold and wet is draining, and it can be very dangerous out there, particularly on long passages. Foul-weather gear has to provide the right protection. Years later, I still think back to that conversation and find myself nodding in agreement. Brian would become a great friend.

Dave, Graham, and I talked feverishly as we drove back to Hull, and I spent the next few days and nights buried in the *Nautical Almanac*. I looked up depths of water at all states of the tide, and the facilities in each port—whether there was water, fuel, and food available and whether it was safe in all conditions. I found the telephone numbers of the yacht clubs and the RNLI (Royal National Lifeboat Institution) lifeboat stations and worked out the exact mileages between ports. Then I split the journey into five stages, each made up of six or seven shorter hops. I planned to travel counterclockwise, to ensure that at the end of the journey, I would have the wind behind me rather than in my face. It was a mammoth task, but I attacked it with such energy and enthusiasm that it simply had to work out.

Two and a half days later I sent every bit of information I could pull together down to Musto, and on 10 April they replied.

The letter, signed by Brian, outlined Musto's fundamental agreement to sponsor me. He'd gone out of his way. He'd found me a sponsor for autopilots and had spoken to my insurers to confirm that the project fell within *Iduna*'s current insurance terms. He also said he might be able to help provide a small outboard engine and weather information. There seemed to be less weight on my shoulders until I read his terms. There were two conditions for Musto's involvement: the first was to have *Iduna* surveyed, and the second was to complete a single-handed voyage of 300 miles non-stop in her. This was a shock, as at the time it suggested to me that Brian and the team weren't confident of my experience and training.

I had never envisaged sailing *Iduna* for 300 miles on any leg of the trip. With good reason, I felt, I had limited my longest leg to just over 60 miles so that at worst it would take twenty hours and in good conditions should take no more than twelve. I didn't believe it was safe to have to sleep at sea in such a small boat, so close to the shore. There is a terrific amount of shipping in the North Sea, and this posed a threat. There was also the shoreline itself. Contrary to what one might expect, this poses the greatest danger to ships, rocks being far more likely than waves to sink a boat.

After discussing it all with Dave I wrote a long letter to Brian, explaining how I felt. My view was that four sleepless days in the North Sea should be a last resort rather than a training exercise. I did, however, promise him that I would sea-trial *Iduna* in fairly serious conditions before I left, to ensure that she was up to the challenge.

I was sure I was right, and I felt we would have a stronger project if we shared our concerns openly. In the end Brian was persuaded, and we ploughed on with the arrangements.

The first job was to get *Iduna* back to the marina yard, where I could work on her with electricity and light at hand. We had long discussions with the Hull Marina management. They decided—to everyone's relief, I think—to let me work on *Iduna* in the yard and keep her on the water free of charge. The deal was that I should carry a sticker from Hull Marina around Britain, and, to be quite honest, I was proud to do so!

From January I worked on *Iduna* all hours that God sent. I broke off only to do a couple of courses on *Alert* and to take my Yachtmaster Instructor examination down on the Solent in April.

On arriving at Hamble Marina, I wandered down to the boat we were sailing for the week-long exam. She was called *Hakuna Matata*—Swahili for No Problem! I wished I felt that relaxed. As soon as I got on board I climbed into every locker and inspected every hatch. I wanted to find out everything about this boat, from where the valves were located in the hull to how I would switch off the gas to where the fire extinguisher was—and that was just below decks!

Our examiner arrived that evening, and all fears of being examined by someone with whom I could not identify were completely blown away! John Goode was a great character, with his spiky, greying hair and old reefer jacket, smoking his favourite pipe. He was incredibly sharp and had an acute sense of humour, and I warmed to him immediately. He was a doer, not a pretender. You will never meet anyone who is more down to earth than John. From time to time, nerves surfaced from the fact that I was doing an exam, but on the whole I tried to convince myself that we were just out there sailing.

On Thursday, John jumped ship to another boat in the fleet, and another examiner, James Stevens, came aboard. James was the RYA's national cruising coach, and we were all very conscious of it. But the weather was easier now, allowing us to use the spinnaker for the first time, and James was only with us for the last day. It was refreshing to undertake new exercises scrutinized by a different pair of eyes.

When it was over we returned the boats to the marina and received our debriefings from John and James. I was suddenly very nervous, feeling I was younger and less experienced than the others, though during the sailing I had tried to blank that out. When my turn came to be addressed, my heart beat faster as I walked into the room. At least I knew the faces there. Both James and John were complimentary but frank about my weak points, the worst of which were my relatively few sea-miles and inevitable lack of experience sailing in different geographical areas. I was expecting the great build-up so that they could let me down gently and say I was not ready. After all, if eighteen was young to take a Yachtmaster ticket, perhaps it was just *too* young to pass the Instructor ticket as well. When the verdict came, it was not as straightforward as it might have been, but I was thrilled. I was told that they would award me the certificate when I arrived in Southampton on my way round Britain. I slept for most of the train journey home.

I now had six weeks in Hull to get *Iduna* ready. There was still much to organize, from the electrics to a full set of the right spares. It was all incredibly hectic, and although I was doing most of the work myself, Dave, Don, and John Duckett also put in hours to get *Iduna* and me to the start of our voyage.

On 1 June I was on the boat well before the sun came up, finishing the final wiring of the spare autopilot. People were gradually collecting on the dockside—Mum and Dad, Fergus, Lewis, and Mac. Lew was going through a very difficult time at that stage. University had not gone as he'd hoped, and he was trying to decide whether he should go back to complete his degree or look for something different elsewhere—perhaps a job. I was grateful to him for his presence. Sarah had come up to see me off too, along with Don, Graham Percy, and others from Don's office. Dave and Maureen were there, of course, and Steve and Shamus, who'd helped me work on *Iduna*.

I put on my oilskins and said my goodbyes. There was no sadness as I spoke to Mum and Dad on the pontoon. Saying goodbye to Mac was hardest, as I couldn't let her know when I'd be back; she just understood, as dogs do, that I was leaving.

I hugged Lew. "It'll be a walk in the park," he said. And that was that.

Although it was going to be a long trip, I knew that all those people on the dockside would be with me in their own way, and I was thankful to them all. I just wanted to stop time and restart it once I was on my way. I didn't cry until I had passed through the locks and was out on the river. I looked back to see Mac stretching high up over the seawall to watch me. A tear slipped down my face for the first time that day. Then I turned back to face the sea. We were off.

It was as if I'd left behind on the dockside every part of my life up until that moment. Ahead was an unknown future, and *Iduna* and I were suspended between the two, waiting for the past to disappear over the horizon. This was the biggest single turning-point in my life, and the intense anticipation was almost too much to bear. I'd been in Hull for just over a year.

CHAPTER FIVE

THE WIND WAS very light on our first day sailing out of the Humber, and progress was slow. The quiet, pale grey sky met the familiar brown-stained waters of the river, and it felt like a very empty afternoon, the only sound the gentle slapping of the water beneath *Iduna*'s hull. Reluctantly, an hour or so after leaving the dockside, I switched on her engine. With the wind so light, we would have to speed up if we were going to make Bridlington for the tide. So we continued to the sound of the engine. It's hard to describe the frustration of trying to sail without wind. I was lucky that I had an engine I could run, but that feeling of quietness was just not there. When the engine is stopped and the bubbling sound of water under the hull returns, it's sheer bliss. As darkness fell the wind seemed to steady, and as I sat back in the cockpit I pulled out my dictaphone for a few words:

> *It's now 2115 at night, the sun's setting and we're sailing along at about three and a half knots with full sail, just managed to get the engine off for the first real time in days and it's absolutely fantastic and peaceful. The wind's about Force 2–3 . . . it's what I've come for. I'm feeling in one of those moods where I wish I could jump off the boat, get in a dinghy and see what she looks like. She must look so beautiful sailing along tonight.*

We approached Bridlington around midnight. I decided to anchor for the night so I could rest rather than wait for the tide at four o'clock in the morning. Though now exhausted, I was happy to be foraging around on the foredeck lighting the little kerosene lamp that Thea had given me. The lights of Bridlington shone over us, and I climbed below and wrote up the log beneath the white glow of the little strip light above the chart table.

The following morning we pushed on up the coast. It began to look like a longer sail to Hartlepool, but when the wind died once more, I decided to pull into the nearest port, Scarborough. I couldn't have had a more cheerful welcome in any port, let alone for the first of the trip. I was met by Tony, the harbour watch-keeper who lived in the lighthouse building on the docks, and I was soon invited into the yacht club for pie and peas with the members. It was a perfect start and an early insight into the kindness I would encounter throughout my trip.

As we headed up the coast next day, the cliffs loomed mysteriously. The breeze was too light to blow away the mist which shrouded the rocks at their base, but soon it cleared as the wind freshened from the south. I made my sandwiches as we passed Robin Hood's Bay, a beautiful cluster of houses sheltered in a tight little break in the cliffs. I had poled out *Iduna*'s genoa, so we had a sail out each side to pull along her little orange hull. For the first time in the voyage, I could hear the water creaming at her bows. I wandered on to her foredeck and sat looking back into our wake, my eye drawn by her little red ensign fluttering away in the breeze. Scotland, here we come!

Our first real setback was Hartlepool. The forecast got progressively worse, and we ended up storm-bound there for two weeks. The waves were relentless, and the wind blew angrily for what seemed like forever. Coincidentally, also in port but undergoing a refit was the Sea Cadets' training ship, the magnificent square-rigged TS *Royalist*. As I arrived she was in her final few days of making ready to sail, and I was invited on board for tea.

She was an incredible ship, covered in brasswork and weathered timbers. Though roughly my age, she was still an evocative link with sailing's past. We ate in the officers' wardroom in the aft of the ship, and I was made to feel completely at home; over the next couple of weeks I had great times on board her, and I made some good friends there. I was even invited to sail as bosun's mate when she went out to brave the mountainous swells. I was intrigued by the teamwork, seeing everyone function together so well. When I climbed the rigging with the young cadets, the wind howled through the ropes and the masts swept violently through the air as her hull pitched through the waves. I was very impressed by the way a job was done if it needed to be done, and by the willingness of the cadets to adjust to their newfound surroundings.

The only difficult part of my time in Hartlepool occurred when Don came to see me. I felt that what we both wanted from our relationship would not take us down the same path. Maybe I felt a little claustrophobic, having had time to think since setting off, and it seemed best to end it there and then, to go our separate directions, rather than let the relationship wither slowly and painfully. My final days in Hartlepool felt like a blur of sadness.

On my first attempt to leave Hartlepool I was piped out by *Royalist* with two blasts on her foghorn, but the swell was too large to motor safely, and *Iduna* and I were flung around so much that I reluctantly made the decision to stay another night.

When we eventually did break clear to continue northward the following day, I felt an overwhelming relief to be moving once again. From the iridescence of the water to the way the evening sun lit the hills of the Yorkshire Wolds as they rolled down to meet the sea, the sheer beauty of it all was breathtaking. I've never had so much time to wonder at my surroundings as during that trip. I sat in the setting sun writing up my daily log:

Puffins flying past just three feet away! Continued north then motored into Eyemouth roads. Anchored up in 5 metres of water, three hours before low water at 1215, then went to sleep. Up for the 1405 forecast—not too good. Eyemouth is a beautiful place, with a beautiful bay. My thumb has gone septic, so I doused it with TCP, pulled out the green stuff then plastered it up! Lovely! Departed Eyemouth at 1700. Sailed out! There wasn't too much wind but I was determined to sail, it's too quiet here to use the motor.

Almost missed St. Abbs! I got my sails off and motored in— taking note of the pilot diagrams. As the entrance opened up I looked across and saw a chap standing by the lifeboat house—

he showed me where to go, and chatted for a bit. He used to go
to sea but is now in the building trade.
St. Abbs is an indescribably peaceful and friendly port. I
was so glad I came. I have had an eel feed on the weed on my
keel and I can see starfish on the seabed—there was some
confusion over where I should berth due to a rock—but
everyone has been more than helpful. I am sitting in the
setting sun writing this at 1948 hrs.

On leaving, I crossed the Firth of Forth, heading north past Edinburgh. It was a glorious day to sail across, passing the rocky but beautiful
Isle of May. Once on the north side of the Firth, I spent the night in
Anstruther. It was getting late by the time we tied up, and I didn't feel
like peeling vegetables for the pressure cooker, so I popped out to buy
fish and chips and wolfed it down as I sat watching the fishing boats.

The night, though, was anything but peaceful. I was kept up with agonizing stomach cramps. By the time the sun had risen, the pain had completely gone, but I'd barely slept. By day, I think I forgot how bad I'd felt.
I cast off *Iduna*'s lines, heading for our next stop—Arbroath. We had all
day to get there, so I decided that even if the wind stayed light we'd
probably make it under sail.

In the heat of the afternoon, the wind died completely and the pains
came back, much worse than they'd been at night. I couldn't crouch anywhere, felt desperately uncomfortable, and feared it might be appendicitis. Although Arbroath was only a couple of miles away, I couldn't get
in because the tide hadn't yet risen. I'd have had to wait until evening. I
decided to carry on to Montrose—it was the only port I could enter,
and with the tide still under us we would be there in a matter of hours.
As time ticked away, though, the pain seemed to get worse. I tried calling home to let someone know what was happening, but no reply. I then
got through to Dad at school, but there was little he could do. I could
hear the concern in his voice, but also his helplessness. Nonetheless, it
was a great relief to hear him. Though I was close to shore, I might as
well have been out of sight of land. Trying to think ahead, I asked Dad to
call Graham to let him know what was happening.

As I approached Montrose I called ahead to the Harbour Control Office to make sure they were expecting me and that there were medical

facilities nearby. "No problem," came the reply, and I was told that someone would come out to meet me. Montrose, almost exclusively a shipping port, was not really recommended for small yachts, but as it turned
out I could not have made a better decision.

As I approached the harbour entrance, I edged my way into the cabin
to call the port authorities to make sure there was no shipping on its way
out. As I reached for the VHF radio to change channels, I was startled to
hear a very large vessel close to me. I peered out through the windows
and saw to my relief that the pilot vessel *Southesk* had come out to meet
me and was right alongside.

They escorted me up the river, where ships towered above the concrete dockside. A shortish man walked out onto the *Southesk*'s side-deck
and indicated where he wanted me to berth. The pain in my stomach
was agonizing. It shot through me every time I moved, so tying up *Iduna*
seemed to take forever. The man I had seen on the deck of the *Southesk*
turned out to be the harbourmaster, Harry; he drove me to the local infirmary. By the time I arrived, the pain seemed to be easing a little. The
doctor assured me that I did not have appendicitis and that the pain
would pass. I was feeling slightly better at this stage, so Harry ran me
back to *Iduna*, where I collapsed in my bunk in an exhausted and sweaty
heap.

I called home later that evening after trying to sleep. My parents had
been discussing the situation, and Mum had decided she was going to
come to Montrose. I was glad, though worried that her trip might be a
waste of time. But I had been away almost a month, and I knew it would
be wonderful to see a familiar face.

That night began fine, but once the final cries from the settling birds
and the noise of the traffic had stopped, I was again racked with intense
pain. I was writing in my bunk, and *Iduna*'s cabin, which had always been
comforting, now felt claustrophobic. I just wanted to curl up and
scream, but I didn't have the space. I was able to hug one leg or the other
to my chest, and I lay there whimpering the night away. I kept reminding
myself that it was not appendicitis and that it would just go away, but it
didn't. There was no relief till I woke with the first movements in the
river rocking *Iduna*.

The following morning Harry came down to see me and asked how I
was. I said that I'd had a terrible night but was feeling better, and that

Mum would be arriving at Montrose Station at three o'clock. He offered to pick her up and handed me a key for the workers' shed. The guys who worked on the docks had asked him to let me have the spare key for their dock shed, in case I wanted to use the toilet, get hot water, or use the kettle.

The pain had eased a bit, so I slept all morning and by lunchtime felt much better. It was wonderful to see Mum bounce off the train at the station, and as we hugged each other, relief flowed between us. Harry dropped us back at *Iduna*, where we climbed down the ladder and I excitedly recited all there was to be told of the journey so far. That night I was ill again, doubled up in my bunk as Mum tried to sleep in the makeshift bunk we had laid down the centre of *Iduna*. It was no use—this pain wasn't going away, and by 0400 Mum was up to see if there was anyone around who could help. I was squirming again, and this time with a temperature. The night watchman kindly gave us a lift to the infirmary in his van. The doctor was fantastic, but he couldn't work out exactly what was wrong. He gave me something to take, and we headed back to the dock. The medicine seemed to ease whatever was going on inside me, and the following day I felt OK again.

Mum was worried about being away from Derbyshire, as so many people relied on her. We talked a lot about what was going on at home, and it was clear things weren't at all easy. Nan was struggling, having had to come home from her exchange program in Germany because of illness. Mum now had to run her to places she'd always walked to. It must have been heartbreaking enough for Nan to have to break away from her studies, let alone cope with the frustration of being so frail. Auntie Thea was also staying in Derbyshire. She'd had a crippling nervous reaction to a painkilling spinal injection after she'd injured her back, and Mum was looking after her. Gran was also unwell and Lew was at home, still trying to make a decision about his future. Poor Mum; as usual she was bearing the brunt and, not for the first time, being strong for everyone. I felt terrible that she had come up to Montrose. I can only hope that her break to look after me did her a fraction of the good it did me. She asked me if I wanted to go back to Derbyshire with her until she was sure I was better, and there was certainly some temptation to do that. But I resisted, telling her that if I went home I would jeopardize the trip and would not make it round. It was disheartening to have been stormbound for so long in Hartlepool, but right now the weather was good and I was going to go for it.

Mum and I found ourselves walking back from town past the dock shed the following morning. On discovering it was locked, I realized I still had the little key tucked away in my pocket. As we opened the door, it was like entering a long-lost den. There were a few dark-coloured seats scattered around, several with the covers suffering a bit through wear. The windows were dirty from the daily forklift and lorry movements, though shards of sunlight were still just about making it through. There were several rather unflattering pictures of semi-naked and naked women on the walls, and a large electric kettle with a few tins, mugs, and spoons in the far corner. As I walked in I smiled; I don't really know why, but I felt right at home in a shed like this; looking back, I think I was just plain proud to have been accepted into the dock workers' world. As we made ourselves a cup of tea and sat down for a great last chat, Mum commented, "Goodness, this is well used," which kind of summed it up.

We said our goodbyes, which in many ways was harder than in Hull. We both had a much better idea now of what I was taking on, although I think this just made me feel more determined. *Iduna* seemed too quiet that evening, but I consoled myself with the thought that the following day she and I would be setting off again.

Monday June 26th
Got up at 0810. Spent the morning fixing the wind generator, making phone calls and washing up. Also spent quite a bit of time passage planning—where to head next. Cut thumb—bad on the aluminium disc. Never mind. Sandwiches for lunch. At 1300 went to get water alongside **Southesk** *pilot boat. Big hassle—too strong a jet which burst my little water tank! Loads of water in the bilges. There was water everywhere, even in the battery box! Luckily I managed to fix tank, it had broken at the inlet! Decided water purification tablets needed. Went into town. Found mega expensive ones in Boots—so tried nearby chemist. Got some Milton! I'm sure it'll do the job. Got back to boat, handed in key to the shed—then departed as* **Southesk** *was due to leave shortly. Still in jeans and T-shirt,*

started up engine and set off—waved goodbye. On way out
called up Montrose port control. Thanked them for their
hospitality and help and said I hoped to come back some
time. The reply was "Iduna—port control, no problem—
you're welcome back anytime"—lovely.

The wind began to pick up soon after we'd left. As I sat in the cockpit with a cup of tea, I could see fog looming ahead, rolling towards us. Above the blanket the sky was clear and bright, and as the air turned grey there was a shimmering on the water as though it was coated in silver. I tried to stay close inshore to keep clear of the routes of any shipping that might be around—I had no way of seeing them other than by eye-balling. I hoisted my radar reflector into *Iduna's* rigging, so that we might have a chance of being seen by the ships themselves, and listened hard for the sound of their engines. We tacked so close into the cliffs that they rose out of the fog high above me while the foaming waves broke onto the rocks beneath.

I called the Coastguard to let him know where I was and say that I was tacking up the coast in fog. I just wanted to let any shipping that was near us know we were around. There was someone else listening in to this radio conversation, though, and soon after-wards they contacted me directly. It seemed that a boat called *MRI 38*—a high-speed rescue boat— was keen to come out and test a new piece of technology on me. Once I was sure that their mission was in no way a "rescue," I was happy to co-operate. Their equipment was designed to find a vessel purely with a radio signal. I carried on up the coast.

The boat loomed out of the fog. Asked over the radio if I
could hear them, my reply was a loud and clear, but they meant
engines! I said "Hang on" stuck my head out of the hatch and
saw their boat on my starboard side, they hung around as I
tried to sail in. At approx 2030 I put on my engine and motor-
sailed—gradually taking down sails—eventually motoring for
the last half hour, very bumpy. Cut finger again!!—blood all
over! Didn't want any on sails though. Waves breaking on rocks
and sea eagles close, very eerie. Followed **MRI 38** *into*
Stonehaven and moored up.

The skipper of *MRI 38* came up to talk to me as I was tying up. His name was Hamish McDonald, and he ran the company which had designed and built the boat that he had brought out to find me.

I needed to get something to eat, and on discovering that the local chip shop was closed, Hamish drove me straight off to his house at the top of the town. I was warmly welcomed by his family, and his wife cooked me bacon and eggs for tea. We chatted till late, and soon after midnight Hamish gave me a lift back to *Iduna*. I turned in straight away, lying back in my bunk with a big smile on my face.

Hamish arrived with the weather forecast next morning and offered to send down one of his engineers to look at a small problem I'd been having with my outboard engine. He also handed me a copy of a book he'd written. Inside was a short handwritten note:

Live by this
Be at peace with nature
Be at peace with your place of work
Be at peace with your tools of work
Realize your capabilities—work to your limitations.

Very best wishes to Ellen, may all your dreams come true.
HM 27/06/95

After the engineer had fixed the outboard, I shipped my lines straight away and departed Stonehaven, sad to be leaving new friends.

It was just minutes later that the dolphins came. I'd be hard pushed to think of another creature that has the potential to make people smile quite as quickly as the dolphin. I was grinning from ear to ear. I had never seen wild dolphins before, and I laughed out loud as they swept past *Iduna*. Though we were moving quite slowly, they leapt at her bow and dived beneath us . . . they would turn their heads on one side and look up, and at the same time I could reach down and touch them. This is what being out here is all about, I thought. If the trip was forced to end tomorrow, I would have already seen such a big part of what I came out to see.

The next stages were calm, a mixture of sailing and motoring. We stopped off in Peterhead, then, after an early start, sailed round the headland to a tiny fishing village called Whitehills. I was starting to worry, though, because we were behind schedule: although we had covered a good distance, we were still below 400 miles of a 1,900-mile trip. We had had our two weeks in Hartlepool and three days in Montrose and should have been nearer the top of Scotland by now. I thought about the options. The plan had always been to pass round Cape Wrath, between Scotland and the Orkneys, but now I was beginning to doubt that would be feasible. We'd had fantastic weather since Hartlepool, and I'd been able to sail most days, but it was not going to stay like that—we had to get moving. I was worried about getting stuck in gales up there in the north—if we got caught, we would struggle to get into port at all. *Iduna* is a very small boat, and her outboard engine simply was not going to be something I could rely on. As our attempt to leave Hartlepool had shown, the engine could be practically useless when the propeller came out of the water each time *Iduna* went over a big wave. I had been worrying about this since the beginning of the trip, and reluctantly I decided to play it safe by taking the alternative route: cutting out those miles around the top by transiting the Caledonian Canal from Inverness to Fort William. I was angry with myself for having opted for this alternative, but I knew it was the right decision. No one else could make it for me, and I was determined we were going to do it.

> *29th June Whitehills*
> *The Harbourmaster thanked me very much for coming to pay.*
> *He took my £6, and asked me if I liked fish and gave me 4 fresh*
> *haddock. He asked me if I could gut them, to which I replied*
> *"No problem" which I was sure I could. I left the shed smiling*
> *and I had porridge for breakfast that I had cooked in harbour*
> *before my departure. I then set about cleaning and filleting the*
> *haddock. Great fun. I tailed and beheaded them first, which the*
> *sea gulls rather enjoyed! I then tried to get the fish off the*
> *bone. Which actually wasn't as hard as I thought. I then ended*
> *up with eight fillets, one of which I fried instantly, it was*
> *delicious. Three yachts passed going the other way to seaward.*
> *They looked like ghost ships. The horizon was hidden in the*
> *mist—they looked like they were floating on glass.*

Next stop was Lossiemouth, where Graham had arranged for me to meet some of the lads from the local RAF base. I was shown round the base and ended up going to the pub and chatting with the guys who worked the search and rescue helicopter. I made it back on board, almost drunk, just before midnight. It had been a long time since I'd enjoyed a big evening out!

Still, I was up early the following morning. The forecast was for quite strong winds, but with advice from the harbourmaster I decided to go for it. He thought I would make Inverness in time for the locks into the Caledonian Canal. He wished me all the best for my journey.

"Yacht Iduna, Yacht Iduna, Yacht Iduna this is RAF 132—do you read us, OVER," and before I knew it there was a Sea King helicopter flying over us! Wow! I spoke to them several times on the radio as they flew around, they said that it was great to see that I was OK, and that I was looking good down there. They circled round a few times, then did a fly-past at great speed— the noise was momentarily deafening. . . . How cool is that!

It was a still evening as I tied up by the lock gates at the entrance to the Caledonian Canal. I closed up *Iduna* and headed to the supermarket, which I'd been told earlier was not far from the moorings. By the time I returned I was surprised to see another mast just behind ours. *Iduna* is small, but this was tiny. It was rare for us to dwarf anything but small rowing dinghies. And the most astonishing thing was that this little thing had sailed over from Sweden. Sebastian, the guy on board her, was tall, slightly unkempt and wore a leather flying hat when things got cold. He'd built his boat, *Arrandir*, in his bedroom at home—he couldn't get her out and had to remove a window! We left Inverness together the following morning and had a great sail down the canal to Fort William before going our separate ways. I was astounded by the sheer beauty of the Caledonian Canal. It took just under a week to sail through, and I cherished every minute of it.

July 8th
*I am realizing today that I am far more content alone than I first was. I am not worried that I am miles away from home with no one I know. I have **Iduna** and she has me and together we shall do just fine. My new home is with me and I have all I need, and more—I am very lucky.*

We're moored up in Kentallen Bay, a magical place. Tea is on the stove, and there is complete silence here. Haggis and vegetables, and maybe I'll try baking a cake in the pressure cooker for afters. Worth a try I suppose, even if it turns into a pudding with custard on—after all it's my birthday today!

CHAPTER SIX

Two DAYS LATER we reached Oban. The sailing from Port Appin at the mouth of Loch Linnhe had been wonderful. I felt like a character in *Swallows and Amazons*, exploring hidden caves and secret harbours. We moored across the bay from the town off a beautiful little island named Kerrara. I had decided to take a break for a day and catch the train to Edinburgh. *Royalist* was about to set off for the biggest event of her year, the Tall Ships Race. Virtually every square-rigged ship for thousands of miles around must have gathered for it, and I was itching to wave them off.

Everyone aboard *Royalist* was on fine form, and the colour and noise couldn't have been more of a contrast to life alone on *Iduna*. There were water-balloon fights with the other ships as they entered the docks, and thousands of people. I had the opportunity to talk to Barry Mattey, the commanding officer of the Sea Cadets, who raised the possibility of my taking a job with them as a yacht skipper. I'd had such great fun with everyone on board that the thought of being an official part of the organization was appealing. There were courses taking place on the Sea Cadets' smaller yachts later in the year, and I had to think about what I was going to do next. It had been wonderful to see friends again, and a small part of me wished I could be sailing off with them. This soon melted away, as my mind returned to my own journey. From Oban I had to make it to Southampton for the boat show.

From Kerrara we sailed through the stunning Crinan Canal, then beyond to Adrishaig, Largs, and Troon.

26th July
1055 I cannot begin to describe what a fantastic feeling it is to
be sailing alone as **Iduna** *is sailing now. She is alive, and I am*
convinced she is aiming to please in every way. We are in
harmony! She gracefully flows over the waves parting the water
at her bows and leaving just an indent, a slight disturbance at
her stern, the only trace of her presence. God has blessed us
with fair winds at last.

We were out of sight of land for the first time in the voyage as we sailed for Peel on the Isle of Man. Rather than making me fearful, this actually filled me with a greater sense of freedom than ever before. *Iduna* and I were off, and I had the most incredible urge just to carry on south and out across the Atlantic. The day was stunning, we were hammering along, and it felt as if the wind-vane self-steering was in control of us for the first time. I laughed aloud at the waves that splashed my face.

Just two hours from Peel things changed dramatically, however. We were downwind of the island, which normally means that the sea flattens behind the shelter of the land. I was looking forward to that final blast in flat sea. Then the wind changed direction and started to increase. I reefed down *Iduna*, as she had begun bouncing around in the waves, and struggled to get things sorted quickly. It seemed everything was against us at that moment. As the winds gained strength they were also turning, blowing us away from Peel. We were experiencing extreme catabatic winds as the air funnelled down the island's hills and out to sea. I felt vulnerable but knew we were just going to have to hang on and battle it out. The waves grew dramatically, and I feared we might even have to change course and head for Ireland—and safety. I tried running *Iduna*'s engine to help us claw towards the harbour, but I could only run it on one tack, as the propeller came out of the water on the other. I tried to stop and start it as we changed tacks, but each time we fell down a wave the engine would scream in complaint as the resistance from the water disappeared below it.

It was the big test for *Iduna* and me, and although the ordeal lasted only two hours, I learned a lot.

27th July
Iduna *and I belong together. She provides me with a home and shelter while I give her direction and adventure. I feel proud to be associated with such a wonderful yacht. How could anyone have abandoned her like they did? She is willing to please if given half a chance. She has carried me through rough and smooth. She has never given up, maybe tested me a little, but we held our own.*

My excitement rose as we headed down towards Anglesey and prepared for our passage of the Menai Strait. The goal was to arrive safely in Port Dinorwic, where I would be met by my friend Sarah and her mum and dad, and then, the day after, by my own family.

I was looking forward to seeing Sarah but found it difficult to relax. I did not feel in holiday mode, as I could not get my mind off the trip. I enjoyed our time together, but I did feel a little bit outside it all. It was a shame—I probably could have done with letting down my hair!

It was similar when Mum and Dad arrived the following day with Ferg and Mac. I wanted to see them and to introduce them to my world, but I also felt distracted. I was definitely not my normal self and was still too absorbed in my trip. Dad, having just retired from teaching, was more relaxed than I'd seen him in years. I was tired, and concentrating hard on not making mistakes. My focus was on making sure that *Iduna* was OK. I had set out to make it round Britain, and that was what preoccupied me. My family had come out to have a holiday, but I was working. I tried hard to relax and enjoy myself but failed miserably.

After just one day in Port Dinorwic I decided to continue to the next scheduled stop—Aberdaron Bay. We had chosen it on Graham's recommendation, as he holidayed there every year. Mum and Dad had brought their tent and I would meet them there.

With Aberdaron Bay virtually in sight the wind shifted, forcing us to spend two hours tacking in towards the beach to reach water shallow enough for anchoring. It was a struggle—the wind was all over the place as it swept into the bay from around the hills and cliffs—one moment strong, the next very light, leaving us at the mercy of the current. The waves picked up by the current were small inshore, but quite vicious, short, and sharp.

We had agreed that Dad would row out to *Iduna* in my inflatable dinghy, which he had brought over in the car from Port Dinorwic, though with these waves in the darkness I dismissed this as a possibility. As I tacked back and forth in the bay, I could just make out the silhouette of a high skyline to windward, and I saw the dark blue-white of breaking waves on the rocks at the far end of the beach. It would not be easy to anchor here. Slowly I edged farther in towards the beach, watching the depth gauge constantly to know when it might be shallow enough. *Iduna*'s motion was horrible, and it took all my concentration to navigate her safely in these conditions so close to the land. Preparing her anchor was difficult, and when I finally let it fall into the water and felt it biting on the bottom, I sighed with relief.

But it didn't hold, and the wind was dragging us out of the bay. The deck swayed from side to side as I pulled up the anchor. The wind was stronger now, and the cold was penetrating my wet clothes. I just needed to make sure we were safe for the night, get dried off, and wait for tomorrow's light.

I glanced towards the shore and picked out a tiny torch beam. It was easy to lose sight of it against the lights from the village. My heart sank when I realized I was watching Dad and Ferg rowing out towards me.

My first reaction was to try to slow our drift by dropping the anchor chain I had just lifted, but it looked as if nothing I could do would stop us from moving farther from the dinghy. I turned on the engine to try to hold ground, and as we swayed around in the darkness, the howl of the outboard as it was lifted in and out of the water only increased my anxiety.

Dad and Ferg looked so exposed, and I was afraid for them. I could not understand why they had come out in such grim conditions. The wind was blowing off the shore, and they would have to row hard to return to land against it. I knew they'd come to collect me, but I could not leave *Iduna* tonight, and while part of me loved them for coming, their recklessness frustrated me beyond reason. Soon their faces came into focus, and I reached down to them as Dad grabbed at *Iduna*'s sides. Incredibly, he was still wearing shorts. Water sloshed around the bottom of the dinghy, and neither one was wearing a life jacket. I couldn't contain my anger.

"What the bloody hell are you doing out here now?" I yelled.

"We saw your signal . . . so we came out."

"There was no signal. It's too dangerous, I have to move, I have to re-anchor—I'm staying here tonight," I shouted. "Come back in the morning, but call me on the radio first."

"OK."

And with that one-sided exchange, the little inflatable ended its squeaking up and down in the waves against *Iduna*'s topsides. Then there was quiet, except for the splashing of the oars and the noise of the weather.

"Signal when you're on the beach," I shouted after them, and I sat in a trance for what seemed like hours as I watched the silhouette of the dinghy edging its way to the shore. There was a flash, and I could see figures moving in front of the lights on the beach. They were safe.

I hauled up *Iduna*'s anchor once more and moved farther along the beach to try to find better holding ground. On the second attempt things improved. The anchor seemed to hold, so I switched off the navigation lights and lit the little kerosene lamp, which I attached in her bows. I climbed down below, foraged up forward for dry clothes for the night, and swapped my clammy wet ones for a wonderful layer of warmth. Though exhausted, I could not sleep. There was the constant banging of the wires within *Iduna*'s mast as she rolled in the waves, and knowing the tide would change in a few hours, I worried that the anchor might not hold. I couldn't dispel the thought of waking to the sound of breaking fibreglass as her hull was washed up on the island's rocks. I thought of Dad and Ferg in the dinghy and had to keep telling myself that they were OK. In reality *Iduna* and I were fine, though sitting in uncomfortable waves; I think I'd just been shaken by the dinghy coming out to meet me.

I must have slept eventually, as I stirred when dawn arrived. I clambered on deck, which was covered in dew, and everything was clear. There was still an orange tint in the sky. I sat outside with my jacket wrapped round my shoulders. I looked up at the tents on the hillside and recognized our little murky yellow one with the car parked next to it. Last night seemed a long time ago.

That evening we all ate on the beach with Graham and his wife, Penny, but before the sun set, I needed to head back to *Iduna*. It had been hard seeing everyone in the middle of the trip, and pulling myself away to set sail once again was a wrench. Graham took a photo of all of us on the beach. In it, Mum is looking at me, and, although she obviously is holding back her emotion, her concern is visible.

After passing the spectacular Pembrokeshire coast, I stayed becalmed for five days in Fishguard, where close friends of Dave King's, John and Margaret, took me under their wing. I stayed in a bed for the first time in months and talked to John for hours about his grandfather's experiences on the clipper ships. While there I carefully studied the charts to Solva, an ancient fishing port which was the next stop along the coast. The entrance was tricky, and I would have to dry out *Iduna* when the tide ebbed, leaving her standing on her keel out of the water, leaning against the harbour wall.

It was a choppy sail round to Solva, but on securing *Iduna* in the harbour, I joined Ian Tite, of the Solva Boat Owners' Association, and his wife, Joy, for dinner. While we ate, I was concerned for *Iduna*. I wanted to be there while she dried out. Half an hour after Ian and Joy dropped me back, she touched the bottom; with a rope attached to the top of her mast to stop her falling away from the quay, all seemed well. I changed into my jogging pants and a T-shirt and slid into my bunk, listening to the water slip down her keel as the tide fell away. Our angle began to feel excessive, however: *Iduna* was sliding away from the wall. I got up slowly, moving gingerly to prevent her from slipping farther, and went up the ladder and onto the dockside. I could see that in a few minutes' time her wire rigging would be taking her whole weight as the keel slid farther from the harbour wall. This would wreck her. I dashed around looking for a piece of wood to jam between her and the wall to try to keep her upright, but I found none. I ran back, my bare feet stinging on the loose tarmac. Her rigging was already touching the wall. I reached out over her and pushed her mast away from the wall. It looked as though I might be able to hold her.

I tried to calm myself and assess the situation clearly. On the one hand, the rigging was safe and she had stopped slipping. On the other, I knew that I couldn't let go—I was stuck there. With a wave of relief I realized I had my mobile phone in my pocket, and I fumbled to get it.

Don't drop it, I thought, for God's sake don't drop it! I pressed a key to illuminate the screen—no signal. I tried calling the Tites anyway, but without success. It was now well past midnight and getting colder.

I tried sitting down, but that was no good as I couldn't reach far enough to hold her mast, so I resolved to stand there till about 6 A.M., when the tide would float her once again. I tried counting the stars, then singing songs, frustrated that I could not remember the words to Kylie Minogue tracks I must have heard a hundred times. I couldn't help but laugh—here I was standing in joggers and a T-shirt, freezing, singing half-remembered snippets of Kylie while I held up a boat.

It didn't seem funny for long, though, and I wondered whether the mobile might be worth another try. When I held it as far away as possible, I got a glimmer of a signal. I dialled, held the phone to my ear, and lost it again. I called again and again, knowing full well that even if I could get Ian to answer, I would only be able to shout into the phone at arm's length. Thankfully, the plan worked. At 4 A.M. I saw his headlights sweep into view. Ian held *Iduna*'s mast while I scouted farther afield to find something to wedge her hull. Once this had been done he bundled me into the car and took me back to his house, where I gratefully slept for the rest of the night.

Our next fixed rendezvous had now been announced by Graham. Robin Knox-Johnston was to make a TV programme sailing his famous yacht *Suhaili* from Plymouth to Bristol. I had been asked if I wanted to be a part of it, and I jumped at the chance. We now had four weeks before we had to be in Southampton for the boat show, and getting to Plymouth by the end of the month seemed realistic. We made good progress from Solva, sailing into Milford Haven and then making our biggest hop so far, across the British Channel into Padstow.

The early stages of the crossing passed quickly; with shipping around us, I worked hard on my navigation. As the sky lost its azure colour, it softened and melted into delicately layered pastels; the water was as smooth as glass, disturbed only by *Iduna*'s bow wave, until a pair of dolphins joined us. I sat on the cabin roof and sang out loud. There was phosphorescence that night, lighting up each fish like a dart as it fled through the water, startled by our progress. The bow wave seemed alight, and I turned off the navigation lights for a couple of minutes, just to enjoy it at its most vivid.

In Padstow the following morning I woke to the hustle and bustle of people, the barking of dogs, and the squeals of children, and when I popped my head out of the hatch I saw that the quiet little harbour had become a gathering-point for holidaymakers. The yacht I had tied along-side began to sway a little, and after a few minutes a scruffy-looking head appeared in the hatchway. The sailor, who was quite young, smiled instantly and asked where I had sailed from and when I was heading off.

"Tomorrow morning," I answered, as he jumped into his tender.

"Do you want to have dinner on board?"

"Cool, thanks," I replied as he paddled away to the dockside.

As I sat in the sun, I reflected on the journey so far. It was incredible how far away mononucleosis seemed, as if that experience was years ear-lier, rather than just eighteen months. I could not believe how my life had changed. I was doing everything I'd ever hoped and had been the recipi-ent of enormous kindness from virtual strangers. But then I thought of Thea. She was still flat out, suffering from her nervous reaction. I had called her from time to time to discuss where I was, or to let her know what was happening, but she should have been out sailing on *Cabaret*, as she had done for the past fifteen years. I knew how it felt to be lying un-able to do anything each day, and I also knew that it would be as unnatural to Thea as it was to me.

The sound of oars brought me back to the present as my new friend returned and invited me aboard. The cabin was dimly lit, and the first things I remember seeing were pots and pans, books, and bits of fluffy carpet on the floor. The boat was a mess! In stark contrast to the clutter of the main cabin, the forepeak held the lovingly well-tended items on board. As I peered into the forward cabin, the setting sun highlighted two thriving cannabis plants.

We dove into a Chinese take-out meal and opened beers; and with the little oil lamp lighting the cozy cabin, we chatted passionately about heading out to see the big, wide world. He was as chilled out as his boat, and we had each other in stitches till the early hours of the morning.

August 20th—St. Ives
Felt a bit down when I got up this morning!—probably due to
bad night and the lack of sleep! Anyway it's now 0922.—have
spent 20 minutes fiddling with fishing tackle to catch some

mackerel. The rocking of the boat should do the job!! Not
having much luck though but it's the thought that counts I
guess. The forecast is crap, and the visibility bad—just over one
nautical mile. I won't see much of Land's End. Continued
fishing and planning. . . . Just waiting for a nibble and the tide.

In the end, Land's End was fairly uneventful, but the Longships lighthouse still felt like a major turning-point. Since Scotland I had been
clawing my way west to round this rock, and now we'd done it and were
heading east to that final corner. We were on the home stretch.

We arrived in Plymouth on the evening of 22 August, with a great
feeling of triumph. I was so proud as we sailed into Plymouth Harbour, I
could have been at the helm of the *Cutty Sark*! That evening, however, I
discovered that my sail with Robin Knox-Johnston aboard *Suhaili* had
been cancelled, and that the filming would not occur. I remember that
evening well, sitting on the head of my bunk with a mug of hot chocolate
and the rain beginning to come down outside. I suppose I'd got myself
quite excited about meeting up with Robin properly after our introduction at the BT/YJA awards, and I felt low about those plans falling apart.
The forecast was appalling, too, with gales for the next few days—a
break in the weather sufficient for departure would take a miracle. I
checked my diary and reminded myself that Nan's birthday was in two
days' time. I needed to send her something tomorrow. I fell asleep wondering what it might be.

Next morning I set about making a little card for Nan. I drew a small
map of the UK, painted in the land and sea, and annotated it with a little
flag for Plymouth, marking Nan's eightieth birthday next to it. I finished
it off with pictures of our adventures in Scotland, the dolphins, and the
storms on the East Coast. Then I wrote: "So sorry I can't be with you."

And as I did so, I thought, I *can* be. I could just catch the train and go
up there for a day. Suddenly I became very excited. I rang Mum to ask
what everyone was doing, though I gave no indication that I might come
home. I was determined to try to join them. Sarah agreed to pick me up
and take me to the pub where they would be eating.

When we moored in Plymouth I'd been struck by two boats branded
with company logos. I recognized them as 67-foot BT Global Challenge
boats. The Challenge was set up by Sir Chay Blyth, famous for his own

solo circumnavigation against the prevailing winds and currents. The race crews follow the same route. I had read that a woman named Samantha Brewster, having taken part in the last race, was going to be sailing a Challenge boat single-handed around the world. I realized that hers was one of the two moored on the same pontoon as *Iduna*, only about 100 feet away. I watched the commotion on the pontoon, and after my efforts to get *Iduna* ready for her trip, I felt I understood a little of what was going on.

Brian from Musto had told me that he was working with Sam on clothing, and he must have said something to her, as she came over for a chat that afternoon. She was small and strong-looking, with a high-energy smile. She was very down to earth and happily took me on board her boat. It made a huge impression on me.

As the sun went down I sat in *Iduna*'s cockpit, sipping a mug of hot tea. I found it hard to stop looking in the direction of Sam's boat, and I kept thinking about what she was going to be undertaking out there.

SARAH MET ME at Matlock Station and drove me to the pub, where to my horror there was no sign of the family car. There was no point in going in, as it was obvious we were in the wrong place, so we headed back home. Sarah left and I let myself into the house. Soon after I heard the sound of the car engine and dashed up the stairs. From my bedroom window I could see everyone getting out of the car. Suddenly, I felt embarrassed. I heard Mum go into her bedroom and decided to follow her. She was on the far side of the bed, getting something from a drawer; as I walked in, she looked up, and for a second I thought she was going to faint.

"Ellen!" she cried, and I ran round the bed to hug her, both of us with tears in our eyes. Nan was quite speechless as I appeared in the doorway. It had been well worth the effort.

My next log entry was for the following day, when I made it back on board *Iduna*.

25/8/95
1328 Back in my world!

I was stuck in Plymouth for a further three days. Each morning, I would get the forecast and decide whether or not it was possible to leave. It was frustrating when each forecast seemed just to hold me back, and we spent another day tied up. I was pretty happy when I finally could get going again.

1700: Speed over ground 6.5—racing another yacht—have sat in bow ECSTATIC!!—I love **IDUNA.** *THOSE WERE THE MOST EXCITING 7 MINS OF MY LIFE—IDUNA WAS OFF!!!*

We had the most incredible time, stopping in ports such as Salcombe, Dartmouth, and Brixham. I was looked after by the Island Cruising Club in Salcombe, welcomed by the glorious castles at the mouth of the River Dart, and built up quite a chatty rapport with Brixham Coastguard on the radio. Each time I left a port and arrived at another I would let them know my passage plan, and by the time I left their region, they'd generally guessed I was sailing around Great Britain. One of them even asked me to send him a postcard from Weymouth.

The longest passage along the South Coast was the trek across Lyme Bay to Weymouth, which, although just under 60 miles, seemed like a major crossing for a 21-foot Corribee. What made the passage even more tricky was the rounding of Portland Bill, a massive natural spit of land leading to a headland. Portland Bill is renowned for its dangerous overfalls and terrifying seas in strong winds. I'd sought advice from several people during the trip, and one piece that particularly stuck in my mind was: "Sail round the point close enough that you could touch the rocks with a boathook." I couldn't wait!

Time passed quickly once I'd rounded the Bill and left Weymouth. I made a stopover in Poole to sleep for a few hours, then made an early start to sail straight up to Southampton.

That afternoon I arrived in Ocean Village and in the grey drizzle tied *Iduna* alongside the pontoon in our new short-term home. As I stowed away everything down below, I heard the sound of an engine coming closer. I peered out of my hatch just as the BT Global Challenge boat that had been tied up next to Sam's in Plymouth pulled gently alongside the dock. There were five or six people on board, and after tying up, one of them came over to say hello and tell me I'd be more than welcome if I fancied popping round for a cup of tea later.

Nervously I climbed on board a few hours later, feeling a little self-conscious. The noise of my feet echoed, and for a moment, I just stood there feeling stupid. I didn't know whether to leave or not.

"Hello," I called. No answer.

Remembering the layout of Sam's boat, I peered down into the living space below the cockpit and called one last time. Still no answer.

Creeping back, I was stopped in my tracks by the grunt of a sleepy giant. A man dressed in very unflattering thermals appeared through a small door just opposite me.

Merfyn Owen clearly had been sound asleep, but having extended the invitation he was adamant that I should not leave. He suggested that I put on the kettle while he got dressed. Five minutes later, as the kettle began to boil, a new man emerged.

Merv was tall and well built, with wild, curly black hair and the loudest laugh you could imagine. It soon became clear that he was a gentle giant more than prepared to give a tremendous amount. We got on famously, and he explained that he was in Southampton with the BT Global Challenge because roughly the same time next year he would be skippering one of the boats sailing around the world.

Merv, like me, had been brought up in the country, but he had not begun sailing until he was eighteen. I talked of *Panic Major* and Hull and discovered Merv knew Robert Nickerson. He talked of the places he had sailed to and the boats he had sailed on, of skippering Open 60s across the Atlantic, of the job he had as shore crew for the BOC, a single-handed round-the-world race that stopped in ports. He'd even sailed on 60- and 80-foot multihulls around France and the rest of Europe. I lapped it up, and as our conversation unrolled, I learned that Merv now made his living as a yacht designer. One of the designs was in the marina, and he suggested we take a look.

Maverick was a unique, incredible boat. Her wide decks and funky-coloured hull gave her an almost dinghy-like appearance. She had no visible cabin like a cruising boat, just a small hatch that went below decks, where there was a tiny bay for a gas stove and four very basic bunks—no more than aluminium frames with plastic mesh stretched over them. The rain began to hammer down, so we climbed inside. Merv leaned back against her hull on one of the bunks, as he could not even sit upright inside, and I sat on the step, entranced. He began talking about the reasons why he designed *Maverick* the way he did, and he described a race known as the Mini Transat. The Mini is a single-handed transatlantic race sailed in high-performance boats the same size as *Iduna*. I was fascinated by what he told me and began to think again about my next step. It had been a long time since I'd had a conversation which appeared to open so many doors.

The Southampton Boat Show got off to a whirlwind start as Musto's Brian Pilcher whisked me away and seemingly introduced me to everyone he had ever known. We called at TV stations and show stands and had lunches during which I poured out stories of every adventure I'd had on the trip so far. Graham Percy was there, too, and between them they set up interviews with local radio and TV and the yachting magazines.

As they'd promised, the RYA presented me with my Yachtmaster Instructor endorsement at the Royal Southampton Yacht Club, and I met up again with the examiners, James Stevens and John Goode. It was odd seeing them on home territory, but I was really pleased to have lived up to their expectations with the miles I had covered on board *Iduna*.

While I was in Southampton I also got back in touch with the Sea Cadets. They'd offered me a week's sailing on one of their smaller yachts out of Gosport immediately after the show. I was unsure whether or not to accept at first, as I was keen to finish the trip, but I knew it might lead to opportunities for the future. I had thoroughly enjoyed every minute of sailing on board *Royalist*, and I realized I would be crazy not to say yes.

After a week in Southampton I was itching to get moving again—I had a week to get as far east as possible before joining the Sea Cadets back in Gosport. So *Iduna* and I left Southampton before the end of the show and headed for the rising sun.

23rd September
1924 hours. Sailing up Chichester Harbour. Fantastic.
Beautiful sunset—red sky and complete silence! Amid this
peace and tranquillity, **Iduna** *creams along, feeling almost*
motionless!

28th September
Depart Northney Marina at 0530. Ran aground on way out of
Chichester Harbour. Very shitty feeling! However, managed to
clear her. There was a starboard mark out. But an ebbing tide!!

I'm writing this at sea on passage to Newhaven just found out
£10 per night there—no free either! The cliffs past Brighton
look rusty along the tops! passed one anchored ship and I
trapped my thumb when disconnecting the Navik. Looe
Channel was a piece of piss! (right now 1317) I feel very tired!
keep thinking about Mini Transat, Merv and **Maverick.**

After a five-day break sailing with the Sea Cadets, the rest of the trip
passed very quickly. The goal was just making it back, and although *Iduna*
and I stopped in several ports, I was so focused that I almost stopped
taking it all in. I knew I had to make it to the mouth of the Humber at
exactly the right time. The Humber is such a fast-flowing and powerful
tidal river that if I got it wrong, even by no more than half an hour, I
would stand little chance of making it to the marina. I could be in sight
of it, but if the tide turned against me before I made it through those
lock gates, I would be carried back out of the river.

The last night was a testing sail, and it passed slowly and foggily. As
the night crept past I was grateful that the fog was lifting bit by bit, and I
was relieved to be able to see the lights of the ships once again. I smiled,
then laughed out loud at 0257 when I heard the familiar voices of VTS
Humber on the radio. I knew I was home.

As the dawn broke on 12 October, the most incredible light was shining through the light mist and gradually crept up into the sky. Everything seemed tinted with silver, almost as though a blanket of moonlight
was covering us. *Iduna* was sailing perfectly, heeling over and making
good speed, the muddy Humber waters once again washing past her tiny
hull. I picked out those all-too-memorable sights on the skyline as we
sailed along—the huge Tetney Monobuoy, Grimsby dock tower, and the
structure of the Immingham oil terminal. As we crept past each buoy it
flashed us, and I picked out its name. I felt as though I was being silently
welcomed back.

All my friends from Hull as well as my family, including Nan, were
there to see me in. There were cameras and journalists, and Robert had
come down with a bottle of champagne. I shall never forget Nan's smile
as she came up to give me a kiss; she seemed so proud. I was surprised
by my reaction to seeing Mum and Dad, too. Of course I was excited,
but at the same time it felt as though the spell had been broken. I had

been desperately looking forward to telling everyone what had happened since I left, but now I felt numb that it was over.

After a day of celebration it was sad to see Mum and Dad leave that evening. Mum had asked if I'd return home, but I had to stay in Hull. In forty-eight hours I'd be joining the Sea Cadets again. *Royalist* was in Dundee, and I'd be sailing her south to Great Yarmouth over two weeks.

As the sun set that evening, I wandered back down from the Nautical School to *Iduna*. She seemed so peaceful as she sat there alongside the pontoon, the radar reflector still hanging in her rigging, her starboard spreader slightly drooping with the load.

"It's over, lass, thank you," I whispered quietly as I rubbed her dewy cabin top.

That night I went up to the marina bar for tea and joined David and his new crew for his weekend sailing course. The familiarity of the scene was reassuring, but I knew that I'd changed. I was still the same person, but now I could see farther. The trip had broadened my horizons and intensified my need to explore them further. I thought about Merv and the Mini Transat, and about the Sea Cadets and the wonderful work they do. I didn't know which way to head yet, but I realized at that moment that I was not going to be happy visiting that bar every night for the next thirty years.

On that trip around Britain, I grew up. When I set out to do it I was going to give it my all, just hoping that we would make it back into the marina in Hull. I had seen the most beautiful, memorable places, and more than anything else had enjoyed the company of people whose openness and generosity never ceased to amaze me. But deep down I was driven—driven not to remain in a place longer than was necessary, even if great people had invited me to stay. I found myself frustrated that on so many occasions I was sailing slowly, or that the winds had simply not come and we'd had to motor. I forced myself to make decisions I'd never taken before. I had sole responsibility for myself and for every move we made. I knew now that there are no magic methods of making a situation better; you just have to stay calm, do all you can, and *believe* that things will improve. Sitting at home alone, you can't anticipate that feeling. It's not just the fact that you are on your own, but the safety decisions: do I go or do I wait? There is never an unquestionably right answer—except, of course, with hindsight.

When I listen to my tapes of that trip I hear such intense unease in my voice. Only now can I understand why I was stressed. There's such a contrast between the highs and the lows: I can hear such desperate anger in my voice when conditions were not as they had been predicted, when I was soaked to the bone, hand-steering because the autopilots would not work properly. At eighteen you look for someone or something else to blame, but I grew to realize that there is no one to blame, that anything can happen and the reasons can never be completely anticipated. Preparation can eliminate some but never all of these problems, because so much is the unpredictable, and it's the unpredictable that you have to learn to handle with flexibility and pragmatism. You simply have to take it in your stride.

I can see the differences in me then, but I can see the similarities, too. I was learning to be philosophical when plans have to change, and I was beginning to realize the extent to which altered plans can and will happen. Good and bad will be thrown up in equal measure, and while enjoying the former is easy, you can't let the latter drag you down.

CHAPTER SEVEN

IN DUNDEE I immediately felt at home back aboard *Royalist*. The sunrise was stunning, with the wisps of cloud forming ornate silhouettes in the beautiful orange sky, and the water was still as we slipped along past the tiny craft dwarfed by our imposing presence. Standing there on *Royalist*'s deck, I had responsibility, shared with the rest of the crew, for the Sea Cadets on board.

I loved seeing how they grew in confidence over the week they were with us. It was constantly rewarding—from the initial days when they considered peeling potatoes in the morning as purgatory, to the end of the week, when we found them singing and joking while they did it. What always struck me was not so much how the week would bring people together as how it made them realize the value of their own contributions.

At the end of the first week we said goodbye as a new group embarked. We sailed the next leg, though, in very different conditions. On the way from Hartlepool to Lowestoft we were stuck in difficult weather—a much-stronger-than-predicted southeasterly which peaked at a Force 9 gale. The North Sea is relatively shallow, resulting in waves that get short and steep very quickly. The motion aboard *Royalist* was dreadful as she pitched and rolled. Each time she punched into a wave, spray and water hurtled over her decks. It was a constant job to make sure that the kids who were off watch were harnessed to the boat as they made a dash for the rail and threw up into the churning water. *Royalist* was unable to sail into the wind in those conditions. The result was that we had to motor, and even that was a struggle, as we managed only a few knots before the night closed in on us, the sky appearing barely high enough to let our masts pass beneath it. I had never before been at sea in such bad weather, and I was fascinated by its wildness—foaming crests crashed again and again as they passed the porthole next to my bunk, and the world outside was submerged with each roll.

Adrenalin surged as I woke from a difficult sleep to the sound of the fire alarm. I sprang from my bunk, grabbed my jacket and the fire extinguisher, and made my way to the deck. The kids were flowing out of the hatches, all wearing their harnesses, and were calmly marching to their muster stations. Some, already green with sea-sickness, now had anxiety etched on their faces. We soon tracked down the problem: smoke and steam from the port engine, which had begun overheating. We shut it down but were now in danger of not making our destination at all, as we could only just creep forward. As a precaution, we lowered the anchor in an attempt to secure the boat in its position while an assessment was made of the damage and needed repairs.

We had to wait several hours for the engine to cool before Dave, the engineer, could attempt to fix it, and as it looked like an awkward job, my offer to assist him was accepted. *Royalist*'s anchor was dragging, and we were starting to drift slowly towards a nearby gas field. Luckily I was able to restrain her enough to keep us safe while we worked on the engine.

Dave and I climbed down into the engine room; as he opened the watertight door, the heat surged into our faces. I took my last deep breath of cool, sweet air and clambered inside the diesel-smelling sauna. Every creak and groan from *Royalist*'s structure seemed amplified down there and certainly made the situation feel more urgent than it actually was. The problem was with the water-cooling impeller, which, because of the location of the engine mount, was very difficult to access. I lay on the engine, stretching to reach the impeller cover, while Dave slid beneath it to get to the bolts from below. The heat was extreme, and I had to move slightly every few seconds to shift the hot spots and remain bearably comfortable as our bodies rocked back and forth with the boat's continued violent motion. I am fortunate that I have never suffered from sea-sickness, but I am sure that if ever it was going to happen, that would have been the time. Sweat streamed down our faces, but around an hour later we finished the job, and Dave tentatively started the engine. Upon emerging back on deck, thankful the job was done, we realized it was not over yet; we still had the anchor to get up and were now approaching the exclusion zone around one of the rigs in a gas field. It was time to get out of there. And so began the laborious task of bringing in the anchor, which seemed unusually slow and difficult. The hydraulics would only winch when the bow was falling into the trough after a wave passed beneath us. The bow then seemed heavy as *Royalist* began to climb the next wall of breaking surf; as the two met, the sea exploded over us, sluicing unyielding walls of water down along the deck.

Eventually the final feet of chain appeared and then the anchor emerged at the surface, but they were not alone; we also had an old cable which we must have dragged from the seabed. With skill and a few years' knowledge, Paul, the skipper, managed to flip the anchor, using the trip point at just the right moment to release the cable. *Royalist's* bow popped up like a rubber duck in a bath, and once more we were able to ride over rather than through the waves, continuing our passage to Lowestoft.

ASHORE IN LOWESTOFT at the end of my trip, I phoned home. Lewis answered, said that Mum and Dad were out, and told me to call back later. I couldn't linger on the phone and got no hint of what was to come.

I called again that afternoon, from the train on the way south. I was bursting to tell them all that had happened on *Royalist*, but my enthusiasm evaporated the second I heard Mum's voice. It sounded empty.

"What's happened, Mum?" I asked.

"Your dad's had an accident. Don't worry, we think he's OK; he's here at home now."

She continued, explaining what had happened. At the weekend, Dad had offered to chop off a few branches from the trees in the school car park. While working with his chainsaw, he was struck in the chest by a falling branch that knocked him out of the tree. He must have fallen about 20 feet onto rocky ground. Luckily someone ran to help him, but in typical, stubborn-Dad fashion, he said he was fine, just winded. This was the same Dad, after all, who had dropped lump hammers on his head and had fallen through ceilings. But he wasn't OK, and an ambulance was called anyway. Finding nothing other than bruising after he'd been X-rayed, the hospital sent him home, but he couldn't walk and virtually crawled into the car when Mum came to pick him up.

That evening Uncle Glyn, the local GP, quickly discovered that Dad had lost some of the feeling in his lower body. On re-admission to hospital he was X-rayed again. The first X-ray had missed the fact that he had smashed one of his vertebrae. It was now thought sufficiently worrying for him to be sent immediately to Sheffield Spinal Unit, where for three months he remained strapped to a bed, unable to move his back in any way. It was a real shock to see him looking pale, helpless, and in pain in a hospital bed. He was always such an active, healthy character.

Throughout his ordeal, he showed no anger, or at least not in front of his children, but it must have been a real trial for him. A day had never passed without Dad having worked in some way outdoors. He could see trees outside his hospital window, and they reminded me of how much it helped me when I was ill to look outside at the eucalyptus. I was glad he could see trees too.

THAT YEAR, 1995, was horrible, and Mum really bore the brunt of it. She's the most honest and gentle person I have ever known and has endless reserves of patience. She seemed to be carrying the world on her shoulders that year,, and I felt acutely aware of how little help she was getting from me. As well as handling the aftermath of Dad's accident, she was helping Lew to decide about his future. By this stage he'd dropped out of university and was struggling to cope with the added pressure of Dad's accident. And the illness that had marred Nan's university exchange in Germany was diagnosed as a form of fibrous cancer in her lungs, which had led to mild pneumonia. Mum was taking meals to her each day and trying to look after her, but her burden didn't stop there. She also was still caring for Thea, who by now had moved up north into my old bedroom. I'm sure that walks with Mac were pretty much the only thing that kept Mum sane through those dreadful months. I told her I would stay at home and help her look after everyone, but she was adamant that she was OK and that I should do what was best for my future. Although I decided to carry on sailing, it wasn't a comfortable decision, and I still look back on it with unease.

My own life at that time was a whirlwind. I was travelling around the

country, writing and answering letters to everyone I had met on the trip
and to those who had sponsored me for it. In mid-November, just two
weeks after my trip on *Royalist*, I received a letter from Barry Mattey,
the offshore commander of the Sea Cadets, offering me a post as a small-
boat skipper. I was sufficiently tempted to arrange a meeting with him
just before Christmas. I was also receiving requests for talks about my
trip with *Iduna* from various yacht clubs, along with the incredible offer
of a space in the pool at the London International Boat Show.

Brian Pilcher, once again, was my guide through the following weeks.
He encouraged me to market myself wisely and to write effective letters. I would have run across the country at my own expense to give a
talk or have a meeting, but Brian taught me to realize that I held some
value. That made a massive difference between having very little or,
worse, nothing. The plain fact was that I did not have any financial reserves. I had spent my last savings in trailing *Iduna* to Derbyshire and was
subsisting on a small amount of money from my first painting commissions, including one of Merv's boat, *Global Teamwork*.

In December I met with Barry Mattey. I knew I loved the Sea Cadets
and I wanted to work with the kids, but I couldn't stop thinking about
the Mini Transat and single-handed races. I had just seen a long article
about the Mini in *Yachting World*, which I'd read and re-read. I didn't
know which way to jump.

I arrived in Portsmouth and, before the meeting, was shown the boat I
would be skippering, a Morgan Giles 43 named *Petrel*. As we walked into
the shed, she towered above us. When I went on board, it was obvious
that she was very much in refit. Most of her interior had been removed,
as fittings were accessed and the engine serviced, but even in this less-
than-perfect state I could see she was beautiful.

I talked about the position with Barry, and with one week in four off,
allowing me to pursue other options, I was convinced it could work. I
wrote to accept the job and was due to start at the end of January.

STILL IMMOBILIZED at the spinal unit, Dad wasn't around for Christmas.
Normally, he would have fussed about in the kitchen with Mum, or fer-
reted around in the fields for holly and mistletoe to hang in the house.
He loves Christmas, and his enthusiasm had rubbed off on his family.

Thea managed to come downstairs on Christmas Day, even though pain forced her to lie flat on the floor. Mac, Ferg, and Lew, who seemed to have grown from the responsibility that came from our father's absence, were also there, and Nan came over. In the evening, we drove to Sheffield to see Dad. Mum, as ever, had been a trouper, and again I felt guilty about leaving, this time to head south for the job with the Sea Cadets.

All too soon our Christmas was over and I had to go to London to prepare for the boat show. I knew the show would be a golden opportunity to meet people who might help me further my sailing career.

Each day of the show I would sit on board *Iduna* and talk to passersby who showed an interest, or go to functions held by some of the sponsors who had helped me get around Britain. I spent a lot of time with Brian, who was revelling in the fact that I had made it all the way round—he was talking enthusiastically about it to everyone.

I'd invited Mum down to London in the hope it would be a welcome break from life at home, and she came along to the show. One afternoon I left her alone briefly with the boat. When I returned she handed me a card left by someone named Mark Turner. Intrigued, we went to meet him on his stand but missed him—a less-than-successful start to a relationship that was to become one of the most important of my life.

We did meet the following day, however. Mark was an athletic-looking guy who I guessed was in his early thirties. He was at the show as an employee of a marine company called Spinlock. He had heard that I had done my round-Britain trip single-handed and wanted to talk about the race Merv and I had discussed, the Mini Transat. Fluent in French, Mark had contributed to the article about the Mini in *Yachting World*, which I had read so avidly and so often. In it he'd mentioned he might be interested in doing the race himself. That was enough for Mark, who is not one to dodge a challenge, and the Mini in 1997 became an unbreakable commitment. We parted on the understanding that if I decided I might be doing the race, we would talk again.

For the rest of the show I wrestled with a dilemma that had become increasingly clear. I knew that I had to make a difficult choice. I began to doubt that I could manage further projects alongside the Sea Cadets job. There was no shortage of reasons why I shouldn't just carry on with the job and move *Iduna* to the South Coast to live on her in Gosport. But the morning after my first meeting with Mark, I had woken with a start. I could sense that burning feeling inside me once more, and I was certain deep down that I had to choose racing.

I knew from my own trip around Britain that a venture demands 100 per cent commitment to be successful. I couldn't take the Sea Cadets job without such a commitment, nor would I be able to pursue racing if I lacked it. I needed advice, and once again I turned to Brian.

He helped me to clarify things. Although he thought the Sea Cadets offered a great opportunity to do something I loved, he saw the danger in starting something to which I was not entirely committed. I drafted a letter to Barry Mattey, explaining that while at the London Boat Show, my exposure to new options had meant I'd come to a decision:

> These options will allow me to get a foothold in the short-handed trans-ocean racing field, which is where my long-term ambitions lie . . . it would be inappropriate to instruct Cadets if my heart could not be 100 per cent devoted to that task.

I concluded that I had "a very real opportunity of fulfilling dreams which have driven my enthusiasm for sailing for some years."

I hoped with all my heart that Barry would understand.

Just four days later, Mum called me to say a letter from Gosport had come for me, and she asked if I wanted her to read it over the phone. I was petrified of what I was going to hear, but asked her to read it nonetheless. Barry began by saying he'd had mixed feelings when he read my letter. He was disappointed that I would not be working with them, but he went on to say, "However I am very pleased for you and if there are any opportunities out there for you as a yachtswoman then grasp them with both hands."

My relief was unbelievable. I could not imagine anyone who might have written a more sensitive or supportive reply. He finished by insisting that I should be neither too proud nor too shy to let them know if my plans went awry for any reason in the future.

Things moved quickly after the show. I needed to make my home on the South Coast, because this was the only place I could learn to race. I had everything to learn, and my limited experience of racing *Panic Major* out of Hull only emphasized that. I decided that I would base *Iduna* on

the Hamble, the river from which I had sailed for my Instructor examination; and yet again Brian helped me out, finding a marina that would
let me leave *Iduna* on her trailer for a few months for free. We were
about to begin a whole new adventure.

MEETING MARK at the boat show had fired my imagination, and by the
beginning of February I was on my way to the Isle of Wight to see him.
He appeared at the door of his office in jeans and a rugby shirt. He
smiled as he welcomed me in, but he seemed distracted by other things.
I followed him up a flight of winding steps.

"I've just got to finish this—are you OK to wait for a while?"

"No worries," I replied. I pulled out the notes I had printed on Nan's
word processor and sat down at a desk at the side of the room. I flicked
through a few documents and calendars I had pulled together to help
make the Mini Transat project work over the months ahead. It was very
much on my list of "things to do," but it was an ocean race, a transatlantic
ocean race. I'd never crossed the Atlantic, and I was desperate to get
more experience. I read through the two-page agenda I'd prepared. In it
were fourteen items meant to show Mark what I personally could bring
to any project, but in truth there was little concrete on offer.

> 11. I have a problem in that I am trying to make a living out
> of all this, so it's just slightly important to get sponsorship!
> I would be quite happy to belong to a company! Do you
> reckon I'd make a successful mascot!

Exclamation marks were a common element in any text I put down
on paper. I was a bundle of energy, just desperate to get on with things.
The list read on.

> 14. Finally—We must go sailing together!!—Who knows,
> we might not get on?

I peered over my papers through the window and caught my breath
on seeing the view. I could see beyond the river, all the way out to the
Solent. The navigation marks were flashing in the channel, and I could
hear the Red Funnel ferry engine as it docked just a few hundred yards

down river. Mark was oblivious to all this and was typing away as if his life depended on it. Anyone could have walked in and dropped something on his desk, and I swear he would not even have noticed. I had never met anyone who seemed so confident with computers. Mark had so many projects going on professionally as well as personally—I saw his collection of posters from the races he had done. He virtually lived in his office, and, seeing the futon on the floor and the duvet in the cupboard, I guessed that he worked some long nights. It was immediately obvious how industrious and dedicated he was.

Although this job was primarily office-based, he clearly was someone who just went out there and got on with it. Incredibly, by the age of twenty-one, he had already sailed in the 1989–90 Whitbread Round the World Race. I learned that he had been to university in Exeter before joining the Royal Navy, where he stayed for six years but left after feeling like too small a cog in a big machine. It turned out that he had raced in 1994 in the two-handed Round Britain Race on Merv's boat *Maverick* when she was fresh from the yard. They had encountered problems and had not done too well, but one thing was certain: I was sitting in the same room as someone who had exactly the same interests as I did— short-handed ocean sailing.

It is difficult to place a finger on what it is about short-handed sailing that is so special. The guys who race single- or two-handed are not necessarily the best at any specific job on a boat, but they do have to be the most resourceful and widely knowledgeable about all aspects of sailing. Unlike racing round buoys in an estuary, short-handers tend to be good on longer events where stamina and the ability to maintain an even level of good performance are more important than flashes of pure brilliance. Above all, there is an unwritten bond that ties the skippers together along with the sea—all realizing how they depend upon each other.

Mark was new to single-handing and, though very positive, was clearly nervous about the prospect of racing in the Mini Transat. We talked about other events using the same boats—the Mini Fastnet and Trans-Gascogne the following year and basically just about every Mini race there was or ever had been. The Mini is an unforgiving but ultimately very rewarding race; it hits home hard that you're sailing thousands of miles of open ocean alone in a truly tiny boat. It's impossible to hide from the dangers of the Mini, and tragically there has on average been one entrant lost each time it's taken place.

We broke off briefly to eat a Chinese take-out meal and then worked on until about 2 A.M., when he gave me a lift in his old Ford Fiesta to my guesthouse. It had been a brief but valuable insight into the life of Mark Turner.

Dad was out of the spinal unit by now and back at home, but he was far from recovered. He had to be very careful moving around and had great difficulty walking. As a result of lying flat for so long, his legs were swollen and uncomfortable, but the hardest part must have been not knowing if the feeling would ever return—only time would tell. The rest of us were just relieved to have him back, but it was upsetting to see in his eyes the frustration at not being able to do all he could do previously. But he wouldn't give in, and that spirit kept him positive. I think Mum and Dad were also very conscious that I was in the process of leaving home. They knew now that sailing would be my career, and they had accepted that it was highly unlikely I would ever go to university.

IN MID-MARCH the day finally came for my move south. I collected my clothes, my bike, and the other personal belongings I needed to move on board *Iduna*. Mum and I planned to drive down in the evening and spend a full day organizing everything before Mum returned to Derbyshire the following day.

We arrived late at our B&B near the Hamble and went straight to our room. As we laughed at shared memories and with relief at having Dad home, I talked to Mum about her worries. We topped up the tea, and Mum spoke about Nan, Gran, and Lewis. By this stage Lewis was looking at moving down to a different part of the South Coast to live with his new girlfriend; it was wonderful to see him so positive after the disappointment of leaving university. Nan and Gran, though, were very ill: Gran had lost a terrific amount of weight and had been at her worst while Dad was in hospital. We had recently learnt that her thyroid was causing the problem, and at least the diagnosis meant there was now a possibility of treatment. Nan, however, was not really improving. The only glimmer of positive news came when the consultant at the Chest Clinic suggested she return to university to finish her degree. I think it was his way of gently letting us know that Nan would not get better. For her, though, it was the best news possible, and something to get her teeth into once again. She would return in September. Although Mum was happy for her, I couldn't help but feel she was a little apprehensive at having to run Nan to college and back each day. But Mum was Mum, and she would go on trying to please others till she dropped.

We had a frustrating time looking for a marina to berth *Iduna*. Moorings were expensive and much sought after, but I could no longer keep her where she'd been sitting on her trailer since I brought her down after the London Boat Show. With each visit, we found the fees still out of reach, and, weary at the end of the day, we reluctantly headed for the last marina on the list. I had been told that it was the most expensive, so we drove in feeling gloomy. It certainly seemed like one of the best places to be. There were all sorts of boats around, racers and cruisers, all sizes—some absolutely enormous. If I was going to meet people to race with, this had to be one of the best options, but I simply could not afford to keep *Iduna* here. I had managed to save just over £2,000—that would not even cover the mooring fees in a marina like this. We drove past the brokerage, the bar, and the offices, and at that point I couldn't help but feel that it wasn't the place for us, but we continued on past a sign saying "Hamble Yacht Services." The clinical feeling that had put us off the other marinas vanished. There were enormous sheds and another pontoon. It was a hive of activity, a working boat yard. There were so many boats everywhere, in travel hoists slung above the ground or chocked up across the yard, that we could not even make out the other side. I now had a good feeling about this place.

We found the dock office in a small modular building by the walkway to the pontoon. I knocked on the door, which was slightly ajar. "Come in," said a voice on the other side, and as we entered we were immediately greeted by a smile.

"How can I help you, my love?" he said, and I began to explain that I was looking for an annual berth. He didn't keep us hanging for his quote for very long and said it'd be £1,000. I could have hugged him to say thanks. Though we didn't know it then, Jim was to become one of the few friends I made on the South Coast.

We returned to *Iduna* after shopping for essentials in Southampton. It was getting dark now and had been raining on and off for hours. We pulled everything out of the car and put it on board. It suddenly dawned on me that Mum was about to leave. In the half-light the yard was grey, damp, and empty except for the two of us standing by the tiny boat and the car. As we hugged goodbye I heard the wind whistle through the forest of masts. Mum's door clunked shut for the last time, and I cried as I watched the rear lights of her car vanish in the rain.

I climbed on board *Iduna*, trying to take my mind off Mum's departure by stowing the remaining gear in the cabin. Everything was damp and I was exhausted. When the only torch I could find began to die, I decided to get some sleep. My bunk was full of gear which was virtually impossible to move, so I wrapped myself as comfortably as possible around the outboard's propeller on the cabin floor and pulled my sleeping-bag over me. As I lay there on my belongings and listened to the alien sounds of my new home, I felt more alone than ever before. "You've got to make the best of this, kiddo," I whispered, and closed my eyes.

THE FIRST WEEKS in Hamble were difficult as I tried to settle into my new environment and work out how my life in the south was going to take shape. I was shocked at how few people I was meeting. When I was in Hull, strangers would come up and introduce themselves and ask what I was up to. In Hamble, it just never happened. The only faces I knew were the guys in the yard—and Jim, of course, who was always happy to have a friendly chat. I suppose a scruffy-looking little 21-foot boat with a handful of stickers on her side doesn't really look like much next to a stunning collection of pristine race boats. I felt very out of place. Everyone else seemed to belong to this boat or that team, and it's not something you can easily break into.

Without company in the evenings, after seeing the sun set along the river I would often walk to the end of the pontoons and sit watching the flashing navigation lights and the water flowing round the boats. Sometimes I would even do handstands and cartwheels along the planked pontoons—it felt fantastic to be able to stretch out after spending so much time working in *Iduna*'s cramped cabin. But the freedom to enjoy this release was restricted at the weekends, when the character of the yard changed completely. The weekend racers would descend on the village, lining the streets with their expensive cars. The commotion would start early in the morning. Gaggles of people would file past *Iduna* while

I sat in her cockpit—sometimes writing, sometimes reading, hoping that someone might come up and ask if I was free because they were one person down. But that didn't happen. By mid-morning, the pontoons would be silent again while the boats raced before returning in the afternoon—everybody rushing in, eager to fill the bars. I hated the weekend evenings. Hamble was buzzing, but I was never a part of it. Eventually I plucked up the courage to visit a pub in the village where I knew the racing crews hung out, but I felt like a fish out of water. My face must have been beet red as I edged my way to the bar, overhearing their tales of the day's racing. I bought a beer and sat at the bar, slowly sipping away. People crammed in alongside me, but I felt as though I was just observing what was going on and regretted having come. The high point of the evening occurred when someone I'd seen in the yard came up to buy drinks and recognized me. We spoke briefly before he returned with his drinks to his friends. I finished my beer and left, thankful for any friendly human contact.

It was weeks before I got to sail as part of a crew racing around the "cans." It was organized by Ashley Perrin, with whom I'd made contact after the last boat show when she was described to me as someone who "has a similar determination to yourself." She was planning to compete in the 1997 two-handed Round Britain and Ireland Race, and we'd stayed in touch. We arranged to meet at the Royal Ocean Racing Club, and I remember being a little fazed by Ashley's confidence; though just over a year younger, she seemed mature for her age and clearly felt quite at home in the yacht club, which along with the surroundings made me feel self-conscious.

I found my first race pretty difficult. I wasn't used to playing just one role on a boat. Everyone on board seemed to know exactly what needed to be done, well trained to the point where it seemed they had been doing this all their lives. Every manoeuvre was like an army drill. It meant each person learned a sequence of events in an almost robotic manner, and the raised voices on board just reinforced the military feeling. My kind of sailing had never been like this. I was used to sailing by the seat of my pants, using common sense and feel. I handled things as they came along, which meant being aware of wind, tide, boat speed, and a hundred other things all at the same time. This was very different; on this boat we had specific, inflexible roles, and I found it difficult to fit in.

As the days rolled by I worked on my computer, writing new proposals for sponsorships and a newsletter to let people know what was happening to me; for many it must have seemed that I had disappeared off the face of the earth. I knew that if things became financially impossible I could attempt to get a job as a sailing instructor, but I wanted to hold back on that. If I was going to give racing a fair crack I had to try harder to gain experience, contact more sponsors, and be ready to grasp an opportunity if it arose.

Not long after returning to *Iduna* from my first race across the English Channel to Le Havre, I received a phone-call from Merv that would shape the year 1996 completely. Merv had been in Hamble for a while, preparing his crew for the BT Global Challenge, and had often supplemented my meagre rations with food left over from his weekend's sailing. This time, though, his help was to prove much more significant. He'd recommended me for a preparateur's job on an Open 60 which had been chartered by his friend Alan Wynne-Thomas. I asked what "preparateur" meant, and he told me it was a French term for the people who prepare racing boats. Merv wanted to make sure I was interested. My job would be to prepare the boat in Plymouth for the Europe One Star (Single-handed) Transatlantic Race, then sail her back from the States with her skipper, Alan Wynne-Thomas, before getting her ready for the ultimate: the Vendée Globe. I tried to sound calm on the phone, but I'm not sure I managed it. I had only dreamt of sailing on a boat like this. Simply to be around one was a thrill.

I arrived in Plymouth a week later, on 1 June 1996—exactly twelve months since I had set off to sail around Great Britain. The sun shone as I checked over the boat. There was no sign of Alan on board, so I put my bags in the cockpit and, as Merv had suggested, went to find him in the bar.

Alan was a short, stocky man with a weathered face, a twinkle in his eyes, an infectious grin, and curly brown hair. Wearing a red-and-black lumberjack shirt and jeans, he did not look in the least bit like a sailor. I liked him instantly. He was laughing with friends in the bar, so I grabbed a drink and sat down. Once Alan and I were alone, we began to discuss the programme for the boat, newly christened *Elan Sifo*. I must have asked Alan a hundred questions about his life. He was a natural single-handed sailor, and at over fifty had a wealth of experience. He seemed to have raced everything across the Atlantic from his own 40-footer, *Jemima Nicolas*, to a 40-foot trimaran, and above all he had already competed in the Vendée Globe, although the last time he took part had almost led to disaster for him.

We talked and worked on board for the rest of the day before Alan returned home to Scotland for the last time before the race. I had to organize the collection of sails for repair and replacement, clean the boat, check the ropes, fix some of the electronics. At times I was out of my depth but knew it, so I sought advice from people in the yard, learning as I worked. I absolutely loved it. I kept reminding myself that Alan was about to cross the Atlantic and that everything had to be right.

Alan returned from Scotland in time to make final preparations for racing before we finally moored her up with the other boats competing in the race. I looked out at a marina packed full of the world's most innovative and high-tech ocean-racing boats and felt inspired. Each one was going to set off across the North Atlantic with just one person on board. As we tied up *Elan Sifo* among them, I could think only of sprinting off around the marina to look at them all.

Everything about being in Plymouth seemed to seal my fate—from the marina full of Open 60s and space-age multihulls to, more importantly, the people. This was what I had to do. I was in the thick of it and felt like I had really arrived. Alan was the best guy I could possibly imagine working for; he would take me to the team receptions at the yacht club, introducing me to many of the other skippers and preparateurs—people such as Yves Parlier, skipper of the extraordinary *Aquitaine Innovations*, and Vittorio Malingri, who'd competed in the same Vendée Globe as Alan. Although we met only briefly, Vittorio said that if I wanted to race with him in the Québec-St.-Malo race in August, I should give him a call—he gave me his brother's telephone number.

The single-handed racing scene was a small world, and I was overwhelmed by how welcoming everyone was. Even the competing skippers seemed really close-knit, and although they were highly competitive, there was no visible hostility among them or their teams. If anything, the opposite was true, as tools were shared happily if a rival was missing something; it was a wonderful atmosphere. I felt embarrassed by my very rudimentary French, which sometimes made communication frustrating in what had become a French-dominated sport.

This was never a problem with Gerry Rouffs, a French-Canadian skipper who, like Alan, was aiming to take part in the Vendée Globe later in the year. He, too, made me feel at home immediately. Ironically, despite the differences in language and culture among the teams, and my own inexperience, I was already beginning to feel like a part of this incredible world.

When start day arrived I think I was more nervous than Alan, and as he went to the clubhouse for his final shower, I checked over the boat time and time again, switching on all the electronics and starting the little generator for a final battery charge. There was no room for error: Alan was going to be out there for more than two weeks, sailing through everything from storms to icebergs to calms. I checked through the water and food we'd put on board, the spares, the fuel; this was my last chance to make sure everything was ready.

I had asked Mum and Dad if they would come down on the day of the start so they could see what I had been doing. Dad was mobile enough now, though still a little unsteady on his feet, and this was to be his first trip of any distance since his accident. Alan had arranged for them to watch the start from his friends' catamaran, which we thought would be more stable than a monohull. They'd seen me in Hull and sailing *Iduna*, but this was completely different. I wanted them to know that this was where I hoped my future would lie. The weather was beautiful and they couldn't have seen it in a better light. I hoped they shared my pride in watching Alan's departure.

He seemed relaxed as we were towed out of the marina. There were a few cheers as we left the dock, and once clear of the first breakwater we unfurled the headsail. When our towboat departed for its next customer we slowly headed out to clearer water. It felt wonderfully quiet all of a sudden, with just the distant applause in the marina still within range.

There was just time to hug Alan goodbye and jump off *Elan Sifo* into a support boat before the ten-minute gun fired. And although I could feel the tension in the air and sense the strain these sailors would be under for the next few weeks, I knew that one day I wanted to take that same start line myself.

Then the start gun fired and they were off.

CHAPTER EIGHT

AFTER THE START of the race, I went home to *Iduna* and followed Alan's progress as often as I could through the Royal Western Yacht Club in Plymouth. Two weeks later I flew to Boston to join him for the sail home. It was the first time I'd been to America, and I hadn't timed my arrival very well. I was due in to Boston at eight o'clock in the evening, but Newport, Rhode Island, was a two-hour drive, and I didn't have a driving licence. Even more cleverly, I'd managed to land on July 4th—Independence Day. Well done, I said to myself, as I walked rather nervously round to Customs and Immigration. I was fortunate to catch a night bus to Newport.

Alan had had a hard race and finished tenth in his class. It had been eighteen days, eighteen hours, and fourteen seconds since that gun had fired and I had watched him sail west from Plymouth.

We had only three days in America, and they flew by. After restocking *Elan Sifo* from the supermarket and making the few necessary repairs, we still had some time to enjoy ourselves. I'd hoped to find Vittorio to talk about racing with him and his brother, but no luck. I would have to ring when I returned to Europe. And anyway, I needed to see how this crossing went first.

Our departure was on 8 July, my birthday. Alan took me to a bar on High Street in Newport, not far from the boat. Though now twenty, I was still too young to drink in America—but we celebrated anyway!

It was five o'clock when we departed. The sky was foggy and there was an air of caution. A hurricane was developing a long way south, but as it was predicted to be five days away, we decided to cross ahead of its path. Whilst there was some nervous anticipation of the crossing to come, I did not worry. I felt comfortable with Alan and knew I'd be safe with him. We saw little of the harbour or coastline, just the last outlying rocks as we slipped away, knowing that if all went according to plan, our next sighting would be the French port of Les Sables d'Olonne. As our world became the ocean, I stood on the bow. Looking back at Alan across *Elan Sifo*'s enormous deck, I reflected that he would be my only human contact for the next two weeks. We were on our way, and it was the best birthday present I could possibly have had.

I learned fast on the trip, through both advice and experience. On day three I had to climb to the top of the mast to retrieve the main halyard. I had only been up tall masts in the harbour before, and as the sea was relatively flat, I jumped at the chance to let Alan hoist me up it. I returned to the deck completely exhausted; I had found it hard enough just to hang on, let alone bring down the halyard.

On one occasion we also lost all power to the instruments, including the autopilot, which meant that someone had to steer all the time. We took turns trying to work out what was wrong before I discovered that a loose piece of antenna aerial in the pilot compartment had shorted and was fizzing away. It was straightforward to fix but drove home how easily one tiny thing can cause such a massive problem. If it had happened during Alan's race, it probably would have been all over for him—nobody can helm for more than a couple of days without a break.

Alan and I got on famously, regularly falling into fits of laughter. He had an incredibly engaging way of telling his stories, which left you no option but to laugh as his face slowly broke into a wide smile and he completely over-pronounced his key words in his eagerness to get the point across. I would question him endlessly, and he would talk patiently for hours about his experiences. We spoke about his last attempt at the Vendée Globe in 1992–93. He had been in fifth position in the Southern Ocean when he was hit by storm-force winds, and his boat was lifted and rolled by a freak wave. Asleep in his bunk at the time, Alan was flung across the cabin, landing on the cabin sole face down in bilge water. That was where he woke, choking and gasping for air. Although he did not know it then, he had broken six ribs, one of which had punctured his lung. A lesser mortal would have drowned there and then in the bilge water, but not Alan. He spent hours lying exhausted, trying to collect enough energy to sew his sails, which were badly damaged after his roll. After several weeks of fighting for his life he struggled into Tasmania. His survival was a mystery to the doctors, who could not understand how his body had coped. No one really knows how he did it; I'm not sure he does himself. But it wasn't just his determination I respected; it was the fact that although he had been through what can only be described as a worst nightmare, he had not only picked himself up but also retained the ambition to get back out there and do it again. I was so lucky to have a teacher like him on my first ocean passage.

After a week at sea we were caught in the tail-end of Hurricane Bertha, which since our departure had swept up the Florida Keys towards Newport. This was my first real storm at sea, and I still have a vivid memory of watching the clear skies disappear quickly behind a solid-looking blanket of black clouds. The water changed from bright blue to dark grey, and the evening lost its yellow warmth as it was suffocated by the advancing front. Though afraid of what might happen, I was comforted by Alan's composure. He was alert but relaxed, still effortlessly bringing a smile to my face.

It was two days before the storm relented. I was transfixed by the sheer size and power of the waves, and fascinated by the way *Elan Sifo* would weave her way through them, rarely faltering even under autopilot. She would regularly fall off the waves, slamming uncomfortably into them, which sent a shudder through every one of her 60 feet. I had felt myself stepping up a gear, and though this was clearly time for calm heads, I was excited and enjoying myself. I would helm for hours as we sped along, trying to carve our way through the waves. Looking back in our log book, I saw that I had reached a surfing speed of 19.54 knots, which was by far my fastest ever—as much a result of the big waves as the 40 knots of wind we were experiencing. Even with the tiny triangles of sail we had hoisted, we were flying along. Alan seemed frustrated by the storm and tired of the slamming, whereas I was raring to get back up for my next three-hour watch and was actually revelling in the challenge. One night-time watch when I was sitting on the helm, I realized just how exhausted Alan must be. After all, he had just done—alone—

three times what we'd been through, and in a race situation. On reflection, I felt particularly responsible.

I was on watch on the morning when the French coast loomed into view. I knew it was coming but had tried to imagine it wouldn't. When I could make out the chimneys of Les Sables d'Olonne through the gentle haze, I couldn't help but feel sad. I hadn't wanted the trip to end, and I toyed with the idea of saying nothing to Alan and turning back out to sea. Although we had been out there for two weeks and sailed through testing conditions, I had absolutely loved it. We really had sailed across the Atlantic, and I knew I was doing what I'd been born to do.

Alan left at dawn the following day to get back to Scotland, leaving us with just a few hours the night before to say our goodbyes and collect our thoughts together. It was a still evening with a clear sky, and we sat in the cockpit chatting for a while before turning into our bunks. I felt quite inadequate that evening, and I desperately wanted to tell Alan just how much the trip had meant to me. Too soon by far, it was time to turn in, and as we stood up to climb below, he reached over to hug me.

"Thanks, kiddo, you've done a great job."

"Thanks too," I said. "It's been fantastic."

With tears of joy hidden by the darkness, I knew there was no need to say more; in that moment, I realized that if there was anyone in the world who understood, it was Alan.

CHAPTER NINE

I STAYED IN LES SABLES D'OLONNE for a few days after we finished the transatlantic crossing. It's a very special place for single-handed sailors. As the start and finish town for the Vendée Globe, it definitely has an aura. While I was there, something seemed to trigger inside me, and each morning at dawn I'd get up and run to the empty beach, strip down to my underwear, and dive into the sea. I was so happy to be there, so happy with everything in my life, and maybe, even then, I was thinking deep down that I'd be back just four years later to start the Vendée myself.

I knew at the end of my crossing with Alan that I had to call Vittorio's brother. The start of the Québec-St.-Malo was two weeks later, and I was going to have to get my skates on.

I still had to raise the funds to get out to Canada, though. While catching up with Merv and hearing about his preparations for the start of the BT Global Challenge at Ocean Village, an opportunity arose to make the plane fare. My paintings of the fleet were going down well with the BT crews, and Mike Golding had asked if I could do a large one. The fee was just right, and soon I was on a plane heading back across the Atlantic. I could think of nothing but the race which lay ahead.

I stared for hours at the maps in the in-flight magazine, looking at the route we would be taking. Though I knew we were sailing out of the St. Lawrence River, I hadn't realized that it would be 600 miles before we cleared its mouth and more than a third of the trip before we sailed past the southeastern tip of Newfoundland. The shortest route from Québec to the English Channel actually takes you to the north of Newfoundland, and even though we would be keeping to its south, this would be nothing like the transatlantic with Alan. We would be venturing into iceberg territory.

On arrival I cursed myself for not trying harder to learn French during my transat with Alan. I managed to get on the right bus, but when the bus driver pointed to the various stop names in Québec, I had no idea which was my destination. I said, "Bateau, bateau de course," and he nodded, though I'm not sure he understood, as when he signalled that I should get off the coach after a journey of several hours, the water was nowhere to be seen. After years of family holidays planned with military precision, I felt I had let down the side—I'd just flown into a country I'd never visited before without so much as an address. On top of that, I had spoken to the skipper I was sailing with for less than five minutes and had no idea who else might be on the boat!

Heading downhill seemed like common sense, and I was relieved to stumble upon the marina after just over an hour's walk. Exhausted and apprehensive, I wandered along the busy pontoon in search of Vittorio Malingri's boat, *Anicaflash*, just glad that I'd made it to the marina before sunset.

Vittorio had designed and built *Anicaflash* with his father, the goal being to compete in the same Vendée as Alan; he failed to finish the race due to steering problems, and then, in true Vittorio fashion, chose Tahiti, 3,000 miles away, as his port of refuge! He was tall and thin, with wild, adventurous eyes, jet-black curly hair, and an almost permanent smile. His brother Enrico, known to all as Toto, had a similar complexion but was short, strong, and solid. With a business career, he had a less wild character and was far more organized. Claudio, six feet and built like a gladiator, had a gentle, friendly nature and, as it turned out, was competing in the Mini Transat the following year. Of all the Italians on the boat, he spoke the least English, which was a shame, as I would have loved to have chatted to him about the Mini. Andrea, a hydrodynamics expert who had worked on several boats' keel forms, was around the same age as the rest of the guys but kept pretty much to himself; as a result, I was more wary of him. Finally there was Giulio, a small, charismatic man who'd recovered from an almost crippling accident in an earlier career as a freestyle sailboarder. Vittorio explained to me that we would work in two watches of three. Giulio and I would be in his watch, while the other watch would consist of Toto, Andrea, and Claudio. I could not wait to get going, and I set about checking lockers and fittings under the amused gaze of the crew.

The few days in Québec preparing *Anicaflash* for the race seemed to be dominated by stocking up on food—fresh coffee, fruit, salami, bacon, eggs, tomatoes, garlic, and of course pasta. This was a real eye-opener for someone who considered a ketchup sandwich a treat and who thought that racing meant you were only allowed weight-saving, freeze-dried "fuel," without worrying about how it might affect your soul.

On our final night ashore we all sat around in the cockpit, talking and drinking beer. It was still warm, and our faces were lit by a faint glow from the cabin entrance. I felt happy, truly content, and calm in the presence of these guys who were making every effort to include me. As I glanced around the cabin from my sleeping-bag that evening, I felt I would develop some very good friendships over the following weeks.

Once the stress of the start was over, we began to take in the beauty of the area through which we were sailing. It was unlike anything I had seen before, the gradually widening river with its lush green banks scattered with little villages that turned to clusters of fairy-lights at night. We were demoralized by mistakes at the start which had left us well adrift of the rest of the fleet, but as each of us, one by one, cracked some kind of joke, our spirits lifted and we began to bond more tightly as a team. By morning we were in the lead of the monohulls, though only briefly, but we had made remarkable progress to catch up with the leaders; it was reassuring to be back in the match! It was a whole different atmosphere out there in a race situation. We had been in sight of another boat virtually all the time from the moment we left, and the strain of balancing on the knife edge of pushing as hard as possible, but not too hard, was really tiring. When I had sailed with Alan on *Elan Sifo* we had used the autopilot virtually all the time, and just steered for fun, but this was different: We were steering for speed, and if that meant spending two or three hours at a time at the helm during your watch, so be it.

On day three we left the mouth of the St. Lawrence Seaway, and although I was looking forward to the Atlantic Ocean once more, I was sad to see the beauty of the mountains disappear into the distance. Over the following few days, we passed south of Newfoundland so were not out in deep water. The Grand Banks and Flemish Cap are renowned for horrendous seas in bad weather, and for the next couple of days, we would be crossing it.

14/8/96 (Day 4)
Vittorio made breakfast, bacon, eggs and toast.
    Strange day. Toto not too good at all. Spent day in bed with flu-type symptoms. Feverish in the night and a painful back. We think he maybe caught something in the water in Québec when fixing the keel. Saw sharks in the evening—I saw two. It was a quiet evening. Our world had shrunk by dusk, as the famous Newfoundland fog had arrived. Visibility down to about quarter of a mile.
    A ship loomed out of fog, not too far away. Light airs, with many sail changes. Hadn't eaten since breakfast, so mixed salad made by Giulio very welcome! Turned in at 2000 after sunset. Had a chat with Vittorio about what it was like in the Southern Ocean—enlightening, but I still feel I have to go there myself!

Our watches were particularly tiring, and I could often be helming for hours as Giulio, who did not steer, and Vittorio spent a great deal of time down below communicating and navigating. At the end of my watch I would collapse with exhaustion into my bunk or onto the floor. I soon realized that the two, three, or sometimes four hours of helming I would do on the trot would become quite commonplace, and I relished the challenge.

    Vittorio finally came on deck after another hard watch at the chart table where he had been studying the charts so closely that he had the Grand Banks imprinted on his forehead. I immediately handed him the helm and dashed to the back of the boat for a pee—I had wanted to do that for a good two hours!

The wildlife farther north in the Atlantic was like nothing I had ever seen before. We'd seen the albino-looking beluga whales as we crossed the St. Lawrence entrance, and pilot whales once we were away from the coast. Now we were seeing massive pods of up to fifty dolphins firing alongside us, whatever the weather. As we passed Newfoundland, we saw several sharks silently slipping along just beneath the water's surface. I was hypnotized by the wildlife, looking out across the waves for any hint of movement, and amazed at how many species were around us when we moved farther from land and into colder water. Even the seagulls were still around, swooping in and out of the waves, their wingtips a paper-thickness above the wave tops. I wrote a great deal about the wildlife during the crossing, just to try to capture the impact it had made on me.

> *During helming this morning I had dolphins for over an hour! In the end there must have been at least fifty, you could see them coming from all directions. About twenty swam under the bow, and the rest alongside. As the waves fell away, they jumped clear, and into the trough of the wave ahead. Giulio took photos but I couldn't (because helming!). As the dolphins left the water you could see them looking at you, as if to say "Hi, guys, we haven't seen anyone around here for a while—we'll keep you company for a bit." From the stern their grey bodies glimmered in the white light of the rising sun ahead; another grey but beautiful day.*

Life inside the cabin was not too comfortable, particularly after the water-ballast tank holding two tons of water sprang a fairly rapid high-pressure leak, leaving its contents slopping about the floor. Claudio and Vittorio were working away, trying to fix it with epoxy resin, so, exhausted after a serious lack of sleep, I made the most of the light winds and dragged my sleeping-bag onto what was thankfully a dry deck. I had slept no more than three hours in three days and had no idea why. I can generally sleep on my head if I need to, but I was struggling here. At last, though, with the cool afternoon air blowing over my face, I fell asleep.

"Hey, Ellen! Iceberg!"

I leapt up and made for the leeward side so I could look under the boom. I expected to see a small floating lump of ice, but what greeted me was a colossal ice mountain that had formed into three peaks, two of them the size of skyscrapers. The cold radiated off them as if we had sailed into a fridge. I knew I could never capture anything so dramatic with my disposable camera, so I made coffee for everyone while they took pictures of each other with the berg in the background. By now Claudio and Vittorio had finished repairing the ballast tank, and I gratefully took my sleeping-bag down to a bunk.

On waking, I heard bad news. We'd run out of gas, and although we had spare canisters on board, they had the wrong adaptor and so were completely useless. The prospect of having to do without a cup of tea for the rest of the crossing was bad enough, but the thought of having to try to fashion something cold out of all that pasta made me wish I'd brought some of Mum's flapjack! The lesson was well learned, though; since then, I've always sailed with a box of her homemade treat!

A more significant cause for concern came through on one of the weather faxes. A big storm was on its way. As if that was not enough, we had just discovered that the ballast-tank repair had failed. Once the mess was cleaned up, we faced up to the fact that we would not be able to use the ballast system. We had already experienced the problems of handling *Anicaflash* with no water ballast, and the lack of that added weight to help us punch through the waves in a storm would be far worse. That night the clouds became more dense and the wind began to build.

As the first hint of dawn washed into the sky, I took over the helm wearing the "full metal jacket" of protective gear the conditions would demand. Only my eyes were visible. I was immediately struck by how much harder it was on the helm. We had a lot of sail up, and it was taking all my strength to hold *Anicaflash* on track as she was taken by the gusts and desperately tried to turn up into wind—a boat instinctively wants to do this when overpressed. My arms were throbbing and pains shot through my elbows. I could only relieve the tension by straightening my arms and using my legs like hydraulic rams. This was sailing on the limit, and much as it hurt, I was in my element. For the first time ever, I sailed at more than 20 knots through the water, and there is nothing to beat it—absolutely nothing!

At about 0100 there was a loud crack, the speed dropped instantly, and the helm died. I shouted for Vittorio, as I didn't dare leave the tiller. The spinnaker halyard had parted, and we had a 90-foot-long, 3,000-square-foot sail dragging in the water.

Everyone was on deck to pull in the material, bit by bit, over the guard wires, but as well as getting the sail on deck, we had to retrieve the spinnaker halyard. We only had one, and Vittorio had no choice but to climb the mast to feed in another. I was steering, trying desperately to stick to as "rock-solid" a course as possible, but the boat still rolled in the waves, which I knew would feel horribly magnified at the top of the mast. I felt that if I made any sort of over-aggressive movement of the helm, I risked shaking Vittorio off—a danger made more real because he had to climb the final few feet without a line to his harness; the only halyard to the top was the one he was to fit.

It was dramatically evident that night just how responsible we were for each other and how much trust we placed in each other. On *Iduna* I had only myself to look after, but now I was worrying far more about the others. The feeling was more acute when Vittorio was literally hanging on for his life, but whether you are helming the boat or making decisions at the chart table, you are doing it also for the others—some of whom will be sleeping helplessly below. I felt enormous responsibility.

That night had only been a mild indication of what was to come, as the weather deteriorated further. The hard thing was that the watches were not getting any shorter, and I was really beginning to feel it. *Anicaflash*'s steering system is basic, to say the least, as she'd been designed to take a wheel, then crudely modified to be helmed with a tiller. The tiller itself was quite long but almost inaccessible, being close to the deck, so we relied on the tiller extension. On top of that, the steering position was appalling. The only place to sit was in the seat part of a legless plastic chair on the deck. I was too light and my legs were too short, so the chair always slid at the crucial moment, and I would find myself steering on my knees, where I could brace myself against a lip on the hatch. After twenty minutes of this, with the blood-flow restricted behind my knees, I'd lose the feeling in my feet, and I also had no way of stopping the water which came rushing down the deck from sluicing up my trouser legs. I would finish a watch soaked beyond my knees and past my elbows. It would always take ten minutes of pins-and-needles hell before I got my sensation back.

*"There'll be some really big ones when the bow just drops
away, try not to fall down there, but go across—and hold on!"
said Vittorio as he passed the tiller across. He then left for the
cover of the cuddy. The waves were now immense, they were
long, and very, very steep. Looking behind was like looking up
at a mountainside, but jet black fringed with lighter water. The
breakers were also getting bigger, some tumbling in behind, in
Anicaflash's wake. Within 60 seconds I had surfed, stalled and
was soaked completely up to my elbows in icy water. As my body
moved I could feel the water working its way up inside my
oilies! Very soon my feet were numb, not so much from the cold,
but from sitting on them! But it's tricky to even shift slightly
for relief as this means a moment when you are not 100 per
cent ready to react with the tiller. When cramp sets in it's nasty
but the helm's more important. The wind died a little, followed
shortly after by a strong rain squall. The stars disappeared,
and the sheets of driving rain were illuminated by the
navigation light at the masthead. Through the distorting
Perspex window, I could see the figure of Vittorio in the candle-
like glow from the cabin lights, clad only in a yellow fleece,
compared to my total protection. My feeling of exposure was
emphasized—like looking through a pub window on a cold,
wet night!*

Never before had I been in so much pain from aches and bruises
without an opportunity to stop and relax. I was abusing my body, and it
was starting to let me know. I had a very painful leg and elbow, and
with the boat's violent motion, it was even harder to get around the
cabin. By now the normal procedure for eating in the galley involved
feet on work-surface edges and head pressed against the cabin roof, and
even that was beginning to hurt. The feeling you have out there is that
of continuous physical exertion—to such an extent that after saving the
boat from a gybe on one occasion, you thank God that you've done it,
not believing that you physically managed it. I felt I was pushing myself
to a point where I could do no more, then having to find twice that
strength seconds later. The wind was now blowing up to 55 knots, the
top end of Force 10, and it whipped the spray horizontally off the tops
of the breakers.

I'm sitting on the windward bunk, with cold feet and wet thermals! Giu's put some music on, which is occasionally drowned out by the drone of the surf. I have so much salt on my face from the spray that it feels like it's covered in sand! A cargo ship has just passed in the other direction. You can only see its lights for about five seconds in every minute—that's how rough it is! It even hurts to move about in the cabin now—it's like trying to walk around in a rollercoaster.

Time 0614hrs. Just suffered a KNOCKDOWN!

I was in the windward berth. We were over well past 90 deg, as the skylights went blue—sea, not spray! The propeller shaft flew across the cabin, and hit the roof! The prop shaft is 10 feet long, 1½ inches diameter, with a bronze propeller still attached! It is mounted inside the floor of the boat, right down the port side—it is not in the water because of the drag it causes there when racing. We really must have been over a long way!! When falling sideways down large waves, it is possible to roll to well over 90 degrees without the mast going in the sea. Our mast was not in! (although I must check with Toto!)

Under my berth cushions were the solar panels, which flew out. My boots hit Giu, and all the remaining vegetables went under the pipe berths down her stbd [starboard] quarter. The weather fax and electric panel, high on the stbd side, are soaked with bilge water! Something we could have done without! I shall try again to sleep!

As the storm was beginning to abate, I came out on watch and clipped on as usual into the helming position. Toto had just finished and was sitting behind me, removing his gloves and passing them to me. Without warning, we were hit by a huge freak gust, and the boat took off uncontrollably.

I yanked the tiller extension towards me as hard as I could, legs jammed against a rim, the handle at my chest. "Toto!" I called, but he was already there, reaching down to grab the tiller extension; we had just managed to settle her when the extension ripped away from the tiller. The boat was now out of control. We both dived towards the tiller and pulled it hard, forcing the wind aft of the beam, and she heeled less and leapt forward through the heavy seas. Spray flew from the bow and off the tops of the waves like snow in a blizzard. Both of us knew she was in charge now, the two of us and our passengers helpless against her massive sail plan. We were going to gybe violently, and we were irrelevant and powerless to stop it. Vitt was up from below now, his face creased in a look of total concern. Almost as if in slow motion, *Anicaflash* heeled over on top of us, the boom slamming across the centreline, its crash like a starting gun for what followed.

Suddenly our lives went into fast forward.

Before we could even let go of the tiller, Toto and I looked forward to see a mountain of water bearing down on us. The boat was already on her side at 90 degrees, her decks vertical above us, like a wall waiting for the wave to break into it. I slid down the deck, my feet jamming on the toe rail, which offered a tenuous foothold from which to leap as the wave approached. Almost as soon as my feet stopped sliding, I grabbed at the mainsheet traveller ropes.

I held on with both fists clenched, as high up as I could, and as my fingers gripped tighter around the ropes, the force of the wave hit me, carrying my body away from the deck as if I were being sucked down a drain. I tightened my grip on the ropes as smothering water sucked my breath away. I was completely submerged.

Desperate for breath, I scrambled up the traveller, using all the strength in my arms to make progress. I didn't know how far over the boat was, or even whether heading up promised escape. I struggled until I felt the air on my face, and then gulped a lungful. My next thought was for Toto, and as seawater turned to daylight, I saw his red figure clinging to the pushpit. Thank God!

He was up to his waist but signalling to us that he was all right. He had been swept about 8 feet along the deck before hitting the pushpit. Getting back to the cockpit was impossible along the deck—it was like a cliff—so he climbed through the toilet hatch, which was just above the water level, and came to us through the hull. As I hauled myself over the cockpit edge, I could feel a burning sensation in my left knee, but it was the least of my worries. I helped Vitt furl the genoa, mind and body working like clockwork. It was not easy, as most of the sail was in the water.

Once the genoa was furled on its stay, we gybed her back and got back

on course with the autopilot. When everything seemed a bit more settled, Toto and I struggled in the fading daylight to relash the tiller extension while the tiller bucked and spat to the autopilot's commands. As we
worked, Toto said that if his back had not hit the pushpit, he would have
gone over—a sickening thought, and the first time I had really con-
fronted the full force of the sea and its mortal danger.

The plastic chair, which was tied on, had been pulled over the side. It
was now flapping against the stanchions like a cardboard box blowing
down a street.

Next morning, Toto and I discussed the incident. He had been in real
trouble and said that when he hit the pushpit, the force of water was so
great on his body, that "Any more and . . . " He crossed himself. I felt
cold and just stared for a moment, unable to focus as I thought about
what might have been.

AS WE DREW CLOSER to the French coastline, the houses gradually became more pronounced and the sunlight painted the rocks, trees, and
roofs with a warm glow. Many of the houses were built high on the
rocky outcrops, narrow and tall with pointed roofs and walled gardens
full of dark vegetation. A couple of cruising yachts passed as we drew
closer, and, shortly after we crossed the transit of the outer pillars, the
Emerald Line Seacat left the natural shelter of St.-Malo. It slowed and
gave a long blast on its horn, as if in recognition of our crossing. There
was a great feeling of achievement at that moment, and looking up towards the bridge wing, I saw the captain raise his arm. I returned the
gesture. Without even seeing his face, I knew it was a sincere, meaning-
ful congratulation.

At the start in Québec, I had been sure that I would develop some
truly great friendships on this passage, and I was right. After just fifteen
days, I felt that we all knew each other, cared for each other, and really
loved each other. The sea had brought us together, and through our
shared experience we'd forged strong bonds which in a normal situation
would have taken years to emerge, if ever. It had been far from an easy
trip, but one thing was certain: we'd each finished with something special—a small but significant fragment of life which we would treasure
forever.

CHAPTER TEN

THERE WAS LESS THAN a month now till Merv set sail, so things were hectic in Southampton. He had had some bad news. Alan Wynne-Thomas had contacted him while I was at sea and told him that he wouldn't be racing in the Vendée Globe. Unable to raise the financing, he'd had to pull out—my first real experience of just how crucial it is to find sponsorship.

I called Merv straight away and could hear the disappointment in his voice. I knew how much it had meant to him and felt awful for him. Having just finished my own race, I felt particularly aware of what he would miss, and I knew nothing I could say would change that. There was nothing I could offer.

BACK IN THE UNITED KINGDOM, I went straight to the Southampton Boat Show and dumped my bags on *Global Teamwork*, Merv's boat, before going off to find him. I'd just had the best time of my life and was bursting to share it with someone. Although Merv was incredibly busy, with just weeks before he left to sail around the world, he still managed to find time for me. It was great to catch up with him, but watching his team stow their food on board for the race made me realize how desperate I was to get out there again.

While wandering at the show I spotted yacht designer Nigel Irens. I'd met him in Plymouth with Alan, but I was nervous he wouldn't recognize me. I needn't have worried, though—as soon as he saw me he said hello. He was a big man with a warm smile and could not have been more gentle-natured. We wandered over to the boats he was exhibiting, and I was bowled over by how beautiful they were, with their low, sleek black hulls, cream decks, and teak rails. Nigel had been designing and sailing for years, winning races himself back in 1983 with boats built from his designs. He was a purist and loved not only the high-performance racing boats but also the older traditional yachts. I discovered that at my age, he too had lived on a 20-foot boat on the Hamble, albeit thirty years before. From the day we met at the boat show he became a firm friend, and I think he could justly be described as one of the nicest guys in the world.

By the time I finally returned home to *Iduna* in Hamble, I felt differently about the crowds who descended at the weekends. I did not feel the same desperation to speak to them, nor did I feel alone or excluded. I had found others who shared my passion and I'd made some close friends. Still, Merv's imminent departure would be tough, and typically, one of his last acts before leaving was to take me around the other boats in the fleet to get painting commissions. I managed about twenty before he sailed, and while not everyone remembered to pay, I'd made enough money to survive until winter.

As I'd expected, things felt very empty after he'd gone. I had become used to having him around and cherished his friendship in a place where that had seemed very hard to come by. But any sadness soon evaporated, as Alan rang to ask if I was interested in going to Les Sables d'Olonne for the start of the Vendée. My answer was never in doubt!

Alan and I reminisced about our experiences in the Transat, but in those quiet moments I could do nothing but think of the race that was about to start. Alan must have been hurting, but I was pleased he would be there for the start, as I was equally sure that in the long run he would have regretted missing it.

On our arrival that grey November day, Les Sables was packed. When we eventually made it close to the pontoons, I instantly recognized *Elan Sifo*'s mast. I discovered she had been chartered by a woman named Catherine Chabaud and renamed *Whirlpool* when Alan had to pull out, to make a late entry into the race. The tension was entirely different from what I'd experienced in Québec, and I think I realized for the first time what these skippers were undertaking. This was in no way a cruise around the world. It was a race, and that was going to make one difficult task a whole lot harder.

I was mesmerized as I ambled along the pontoons, stopping to look at every boat. I stood on tiptoe to peer into cabins, and examined every piece of rigging termination in an attempt to learn what was going on in these guys' worlds. I smiled at skippers I knew and sometimes chatted to them if they had time, reeling at the enormity of the whole event. There were thousands of people around—some hailing skippers asking for autographs, some simply watching and talking about the boats to each other, some just touching the hulls of the boats that they knew were about to set off on an almost incomprehensible challenge, a non-stop race around the planet. Englishman Pete Goss was there with his state-of-the-art 50-footer. I chatted briefly with him, and though he looked tired, he was clearly elated to have made it, against the odds, to the start of the race. I saw Gerry Rouffs and Tony Bullimore, and Yves Parlier with his space-ship-like *Aquitaine*—it was fantastic just to watch what was going on.

I came across Mark Turner on the pontoons, there with Spinlock. We met only briefly, but it was a reminder of my big question: what next?

The following day, watching the boats from a flat by the harbour as they sailed away was an emotional experience. My heart was pounding before that gun went; for reassurance I looked over at Alan, who was putting on an admirably brave face. He had an uncanny knack for being pragmatic at some of the most difficult moments. I wanted to be alone as I watched the boats disappear into the distance, and I pressed my face against the window to watch the tiny sails on that grey seascape. I had to be here in four years' time, I thought; no matter what it took, I had to be on that line. I could not put my finger on what it was about the Vendée Globe, but back then, standing in a window watching a cold and open ocean, I knew it would be the ultimate.

AFTER RETURNING HOME, I discussed the future with Nigel. He spent most of his time in France and was well aware of the races I was interested in. The Mini Transat seemed like the best immediate option, although I knew I had to find a sponsor. Nigel was a wonderful support that winter, at one point taking me with him to a conference at Disneyland Paris to discuss a new event called simply The Race. It was a new concept for competition, using boats of any type, any size, and any number of crew to race non-stop around the globe. As I looked around, I spotted sailing stars I would normally only see in magazines. It turned out that the majority of them were people Nigel had known for years, so meeting them felt entirely natural to me. It was not until years later that I wondered what they must have thought of me. I was twenty years old, and probably the youngest person there by at least fifteen years, but Nigel gave me confidence.

Later that evening we were approached by a man who introduced himself as Hugh Morrison and asked if we had any plans for dinner. He was involved with the business side of Disneyland and, indirectly, The Race. I sat very quietly through the beginning of the meal, but when Hugh asked me a question, I talked feverishly about *Iduna*, my transatlantic crossings, and in particular my plans for the Mini Transat. I think that my mind was made up in the course of that discussion—little did I know that it would change my life.

I WAS BACK on the South Coast in mid-December 1996, when I began my first-ever official job working at a boat yard. At the Southampton Boat Show, I'd been approached by Mark Orr, general manager for Bowman Yachts in Southampton. He had worked with Pete Goss, who had just left on the Vendée Globe, and, having watched Pete's struggle to get to that start line, wanted to help others do the same. He offered me a job at Bowman primarily so I could earn some money, but also so I could have the use of the office facilities after hours. The yard, with its large boat sheds and complete woodwork shop, had been there for years. Bowman's reputation was based on tradition and quality, employing many craftsmen who had been building boats all their lives.

After I'd spent a couple of weeks cycling to and fro between Hamble and Southampton, Mark suggested I bring *Iduna* to the boat yard and moor her on Bowman's own pontoon. This made longer hours possible, and I was able to use the office in the evenings both for warmth and for writing letters to seek sponsorships.

Often the electricity cable running to *Iduna* would trip out at night, and rather than climb back up the long rusty ladder, I would resign myself to having no heater and ice on the decks, and waking with freezing feet. I exhausted myself during that time in the yard. I was still getting up at 6 A.M., writing letters or planning before everyone came in, then working as many hours as possible at Bowman's to earn enough money for the batches of stamps I was buying to mail my letters. I would then work in the offices at night, sometimes until two, three, or four in the morning, trying to write as many letters and address as many envelopes as possible for the following day. I would finally wander down the yard, away from the buildings, clutching another pile of mail, hoping the next day might bring a reply from someone. I still wince when I think of the day I posted letters bearing stamps worth £300. The reality was that it was a fairly grim life, although at the time I didn't see it that way.

The possibility of teaming up with Mark Turner was still nagging away at me. I knew that he was searching for a sponsor, and we'd talked several times about working together.

At the London Boat Show in January I had a decision to make. Was I going to try to mount a challenge in the Mini Transat alone or try to work with someone I hardly knew? Everyone I talked to spoke very highly of Mark. This was reinforced by what Merv had said after Mark had raced his boat *Maverick* in her maiden event. Brian Pilcher once again acted as a sounding-board. I trusted him implicitly, and he could usually reason away my worries in no time. With this issue, though, we were struggling. I explained that I was worried about jumping in with someone else. I knew my own strengths and weaknesses, but I also knew that if I decided to go with something, unless things went seriously wrong, then I would stick with it, and I did not want to make the wrong decision. I knew that we would be stronger as a team, but at the same time we were going to have to raise twice as much money for our two entries. Mark did have an incredible number of contacts in the marine industry, though, and had already tried, albeit unsuccessfully, to compete in a Mini race the year before, when we had discussed how we could work together to our mutual benefit. I think I knew that whatever the decision, it wouldn't be easy—almost like marriage, I guessed.

I decided to go for it, and although I found Mark's reaction incredibly businesslike, he too seemed to get a boost from the partnership project. But despite the importance of the decision to team up with Mark, my strongest memories of the London Boat Show were of the stories that emerged from the Vendée Globe. The previous month Isabelle Autissier had limped into Cape Town with a broken rudder, but now people I had seen with my own eyes just weeks before were clinging to life deep in the Southern Ocean. Tony Bullimore and Thierry Dubois had both turned upside down, and no one knew whether Tony was alive and on board, in contrast to Thierry, who was waiting for rescue literally clinging to his upturned hull. We had already seen the dramatic rescue of Raphael Dinelli by Pete Goss shortly after Christmas, and we were lucky enough also to see the rescues of both Thierry and Tony. But far less publicized in the UK was the loss of ARGOS transmission on 7 December from Gerry Rouffs on board *Groupe LGII*. Several boats from the fleet diverted to his last reported position, but no trace of the boat could be found. The sailing world hung on, hoping Gerry would miraculously reappear, but the tragic reality of his death was confirmed on 17 July, when the wreck of his boat was spotted by a ship off the coast of Chile. He remains sorely missed.

A few weeks after the boat show, Mark and I forged our new partnership by taking a weekend trip to France to see which Minis might be available for me and to get a greater sense of the scene. Even today, France is very much the heart of the Mini Transat. We were to meet Thierry Fangent, who ran a yard, AMCO, and whom Mark described as the "all-time guru" of Minis. Mark talked about his first visit to the yard when he'd unsuccessfully tried to compete in a Mini race the previous June. I could tell that he was frustrated at not having pulled it off, and this was being channelled into getting this season right. There was something about Mark, some inner drive which pushed him to do everything he did as well as he possibly could. I was sure this was also in a small way his downfall, as he would work himself into the ground to complete things. He was also a risk-taker, to a far greater extent than I, though I was beginning to realize that I would have to stick my neck on the line too—the life I had chosen was not going to fall into my lap. I asked Mark questions about his childhood, trying to find out what made him tick. I felt that in many ways we had a lot in common—his parents sounded quite down to earth, and I sensed that we'd had a similar upbringing. But I knew deep down that there were some fundamental differences. Of course, back then many of these stemmed from my own lack of experience and exposure to the big, wide world, in contrast to Mark's early navy career. I must have been a nightmare to be around, continually asking questions about anything to do with the Minis, the ocean-racing fleets, and Mark's career. As we drew into AMCO's car park, I don't think there had been five minutes' silence during the whole journey.

Not speaking French, I felt fairly helpless once we'd arrived and once again wished that I had devoted time to learning the language. Mark, though, appeared fluent, and he spoke with confidence. Thierry was tall and wiry, with piercing eyes and a mop of tightly curled black hair. He stood talking to Mark with a half-smoked, unlit roll-up in his hand. I was wary at first, as he seemed to be keeping us at arm's length, and their conversation appeared to be going round in circles. Eventually, though, Thierry reached down, relit his roll-up, and wandered over to another door in his office. He took us down a dark and dusty corridor, and I instantly smelt the fumes of acetone and epoxy resin. When Thierry opened the door I had to hold my breath; we were standing in the doorway of a shed at least 100 feet long and 50 feet wide—full of Mini Transat boats. I grinned at Mark, then up at Thierry, elated to see him smiling back. In that instant my understanding of Thierry's character changed—from being a cool Breton who quite rightly did not want to waste time letting his shed be used as a museum into someone proud and passionate about what he was doing. He became a comrade.

I wandered around the shed, in and out of the keels, looking up at the hulls, running my fingers along them. I could see *Omapi*, the boat that had won the previous race, and Thierry's own *151*, which finished second, sat looking immaculate in her cradle. But there was also another boat, looking back at me as I looked at her. She was distinctive, her entire hull covered in painted fish scales and her bow decorated with eyes and a mouth; her name was *Le Poisson*. Without having so much as set foot on board, I knew that I had just found the boat I was going to race. It was love at first sight—literally.

I MADE MY DECISION that I had to leave Bowman Yachts when I returned home. It was grinding me down, trying to work in the yard all day and toiling in the offices all night, although the big plus was that I was managing to save some money. But during our trip to France, Mark had talked to me about working for him on his boat for the Mini, which he was completely refitting, and when he offered to pay me £5 per hour, I decided to run with it.

Within a week of arriving back in Hamble, and at Nigel's suggestion, I moved up in the property world. I rented a 12-by-9-foot modular shed and moved most of *Iduna*'s contents into it. I needed a land-line to make phone-calls to potential sponsors, as my mobile calls were proving financially crippling.

I bought a scrap of carpet and the cheapest futon I could find, and I plugged in the sandwich-maker and kettle. I had no running water and had to carry bottles across the yard, but I reckoned I had the best home in the world. After all, I had a heater and I could stand up—it was palatial!

Working life settled into a pattern. I divided my time between working on Mark's boat and phoning companies and preparing documents to try to attract sponsorship. The boat shed was cold, draughty, and empty at night, though the sound of my sanding would keep me company with its echo. Sometimes I would have the radio on, knowing full well that when the DJs went off air, it was time to stop, but I didn't. I just kept at it—after all, the job had to be done. As I worked on Mark's boat, my mind would drift off, dreaming about preparing *Le Poisson* for the race. Then reality would intrude. Don't be stupid, I'd remind myself, you haven't even bought her yet.

Occasionally in the evenings and at weekends, Mark would come over from Cowes to see how things were going. He would join me on the night shift. I would teach him how to laminate fittings onto his mast, and we'd discuss the latest developments on the boat or any positive contact I'd had with sponsors. Mark, too, was on the search for sponsorship and was sending out proposals to several of his contacts. His situation was different from mine, though. He had begun his struggle being able to buy the boat himself, so he stood more chance of attracting support with a material object—collateral, really—around which to base his proposals. He was also able to borrow money—something I knew I didn't have a hope in hell of doing. When I'd tried to buy a mobile phone, I'd been turned down because of my credit rating. I don't think I even had one!

I applied to organizations such as the Foundation for Sports and the Arts, and had a meeting with the Royal Yachting Association. That morning I put on my smartest shirt and trousers and scrubbed myself red-raw trying to get the paint and resin off my skin, but the verdict could not have been more stark. I did not qualify in any way for grants or support. In fact, I was told that they were unable to support single-handed sailors in any way whatsoever. I had been an RYA member since I went on my first dinghy training course on Rutland Water ten years before, and I had trained up through their schemes to Yachtmaster Instructor. I couldn't help but feel disappointed.

> After approaching a number of companies from outside the marine industry, I have come to the conclusion that unless there is a representative within the company with a passion for sailing/racing I am very unlikely to get the chance to convince the Board that their involvement with this campaign could provide unique benefits. These range from international and national media coverage to corporate opportunities (Cowes Week, Martinique, etc.) as well as internal company incentives related to the stimulus of adventure—through talks (see CV), and following the race, etc.
>
> Funds to support, programmes to follow and schemes to assist are not available for sailing of this kind. It is for this reason I write, as I feel the truth from my position is that I have to build my own ladder before I, and others, can climb it. I only hope that in doing this, I can inspire others, showing that it really is possible.
>
> If you are involved with or know of a company which might be seriously interested in this campaign, or feel that you can help in any way, PLEASE get in touch ASAP. Either call me, write to me, e-mail me or fax me (details below)—I'd love to arrange a meeting to share a little enthusiasm!

Although the response to various letters was disappointing to say the least, I had in no way given up hope. But before long, the lack of replies made me realize that if I was going to find the money, I was going to have to buy the boat first. I had no income other than the money from Mark—and I soon realized that it, too, would soon run out. I took my time-sheet off the wall and stopped counting. I knew all too well that Mark had no money either, and while I had joined as an employee, it was obvious that we were in it together—we were partners. I had to content myself with the fact that when my money ran out, he could pay me subsistence, and he was still paying the phone bill. I had no house to sell, no car to sell. All I had was an old bike that was too knackered even to give away since it had been vandalized at the railway station.

Mark and I would talk through most of the night about our thoughts, contacts, and ideas, while I would attempt to make us something to eat from what was in my food box under the table in the corner. It was usually cheese and rather sickly looking broccoli shoved into the sandwichmaker. The choices were slim, really—it was virtually impossible to keep food without a fridge or to cook without a hot plate or an oven, and I limited myself to £10 a week for food.

In the not-so-early hours of the morning we would crash out on the futon. I only opened it out when he was there; the rest of the time, I just left it folded, lay down, and stuck a bean-bag under my feet where they hung over. I know many people thought that Mark and I were emotionally involved, and I guess in many ways they were right. But it was more like a brother–sister relationship than anything else. We were inseparable, bonded together by the burning, sometimes seemingly impossible goal of both making it to the start line of a race.

At the end of March 1997, Mark went to France to see Pete Goss and Catherine Chabaud finish their Vendée Globe. He was completely blown over by the intensity of what he saw. When he returned, he described the atmosphere and emotion displayed by the huge crowds that had showed up to see the boats. I wished then that I had been there, and while I'd convinced myself it had been better to stay in the UK, I made a pact with myself that I would be there myself in four years' time.

The future, while daunting, wasn't all bleak. I had been in touch several times with the owner of *Le Poisson* and had had a survey carried out on her. There was also, at last, the prospect of a loan from a businessman who'd been a supporter since my trip around Britain. The only condition was that we brand *Le Poisson* with his company logo. Mark, Brian Pilcher, and I arranged a meeting to discuss the details and then planned our trip to France to buy her.

The afternoon that I'd arranged for *Le Poisson* to be trailered back to the UK, I received a fax from my friend's solicitor that made my world fall apart. The additional terms and conditions were just impossible. I slammed my fist on the desk and sobbed with frustration. I couldn't believe we'd got so far only to have our expectations shot down. The fax set out the amount I had to sell the boat for, and by what date. It stated that they had to remain the prime sponsor, and that the costs of the rebranding had to be covered by me. I was sorely tempted just to sign the thing, and to hell with the terms, but I knew I couldn't. I counted on the value of the boat when I had finished, and to have to sell her by an arbitrary date crippled the chances of her holding her value. Selling a boat can rarely be forced, especially when the race for which she'd been specifically built only occurs every two years.

The following morning, in desperation, I looked into borrowing the money some other way and tried to find loan companies that might allow an unguaranteed loan. Things looked likely to get very messy. While I was at my lowest ebb, Mum and Dad called to ask how things were coming along, and when I built up the courage to tell them about the loan falling through, it was impossible to mask the disappointment in my voice. I told them I was going to borrow the money and asked if they would be prepared to act as guarantors. It was as much of a shock for me to ask them as it must have been for them to hear. I never imagined I would end up in debt, and in fact had always been determined to avoid it. But now I felt I was in a position where it didn't matter any more; I needed the money, and hang the consequences. Then Mum and Dad said that between them they could raise £15,000—Dad had been awarded some compensation after his accident, and they said that in these circumstances, they would be prepared to lend me the money. I felt giddy with happiness, while knowing that it wasn't as straightforward for them as the simplicity of the offer had made it sound.

I'd boarded the ferry to France still uncertain that I would be able to raise enough money to bring home Le Poisson. Despite a massive leap forward, thanks to my parents, I still needed a further £2,000 before I could buy her. As I was standing just a few yards away from her owner in La Trinité, a call to Mark Orr saved the day—he lent me the final amount. The belief and faith in me that Mark and my parents had shown were the next critical stepping-stones towards that dream.

That evening, Nigel, the lorry driver, and I reached St.-Malo too late to make the evening ferry. We went to look for a hotel, finding one in the outskirts of town. It was dark, and Nigel hovered by the entrance, waiting for me to go in with him. I looked over at Le Poisson.

"I'll stay on board," I said.

In truth, I couldn't afford the hotel. I found a comfortable place on the cabin floor, put on an extra sweater, and buried myself in an old spinnaker. I woke up half frozen, but I was over the moon.

I SPENT THE NEXT MONTH checking over *Le Poisson*'s equipment and working on her as much as possible before she went into the water. The jobs I decided to do were those I could afford and attempt myself—not necessarily those I would have liked to complete before the race. For a start, my mast was shorter and heavier than the others; and all the sails I had were to fit my smaller mast. If I changed the mast, I would need all new sails, and I could never afford that. I had to stick with what I had. Mark's contacts within the marine industry were proving vital; it was their trust in us which often allowed us to change essential fittings.

Hamble life was becoming more enjoyable by now, as I had made some friends with guys from a boat preparing for the 1997 edition of the Whitbread Race. They provided good advice on setting up *Le Poisson*'s rig, but beyond that, they were just fun to be around. I was surprised how friendly they were, and astonished at the difference from others' reactions to me only a year before. Two of them, Jez Fanstone and Jan Dekker, went out with me on *Le Poisson*'s first UK sail. It was a fantastic feeling, and an emotional release as well. We ended up becalmed off the mouth of the river and accidentally splashed her sails with red wine as we celebrated her maiden sailing. I laughed more in those few evening hours than I had since the project began. I felt as though we were on our way.

Mark, meanwhile, had received his first really positive news on the sponsorship front. Charles Dunstone from Carphone Warehouse had decided to sponsor him. Mark immediately threw the money into *our* project. With a sponsor behind us, we could announce our 23 May launch.

This took place in Cowes. Although it was a small event, we had the boats ready in time and branded them with our new sponsor's logo. It was also an opportunity to thank everyone who had helped us. Seeing the two boats side by side was a very proud moment, and although we were stretched to the limit financially, we felt we had already achieved a great deal in just getting them both this far. That evening, we relaxed for the first time in months, with the Pier View pub being the main beneficiary!

Two weeks later, Jez and I took *Le Poisson* out to compete in the Round the Island Race. We didn't do terrifically well, but it was a great sail and a very worthwhile test. Not only was Jez a great guy to sail with, but he made more difference to my sanity over those months than I'm sure he ever realized. He had arranged for a friend of his, Keith Willis, to race with me in June on one of the two available qualifying races for the Mini Transat. It turned out to be a race to be reckoned with, setting off from Trébeurden on the northern coast of Brittany, round Fastnet Rock on the southern tip of Ireland, then back to Trébeurden. There was the inevitable struggle to get the boats to the start line, not helped by dreadful gales. As neither Mark nor I was ready to sail the boats there and risk damaging them on the way, we opted to take them by trailer. Working until the very last minute, we reached the ferry with only ten minutes to spare. With fittings still being attached and *Le Poisson*'s mast needing work, we were lucky to make the start. Mark's boat, too, though now beautifully painted, was far from ready. We worked frantically to prepare them, knowing that the start date of the race was firm. Dark, depressing skies, horrendous wind speeds, and the relentless rain seemed an appropriate backdrop to our efforts.

Somehow, and I shall never understand how, we both set off on the race. A photo was taken of Mark on the morning of the start, and in all the years I've known him, it is by far the most revealing—his eyes are sunken, and he looks as if even keeping them open was a struggle. He looks as though he could give no more. And he hadn't even started the race.

Fortunately, there was a light patch in the weather for the start, but it didn't last—another gale was on its way. Mark and his crew, Fred, and Keith and I set off knowing it was going to be tough, and we were right. We ended up spending several hard, stressful days fighting through Force 7 winds on our way to Fastnet Rock before turning round to weave our way through the steep Atlantic waves. The conditions were physically some of the hardest I had been through, and the Minis are not your average boat. They're light and flat and surf like little skiffs. The big difference is the size of their masts, and the absurd amount of sail they carry. *Le Poisson*'s mast was well over twice the height of *Iduna*'s, and the boats are pretty much the same size. Being racers, they offer little protection from the elements. The cabin was wet, as was our clothing, and when we tried to sleep, exhausted, we would lie against the hull down below without removing our waterproofs in an effort to keep the freezing cold at bay. The motion was horrendous too—we were pounding into the wind and massive waves in a boat the size of a large dinghy. We would hold our breath on deck as waves passed over us, and close our eyes down below as *Le Poisson* fell off the top of one wave and into the next. With her heeled over—up to 45 degrees or more as the gusts hit—doing anything on deck became brutally difficult. There were simply no creature comforts, just an empty fibreglass sandwich shell which resonated like a loudspeaker, amplifying every squeak and groan on deck for the benefit of anyone in the cabin. Keith was sick on the worst day, so I found myself on deck longer, feeling the cold that little bit more. After the first twenty-four hours, I'd virtually given up the possibility of feeling my feet again, and with every wave trying to wash us backwards, progress was painstakingly slow. We dreamt of getting round the rock and charging back towards Trébeurden at three times the speed with the spinnaker up.

Sadly, the return leg wasn't the long downwind sprint we'd hoped for. After several incredible hours we broached, damaged the spinnaker, and broke the boom before finally finishing in eighth place. But we'd had it good compared to Mark and Fred. A few hours after rounding Fastnet, they'd been dismasted, and as we sailed towards Trébeurden, we saw them limping along with just half their mast—a large part of the transom had been ripped away. Better now than in the Atlantic, I thought. At least they were both safe.

I RETURNED TO DERBYSHIRE for my twenty-first birthday at the beginning of July. Having missed being with the family for my three previous birthdays, it was time to go and see everyone. It was very much a double celebration, as Nan had just passed her European Languages degree with honours—an astonishing achievement at eighty-three. After her long struggle, not least against illness, it was precious to see her eyes sparkle as she spoke of the lecturers and staff who worked in her department. The degree ceremony itself was still a long way off, at the playhouse in Derby after Christmas. I hoped I'd be there.

After my brief break at home, I was back with Mark in France to prepare for the Trans-Gascogne Race down to Spain and back across the notorious Bay of Biscay. The race would fulfill the single-handed part of my qualification for the Mini Transat. I was really nervous about racing alone—it would be my biggest test so far. Any chance of Mark's competing had been wiped away by the extensive damage to his boat, which was still at AMCO being repaired.

The race got off to a terrible start, with a collision after only an hour, just when I had everything settled down. We were heading up to the first mark when a boat tacked beneath me. I saw the tip of his mast just a fraction of a second before the splintering crack that stopped us dead in the water. The damage to the bow was ugly but did not look structural. I decided not to retire from the race but to keep checking the damage regularly, and I was fortunate that things did not worsen.

I finished eighth overall in the race, and I was happy with that, especially after the smash-up. Spain not only offered the chance to effect a temporary repair but ironically also marked the first time I managed to hold a conversation in French, bumbling and slightly alcohol-fuelled. It was a wonderful feeling to be able actually to communicate, though, and to realize how keen people were to help you speak their language.

After a tiring return across the Bay of Biscay to Port Bourgenay, I sailed on to La Trinité, where Mark was back with his boat. I was ready to drop, but on arrival in La Trinité, I turned straight round again, as Mark had arranged a photo shoot with a helicopter for publicity images. I was absolutely shattered and spun around beneath the helicopter in a fury, oblivious to the necessity of getting these shots to promote our efforts. Their worth was confirmed, though, when Mark's boat appeared on the cover of the next *Carphone Warehouse* magazine.

The following day, I woke drowsily to the sound of church bells. I remembered driving somewhere with Mark the night before, but as I opened the shutters, I was taken aback. Below me was a market bustling with people. The church was just across the street; to the right, just beyond the little market-place, was one of the most beautiful stretches of water I had ever seen—the Golfe du Morbihan. The house belonged to a photographer friend of Mark's, Thierry Martinez, and his generosity meant that it was to become home for the next two months.

There was still little cash, and we were burning through the sponsorship money quickly with race entrance fees, travelling, and eating. But setting aside time to find a sponsor was almost impossible. Mark had his job to do, and I was in France trying to repair my boat. Things would be really tight.

Just days after arriving in La Trinité, *Le Poisson* was out of the water and in the sheds at AMCO. I would often stay there working away till eleven or twelve at night, as there were always errands to run during the day to the sail loft or to the machine shop where I had some pieces made. Often I would go into the little room by the offices, make myself a cup of potent coffee, and sit there, my head in my hands, trying not to let myself fall asleep.

To make matters worse, I also knew that I was missing important equipment. In the last two races I'd found a few creaks and leaks in my four-year-old equipment. Safety-wise we were OK, but from a competitive racing point of view we were struggling. What options did I have, though? I was maxed out, financially and mentally. I suppose all this was building up inside me while I was working like crazy to repair my boat in a stinking hot shed. Watching the magnificent progress of Mark's boat next door—financed, it has to be said, by the insurance money from his Fastnet disaster—just seemed to be rubbing my face in it. As it neared completion it looked like a totally new boat, with a new rudder, bowsprit system, mast and sails, and every little detail done and dusted. All the ropes were beautifully coloured, while I had to make do with what was left. I was angry that things appeared so one-sided. Mark's boat had the best of the new gear we'd received, and I just felt like the kid tagging along. We'd set out to work on this together, and in my book that meant we should have been sharing everything.

One Sunday afternoon when Mark came down to the yard to see what was going on, I lost it. I felt like the underdog, and I had to let him know.

Mark's reaction only fanned the flames when he said that he was the person who had to worry, that except for the Mini Fastnet, he had hardly sailed his boat. That tore it. Desperately needing to let off some steam, I yelled, "That's it, it's always Mark f*****g Turner!"

A few equally inelegant sentences later, he was gone. He did not even appear to be listening. He just walked out.

A few hours later, and with both of us feeling we'd been dragged through it a bit, we were fine. The bottom line was that we needed each other, and Mark actually had a fair point: he *was* in a weaker sailing position than I, and although he had more race experience in general than I did, he had far less experience sailing alone (he was to start the race with only eight days of solo experience). I was the kind of person who would simply charge headlong at something, and I relished being alone at sea. Mark, in contrast, seemed to be pushing himself into racing single-handed, challenging himself. It wasn't until then that it sank in—the sailing itself held a fear for him that I'd never previously understood. For Mark, this was the coming-together of a ten-year campaign, and, as he saw it, his boat just had to be as right as possible for him to succeed.

I WAS DOING ALL I COULD to save money. Lunch would be a baguette and a couple tomatoes, and dinner was more often than not out-of-date freeze-dried food packets that were kicking around in boxes on the floor.

I grew to love the French. Their way of life and passion for sailing were second to none. At the AMCO yard, I talked with Thierry, learning new words, understanding more as he generously shared his knowledge. I would often watch him at work, laminating rudders for the Open 60s, or working on Mark's Mini, so meticulously and accurately that anything he did was an absolute work of art. My French was coming along in leaps and bounds, although it was by no means classical. I was learning French boat-yard slang—phrases such as "a donf," "A+," and "ça roule (ma poule)": "go for it," "see ya," and "that rolls my chick"—or, more literally, something about hens!

We were getting ready to leave La Trinité. Mark's boat was finished and he had just completed an extremely hairy single-handed qualification to Spain and back. We were on board his boat, having tied alongside, discussing his trip and bailing out water that had collected in her bilges, when we noticed some small water droplets on the inside of her hull. They were the first signs of total disaster.

As a safety precaution we had her lifted out of the water, then asked Thierry if he would come down to have a look. He climbed down into the tiny cabin and spent a few silent minutes examining the hull. He then shook his head slowly, before looking at us with a pained expression. When he spoke, we could tell by the tone that it was serious. His verdict was that there was virtually no inner skin, and what was there was not bonded well. Basically, Mark was in danger of losing his keel, and with the foam core wet, there was no time to repair it safely before the start. A second verdict from Nigel Irens was the same. We had no money, and one boat between the two of us in which to race. It would take a miracle to get us to the start line.

As we wandered back along the pontoons to *Le Poisson*, we were joined by another competitor, Thomas Coville, whom we'd met through Thierry Martinez. Thomas had heard what had just happened, and he walked up to Mark and simply said, "You have to make the start, Mark," and handed him a cheque for 10,000FF. Mark has never cashed that cheque, but its message has never been forgotten.

In the evening we returned to Thierry's house and sat together on the sofa. Mark was emotionally drained, his eyes tired and sad, but there was still a spark of defiance in him. We talked late into the night. It couldn't all stop here, not after what we'd been through. The only way to race was to find another boat, and the only way to do that was to find more money. We knew the cost of chartering a Mini, and it was totally out of reach. Without money we didn't stand a chance. We just kept coming back to the same place. At 2 A.M., we typed out an e-mail, really no more than a cry for help. It explained what had happened and what we were going to have to do in order to make it to the start line.

Both Charles Dunstone and Hugh Morrison contacted us the following day. Hugh, to whom we had barely spoken for six months, except for the odd updating e-mail, called to ask for our bank details and offered to transfer £10,000 immediately. Charles agreed to up his original £10,000 to £15,000. This generosity was awe-inspiring, but it didn't solve everything by any stretch of the imagination. We could move forward, though, and while it was going to be a real struggle, we were driven by the challenge of making it happen. While my boat was renamed *Financial Dynamics*, taking on the name of Hugh's company, the money itself was used to try to get Mark back into the race.

The few days until the start in Brest seemed like months. Mark managed to find and charter another Mini not already taking part in the race and hired a wonderful preparateur named Jeanne to transfer much of the equipment, including the mast, electronics, boom, and sails, from his old boat onto the new one. It was going to work. Meanwhile, Mark also laboured away on the publicity side. He was a natural at making sense of this. He knew instinctively what needed to be communicated, when, and to whom.

Meanwhile, I returned to the UK to make a flying visit to Southampton during the annual September Boat Show to collect my final equipment from Hamble. By pure chance, I remembered to check my mail when I stopped to thank the yard staff for all their help. A life-changing letter had arrived that very morning. It was from the Foundation for Sports and the Arts. They had considered my application and stated that "it would be our desire to offer a grant." They had offered me £6,000.

I called Mark, unable to tell him fast enough. After all the bad luck, someone must have put in a good word for us! They couldn't have known just how crucial their backing was. I now had the chance to buy that much-needed equipment for the race, and I spent a frantic afternoon at the boat show, sprinting from stand to stand, picking up everything from an extra sail to the autopilot I needed so badly. In the end, I just managed to make the ferry, but only because the man who sold me the generator gave me a lift.

We were only a week from the start when I arrived back in France, and with a whole hoard of new equipment to fit, I felt woefully ill prepared. Work on board Le Poisson—now Financial Dynamics—was hectic. If the race had come down to the amount of gear each boat had lying on the pontoon, we had the rest of the fleet licked.

Every single skipper on that start line had struggled in some way. Most had been living on board their boats for months. Those struggles brought people closer—there are few races where skippers will donate their unwanted sails to other competitors who are struggling, or discuss their weather tactics with each other in such detail. But everyone in the Mini shares something and everyone gives something. There were fifty-two boats in the fleet, and it was one big family.

More than 70 per cent of the boats in the race were French, and most of the rest were Italian. But as the only two English competitors in the race, Mark and I had our following, too. It made for a busy time, as we were not only preparing the boats but also trying to give interviews to all who asked for them. I was unprepared for how many there would be and how time-consuming they would become. More unsettling, though, was being asked continually about what it felt like to be the only woman and the youngest competitor in the race. I wasn't sure how to answer. I had never considered it and had never known what it felt like to be anything else. The question drew attention to me for all the wrong reasons, and I hated being singled out. I just tried to play it with a straight bat: "It's an impossible question for me to answer. I don't know how it feels to be a guy or ten years older."

I thought a lot about it afterwards, though. Why should I be any different? Of course, I was happy to be there, like everyone else. I was nervous, excited, and impatient for the start—but so was the rest of the fleet. It was the first time I had even considered being any different. I had not thought of myself as the fleet youngster, or the token woman. I had never felt that I was being treated any differently from the way Mark was, for example. Yes, fine, I was a woman, but I had sailed and worked with guys for the previous four years, and I had always considered myself to be absolutely one of them. I had my own strengths and weaknesses, but so did every other skipper. Ultimately, there could be no difference. We'd be in the same boats, in the same race, in the same seas. And no storm would make any distinction among us.

MUM AND DAD had come down for the final day before the start, so they could send me off with home-made flapjack, and they were surprised to find that they, too, were a target for interviewers. We had begun working on film of the race ourselves, so they were also filmed and interviewed by Dick, our cameraman extraordinaire. Mum said far less than Dad, but she was clearly nervous about the race. Dad tried to be braver, although as he finished his sentence, I could sense his voice was breaking. "If I worried about Ellen in the same way, I probably wouldn't sleep. I don't think it's logical to worry, we've tried to understand what Ellen is doing, and we've helped her as much as we can, and as Dave King at Hull, where she did a lot of training, used to say, 'The sea will look after her,' and if it does, then what more can we do?"

On the morning of the start, I felt anxious. People tried to talk to me, but I struggled to communicate. My mind was elsewhere, and all I wanted was to be away. I wished I could just have been transported out to sea. I had my last real chat with Mark: almost mechanically, we went through the weather situation and discussed our tactics. It was a comfort to know that no immediate storms were forecast; we were due to have a fresh, but not tempestuous, start to our race.

When the time came to leave, before saying my final goodbyes, I had to see Mark again. We had not really parted earlier, and I could see that farther along the pontoon, he was preparing for his tow to the open water. I wandered along, acknowledging many other skippers as I went. The French just say "merde" as their equivalent of "break a leg," so there were many "merdes" as I walked along. I could see that Mark was standing with his father, and the first thing I noticed as he looked over at me was how red his eyes were. He didn't appear to be finding it easy to say goodbye. I stood back for a while, just watching. It struck me again that I did not share the fear that Mark appeared to be wrestling with. I did not for one instant think that I might never return to those who loved me. For me, this was an incredible moment.

I walked over to Mark. I have no recollection of the final words that passed between us before he stepped on board his boat and left, but I felt I had to be the stronger one, and I remember his arms wrapped tightly around me and the look in his eyes as he let go, which said it all. Whatever happened over the next weeks out there, we had already achieved an incredible amount together.

Mark slipped away, and as his concentration focused on the boat, I walked back to say a final goodbye to Mum, Dad, and Dick, who were waiting by *Financial Dynamics*. I didn't feel like crying at all as I prepared to sail away. I still felt oddly detached and focused more on getting out and over the start line safely. I hugged Mum and Dad. I looked Dad in the eyes, and he smiled back to tell me he was OK.

"Take care, Mum," I said, and jumped on board. I was off.

Almost as soon as I arrived in the start zone, Mark called on the radio. It looked as if his autopilot wasn't getting a reading from the electronic compass. I told him what to look for and where I thought it might be, while assuring him that I would sail round to him while he was down below to make sure there was no collision. I stayed with Mark for more than half an hour while he tried unsuccessfully to fix the problem, speaking to him every couple of minutes on the VHF to reassure him he was in no danger. I guess it was good for my nerves at this stage to be worrying about someone else's problems!

I soon had my own to occupy me, however. As I turned the windward mark after the start, I went up to the mast to hoist my new spinnaker. In the rush of preparing for the race, it had been overlooked, and this was the first time I'd used it. As I pulled the halyard through the clutch, I watched it flow out of the bag. I couldn't believe it—it was too short, a long way too short. I cursed myself for not having had the exact measurements when I ordered it at the boat show. The guys had been good to build it and get it to us in time, but I was still angry—I'd thought I'd given them enough information.

I knew I had to live with it, as without it I'd be one sail down. It was just a shame that we weren't allowed to modify our sails when we stopped in Tenerife after the first leg. My only large spinnaker was so damaged that I could breathe through it. I gritted my teeth; it was simply going to have to last.

As I headed away from Brest, I was badly placed. The wind was dying, the sun going down, and day one was drawing to an end. By this stage I had changed my spinnaker for my older and now largest one. The last of the support boats had turned back, leaving me very quiet and almost deflated, slowly creeping out to the west through the silhouetted rocks. All movement, sounds, and thoughts seemed very small against the magnitude of the ocean, as the sky gave up its gentle orange for an inky black. The sleepless nights, financial worries, and sheer bloody-mindedness over the previous nine months had all been for this. I had a video camera that Dick had given me and a small Dictaphone, and that evening I made my first comments.

> *It's not half good to be out here. This is it, this is the Mini*
> *Transat. I can't believe I'm here, I can't believe it. It's almost*
> *too good to be true. . . . Incredible. I just wish the people*
> *who've helped me to get this far could be living it with me. I'm*
> *doing about 12–13 knots, kite up, and after all that's happened*
> *it seems like magic that there are three dolphins with me right*
> *now.*

The following morning, I heard on the radio that many people had broken bowsprits or spinnaker poles. We were required to call up by VHF radio at a set time each day; these "scheds" were only possible if we were in range of one of the four support boats that followed the fleet. We also had ARGOS beacons, which informed satellites of our position, allowing the organizers and then supporters to know where we were. These positions were sometimes broadcast on Radio France, along with our weather bulletin.

Even when I did manage to get some sleep the following day, it was only for ten or at the absolute most fifteen minutes; and generally it would be lying on the cockpit floor in full thermals and waterproofs. I would stretch out with my head on the life raft, watching the speed as my eyes closed. It's incredible when you dream, wake, and look at your timer—only to find that you've been asleep for a mere eight minutes. I think it has something to do with the comfort factor, too: at the end of the day, not even having a bunk in *Financial Dynamics* didn't allow my body to lull itself into the false thought that it was tucked up in a nice, warm bed. For the four weeks I was at sea, I didn't climb into a sleeping-bag once.

In Biscay I was joined by a little bird resembling a yellow wren. He didn't seem to know where else to go. That night the little fellow hopped into my tiny cabin and roosted for the night in a small loop of cable that was hanging loose. I was devastated when in the early hours of the morning I startled him and he flew off in a panic. He never returned, despite my efforts to guide him in with a torch.

Farther south, as we approached Finisterre, the wind died and we all had to fight to keep the boats moving. It's even harder when the fog comes down, as the worry of being too close to another boat or, worse, a large ship is completely consuming—sleep is virtually impossible.

There are a few ships quite close. Luckily I can hear the fog signals, which makes things quite a bit easier. But there are whales too. I'm floating around with no wind doing about 1.5 knots, and I can hear a "blow" just 20m away on my starboard side. . . . That's quite scary.

When conditions changed and the wind increased, things did not improve. The following night we were surfing along at 10 knots, not even able to hear the fog signals through the sound of the waves. I felt pretty helpless, unable to see anything and just ploughing on into the unknown. But then, what are the options? It's even worse to be slow—at least keeping a constant course and speed gives a ship's radar operator a better chance of seeing you.

I managed to call up Mark on the VHF radio, and we discussed conditions and experiences. He, too, had been through the shipping lanes with no wind, which he felt had been a far-too exhilarating experience. He told me he'd spoken with Thomas Coville, who was narrowly ahead of him. He had missed a cargo ship by feet, slamming his boat into a gybe to miss it. His spinnaker was lost as it snagged on the side of the ship. He must have been seriously shaken by this, and it preyed on my mood for the rest of the day.

During the final part of the first leg, we approached and finished on the island of Tenerife. The lack of sleep was beginning to take its toll, though—I could not have been getting more than three hours in every twenty-four. The last miles of the race resulted in a desperate struggle to find wind, and for the first time, I was close to cracking. I sat off the island for hours, caught in its wind shadow all night, and had to endure the sight of three boats sailing past me just a little farther from the coast. I knew I had to come in wide, but when the wind had died, the current had taken me closer to the shore and I was stuffed.

I crossed the line in twenty-sixth position. I was bitterly disappointed with my result and vowed that no matter what I had to do, I would do it to achieve a better result on the second leg. I spent hours trying to analyze every move and where I had gone wrong. I knew that I had struggled at the start and that my spinnaker had lost me miles that I would have to struggle to regain, but I worried about my weather knowledge; although I understood the weather systems themselves, I felt I needed to know more about the tendencies in specific regions.

I was upset that Mark hadn't been by the waterside to see me in, but I quickly learnt from the other skippers that after finishing ninth, he'd literally fallen into his hotel room, completely exhausted, and couldn't be woken. By the time he came along the pontoon, I was glad my anger had blown itself out. It was great to share and celebrate his impressive performance!

WE SPENT JUST UNDER two weeks in Tenerife preparing for the next leg. It was a long break, but one engineered more around the weather than anything else. September–October can still be quite an active time for hurricanes on the other side of the Atlantic; so the longer you wait, the less your chance of getting caught up in them.

By sheer coincidence, Sir Chay Blyth was in Tenerife while we were there, for the start of the first edition of his transatlantic rowing race.

We'd met before at the London Boat Show which I'd attended with *Iduna*. He'd been quite rude about her, calling her a cockleshell, and I vigorously defended her honour! He recognized me and called my name. We also discussed the round-the-world record against the prevailing winds and currents which Sam Brewster sadly had failed to beat. It was still held by Mike Golding, and clippings from that attempt were still tacked to my bedroom wall in Derbyshire. During a meal later that evening, Chay surprised me by offering me the chance to skipper an attempt to challenge Mike's record. He had a sponsor lined up and said I could choose any designer to have a boat custom-built. The offer was extraordinary, but I tried not to show my excitement. In effect, he'd just offered me the complete package—the chance of a lifetime. At the same time, it would still be Chay's project. My gut feeling was that I should do my own thing, though I knew I needed to think hard about his proposal.

The restart was a nerve-racking process. All the skippers agreed to delay it for twenty-four hours to allow one of the competitors to finish repairing his mast, during which time the wind built steadily. Everyone was nervous, and the atmosphere in the port was almost subdued as each boat slipped out and was towed to the entrance of the adjoining harbour. There was another question, too: the weather. Mark had been in contact with an American weather-router who had sent a fax offering his present synopsis and views on the leg. The stable area of high pressure which normally causes the trade winds was simply not there, meaning that the trades were much weaker. Although he recommended that we head south to sail close to the African coast before crossing, there was another option: to follow the more direct northern route. As Mark and I discussed options, I was still not really confident in my knowledge of the Atlantic systems.

I decided to go south. *Financial Dynamics* was not by any means an efficient boat upwind, so the northern route would be a meteorological as well as a tactical risk. Even if there was less wind south, I would have to run with it. . . . By the looks of things, this was going to be a tough leg.

By the time we started, the wind was really blowing, making it hard going and reducing much of the fleet to two reefs and a storm jib. The radio was wild with voices as several boats were dismasted; one was run down by a ferry and another lost a rudder. It was carnage as we fought our way between the islands in the choppy weather, watching out for one another. That night I had my own nightmare when I caught a 60-foot, 2-inch rope round my keel; not so easy to remove with a boathook in the darkness. In the morning I was worn out from lack of sleep and frustrated, as the wind had dwindled to nothing. It was murder trying to keep *Financial Dynamics* moving, knowing that each time I closed my eyes, the tiny puffs of wind might change direction by 10 or 20 degrees, and I would occasionally wake after my twenty-minute snatches dead in the water. Again I kicked myself for not buying new sails for the race. My big, old spinnaker was in a terrible state now, its fabric resembling tissue paper and fraying at every seam. My gennaker was even worse—knackered, and flying from the bow rather than the bowsprit, it never set well and rubbed against the shrouds. I'd have been faster if I'd thrown it over the side.

I managed to raise Mark on the radio. He was currently in first position and had a light but steady breeze. I knew also that once the wind had died, we would not be able to contact each other again. Our only form of communication was VHF radio, which has a maximum range of about 60 miles, and once this distance separated us, we would be on our own and would only have the French weather reports for company. The Mini is unique in leaving competitors so isolated.

As the wind filled in bit by bit from the northeast, my hopes grew with it. We crept up from thirtieth position to nineteenth.

> *Even if I am not breaking any records and my speed is not as fast as I would wish, it is wonderful sailing! There are fantastic flying fish, one that seemed to glide for simply miles. I have just realized that it is 1 November and that it will be Bonfire Night on the 5th. It feels very strange to be at sea on Bonfire Night. I think of everyone back in Derbyshire, fireworks and toffee apples. It is all a very long way away from here.*

The breeze was a false dawn, and over the next achingly frustrating windless days we slid back down to thirty-ninth place. As I sat in the cockpit clutching my radio, I was further discouraged to read that the wind was not forecast to improve and that the boats to the north were barrelling along—the leader was 250 miles ahead after only a week's racing. Conditions on board were sweltering, and racing *Financial Dy-*

namics in these airs was hardest to cope with. Each time we had the weather, we had the position reports. They were all equally bad. I felt as though I'd been kicked in the guts each day. I was exhausted, pushing myself harder and sleeping less to keep us moving in the desperate heat. There were no options, though—you just had to dig as deep as you could and get on with it.

> *There can't be many boats in this situation, this is crazy just crazy, you can't do anything; just helpless . . . [pause] . . . Anyway just got to keep plodding on, and keep trying and when a little bit of breeze comes take it and get the boat moving, then eventually we'll arrive.*

I calculated that at the current rate of progress it would take us forty days to reach the finish. I knew that this wouldn't happen, and the wind would come, but *when* was the big question . . . it was a depressing thought.

The windless days ended abruptly with an enormous electrical storm. It was a daunting afternoon before it hit. I'd heard on the weather report about an area of high electrical activity with its epicentre just a few miles directly in front of us. I slept as much as I could before nightfall, when I knew a storm like this would intensify with the cooling of the air.

What began as a low line of dense cloud in front of us slowly enveloped us, its slashing lightning strikes becoming increasingly vigorous. I was soon in its centre, and I'd never experienced anything like it before. The sky lit up as if it was day, and as I worked reefing and changing the sails in the squalls, I could see everything I was doing. The air was dark with rain, like a cloak around us, snatched away with each fork of lightning. I felt the thunder as much as heard it, and the wind snapped from nothing to 20 knots and back again as it whipped in from constantly changing directions.

Following the storm, though, the heat returned. This time, the barometer read 98 per cent humidity in a temperature of 33°C. I didn't care; the wind was back, and we were eating up the miles.

> *It's so hot that the sweat is pouring off me and when I sit down in the cabin I leave behind a little pool. The skin on my legs has*

come up in little spots, which although they do not hurt and
are not even sore, look pretty horrible. I also have sores on my
hands, but even if a little battered I am in good spirits. We are
sailing well, averaging about 7–8 knots thanks to this precious
breeze.

Then there was even better news: It turned out that the boats to the
north were becalmed—albeit temporarily. When the next position report came through, I leapt so high I was lucky not to crack my head on
the deck head. We were in thirteenth position—I'd overtaken seventeen
people in forty-eight hours! I was back in the match, and I'd completely
forgotten the gloom of the preceding days. On a high, I felt as if nothing
could stop us; it just proved that you can never give up.

I am surfing at 12.4 knots. I have clouds behind me and in
front but they do not look vicious. It was a long night but I
should now be west of the storm area. I have better weather,
a good wind, and I am averaging 9 knots. I have 800 miles to
go. . . . I've been thinking about Chay's suggestion. But it does
not thrill me at the moment. I know that all I want to do is to
race like this.

I slept for no more than a total of an hour or so in the final few days,
and the last 500 miles was a hard grind. You can smell land when it
draws closer—the French call it "smelling the stables"—but you just
have to keep going and not let your concentration slip at the final hurdle.
One mistake and it could all be over. I thought a lot about my option to
the south and whether or not it had finally been the right choice. My
verdict in hindsight was that I *had* done the right thing—with the boat I
had. I had less sail area than most others, and our poorer upwind capa-
bility meant I just wouldn't have been competitive if I'd tried to stay
with them. But then, if the wind had come in a day later—or, indeed, if
it had arrived days sooner—it could have been a very different story.

I now feel so wonderfully in tune with the boat and the sea
that I know I shall really miss this once the race is over. At
night I watch the sun go down and in the morning the sky is

there above me, a wonderful feeling of space and timelessness.
Today the sea is blue and ahead of me the sky is clear and so
very fresh. I shall be very sad to leave all this behind.

My feelings were mixed as the lights of Martinique appeared—I even regarded their presence as a bit of an invasion of privacy. As I approached the tip of the island, I had to turn and could see just one boat astern of me. This turned out to be number 333, who, though I could not see it, had just lost the top half of his mast. We were in for our fair share of problems, too, though, as when we were almost at the headland, the wind changed violently and we broached. *Financial Dynamics* was lying on her side, and as I blew off her spinnaker halyard, I realized that finally our precious "tissue" spinnaker was completely in tatters. I dragged the sodden mess out of the sea and changed as fast as I could to the smaller, bright pink spinnaker, though I took that down shortly afterwards when the wind changed once again.

Our final straight-line course was along the southern coast of Martinique; though only short-lived, it was awesome. We were reaching a high speed with waves washing over us as we raced along. I sat on the side-deck and steered with the warm, scented air blowing off the land into my face. Below me, in the water, a pod of dolphins played, and the sky above was littered with stars bright enough to silhouette the island.

I crossed the finish at just after 3 A.M., after almost twenty-four days at sea; relief surged through me, and satisfaction that we had clawed our way up through the fleet from way, way behind. I had achieved my goal to do better in leg two. As before, and it was less unexpected this time, there was no sign of Mark on the dockside as I arrived; he had finished in fifth place overall the afternoon before and was no doubt enjoying his first real sleep. I threw my lines to the guys on the dock, who swiftly tied up *Financial Dynamics*. I spoke briefly to Dick's camera as I began tidying my little world. I popped down below to drag out my sodden spinnaker and smiled as I looked up at the electrics panel: no need to check that the batteries were charged tonight!

I was alone on *Financial Dynamics* now, and I wanted to say goodbye. I had no urge to leave her, but I knew it was time to go—Dick was waiting for an interview. "OK," I said, "I'm coming." I stepped onto the pontoon; I slid my hand along her guard wire until I reached the bow, kissed her gently, and then patted her goodbye, silently wiping away a tear. She's a pretty cool boat, that one.

My position coming in tonight, 13th, I was very pleased with. I know there are many boats out there faster which is a big thing and I couldn't have pushed any harder I don't think. . . .

The feeling inside is one of nervousness, of being aware all the time and trying to make the boat go. It's very hard to describe; but you're doing a job out there, you are in a world where you have your 6.5m by 3 metres and you are in control of it, and that is it.

After our interview, Dick took me back to the hotel. He told me that as he'd come out to welcome me in, he'd banged on Mark's door trying to wake him, but he was dead to the world, so Dick had had to come alone.

When we eventually managed to wake him, Mark and I talked as if it was the last time we could about all that had happened to us out there. Mark described hallucinating on his trip, which scared me a little. At one stage, he was sailing along with a team of guys on board who were trimming the sails for him, but more worryingly, on another occasion he had actually taken down his spinnaker without really wanting to, after cursing his imaginary companion for not taking it down. Twenty-four days is a long time when you're exhausted and pushing yourself harder than ever before. Mark spoke of the weather front he had sailed through, battling with high winds, and his time spent sailing close to Thomas Coville, the conversations they had had on the radio, and of his second-night disco. Unable to contain the excitement he felt at hearing he was in the lead, he pressed "transmit" on his VHF radio, then yelled out in a very uncharacteristic DJ fashion: "Yo, get down . . . it's Carphone Warehouse party night," then played some of his favourite tracks. He hadn't thought there was anyone to hear him, but he was caught, and, of course, word spread quickly!

During our time in Martinique, Mark and I talked a lot about the future, and it was great to spend time together without the overwhelming pre-race pressure. He was going to return to his job at Spinlock, whereas I had nothing to go back to other than a burning passion to progress with my racing. There were a number of options, but I always knew that the Vendée remained the primary goal. The debate was about how to get there. To be ready, I needed more experience on bigger boats. The Open 60s that competed in the Vendée were nearly three times the size of *Iduna* or *Financial Dynamics*. I was also keen to have sailed in the Southern Ocean before tackling the Vendée, and there was a race which could take me there—the single-handed Around Alone—round the world with stops. But there was no time to raise the funds to charter or build a boat for such a long race, which started in less than a year. We couldn't risk being badly prepared.

Another option, though not one that would take me into the far south, was the Route du Rhum, a race that I knew little about before meeting Mark and being introduced to the French scene. For a single-handed sailor, the Route du Rhum is probably the most competitive trans-oceanic sprint in the racing calendar. It runs from St.-Malo to Guadeloupe and attracts the best of the best, sailing single-handed in Open-class trimarans and monohulls, most of which, like *Elan Sifo* and *Anicaflash*, are 60 feet. Mark had been to the start of one of these races and was sure that it would be the right move. I agreed, and the Route du Rhum became our immediate aim: not only was it high profile, but we felt sure that after training for and competing in it, I'd be ready to challenge for the big one, the Vendée.

In the end, Martinique was far from a holiday paradise for us. After those initial days fuelled by the adrenalin of finishing, we knew we faced the enormous task of getting the boats freighted home. We were badly let down by our first shippers when a written quote turned out to be nothing more than a barefaced lie. After the agent reneged on the deal, I ended up paying double the price, but thankfully to a different company found at the last minute. I was furious.

Since finishing the race, Mark and I had become listless and tired, and the consequences were beginning to show. Emotions were inevitably running high, but my frustration overflowed on the final night when Mark asked me to pay for our hotel. I left the room where he was working on his laptop and wandered off barefoot into the hotel complex. My blood was boiling, and I didn't know where to turn. Anger was consuming me, and I hated it. I knew I had to get over it but had no idea how. There was resentment and fatigue, frustration at not standing my ground, and lots of bottled-up emotions. I was frustrated by the fact that we were staying in a smart hotel, while many of the skippers were living on their boats or in cheap hotels in town. We had no money, but Mark viewed the end of the Mini as the end of a ten-year campaign—his last big single-handed race. He felt he'd earned a reasonable rest and knew that in the grand scheme of things, the cost of a couple of nights' decent sleep was unimportant. At the time, I just couldn't see how much sense that made. All I knew was that we had to stick together in order to make all this happen. I gritted my teeth and hammered my fists a few times into the concrete steps I was sitting on. After a long think, and time to cool off, I returned to the room feeling deflated but a million times more positive. Mark and I were fundamentally different in this respect, but it didn't mean that we couldn't or shouldn't continue working together. He was completely unaware of my frustration, and the following morning I just gritted my teeth again and put the entire hotel bill on my credit card.

With the boat shipment arranged, I was finally able to put all this behind me when we caught a ferry to Guadeloupe, from where we would be flying home. We were staying for a couple of nights with Mark's friends Pipo and Marie Cairo and their daughter Mathilde. They couldn't have made us feel more welcome. Deciding to make the most of our time on Guadeloupe, Mark and I hired a small car for twenty-four hours and took it over to the mountainous side of the island. I'd never before seen such lush scenery. Strange animal calls and steam rising from the dark green slopes made it seem impossibly exotic. I was fascinated by the isolation and density of the forest. I felt intensely alive, savouring all the new sights, smells, and sounds. Mark travelled with a less obvious sense of wonder, having seen the world with the navy by the time he was my age, but still his curiosity and appetite for living were undimmed. It was all so far removed from the rest of my life.

As we drove back to Pipo and Marie's, relaxed after a wonderful day, we discussed the Mini. And I began to understand more the differences between us. We had teamed up, trusting our instincts, and that decision was dramatically shaping both our futures. Mark was competing to challenge and test himself, whereas I was there primarily to be out on the ocean. For me the racing side was a bonus which made it tougher and without a doubt made me push myself further, but the reason was not the race itself. I relied on my natural competitive instinct to push me harder when I was out there. I didn't need it to force myself to the start line.

I was intrigued by the difference in our views and understood why our partnership worked. Mark had needed my support as much as I had needed his; he was looking for someone with whom to share this experience. He had known that his drive and knowledge of the racing world would help me get to the start of that race and most probably make something happen which could otherwise have taken years longer. But he knew equally well that in order to get to the start line of that race himself, he needed someone there too.

Mark told me that the skippers of the top three boats had all said that by the time they arrived they were dying to get off their boats. I hadn't wanted the race to end, and I wondered if this meant that I would never be a winner because I might not have put in enough to hate it. I knew, though, that greater success in the Mini wouldn't have changed the way I felt at the finish. I thought about everything I had done, every decision I had made, and about what had gone right and wrong for us. With hindsight, maybe I would have done better in the north, taking the same route as the winners, but since *Financial Dynamics* performed less well upwind I was convinced that I would have really struggled up there. I had put in everything I'd got and relished every second, good and bad. And I told myself that what I'd felt was not a fault or a weakness but a strength.

CHAPTER ELEVEN

LIFE WAS HECTIC on returning from the Caribbean, and it seemed strange to come back to a modular shed in a quiet boat yard in the cold of winter. Mark and I brought back from the Mini some of the best memories of our lives and a list of great new friends, but we were financially drained. Both of us owed large amounts of money, but at least Mark had the income from his job, while I was in a more difficult situation. It was then that Mark asked me if I would like to become a joint partner in the company he had set up a couple of years before. Although the business had done little up to that point, it seemed a good idea to become part of an operation through which we could run our future projects. After what we had been through together, I made up my mind quickly and decided to go with it. Working with businesses was a big part of our projects; I had to learn fast. A few weeks later I became joint owner of Offshore Challenges.

I wasn't long on the South Coast before I headed to Derbyshire to see everyone. It had been a long time since I'd managed to visit Gran and Nan, both of whom were unwell. Gran had been into hospital for heart surgery and despite some complications was improving; but Nan was struggling. She had finished her degree course by this stage and had given just about all she had left in achieving it. She seemed so happy to see me, but while her eyes still shone, she was clearly very frail and weak. Dad was getting stronger and wearing his back brace less and less. But even as he recovered and was spending more of his time outside in the yard and around the barns, he remained incredibly frustrated that he was still not fit enough to do even half the chores he loved.

That Christmas was wonderful, really normal. Dad played his Scottish pipe music extra loud on Christmas Eve, more than making up for the fact that he had missed out the year before. On Christmas morning he went over to collect Nan and we all sat around for a fantastic Christmas lunch of turkey, rounded off with one of Gran's famous Christmas puddings looking splendid with the sprig of holly on top. Dad poured on the rum and lit it, and after lunch we sat down around the fire and opened our presents. Thea came down from her bedroom, and we talked about all that had happened in the Mini and the conditions Mark and I had experienced. We talked about the Route du Rhum and reminisced about our fantastic adventures on *Cabaret*. I walked Mac in the hills—sometimes alone, sometimes with Mum. I was relaxed and happy, and the time at home did me a world of good.

THE BREAK ENDED all too soon, however, and I returned to the boat yard to prepare for the London International Boat Show, starting on 9 January 1998. It was a crazy show for us, meeting yet more people, and I gave a presentation about the Mini Transat. I had done several presentations by this stage, but none with quite the same pressure of venue. Several people approached me afterwards, asking about the race and whether I had any secret tips on how to make it to the start line. I was embarrassed not to be able to offer more help, saying only that learning French and spending as much time as possible on the water before the race was important. What people really wanted to know, though, was how to find sponsorship—a difficult question to answer in finite detail, and probably the hardest aspect. I knew well enough from my own experience and couldn't help but think that Mark and I had set ourselves a new impossible task in finding sponsorship for the Route du Rhum.

The most promising development for me at the boat show was the possibility of a new challenge on board an Open 50. The boat was about to be bought by a family named Rowen, and I was asked if I would be prepared not only to manage the boat but also to co-skipper with David, the son, in the Double-handed Round Britain and Ireland Race. I was reluctant to commit myself long term, but their offer made sense. Not only was it a great race to compete in—clockwise round the UK and

Ireland in short sprints—but, more important, I would also gain valuable hands-on experience in the Open-class world.

The boat the Rowens were interested in, *Jusqu'au Bout du Monde*, was lying in Brittany, and soon after the boat show we went there to look her over. Merv, who was now settling into life after the BT Global Challenge, joined us to do the survey. He was living in Cherbourg, where he was managing the building of a new Open 60 for Mike Golding—Golding's next project after winning the BT Global Challenge. We all chatted away like a bunch of old schoolfriends, which was good news, as David and I would be going through a tough race together. David seemed shy at first, but he had a wicked sense of humour and a very definite passion for sailing.

Things happened quickly. David and his father bought the boat, and on Merv's recommendation we sailed her to Cherbourg so the bulk of the work could be carried out there. By the end of January we had her in a new base, had arranged for the cradle, had her out of the water, and had started on the list of work to be done. She was to have a new engine and a new water-ballast system, and we were going to repair her keel, which was not very symmetrical. Merv suggested that during the three months I would be there, I could stay with him in the beautiful cottage he had rented, about half an hour's drive from Cherbourg.

On 23 January, while I was still in France, the rest of the family joined Nan, now very ill, at Derby University for her graduation ceremony. She was understandably thrilled not only to be receiving her degree but also to be asked to give the thank-you speech on behalf of all the graduates. It seemed a fitting recognition of a lifetime's determination.

As she finally collected her degree, she got the loudest cheer of the day; when she gave her speech, she held the 2,000-strong audience in the palm of her hand, mixing humour and warm anecdotes that kept everyone in the hall transfixed. Her final line read: "I was glad to have been made aware that life holds a lot of treasure—still to be mined in one's eighties!" She had been living for that day all her life. At long last, she had achieved her goal.

Just three months later, she died from the cancer she had been fighting.

The springtime after Nan's death was bleak, but while we were devastated to lose her, we were comforted by the fulfillment of her dream and the end of her suffering.

* * * * *

I TRAVELLED HOME as often as I could and whenever possible met up with Mark to discuss any leads on sponsorship and progress on trying to find a boat for the Route du Rhum. There were few around, though, and we knew that without sponsorship, the task would be virtually impossible; with Mark desperately trying to catch up at Spinlock, and me with my head buried in the Round Britain and Ireland project, it was difficult to make headway. At least by April I would be back in the UK for a month to prepare for the Round Britain. I hoped that being nearer would make things easier to complete and achieve. To complicate things even further, Mark had decided that he was going to compete in the race as well, but in a 40-foot catamaran named—ironically, as it turned out—*Fingers Crossed*. It was all go once more.

My only break from a life revolving around the dockyard was a five-day trip on one of the BT Global Challenge boats. Two of these had been chartered by a company named TMI, and I had already met one of the directors, Antony Lane. Antony had sailed with Merv on one of the legs of the BT Global Challenge and had always been a sailor, as had his brother Chris. We had a rough start to our trip—a race against other Challenge boats around the Fastnet Rock. Every boat in the fleet turned back, though we were the last to do so; when we finally called it a day, the majority of the crew of twelve were seasick and the rest were too inexperienced to carry on safely. Below decks was carnage—pieces of clothing slopped around with bits of revisited breakfast from one end or the other that had failed to make it into, or had fallen out of, the buckets. Rather than continue the punishment, we spent the last few days cruising in the West Country, and we laughed so much we didn't know what to do with ourselves! The memory that sticks with me, though, is of a fourteen-year-old girl named Hemma. She had been invited on the race by an educational trust created by TMI that aimed to provide youngsters with otherwise-impossible opportunities. Hemma, from inner-city Birmingham, had never been on the water before, let alone lived on a boat with a bunch of puking adults, but as our trip drew to a close and she stood at the helm in complete control of the boat, I don't think I had ever seen anyone's eyes shine so brightly.

Back in France, the hard work resumed. I never seemed to leave the dockside until after dark. Although *Jusqu'au Bout du Monde* was out of the water, making it easier to work on her, the docks near the ferry terminal where we worked were horribly exposed to the bitter Cherbourg winter. While I felt sure I would lose my fingers from frostbite, I never lost my enthusiasm and was never more than a couple of minutes away from a quick hot chocolate and a warming chat with Jean-Marie Vaur, the manager of the JMV yard, about the work that was going on. In the evenings, we would talk about the Open 60s, and he would show me around the yard, explaining what each piece of machinery was for and how it functioned. He showed me the types of construction and the various materials that were used in these modern racing machines. His pride in the yard was transparent, and I was fascinated. Merv was still there too, working on the final stages of Mike's boat, *Team Group 4*, and when we both had a few minutes to spare, we would wander around talking. I also got on well with the guys working with him and would sometimes join them after hours for a beer laid on by Merv. He was sensitive to the guys' feelings and had built a great relationship with them. He was aware that a boat's eventual level of performance would be a direct reflection of the amount of energy and care put into building her.

During the final stages of my time in Cherbourg, Merv and I realized that we were becoming more than just the close friends we already were. We shared so many of the same passions and dreams. In the evenings we sat in the cottage tapping away on our laptops and chatting about Open-class boats and the Southern Ocean. We had lived together for two months, gone running in the evenings, and cooked meals for each other (though mine rarely stretched to anything more glamorous than crêpes). We saw that this could be something longer term. It was a wonderful feeling, almost a relief, to start a relationship with Merv. He understood me, watched out for me as I did for him, and took me for what I was. I felt like the luckiest girl on earth. He was a caring, loving man who would go out of his way to help people. He was as solid as a rock and wore his heart on his sleeve—both qualities I appreciated immensely. After only a few precious weeks, it was a wrench to leave him behind in Cherbourg and head for Plymouth with David to prepare for the race.

IT WAS AN ODD TIME in Plymouth. I felt nervous and very responsible, as for the first time my work was important directly for David, too. There was a real mixture of boats in the race, from our 50 to the monster 60s, and several trimarans around 45 feet in length. It's a special race, run in stages with exactly forty-eight hours in each stopover—which, though busy, normally also end up as quite social occasions with the other skippers.

David and I had a great time on the Round Britain and Ireland Race. We not only had some hard and tactical racing but also laughed a lot. We got on famously, and it revealed once again the incredible spirit it is possible to have on board when people are compatible and have to work hard together for something. Mark, on the multihull *Fingers Crossed*, was desperately unlucky when the catamaran's mast began to come down just 60 miles into the race, forcing them to turn back before they ever really got going. But for the lucky ones, the route was beautiful: the Outer Hebrides were stunning and we were blessed with wonderful weather and light winds—eternal daylight was breathtaking as we headed farther north. The race was not without its problems, though. During a rig check in Lerwick I discovered our forestay was breaking, so we spent a laborious and rather chilly day removing it. It was nippy spending hours up an aluminium mast as far north as Cape Horn is south!

It was a foggy passage through the North Sea and past the River Humber before a real bashing down the English Channel, where we developed problems with our other forestay, which led to an incredibly stressful final night in a very black and vicious storm. We made it back to Plymouth, though, and the icing on the cake was that we won our class in the race.

But there was a lot going on ashore while I was racing. Mark made a big life-changing decision; he resigned from Spinlock, having decided that he had outgrown his post there. There was no doubt that the Mini Transat had changed his outlook; in fact, it had changed us both—and my goal of the Vendée Globe was sitting there just waiting to be seized. The Mini had taken us a long way towards that. At the time of the start it was the unimaginable culmination of all our hard work; by the finish, it had become the foundation on which we could build the campaign for the Vendée. The biggest step forward for both of us was simply our decision to work together.

Returning from the race, I sailed with David back to Hamble, where the boat came out of the water. I made a quickly filmed BBC *Waterworld* programme about my plans for the Vendée Globe; then, in a car BBC was kind enough to hire for me, I drove to Falmouth with some parts for

Merv, who by this stage was preparing *Team Group 4* for her first race. It was great to see him again, and I even had a few hours' sailing on the boat, which was fantastic. Mike Golding was going to race over to America in the feeder event for the Around Alone, the same race we had looked at; but with stopovers, it meant that Merv would be following him—I would be seeing little of him.

After my brief trip to Falmouth, Mark and I once again set about looking for sponsorship and a boat in which I could race in the Route du Rhum. A seemingly obvious option for the latter was the 50 I had just raced on. She had been bought very much as a boat for a single purpose, and now that race was finished. I also knew her well, and since several discussions touching on the subject had already occurred, we thought we should ask the question properly.

We had several meetings with David, his father, and their business associates; contrary to what we had initially thought, they seemed quite keen to take it forward as a project. We came to an agreement whereby I would be able to sail the boat in the Route du Rhum. The boat itself would be further enhanced by work that we would do over the rest of the summer, ideally including a new mast and new sails. Her visibility would be significantly raised in France, which would greatly improve the prospects for selling her.

We were over the moon to be working with people whom we had come to know and trust over recent months, and as we had learned with the Mini project, having a boat meant we were on far firmer ground in our search for a sponsor. Finding big-name sponsorship was undoubtedly going to be hard, but using the success we had had with our Mini sponsorship, we explored every avenue. Dick had already made a programme on the Mini Transat using footage I'd shot, and he and Mark and I set about producing a sponsorship video which we could show at meetings. Along with this, we developed a computer presentation with more particular talking points which could be shown on a big screen.

Every billboard or poster seemed to suggest a new opportunity or sparked an idea for a potential sponsor. As I curled up in my little shed, I would close my eyes and drift off to sleep, always keeping a notepad on the floor next to my pillow—nine nights out of ten, I would switch on the light and scribble down a thought or idea, whether for pursuing funding or for modifying the boat.

The pressure was definitely mounting. As each day passed, there was more and more to organize. Mark was in the process of completing his three months' notice at Spinlock; we still owed serious money on our Mini Transat boats and could not risk spending the money I had earned working on the 50. I decided to move out of the shed, which was costing us over £30 per week. While *Team Group 4* was out at sea, I could join Merv, who was staying with friends in Cowes. Some nights, I would stay at Mark's mother's house on the other side of the Isle of Wight. Meanwhile, Mark and I arranged to share an office with a good friend, yacht designer Chris Stimson.

Cowes Week in August provided an opportunity to meet potential sponsors for the Rhum. I'd met one of my sponsors for the Mini Transat this way, so the omens were good.

In the end, Cowes yielded fewer contacts than we'd hoped. It hadn't helped that I'd been ill for most of it, sleeping on the floor of Chris's office right in the yard, where nightly celebrations were held in the beer tent. Not only did I hear the commotion of thousands of people enjoying themselves outside, but at about 10 P.M., the nightclub started up for the all-nighters in the giant boat shed adjoining the office. I would lie there on any cushions I could find from the chairs and, in a fever-like sweat, try to block out the thumping bass by listening to music on a portable CD player. I knew I was not supposed to sleep there, so I would keep the lights off when darkness fell; if I was working, I would rely on the glow from the computer screen. It was a small office, and as it was a basic single-skin brick construction with single-glazed windows, it got cold at nights. But it allowed me to work and live in the same place, saving money, time, and energy. We were able to meet up with and interview a French girl, Marine Crenn, with a view to her working with us at Offshore Challenges. She was young, very outgoing, and a good dinghy sailor. She had grown up in a world of single-handed sailors on the north coast of Brittany and spoke good English. Now having a base meant that we were able to be more than just Mark and Ellen, and as Marine spoke French, she would be perfect to take over from Nick, the student who had been helping us as a summer job. We made a hasty but life-saving decision to go with it: she joined us on 14 September and could not have worked harder for us.

I stayed in regular contact with Hugh Morrison at the time, and I kept him up to date with the latest developments. He has always been an incredible idea man, constantly coming up with different suggestions or a new angle. People such as Hugh helped keep us going. I know that enthusiasm on our part was not lacking, but when the chips were down— and we were about to discover how that really felt—his support was priceless.

Hugh,
I had a phonecall the other day from Antony Lane, the Chairman of TMI (UK). He had a fantastic offer, which needs a little explanation. . . .
His brother Chris, the Chief Executive, was one of the founders of the company and during their first years, when they were really quite small, Chris managed to get British Airways to take them on to train 38,000 staff in 18 months! At that time TMI had five employees! They did it, and the company has never looked back.
Now, there is a story behind their offer to help me that I must tell you. . . .
A friend of Chris's, a musician at the Royal Shakespeare Theatre in Stratford-upon-Avon, had a teenage son who was an incredibly talented flautist. He was winning competitions all over, and was accepted into the finals of the Young Musician of the Year award. His flute was good, but certainly not up to award standards. . . . He said exceptional talent will only take you so far, you also need an exceptional instrument . . . true, I suppose!
Chris was having this discussion with the boy's father in a local pub, and after a few beers he suggested that TMI could sponsor a top-class flute made specially for the young man at a cost of about £10k. The boy's name is Julian Cawdrey and he has never since been parted from his flute. He now plays as a soloist for the world's top orchestras and is much sought after as a teacher. This was the "ethos" behind their offer of help.

Chris and Antony set up an "education" trust fund, which is what they want to use to help me. Their solution to the problem is to pay some of my "billed items," and they are not asking to have their name on the side of the boat. They simply want to get me to that Start Line . . . fantastic. . . .

Their company is a training company, with courses predominantly on team building, time and stress management, customer service, etc., etc. The courses are fantastic, inspirational, really hitting home. Their intention is to send me on some of these courses, and for me, in a few years' time to work with the company delivering messages. I will take this on as a challenge, I enjoy speaking . . . who knows what this might lead to? Their courses are for companies such as Esso, ICI, etc., so could lead (and I know they're considering this) to some great opportunities, and an income of sorts. . . .

Wonderful, wonderful news . . . with their intention that I can still find a main sponsor!

Feeling quite run down right now, I'm homeless as the Portakabin *[prefab shed]* was towed away last Friday. . . . My life is in a lockup, and I'll be free till the beginning of October! What a story . . .

Will be in London for meetings next week. I'll mail with more details. . . . Thanks for all your support, Hugh.

Ellen

Antony had been fantastic in giving us a break that we so desperately needed to survive. Despite this, however, we still had few financial reserves left. What we lacked was hard cash. The support from TMI was very much a reality, but as it was a trust fund, we would only be able to refund from receipts. By now, we were really facing trouble—we had still not been able to pay the £5,000 entry fee for the race.

We suffered what felt like a knockout blow immediately after Cowes Week. Mark called, and I knew instantly from the sound of his voice that something was wrong. He had received a fax from the Rowens, stating that they had had advances from a potential purchaser of the 50. With those few words, we knew they had withdrawn the offer of the boat, and we felt devastated.

I forced my eyes to shut so tightly that I could feel the blood withdraw into my head. I wished I could turn back time and just be getting on with the project. Why had we not had a face-to-face meeting about this a month earlier? Although we had still been waiting for the contract, we had had the verbal agreement for weeks.

In anger and frustration, I hammered out on paper my thoughts for a reply. I knew I just had to get it out of my system.

> I honestly believe this is your loss . . . and unfortunately, as a result . . . our pain, and our explanation to those who have helped us get so close. . . .

My teeth were gritted together firmly as I wrote:

> Now we have only our own enthusiasm, and that of those who believe in the project to make it happen . . . and who shall see it to the end. We shall find a solution, but for now our work has been made far, far harder.

Finishing the letter, I let my head fall into my hands. What was the use? She was their boat, not ours: their call. If we were going to make it to the start line, we would have to find another boat. I think both Mark and I knew that with less than ten weeks to the start of the race, this one was going to hurt. I was confused, too. David and I had got on so well during the race, and I couldn't help but take their decision personally. Ironically, the 50 wouldn't sell for another three years.

Mark and I got to work immediately, contacting every person we thought might know of a boat, but with two massive ocean races already in progress, we had our work cut out. It looked as though there were just two options in the whole of the Northern Hemisphere: a 60-footer named *Coyote*, which we could buy for more money than we could ever dream of attaining, and *Great Circle*, a 50-footer lying in Bermuda, charter price negotiable.

In the end, Merv turned out to be our saviour when he e-mailed Brian Hancock, the owner of the boat in Bermuda. E-mails were soon flying back and forth between us. Brian had been planning to race his boat *Great Circle* in the Around Alone Race, but after a fruitless and frustrating search for sponsors, he was reluctantly concluding that it wasn't going to be possible.

It was mind-blowing to see the support we received at this point: the Lanes, for a start; Merv, for his time spent on trying to find another boat; Ashley Perrin and her family, for offering me airline companion passes so I would be able to travel at a fraction of the usual cost—very handy when a trip to the States was in order.

In a few days' time Mark was due to fulfill his final commitment to Spinlock—a series of meetings on the U.S. East Coast. Coincidentally, this was where Brian Hancock, a South African, was now living. I could join Mark a few days later. Brian had said he would fly to Bermuda and sail *Great Circle* back to Marblehead, allowing us the chance to see her there the following weekend.

Before this, however, I'd promised Mum and Dad I would join them in Scotland on holiday. My plan was to pass through London to see Hugh Morrison, then catch the train north to Derbyshire. As usual, Hugh was full of enthusiasm, bundling me into a cab at the end of our chat with a packed lunch from the canteen. He really did understand.

I spent a night in Derbyshire before driving north with my parents. As we drove, a million things spun round in my head, and I could not help but feel that I shouldn't have been there. I desperately wanted to spend time with Mum and Dad, but it was very stressful. Each day we would go out in the car, and I would connect my laptop to my mobile to read e-mails. I was waiting to hear from Brian. Although I realized he would be at sea for a few days, I needed to know that all was well before catching the flight to the States. I was stumped when I received an e-mail from Brian, clearly sent from the boat's e-mail address—short of characters as each message is paid for by its length.

Date:Tue, 25 Aug 1998 00:31:39Z +0000
To: Offshore_Challenges_Ellen@compuserve.com
HiEllen Cant GETthro2U from here. Here isTHE situation asICit.
Letsmeet inMarblehead ths weeknd & sort allBOATdetails I will
SAIL2Azores from here W/U. Boat willB redy2leave whenURredy.
Please GIVEme somedates 4depart BDA that work4U soTHAT I can
makeMY flt res4 return 2 BDA. Please understand that by
yourREPLY Iam finally givingupon my campaign&working w/U &
willHOLD U2 our agreement outlined invarious e-mls.Pls reply
ASAPvia eitherMYWIFE orMERF. LK fwd2seeingU Brian

This was odd—Brian was still in Bermuda (BDA) and was suggesting sailing back to Europe from there. I was getting worried by this stage, and it was impossible to reach Mark to discuss the situation. I felt as though I had the weight of the world on my shoulders.

Although I was distracted during the trip to Scotland, I think ultimately that holiday allowed me to carry on with that year. I was absolutely exhausted when we arrived there, although I'd slept for most of the way in the car. I felt drained and on the second day developed very swollen glands. I worried that my mononucleosis was coming back. A blood test by a local doctor put my mind at rest on that one, but I was forced to slow down—I had only two days to get stronger before leaving. As I lay in bed that night, I began to breathe deeply and slowly, and I closed my eyes. Mac was lying on the floor next to me, and I let my hand fall to stroke her. I simply had to get better, I could not let everyone down. On the last morning, I woke and wandered into the living area of the cabin. I could see the hills disappearing into the distance, and the light mist softening each feature. I could see the shepherd in the farmyard preparing to leave for the hills, and the rabbits that had come out for their first lollop. Mac sat by the window, ears pricked up, watching every move outside, while I made a cup of tea and curled up in a ball on the sofa with a thick scarf round my neck. I loved that time in the morning. I reckoned I'd be OK.

I QUEUED NERVOUSLY at the gate at Heathrow, the last person to board and lucky to get a standby seat. Mark picked me up in Boston and we drove north to meet Brian Hancock. We talked feverishly in the car—I felt better now, relieved to be back on form.

Brian had boundless energy, and it was evident just how much effort he had put into his own campaign. He seemed to live by its slogan, "Goals are just dreams with a deadline." He had bad news, however, which finally made sense of the e-mail I'd read in Scotland. He had attempted to sail *Great Circle* back to Marblehead for us to see, but on leaving Bermuda, he'd been caught up in a tropical storm and gone onto the reef. The boat had been damaged—the forward fin ripped out, the keel scraped, and the rudder broken. We now had even more on our plate. Brian could see we were struggling, and he had decided that if *Great Circle* could not race around the world, she would be far better off racing in the Route du Rhum. He let us charter her for a fraction of the cost of other boats.

The plan was to fly to Bermuda just two weeks later. Things were going to be very, very tight, and there seemed to be an impossible amount to do back home.

Hugh Morrison was trying to set up a meeting with a company he thought might be a potential sponsor for us. In the UK, Kingfisher PLC owned well-known brands such as Woolworths, Comet, Superdrug, and B&Q, and Hugh explained that they had similar brands in France and other parts of Europe. He felt that it would be a great match for us—we were English, wanting to compete in a French race but in no way going out there to "take on" the French. Both of us felt European, and Kingfisher was a pan-European company—perfect. Hugh might give us the opportunity to walk through the boardroom door and make our case.

We worked with Dick on the sponsorship video and put together a new presentation for the meeting. Although our most pressing battle was simply to get to the start of the Rhum, our strategy was to present a campaign culminating in the Vendée Globe; while that remained the ultimate, we planned to present the Route du Rhum as an imminent trial run for us and our sponsor. We would offer main sponsorship for the Rhum at a tiny price, but enough to give us a chance to show the sponsor what we were capable of doing. We simply had to give the meeting our best shot.

At the same time, we prepared for a press launch at the Southampton Boat Show, now just a week away.

> Mark,
>
> I've spoken to Hugh, and he was great . . . as usual, more helpful than imaginable. . . . I said we could (just feasibly) have the video done for next Friday. . . . He said I must let him know if we're really scraping for money, and that he'd be there to try to "unstick" us if we got "stuck!" He also remarked how experienced we were at getting these projects together at the last minute! He's such a great person. . . .
>
> He said he's likely to have an answer from the KF group by the end of next week.
>
> I desperately need to get practicing "close racing!" . . . This, plus the weather routing . . . needs to happen. . . . I've got to get some things right!

Hugh's final words were to contact him without any hesitation whatsoever . . . if there was anything he could do,
or we were stuck. . . . His final words were . . . "No worries, mate, I think you're worth it!"

It's priceless to have people like this around . . . never
doubting, never pausing . . . always supporting, helping
and encouraging . . .

And Mark, you are the same. . . .

There is always a way, we can always succeed, and we
will get there. . . .

Thanks for everything. . . .

see you later . . .

and smile!

e

xx

I had also been asked to give a speech at the opening lunch of the
Southampton Boat Show. Once again it was going to be a busy show, and
we had a lot of ground to cover in our time there. We borrowed a tank-
test model of an Open 60 from Thierry Dubois, a French sailor who has
always keenly encouraged newcomers into the sport. We painted it silver and put stickers announcing "GLOBE 2000" on its side. We had to
give out the right message, and we wanted no one to be in any doubt
about the ambition and substance of our plans. Our first press release
together under the banner of Offshore Challenges read:

GLOBE 2000—SINGLE-HANDED, NON-STOP, AROUND THE WORLD—TO WIN

Today Ellen MacArthur announces her campaign for the
Vendée Globe single-handed, non-stop, round the world
race in the year 2000. Whilst there are nowadays a number
of round the world events, the Vendée Globe clearly remains the pinnacle of human challenge—and nowadays as
professional and competitive as the Whitbread/Volvo
Race.

Short-handed racing is growing fast in popularity in the
UK, with as many as ten skippers signed up for the next

Mini Transat, and for the first time British born and based professionals entering the professional French Figaro circuit.

Teaming up with fellow solo skipper and marketeer Mark Turner, and his company Offshore Challenges, the search has begun in earnest for a business partner and sponsor. The objective is clear—to win the race, but also inspire as many people as possible along the way, whether from their armchairs or for their own campaigns. The budget for Globe 2000 is £1.5 million.

The path has been a fast one for 22-year-old MacArthur—and the learning curve steep—but the results prove her incredible ability to learn, and her competitiveness. With more than 30,000 miles in Open 50s and 60s, a victorious two-handed Great Britain, and the tough 1997 Mini Transat under her belt, she is moving on to the next stage of Vendée Globe preparation, the Route du Rhum.

Departing from St.-Malo on 8 November this year, this the most famous of French races (an event recognized by 30 per cent of the French population as a whole) will provide the first solo big boat test for MacArthur. The 4,000-mile race includes some of the top names in the single-handed circuit, and takes the solo skippers from the north of France across the Atlantic to Guadeloupe in the Caribbean.

The boat she will be sailing is a lightweight all carbon Open 50 previously named *Great Circle*. She was built in the USA by Concordia Yachts for over 1 million dollars, and has since never raced competitively, narrowly missing the qualification date for this year's Around Alone race . . . maybe she has something to prove?

By the end of next week MacArthur should be at sea on the delivery of the boat back from Bermuda, ready to change sails, and fit an engine in preparation for the start. The programme is charged, but the participants motivated to overcome the hurdles!

From a small beginning just three years ago—a round
Britain solo voyage in a 21-foot Corribee—Ellen
MacArthur has progressed way beyond most people's expectations. There will be no change of pace. With her are a
fantastic group of sponsors and supporters—from inside
and out of the marine industry—without whom this
would be impossible.

On the day of the project launch we received a call from Hugh Morrison to tell us that we had our meeting with Kingfisher—the meeting
that we hoped would allow all our plans to become reality. It was
arranged for the following Friday, just seven days away.

That evening I went back to Ashley Perrin's place. Ash was brilliant,
keeping me fed while leaving me to get on with writing. This time I just
got in and collapsed on a bean bag in the corner of the room, snatching
only a couple of hours' sleep before getting up to prepare my boat show
speech.

I knew that it had to be a good one. The show was launching a new
campaign called Big Blue, aimed at inspiring kids to get onto the water. I
wanted to show support for that cause and to demonstrate that things
really are possible if you give them your all. I knew that I had to communicate my passion. I would have to stand up there and wear my heart on
my sleeve.

I was incredibly nervous as I stood alone at the microphone, hearing
my heart pounding away in my chest.

Normally when invited to lunch, I would politely decline,
and ask if I could please have the money instead. For ten
years I collected my lunch money, on a mission to save for
a boat, each day placing the 70 pence in my tin! When I
asked Denzil if this was possible today, he cunningly suggested I make a speech instead . . . maybe I should have
kept my mouth shut!

Since then things have moved on. I have spent four solid
years working on projects, racing, crossing oceans . . . and
really living. The decision to sail full-time was, and I hope
always will be, the best decision of my life.

Many of you will remember the Mini Transat, the biggest project for me until this year. Over 4,000 miles of "hardcore" racing in 21-foot skiff-like boats, cabins resembling the interior of washing machines (size included!), no bunks, no sleeping bags, freeze-dried food, and the ocean. A wonderful race—I learnt so much about campaigns, racing alone, myself, the world, and about others. I made some fantastic friends, and through this race have teamed up with Mark Turner, with whom I now work on future projects. Not only for ourselves—Offshore Challenges is a company designed to help and inspire others, and to work with them to achieve their goals.

As with any industry, we face huge hurdles. Just eighteen days ago, and weeks from the start of my next race, the Open 50 we'd been promised for the Route du Rhum was withdrawn. Since then we've travelled over 8,000 miles in search of a new boat. Having found one in the States, I fly out next weekend to sail her home to a race start just three weeks later.

Tiny things can make an immense difference, and people's kindness and support in whatever form is priceless. But this is not about asking for charity; it's not about pleading for help. The bottom line is business. Single-handed sailing in particular has the potential to break through the barrier of people's perceptions. It can dismiss the elitist image, bringing passion, emotion, and feelings into people's homes. If someone is exhausted, happy, or emotional, anyone can understand, anyone can relate. You don't have to be a sailor or even have set foot on a boat before.

Eight hundred thousand people will descend on St.-Malo for the start of the Route du Rhum in two months' time. The event is covered extensively, the start shown "live" on national TV and radio, and it's virtually as popular in France as Formula 1 Grand Prix.

Their sailors are heroes. They are setting goals; they are winning. Young people in France believe that they can do that too, because they can see, and have access to, this success. Each and every one of them feels a part of it, and I believe their nation feels this.

Exactly three years ago, I was here at the show. I knew no one in the industry but was so quickly supported and accepted. I have been lucky—I was a wide-eyed teenager, finding my feet during a single-handed round Britain sail. I was young, naive, and soaking up the atmosphere. People have helped me, supported me, and believed in me. The BMIF took me under their wing and gave me chances to speak, to talk to people, and to learn more. I hope that in time I not only can return this, but put more back in.

I do not know where my motivation has come from, but I feel it is my goal to pass it on, to help and encourage others, and to sow the seeds of inspiration, which transform dreams into reality: to race, to compete, or simply to enjoy the water.

In the next ten days I have to find £25,000 to make this race happen. New sails, a new engine, travel, and a roof over my head. This end of the sport is expensive, but so vital for the future. The football industry will not promote sailing, the Formula 1 industry will not promote sailing. It is down to us.

One thing I've learnt over the past years is that if deep down in your heart you have a goal, you can achieve it. Getting to this stage has pushed me hard, harder than I ever imagined, but I have experienced moments more rewarding and more beautiful than in my wildest dreams. Yes, it's true, luck does play a part in it. But if you believe, and are determined, you can build your own luck . . . and realize that vision is really not so far away.

As I spoke my final words, there was silence. I had to pause for breath between the sentences to try to calm myself. I was completely exhausted, and letting all that out in one hit had just about finished me off. As I sat down, the world closed around me—I could make out faces, but their words didn't connect. I suppose it was the relief of having shared so much. The bottom line is that we could not have coped without the support of all those who rallied around us.

After the show, work on both the race and our crucial sponsorship presentation continued at fever pitch. The speech had immediately resulted in offers of everything from free berthing for *Great Circle* to a free engine and other bits of gear for the boat.

> *Date: Wed, 16 Sep 1998 02:21:39*
>
> *We were working on the promotional video tonight . . . still up as usual! 0059. We have a meeting on Friday with a sponsor we hope will come in for the next three years. However, there's a fair bit of persuading to do on this front, and we've never met him before. . . .*
>
> *We're in a bit of financial strife here! We're cleaned out after sail deposits, charter fees, insurance premiums, flights and "everyday bills." . . . All fairly stressed.*
>
> *We should have had the entrance fee in by the end of last week. but they've given us till this weekend to come up with the money. £4,500. . . .*

Later that day I called Mum, and though I had phoned sporadically to keep her up to date with all that was going on, I don't think she realized until that moment quite how bad things were. I was desperate and just needed to share the burden. I had held back before, as I didn't want to worry my parents, but right now I just had to call. We had less than forty-eight hours before, without the entry fee, we would be out of the race. Since the holiday in Scotland, Mum and Dad had clearly been discussing things between themselves, because after first listening to me without saying a word, Mum then said quietly that there was some money available. I was puzzled; I still owed them £15,000 for the Mini Transat.

"Your Nan left you £5,000 in her will." Oh, Nan! My eyes welled with tears—she was still making the difference. It may have been the last minute, but we'd be on that start line now. I gave Mum the race organizers' bank details.

The surprises didn't stop there, though. That same evening, I was asked if I would present the prizes for Cowes Week. I was supposed to be with Mark and Dick working on the video, but I decided to go anyway.

I arrived in a terrible state. I'd bailed out of Ashley's that morning and had run from the boat show with all my bags. As I arrived, I was flushed and sweating. I took a deep breath in an attempt to make myself look presentable, and as the lift headed to the top floor, I leant back against its cool wall and took advantage of the brief moment of peace to drift away.

I was shown round by Bill West, whose company was behind the awards, and recognized Johnny Caulcutt, who'd supported our Mini Transat campaign. We all talked, and I couldn't hide the fact that things were pretty dire. I explained that we'd just managed to charter a boat and just managed to pay the entrance fee. How we were still in the race by the skin of our teeth.

Our conversation was cut short by the prize-giving, and after a brief introduction by Bill, I handed over each prize in turn.

As things were drawing to an end, Johnny leapt up on stage without warning and began to recount our conversation, finishing emphatically, "Now, this girl needs support right now! I pledge £1,000. Bill, you'll pledge £1,000, won't you?" And within five minutes, we had raised almost £5,000. I've no recollection of what I said when Johnny encouraged me to say a few words. I just know that they ended with the most heartfelt thank-you. I only hoped that each person who had supported us had just an inkling of what a difference they had made.

I wanted to hug everyone in the room. As soon as I could, I raced outside to call Mark and tell him not to despair. He immediately recited a string of problems with the video and he sounded very depressed. The computer had just crashed, and they needed to start a whole section from scratch.

"Mark," I said, "I've got some good news. We've got £5,000. Johnny Caulcutt just stood up and raised £5,000."

I'm sure Mark thought I was winding him up, as he failed to react at all, saying little more than "I have to go, see you later" before hanging up.

Date: Thu, 17 Sep 1998 23:11:03
Another fairly full on day. Found out today that the rudder for **Great Circle** *is being rebuilt, and will not be flown out (nor will the owner, as he's coming with it!) till Monday 21st!!!!*
The more I think about the problem, the stronger I feel. There is such determination inside me; I can feel it. . . . We will not give up, and we will get there . . . and **not** *just for me.*
There is a way, and I shall run and run until I find it.

Friday was suddenly upon us. Since starting on the video, we had worked non-stop, snatching no more than eight hours' sleep altogether in three days. At nine in the morning on the day of the presentation, we were still getting documents bound.

It felt like all or nothing. The following day, I was flying out to Bermuda and now we were heading for the meeting that held the potential to change everything. Mark and I met Hugh in London, and we all jumped in a cab to head for Kingfisher's office. Hugh was a calming presence. If he was nervous, it was impossible to tell. He'd obviously done a lot more of this than we had.

It was intimidating to walk into an enormous boardroom to which we felt so unaccustomed. But we thought the meeting went well, and by the end I think that CEO Geoff Mulcahy's interest had certainly grown for the project. Hugh had sat down on the opposite side of the table from us; Mark and I were there to sell the project.

We talked predominantly about the Vendée Globe, showing the video we had produced with Dick and talking through slides we had created. We were passionate about the fact that a project such as the Vendée Globe could work, and that we were not asking for the money just to enable us to stick their name on a boat's hull and go sailing. We wanted to work with the company to make the sponsorship work for them, both internally and externally. We felt that some sailing sponsors had been "used" in the past, and we emphatically were not going to allow this to happen. As far as we were concerned, we would all be in it together and would work as a team.

What was initially a chance meeting on leaving the boardroom would later become a critical factor. Geoff left the room to answer an important call and briefly greeted a man who was leaving the lift. Hugh whispered to Mark, "You should engage this guy." Mike Hingston was not only a keen sailor but a perfectionist with vision.

Three months later, he became Kingfisher PLC's Director of Corporate Affairs and a key decision-maker when it came to sponsorship.

CHAPTER TWELVE

WHEN I MET Liam and Chris at Heathrow, I don't think they had a clue what they were letting themselves in for; they were willing volunteers for the delivery from Bermuda. Liam had been working at Ocean Village on the trimaran *Spirit of England* when I had been working on the Open 50 that David and I had sailed in the Round Britain and Ireland Race. We had kept in touch since then, and both Merv and I thought he was more than up to the job of helping with the delivery of *Great Circle*. Liam was from Liverpool and had a great sense of humour; his laughter proved to be a precious commodity in the weeks that followed.

I barely knew Chris. He was hoping to do the Mini Transat the following year and had already bought a boat. He was about to take part in the Atlantic Rally for Cruisers (ARC) to get miles under his keel, but before that, the trip back from Bermuda was a great opportunity to gain open ocean experience. I think he got a bit more than he bargained for!

When we arrived in Bermuda, the weather was deteriorating. We headed for the Customs House in St. George's, where the boat was lying. Once on board we made ourselves at home, and I was impressed with how well built *Great Circle* seemed. Everything was clean and tidy, and there was even enough food on board from Brian's trip to fashion a meal later. There was a bunk on each side of her, and in the centre she had a canting chart table facing a Recaro race seat. I dropped my sleeping-bag on it and gave the guys the bunks—I'd need to get used to sleeping in it anyway.

We soon jumped off for a swim. I wanted to see what state the keel was in, as we knew that she'd suffered damage on the reef last time she was sailed. Besides, we'd been travelling all day and it was stinking hot.

Hi Mark,
Just to let you know the situation with the boat.

We're alongside in Bermuda. The boat is relatively OK, although the mainsail and rudder are a large problem. Brian has not arrived yet; he should be flying in today. Apparently he had problems getting the rudderstock through Customs. The new one is fairly heavy . . . like three times the weight of the old one! No choices on this one now, though.

The mainsail will, I hope, last the trip, but we haven't had it up yet. So far things have been very, very hot, very, very windy, and very, very, very wet. We've had squalls so strong the aircraft have not been able to land!

The rudder is another problem. There's a lot to do on it. We literally have some foam shapes here, that's all. They're not even really rudder shape! A big job, and more I will only know when Brian arrives. It seems a little suspect to me. The thought of glassing foam fairings onto an aluminium stock does not fill me with a feeling of security! I will mail Merv and Nigel now to ask for advice.

As far as life in Bermuda is concerned. Great people, extremely hot, warm water, but very, very expensive. Food is at least twice its price in the UK. We have cooked for ourselves here, but each meal is costing at least 40 dollars! Money is going quickly. I am worried about stocking up for the trip back. I guess I just have to go for it, but it will be hundreds. . . .

The generator will not start at all right now. We've played with it a little, although I'm loath to play with it too much, as Brian obviously knows the systems much, much better. The Ockham electronics are "half working." Heading works, but no wind-speed, wind direction, etc.

Fitting the engine will be fun too. If we change one for the other, we'll have the sail-drive leg sticking through the rudder tube! Problems. . . .

The mast leaks like mad around the base. Minor problem right now though.

Hope all's well there, thanks for everything,

Please mail back with any news. We'll be at least another three days here . . . a bloody expensive three days at that.

Ellen

xx

As planned, Brian flew in for a couple of days with the new rudder-stock, and we immediately rose to the challenge of preparing the boat with enthusiasm. But as the whole thing began to take shape, I realized that the key-way at the top of the rudder was back to front. This meant that we could only fit the rudder in the boat backwards— worse than useless. This was disastrous: we were already delayed and now had to find a machine shop which might be able to mill out a flat area on the other side—which we could only hope would be a solution. After making a number of inquiries, we managed to find a machine shop where the stock could be ground down to fit. At least the time it took for the stock to be milled gave Brian and me a chance to go through the electronics and instruments on board, and to spend an evening together on the dockside discussing the sailing of her. The day after we'd collected the rudderstock, Brian flew back to the States.

We were on our own, but throughout, the warmth of the local people and their willingness to help were priceless. One of them was the retired harbourmaster, Bernard Oakley or "Bitzy," who would come down to see us every day on his moped—a lovely and unbelievably helpful guy who deserves a medal for his services to sailors. His brother owned the local hardware shop, and as there was no real yacht chandlery, we became very dependent on Bitzy's brother.

Cannon Ball, a big friendly guy who wore his baseball cap under his crash helmet, also made Bermuda feel like a different place. He came down on his moped just to ask, "How ya doing?" It's a measure of how bedraggled we must have looked that he showed up one day with a bag of clothes for us from the local charity shop. Chris was particularly taken with a pair of bright green trousers, which needed the ankle cuffs cut off and the waistband folded down just to fit.

I felt immense pressure during our days in Bermuda, and though I desperately wanted just to have a laugh with the others, I felt completely detached from them. On a couple of evenings they went off into the town for a few beers, but I could not go with them, as I dared not spend any more money than we had to, and my mind was completely preoccupied. I was worried, really worried—we had a rudder to repair, there were three hurricanes tracking towards us, and we just *had* to get out of there. As they recounted their tales the following morning I smiled but felt a million miles away.

Still, the guys ground out the day's work, although I think that Chris in particular wondered what on earth he was doing there. I don't blame him. They were both amazing, and it made a massive difference to have their help and support. They both did it all for nothing. We had paid for their flights but could not pay them for the work that was necessary just to make *Great Circle* seaworthy.

The rudder was a massive job that took the best part of a week to complete. When finished it was by no means perfect, but it had to work. However, getting the stock up inside the boat might well have turned out to be a hellish task, as she was moored alongside the dock. I envisaged the 120-kilo stock sinking to the bottom underneath the boat. As it turned out, once we had actually repaired it, it floated despite its great weight. While this made fitting it easier, it also created its own set of problems.

Amazingly, local people appeared from nowhere to watch the event—they all came to see what was going on. We couldn't have wished for a more helpful audience. With the rudder floating, we had to find a way of sinking it, so some of our audience disappeared in search of something appropriate, returning later with an enormous piece of cast-iron drainpipe. This we tied to the rudder in a way that allowed us to control the depth to which the whole weighted arrangement sank. Liam and I swam beneath the boat—diving under, holding our breath, making sure it was aligned with the hole. When released, the rudder floated up underneath the boat, and I think everyone was amazed when this strategy worked and the stock fitted exactly in place.

We had been told that the old sails on the boat were adequate to deliver *Great Circle* back to the UK, where we planned to replace them. As it happened, they were rather less than adequate—particularly the mainsail. In fact, they were barely in one piece—one side of the main had even been completely covered with adhesive sailcloth in an attempt to hold the whole thing together. The existing inboard engine was also in a shocking state and could be started only by shorting it out with a screwdriver. We got it going, but once it was running it made a variety of frightening rattling sounds.

On the final morning, we started the little emergency outboard engine (our only propulsion, as the inboard engine was only for charging batteries) to make sure all was OK. We'd tested it a couple of times and had got it going, but weatherwise we were looking at sailing into a large high-pressure system, which was good news on the hurricane front but bad news on the wind front. With this in mind, Liam suggested it would be a good idea to check over the outboard and clean the spark plugs. He went at it with a spark-plug wrench, and quite soon a loud "f***" told us that a spark plug had sheared off inside the engine. My heart sank.

The nearest machine shop was a taxi ride away, and we used our last $20 to get the engine there. I walked in and told the guys what had happened. We fought with the engine for three hours, but the thread was completely corroded to the cylinder. The engineer shook his head. If it had not been for the incredible help we received there, we might never have left—they called every outboard engine supplier on the island, and on their last call found a man who had a suitable engine costing $2,500. I knew full well that only one of my credit cards might work, and that a $600 transaction had already been refused. I phoned the credit card company in a final attempt to beg for a higher limit. I began to explain the situation, but as soon as I mentioned Bermuda, I was told that there had been a problem with the lines and that my earlier attempt should have been OK. I had barely enough, but enough. Thank God.

This piece of good news was followed by a much better one. Just before we left Bermuda, I called Mark. His news took my breath away. Kingfisher had confirmed that they would sponsor us for the Route du Rhum. Absolutely elated with the news, I ran to tell Chris and Liam. Although it didn't make much difference to our immediate plans, it lifted all our spirits, and we left Bermuda on a high. I knew that our quest for the Vendée Globe was starting to come within reach.

As we left we hoisted the sails behind two cruise ships. We were elated. On several occasions problems had looked insurmountable, and it seemed that there would be no option but to fly home. We hadn't showered in ten days and had lived in clothes covered with carbon, grease, and resin. The conditions in St. George's had been pretty miserable. Only the wonderful support of the people in Bermuda had made things possible. Now at last our destiny was in our own hands again.

MOST DAYS on the *Great Circle* epic from Bermuda—as it was soon to be dubbed—we worked on the sails, fixing holes and just trying to get them to stay together long enough to see us home. As we helmed, there was a regular shower of glue and flakes falling on us—the sails were literally disintegrating over our heads.

But as though the sails were not a big enough problem, the weather was also about to test us. Hurricane Lisa, instead of following the normal hurricane track—heading west and then north from the Caribbean—instead came charging northward up the Atlantic towards us. Roughly 1,000 miles into our trip we had to turn back towards Bermuda for two and a half days to avoid the storm. It was massively frustrating, but it would have been idiotic to try to battle it out, especially with the mainsail in its fragile condition. We just couldn't have managed it. We fretted about the possibility of breakages from the rudder on up, but our major goal was to get back across the Atlantic to Britain and then sort things out. We were not racing, but we had to make it to the other side; that was our sole aim. We had planned to replace the rigging once back in Southampton—new sails were being made as we sailed—and back in Cowes a lot of effort was going into the project. Mark was spending all his time trying to work out a schedule for us, and the list of jobs was growing by the minute.

We were sailing as conservatively as possible, but even so, I remember that at one point we were sailing in a fair amount of wind with three reefs. We were under-canvased, but we did not want to go back to two reefs, because then we would be carrying slightly too much sail. In the end, though, we were forced to go back to two reefs simply because the third had all but pulled out of the sail. The second reef appeared to be the strongest of all the points. To say that things were far from ideal would be an understatement. We had to do the best we could in the circumstances. Despite everything, humour on board was outstanding. I don't think we were demoralized, and the guys were fantastic. We all just got on with the grim situation, which perhaps just seemed too farcical to be anything but laughable to them, and certainly they always tried to see the funny side of each situation. We occasionally trailed a line, never really expecting to catch anything, but one afternoon Liam and I caught an enormous dorado off the stern deck. Our on-board diet was fairly basic, so it was great to enjoy fresh fish—we ate the whole thing by sunset.

Great Circle didn't perform as I had imagined she would, but I hoped that with her new sails and faired rudder her performance would improve. The stakes had been raised greatly with the news that Kingfisher was sponsoring us, so while I needed to learn more about the boat, I also had to deliver in the race to secure our future. It was a real concern to think how unprepared to race she was.

About a week into our trip, the luff of the mainsail was ripping apart, tearing at the batten seams. Everyone's patience was tested to the limit, as virtually every stitch had to be preceded by a brad-awl hole, or else a second person was needed on the other side to retrieve the needle. We ended up sewing webbing straps around the sailcloth in an attempt to hold it together. We sewed for days on end, and that was the most demoralizing thing for Chris and Liam. They'd signed up to sail across the Atlantic, not to limp across as tailor's apprentices. I felt guilty, but they never complained.

We made a decision to put into the Azores, where we could replace the mainsail. But as we approached the islands, my mobile came back into reception for the first time in just under a month, and I spoke to Mark, uncertain of which course of action would be best. We would have to wait two days for the sails to arrive, so I suggested that we head for Spain instead—it would be much easier for Merv and Sam Davies, a new member of the team, to transport the sails there. I found it hard to tell this to Liam and Chris. We were a mile off the entrance to Horta in the Azores and could practically taste the ice-cold beers!

The disappointment was exacerbated by the next few frustrating days, probably the most difficult of the whole trip. We had no wind, and I wrote in my log:

Battered and exhausted. Mentally tested and just "hanging;
hanging in." If there were ever a test of endurance as far as I've
ever been tested anyway now is it. How late can this RUN? It's
never time to give in, we're almost on European shores and we
shall not give in until she reaches them with the three of us on
board.

When we finally arrived in Spain, it was far from over. That evening I planned to set sail once again to the UK with new sails. We had just thirteen days before we were due in St.-Malo for the start of the Route du Rhum, still with a million repairs, an engine to fit, and a delivery to the UK, then France!

Another new priority was to take a few promotional photos that needed to be sent back—of me wearing my first Kingfisher shirt, the only clean piece of clothing I now possessed! I'd spoken to Merv a few times from Bermuda, but it was wonderful to see him again.

Late in the afternoon, Merv took a call from Mark. Even recalling it now makes the hairs on the back of my neck stand up. I was lying on the gravel in the car park, trying to attach one of the batten fittings. Merv handed the phone to me, and I knew something important was about to happen when Mark said, "Make sure you're sitting down."

"Don't worry, I'm lying down," I replied.

He then told me I needed to get on the next plane home to Britain. It took a long time for his words even to register. I told him he was nuts. I still had to sail the boat back for the qualifier, and I didn't have time to fly home for some meeting.

He had difficulty making me understand, as my mind was racing at such a pace that I wasn't really listening. He told me I wasn't going to race *Great Circle* in the Route du Rhum. I feared the worst and felt sick deep in the pit of my stomach. I was light-headed and confused. Entirely without my knowledge, Mark had negotiated some additional funds from Kingfisher to charter *Aqua Quorum*, the boat in which Pete Goss had competed in the Vendée Globe, and he had just received confirmation seconds before calling. There were no more flights to the UK that day, so I had to spend a night in Spain. With no necessity to work on *Great Circle*, it was the first time I had relaxed in months. There was nothing more I could do. Indeed, we all talked and enjoyed each other's company, laughing about things which at the time had seemed obstacles beyond belief.

Next morning I jumped on the first flight back to Britain, while Merv and the others finished the final jobs on *Great Circle*. As I sat on the plane I felt a pang of regret that after all we had been through, *Great Circle* and I would not be racing together. But I couldn't help but feel it was our only choice. We had been delayed so many times now that we would only have been able to spend a few days in the UK—not really enough to complete the jobs that were necessary for her just to qualify. It was sad for Brian Hancock, too—after being forced to pull out of one race, he had lost the glimmer of hope that the boat might race in another. I wrote him a letter, which finished:

> I am sorry not to have taken *GC*. I was sad as we drove off to the airport. You do develop a relationship with a boat over a period of time. I was never worried about her strength. She lives for the surf, and is very easy to sail.
>
> Life works in strange ways. . . . Goals *are* dreams with deadlines. That's the problem! It's a shit fight out there.
>
> Brian, thanks for all your support.
> Will be in touch.
> kind regards
> ellen

CHAPTER THIRTEEN

WHEN I LANDED in London I took the train down to Southampton, spent a few hours in the office in Cowes, and met with Nigel Irens, who was driving to the West Country that evening. This was a happy coincidence, and it was wonderful to discuss all we had been through with someone who understood the situation. We drove through the night, arriving in the early morning hours at Nigel's office in Totnes, where I slept on the floor.

As I woke the following day I was tired but excited. I had read Pete Goss's book, *Close to the Wind*, on the way back across the Atlantic, but the possibility of chartering *Aqua Quorum* from him came as a complete surprise. My understanding was that Andy Hindley was going to sail her in the race. However, Andy, a member of Pete's team, had not been able to find sponsorship. When I arrived in the boat shed Andy was there, directing the work on the boat. I felt for him, and could only imagine the sorrow he had to be feeling at being unable to race.

The boat had been laid up for some time, so there was a tremendous amount still to do to get her ready in time for the race. The mast wasn't in, the keel wasn't on, and some of the electronics were missing, but somehow we got everything done, and when the logos were finally applied, she looked fantastic. I was desperately trying to get some rest, as well as to be down in the yard for the important jobs that were being done. There were interviews, too. A French TV crew came over to Plymouth, wrapping up by asking, "So tell me, Ellen, what is your favourite French phrase?"

I thought about it briefly, then replied, "A donf!" Slang for "Go for it," this was seized on by the French public watching the programme, and it has become the slogan for all our campaigns.

We were hampered by gales all week, but just before we left for St.-Malo, I went with Pete for a test sail in Plymouth Sound on *Aqua Quorum*, now renamed *Kingfisher*. It was blowing about a Force 7, and I doubted that we would be able to make it out against the wind, but Pete knew her well, and we had a cracking sail for an hour or so. Ashore, the team was fantastic, and Pete's team couldn't have been more helpful, which meant I was able to take a little time away from the boat. Although I found it difficult not to be there all the time—and particularly not to be doing the jobs myself—I knew that the next weeks were going to be tough, and that this really was my last opportunity to check over charts and weather tactics and to spend a couple of mornings with Merv before I sailed off to St.-Malo. Merv himself would be flying to Cape Town in a few days for Mike Golding's next stop on the Around Alone Race. I would have loved to have had him nearby for the last week before the start of the race.

NOTHING COULD HAVE prepared me for St.-Malo—and the atmosphere before the start. I was aware that the Route du Rhum was a massive event, but it still took me by surprise to see the thousands and thousands of people who came to see the start. By the time of the start, cars—all facing into town—were parked bumper to bumper for miles on every approach road. The dock held thirty-six of the most beautiful boats I'd ever seen. They were lined up on the pontoons, decorated with flags and lit by floodlights. I felt very privileged even to have a slot there.

I had never before been asked for my autograph, but here I could not leave the cabin without hearing my name. I spent hours signing autographs and found it difficult to walk away when so many people were still holding out their programmes and pieces of paper. It was quickly apparent that sailing in France is far from an elitist sport. People were coming to see us not because it was their hobby but because they enjoyed what we did and wanted to show their support by wishing us "bon vent."

As the week slipped by, I found I was talking to journalists for hours on end. St.-Malo was wearing me down. It was increasingly hard to spend time anywhere other than hidden away. And as the number of people arriving in town increased, so the number of interviews seemed to explode exponentially. I was still very wide-eyed and keen to soak it all in, but there is only so much of this you can do before becoming saturated. Luckily, the euphoria of being there kept me going, and Mark was in the same position. His brain was working overtime as he tried to juggle the demands for interviews with time for the team, discussing final adjustments that needed to be made to the boat.

I spent what free time I had learning about various emergency procedures, the electronic systems, and the hydraulic keel with Jim Doxey, from Pete's team, who had worked on the concept of the boat. There were always solutions needed on a boat designed for a 6-foot-tall mariner (I am only 5 feet, 3½ inches tall)—I could not even reach some of the cleats on the mast and had to jump up to them each time. I spent several evenings poring over the weather charts with Andrew Cape, "Capey," the new team expert, but I was so tired I could hardly keep my eyes open. Most of the weather reports, it seemed, contained bad news—big depressions, a string of them—and it was obvious that this was not going to be easy. One weather fax had "bomb" plainly written on it. Even Capey said he'd never come across that before. Great, I thought, that's all we need!

That day, we had our first visitors from Kingfisher PLC when CEO Sir Geoff Mulcahy and Mike Hingston, who had both been present at our initial meeting, fought their way through the crowds to come aboard. I didn't know whether to shake their hands or hug them, as I knew it was only through their support that we'd progressed this far. Geoff was very tall, but despite his imposing presence, he remained approachable. Mike, responsible for corporate PR, was also a passionate supporter of ours. You knew that once he was committed to something he'd give it everything he had. Geoff asked about how I put the spinnakers up, and as I described the process, I was conscious that I had only seen one of the four spinnakers out of its bag. I was confident, though, because this was our big chance. I felt sure that Kingfisher had said yes to our project for a reason, and I drew strength from that thought.

That evening, as we took *Kingfisher* through the locks for the start the next day, the crowds went wild, and I tingled from head to toe at their warmth and encouragement. I waved back at them and shouted inadequately, "Merci, Merci." It was now nearly midnight, and literally thousands of people were jamming the sides of the lock and the docks. It was early in the morning when I eventually crawled beneath the sheets to sleep. I made a quick call to Merv and drifted off. I was tired but still relaxed.

AT 1302 THE GUN went off.

Just ten minutes earlier, all the team had clambered off the boat. It was a powerful moment, the reward for months of determination. As he left, Mark was unable to articulate the intensity of his feelings, but he didn't need to; his face said it all. We had succeeded. We were on the start line.

After the gun, as the boats jostled for position, I was more concerned for our safety than anything else. There were race boats everywhere, and I didn't want to have a collision so close to the start. I was out there racing with a large proportion of the best single-handed sailors in the world. This was it; my turn.

It was hazy and drizzly, but thankfully there was wind. I was farther out than other boats, so I spent the first hour more alone than with the fleet. Mum and Dad, who'd arrived the day before, came alongside in a RIB to say goodbye before watching their daughter sail off into a gale. I caught my last sight of them before they turned for home, their faces betraying a mixture of pride, happiness, and concern.

They very nearly failed to make it at all, however, when the boat they were in broke down right in the path of Mike Birch's trimaran. The understandable abuse that came their way during his avoiding manoeuvres is surely among their most vivid memories of the day.

As we approached Cap Frehel, we were still surrounded by spectator boats—from tiny fishing dories to family cruisers and cross-Channel ferries. All shouted encouragement. The clifftops of Cap Frehel itself were also lined with excited people, all cheering "Allez, Ellen!" or "A donf!" There were tears in my eyes, and the emotion inside was hard to contain. Both praise and support were relentless. These people were proud of us, too. It almost seemed that they understood the strain of the past months. Their smiles and good wishes were telling me that all would be well and that all the trouble had been worth it.

BY MIDNIGHT on the first night, it had blown up. The barometer fell and the wind howled through the rigging. Changing sails on the foredeck was lethal. *Kingfisher* tried her best to cling to the water's surface, while I just tried to cling to her. I was being pounded, thrown again and again onto the deck as her hull flicked up to hit me while I was slammed down by the motion of falling from the wave before—it was unrelenting. With each impact I closed my eyes and gritted my teeth, hanging on as tightly as possible. I tried everything to calm her, but the waves were enormous, and whether we charged over them or fell down them, it was going to hurt.

A hard lesson learned, though—Pete's boat was unusual in the fleet, as it did not have furling foresails, which allow the sails to be rolled around the forestay by a control line worked from the safety of the cockpit rather than requiring a sailor to handle them on the foredeck. Foredeck work in heavy weather is fairly full on, and Pete was clearly stronger than I. He had gone for the reliability option in the Vendée by not taking furling sails. It was a shame we had not had time to fit them before the start of the race.

The wind continued to rise during the first few days. On the third day I was changing down to the storm-jib on the foredeck when I was thrown off my feet and cracked my head hard against the inner forestay rod, resulting in an instant lump and a strange nausea. Soon afterwards the front passed, only to bring even stronger 55-knot gusts in a steady 45-knot wind. It was an unreal, crazy situation; just trying to hang on inside the boat took every ounce of my strength. Food was hurled around the cabin, along with water containers and spares, while I tried to scrape things up and put them back in the boxes. My hands stung, my eye was swollen, and my wrists were already covered with open sores. The Québec-St.-Malo had been very tough physically, but nothing like this. In fact, conditions were so bad that Mark Gatehouse, an experienced English single-handed sailor and a friend of Alan Wynne-Thomas, had been thrown across the cabin and smashed his ribs, forcing him to head home just days into the race.

Dawn brought some respite. My core temperature warmed after the freezing night, but whenever I sweated through the physical exertion of a sail change, I'd once again cool to a shiver when I finished. Sleep proved virtually impossible—just snatched ten-minute bursts ended by cold.

Sent: 9/11/98 2:50
Received: 9/11/98 6:34
From: Kingfisher, 423420410@c-link.net
M. FullOn but allOK bar unbearable shddering. Survival suit s
godsend. 45 knts plus. Fredeck is hell!
Lst night was bad, so very cold. If my eyes closed to sleep They
would opento find me shvering. Decsion making hard, getting strm
jib ondeck yest pm felt like climbing everest. Fightingthis cold and
enrgyless state. Can hrdly type, thnkx fr messges. [Very] welcme!
Love to M&D. Love from a batered e! (glad 2 be off tho!) Exx

Just two days later conditions began to worsen again. Doing anything
was not only difficult but also painful. My hands were red-raw and
swollen, and my head was aching—even more so when the freezing
water washed breathtakingly over it each time I went forward to change
sails. It became more and more obvious that the boat had been designed
for Pete Goss. Shifting the sails was hard, brutal work. Each time I
needed to change one I would pull it forward, clipping myself on, and
hanging on for dear life. Waves would continuously power down the
side-decks, often washing the sail and me back several feet, forcing me
to hang on and tighten my grip on the sail tie even further. I would often
cry out loud as I dragged the sail along; it was one way of letting out
some of that frustration and of finding the strength to do it. Once forward, I had to use my freezing fingers to clip on each sail hank by hank.
After each sail change I would collapse into the little cuddy seats out of
the spray, close my eyes briefly, and try to recover.

After a week things finally began to calm, and with my backside red-
hot and sore, and my wrists and fingers swollen, I finally enjoyed the first
opportunity to remove my survival suit. Though the relief was wonderful, the smell was not!

Sent: 14/11/98 15:23
Received: 14/11/98 17:50
From: Kingfisher, 423420410@c-link.net
HI . . . OK my words, but first. . . . An overwhelming thankyou.
There is noway in thisworld I could be here without you, I have been
doing a lot of thinking over the past days, and can offer little more at

this time other than offer my eternal thanks, and win the bloody race!

. e xx

4 hrs at 12-19 knots! Great to have KINGFISHER going like a train. WE're hanging in there in the 60 fleet, and proving our own as being 2 of the smallest in the fleet! Herself and me!

Its been fantastic [to be] able sail her rather than simply survive! The storms of the first week were horrendous, and now, after I had a chance to walk on her decks rather than crawl, and place someing on a surface without it ending up in the bilge! Today I removed all the food I could fnd from in the spares boxes, under the anchor and behind the bunks. Each of the food boxes crossed the cabin at least 6 times each during the storm, dispensing hteir cotents eerywhere they could!

Got to go.

exx

love

e

xxx

After a frustrating, windless time around the Azores, worse was to come.

The survival suit went back on. It was the fourth depression—ten days into the race. We had winds reaching 65 knots over the deck, and as the front passed, a constant 50 to 55 was not welcomed with open arms. Tacking the boat was interesting in such strong winds, the swing-keel timing playing a vital role in her somewhat wave-driven dance. The wind was to switch to NW with the front, and this was the debut of our sleighride to Guadeloupe (or so we thought).

After this fourth depression, disaster struck. I was having a rather bad time, as I'd spent five hours of a 35-knot night resewing the leech on the staysail. A piston hank had come undone, allowing the leech to flog. I was exhausted by the time the crashing waves slowly became visible in the approaching daylight, and my fingers were bleeding with punctures. Elated that I had finished the job, I went below to grab a snack—it was almost time to put up the staysail again. As I foraged in one of the food boxes I noticed some water on the floor, and although there was usually a small amount from drips, this seemed like a bit more. I checked forward and was shocked to see water there. It was ankle-deep, so clearly the forehatch must have come undone over the last few hours.

I decided a complete bail-out was in order before a sail change, so I started the process of drying out each compartment in turn. I sealed the forehatch, and while trying to balance with the horrendous motion I took a good few bucketfuls out of the forepeak.

I thought I should check the aft compartment too, in case water had leaked in through the rudderstock seal. This had already happened a few times, so before finishing off in the forepeak, I decided to bail out the back. There were a few bucketfuls in there, but the horrific motion made it a frustrating job. With the new wind direction, we were sailing straight into the waves, which makes it hard for the boat to stick to the water. I was being flung up at the deck-head and then back down onto her hull, which made it virtually impossible to keep the water in the bucket. I was sliding around and cursing at myself as the bucket's contents repeatedly ended up in my face before I could get it out of the hatch. And if it wasn't the contents of the bucket, it was a wave coming down through the hatch as I opened it to empty a bucket.

Suddenly I felt something was very wrong. *Kingfisher* began leaning more and more, and I heard a useless whine coming from the motor that controlled the swinging keel. I scrambled out of the hatch and across her now precariously steep deck to the cockpit, hanging onto anything I could as I went. I bore her away from the wind to bring her as upright as possible, reset the autopilot, and went below to begin my crash course in advanced hydraulics.

My first slightly panicked call was to Mark. He answered from a marine equipment show in Amsterdam: "I know you'll work it out."

He hadn't said much, but his confidence in me was reassuring.

After I'd closed the "last-resort, lock-me-in-place" valves, the keel was still swinging as freely as ever. After a tedious session of trying at least forty bolts, I at last removed the appropriate section of the keel box lid. The problem was immediately obvious—the box was swilling with litres of oil. The hydraulic pipe had burst, and the system itself was drained and lifeless. I called Merv, who was with Jim Doxey in South Africa on the stopover from the Around Alone. Jim had designed the system, and he discussed with Merv what to do. Although we had been through the system before leaving, this was clearly a more critical problem, and it was difficult to understand exactly what went where, especially as I was already so tired. At the end of the day, though, what were the options? There was only the one, so I just got on with it.

Spoonful by spoonful, I began to refill the 10-litre reservoir with the spare oil I had on board. Lying on my back wearing a survival suit on a rolling boat, I was covered with hydraulic oil and had grease from the valves all over my hands. There was still some water in the cabin, and the contents of my food boxes were swimming around in it. It all seemed so bizarre I could only see the funny side. What a state we were in!

Five hours later I had the keel jammed in the centre and was in a position to race once more. And despite the now-inefficient keel and relative lack of stability, we enjoyed the fastest average in the fleet over the next four position reports.

After this disaster, I did the usual full check through the boat and was alarmed to find a crack in the forward bulkhead, stemming from a drain-hole at its base. I went on deck and slowed her down, sitting next to the damage for an hour or so to see if it moved. I could see nothing, but the slow movement through the water was causing the boat to slam more. I marked the ends of the crack so that I could keep an eye on it, then I gradually increased sail until she felt comfortable. I had been in the fore-peak before the storm to check that all was well, so the crack couldn't have been there long before I found it.

Before the keel had gone, I was just a few miles behind one of the newest Open 60s in the race. But it's easy to lose miles and a damn sight harder to gain them back. The tiredness and the heat were a problem, but most difficult of all was the disappearance of the wind between depressions. One day we would be in a full-blown storm, the next we'd have a boat speed of barely 3 knots and mere whispers of unreliable wind. I found it frustrating beyond belief and knew I had to learn a more pragmatic approach to this kind of weather. It was up to me to better understand why and how the wind dies, then work to use that to my advantage. Races can be won and lost in light airs.

> Yesterday was awful. Really light breeze. 23 sail changes—from kites to jibs . . . Hard work in the windless scorching sun, time when it becomes obvious I am 50 not 60feet. FOr 4 hrs there was literally nothing as the trough passed over us. I wonder if the rest of the fleet have had personal clouds too?
>
> Helplessly sitting, as the position reports showed othersmoving. A time to reflect on things far, far away . . .

My hands were still raw, painful, and riddled with salt sores and scabs; in the still heat, sweat stung as it found its way into every abrasion. Even the easiest task, such as sitting on my backside, became an uncomfortable chore!

Thank goodness we had a good breeze for the last few days on our run into Guadeloupe. Just a few miles out I was told I had a call from Robert Nickerson, my old friend from Hull. I wondered why on earth he was calling me on board. I phoned the number I was given, and he answered.

"Where are you?" he said in a familiar, friendly way.

"In a race called the Route du Rhum."

"I know that, I've heard—what's your position?"

On his Round the World sail with *Panic Major*, Robert was coming to meet me! He joined me early on during the final painful day as we drifted around without wind in the lee of the island. Most get caught here with the finish just out of reach, and we were no exception. We eventually crossed the line that evening after dark.

There were horns and sirens, and a flotilla of boats of all sizes came out to greet us. After the becalmed final day, the noise and colour were overwhelming. Not only had we won our class—the 50-footers—but only four of the twelve Open 60s that started had beaten us. Adrian Thompson, *Kingfisher*'s designer, and Pete Goss had built a 50 which was quite at home racing among the 60s.

All the same, the end this time felt very different from the end of the Mini. I was ready to leave her. Although I patted her goodbye and said thank you, I was acutely aware that I had been sailing Pete's boat. I had felt a little like a guest on board—albeit a lucky one. She was a great boat. I climbed off her, still sticky with sweat from our final hours of fight. Except for the rain, I had not washed for more than twenty days, and my face was sore with sunburn. But I knew I was glowing—not just from the heat, but with relief.

As soon as things began to die down, I crept off with Mark and sat in his rented car for five minutes while he made a phone call. I was almost delirious with fatigue, but my eyes were wide open, just soaking in the atmosphere around me. Mark said that we were going to a hotel for the press conference, and I rested my head against the car window as we sped through the streets in the dark.

CHAPTER FOURTEEN

MARK AND I spent less than a week in Guadeloupe after the race, although we did manage to catch up with Robert and Marie and Pipo. The response to our performance in the Route du Rhum was extraordinary. The number of congratulatory e-mails and fax messages we received opened my eyes to just how many people had been following us out there.

> To: e.macarthur@rhum98.com
> Subject: congratulations!
> You are the English girl in the race.
> We don't know you but are happy to tell you "bonjour"
> Sincerely Yours.
> Famille Macabies
> (We live in the Alps)

And

> From: AMCO
> To: La Reine Ellen et le Roi Turner
> Well done the Glaouchs *[Breton slang for the English]*—you have
> really stuffed the French, and the rest of the world!! Good luck for
> your future projects.
> A+ Thierry

There was also a handwritten fax message sent from a small office services company in Derbyshire:

    congratulations
    well done!
    with love from all at
    home including
    mac
    macarthur true grit all
    the way and from head to toe.

The race marked a significant turning-point in so many ways. Both our futures had rested on how we performed, but now we were faced with starting again from scratch. To compete in the Vendée, we needed a boat, a team, and sponsorship, and Kingfisher PLC was not committed beyond the Rhum. We had proposed the Vendée project to them initially and were wondering if we had done enough to convince them to continue working with us. After the Route du Rhum, a photograph of *Kingfisher* finishing appeared on the front page of the *Times*. I don't think in our wildest dreams we had thought the race would get that kind of recognition. We knew we had a powerful story, but that was never any guarantee. We felt this was an incredibly positive sign. It showed us that we were communicating what we were doing in the right way, and that sailing could reach the front pages for the right reasons. Sadly, since the arrivals of Sir Francis Chichester, Sir Chay Blyth, and Sir Robin Knox-Johnston, single-handed sailing in the UK had more often than not been covered when things went wrong. We were in no doubt that Kingfisher would be over the moon, too. As a stepping-stone for the future, the Rhum served us well. Mark and I believed that with Kingfisher we had something special: the relationship worked well, the formula worked well, and the publicity had been an outstanding success, both in France and in the UK.

I could sense that one of the biggest difficulties facing Kingfisher PLC was that they felt responsible for me and were concerned about sending someone in her early twenties out to race around the planet. I understood their point of view and knew that an article quoting a top single-handed sailor who said I shouldn't be going for the Vendée Globe hadn't helped. I had talked to other sailors who had taken part in the race, and I knew that some of them felt I should be racing in a 50 rather than a 60.

But I had sailed two transatlantics on 60-foot boats and knew that the size simply wouldn't be a problem. I also knew deep down that, whatever happened, I would be in the next Vendée, with or without Kingfisher. The race was just waiting to burst out of me. But if things were going to happen, they would have to move ahead very quickly—we would have to be building the boat by summer.

It was time for me to write an honest letter that would let Kingfisher know in no uncertain terms that there was no way I would do it if I wasn't ready, and that there was no pressure on me to compete in the Vendée other than the pressure I put on myself.

Dear Geoff & Michael,
I have spent my life dreaming of the ocean, since 1994 I have done nothing but sail. It is my passion, my life, and undoubtedly is my future.

The Route du Rhum was a demanding race, both the conditions and the boat made it very testing, but it became the most incredible proving ground. . . .

It is firmly cast in my own mind that I can do this. I had sailed the boat very little before the start, was learning the whole time, despite getting thrown around somewhat, I never felt out of my depth. I am a tough cookie, not someone who gives up. That is why I am ocean racing alone at 22.

There are real dangers, we all know what has happened in the past, but I believe I have a very level-headed approach. I will be getting around not only for Kingfisher, but also for my family and friends.

From a non-sailing point of view, the work with both Mark and Gwenola [Gallois] on the public relations side has also been a success. I have proved to myself that I can communicate, even when things are tough, and the world outside has been able to actively follow our progress. This has led to an explosion in both UK and European press. It has amazed us all, and I can see no reason why this should not amaze us all again.

Being part of such a fantastic team, working with such
enthusiastic people has been a real pleasure. . . .
   I may sail alone out there, but without a committed
team it could never happen. I can do this—just as we can
do this.
   It is inside me to compete in the Vendée Globe. . . . I will
be on that finish line.
   What more can I say, than,
Thank you to all at Kingfisher for the support so far.
   Ellen

I had never written a letter trying to sell myself as confidently as this
before, but I knew I had to show that I could do it and was determined.
We would have to wait to see what the response would be.
   Our stay in Paris following the race was notable for a couple of reasons. I was astounded and touched to be told I had been awarded the
Jeune Espoir de la Voile, or Sailing's Young Hope. With a little help from
Gwenola on the translation front, I gave my first speech in French, ad-
dressing hundreds of people during an enormous dinner. Every other
name on that trophy was French. It was a further measure of the impact
we'd made with our campaign for the Rhum.
   More significant, however, was a phone call from Kingfisher confirm-
ing that they would sponsor us for another two years. Mark and I were
crossing a busy Paris street as we took the call on the mobile. By the
time we'd reached the other side, both our lives had been changed forever by the news. The new sponsorship meant that both of us were now
by any measure professionals. And with this status came obligations.
We'd always maintained that we had more to offer any sponsor than simply the opportunity to display their logos on the boat. We wanted it to
be a partnership, and this meant that our commitments to Kingfisher
were to form a vital part of the preparation for the Vendée.
   At Christmas, I returned to Derbyshire while Mark, as was his habit,
headed to Australia on a one-month work contract and to compete in
the Sydney–Hobart Race. Although I had bought a Christmas card for
him, I was too late to send it, so I included its message in a festive
e-mail:

Mark,
Just wanted to say the biggest thank you I can electronically!
    It's been bloody hard this one, and we're both tired.
    You can't believe in half the things you hear,
    You can't believe in most of what you read,
But you *can* believe in all of what you do. . . .
We WILL get there. . . .
    Message from Xmas Card I bought for you! . . .
"I was going to give you MONEY for Xmas . . . "
(TURN PAGE)
"But the Police dragged me out of the fountain before I could gather
together a respectable amount!"
    NOT FOR MUCH LONGER!? . . .
Love and best, best wishes,
sail safe, keep well,
  E
  Xx

Mark's race turned out to be a tragic reminder of the sheer power of
the Southern Ocean at its rawest. A freak storm intensified, smashing
many of the boats and causing a terrible loss of life. Mark was one of the
lucky ones.

Christmas was cut short for me the day after Boxing Day, when I
drove down to the marina in Plymouth where *Aqua Quorum* was now lying after her delivery home. I spent a day on board trying to clean her,
remove our belongings, and leave her ready for handing her back over to
Pete. I did all I could there and collected our belongings with her engine
running to heat the cabin a bit. It was a sad final goodbye to the boat as I
struggled along the pontoon in the drizzle with the last boxes of gear.
Pete was upset about the crack I'd discovered in the forward bulkhead,
as well as external damage from having hit something at night, but I was
hurt by his suggestion that I'd pushed her too hard. I could only reassure
myself that I'd been as protective of her as I have of any of the boats I've
sailed—thinking of the boat before myself even. I understood Pete's in-
stinctive reaction to the damage caused by the extreme conditions. I,
too, would have felt wounded by it. It was a shame, though, because we
should have been celebrating together, and I hoped that day would still
come.

* * * * *

ON THE FIRST DAY of the London International Boat Show in January 1999, we announced on centre stage that Kingfisher was sponsoring a fully funded Vendée Globe campaign. As I stood there and spoke in front of the journalists, my knees shook. This was really it, this was the start of our dream. Our relationship with Kingfisher was building day by day in the planning, preparation, and organization for the project, and I found it both stimulating and rewarding to be involved in the meetings. We also made presentations to various divisions of the company, the first of which took Mark and me to Germany to talk to an audience of senior management. My right knee shook again, and my mouth became so dry from nervousness that I could hardly finish. Their support and belief in us were overwhelming, and the implications of our relationship took a while to sink in. It simply changed everything—what we could do, how we could do it, and what we could aspire to. It was important to us that they knew this—that we were able to convey how offering an opportunity can change people's lives. And that we'd never take it for granted.

Mark and I soon had to make the biggest decision of the year so far: selection of a designer for the new *Kingfisher* 60. It's more than just a question of finding who can design you the fastest boat. The Vendée is notorious for its duration and remoteness, and any boat taking it on has to be strong, safe, and reliable—your life is in the designer's hands.

Initially, we sent out a tender document to a host of designers, then we reviewed the replies. All the responses were credible, and it was a difficult decision to bring it down to our final two. One of these was Marc Lombard, a French designer, and the other a team comprising the Owen Clarke Design Group, Rob Humphreys and Giovanni Belgrano. It was a tough decision, but the team approach, with its wide base of knowledge, appealed enormously. Our only concern was that the Owen of Owen-Clarke was in fact Merv, who had set up the company years before with his partner, Allen Clarke. But we knew that there were few others available with such extensive knowledge of modern Open 60s, and in our final decision, we felt that our personal relationship would help make her a better boat. Merv was committed to his work and had already suggested he would be prepared to project-manage the building of the new boat. This was a big plus. We strived to do something a bit different, and though it was not our intention to take too many risks on the development front, we did not want a clone of the other boats. With the addition of former Vendée winner Alain Gautier, the team became the Kingfisher Design Team.

The design decision-making process had been stressful. I had not discussed my views with Merv outside the office, and this wasn't made any easier when we moved into a rented flat together. I think, in retrospect, that even at this stage the project had begun slowly to grind us down. And although our relationship perhaps contributed to the care and incredible attention to detail that would be so evident in *Kingfisher*, at the same time she put us both under the first layers of pressure.

We also went with the decision to build *Kingfisher* in New Zealand. I had made a brief trip out there to see Merv at the end of January. He was there as part of Mike Golding's Group 4 campaign before he'd run aground off New Zealand's North Island, which ended his race. I fell in love instantly with the country and its people. Another attraction was New Zealand's incredible sailing industry. Thinking aloud, Merv said that it would be a great place to build an Open 60, and we realized it would be great experience for me if I sailed the boat back to Europe.

Initially, we'd considered New Zealand too far away from Kingfisher PLC's interests, but on further reflection it began to look like the right idea. If we could build within the schedule, it made sense to use the journey back from New Zealand as a sea trial for the boat and a chance for me to gain experience not just with her but with the Southern Ocean. There was also the added bonus that New Zealand was hosting the America's Cup. This would be fantastic to be around and watch, and the country also would be buzzing with journalists from all over the world.

By April there were a couple of new faces on the project team. Mary Ambler joined us to take on some of the media work, which, with the launch of the Vendée campaign, had grown enormously. Dana Bena came to take care of some of the logistics while Ian McKay, a graphic designer, began to work wonders with logos and press packs. Back in January we'd announced that I would be competing in the Vendée, and now we were launching the whole project in detail, announcing our design team, building location, and training programme, and we brought journalists over to the UK from France. We wanted the whole launch to be as professional as possible.

We were asked many questions about our hopes for the project and about what was possible in the race, and here our emphasis had changed over recent months. We'd set out just a year before saying we aimed to win, and of course that had to remain our target, but we knew we had to prove the boat before we could make any real predictions. The competition out there would be the best in the world, and, as had been seen in past races, anything could happen at any stage. Leaving in November always poses a threat to the fleet, with the winter gales beginning to roll in. In order for the campaign to be seen as a success for both us and Kingfisher, we couldn't allow it to hinge on winning alone.

From a personal point of view, one of the most important parts of the launch was announcing my own intensive training programme. It was designed with one clear objective—to plug as many holes as possible in my knowledge and experience. I knew as I stood on that stage in April that I was not ready to take on the Vendée Globe, but I also knew that twelve months later I really could be.

The programme contained a number of different elements, including single-handed and crewed offshore racing, dinghy racing, meteorological instruction, first aid, and straightforward fitness training. All of this would be supported by Kingfisher's sponsorship, which meant we could include what was necessary rather than simply what was possible. We were able to approach things professionally, albeit in a somewhat compressed manner.

Training began back in France aboard boats called Figaros. These small racing boats, just over 32 feet in length, are used for highly competitive single-handed racing in France. A Figaro campaign is not overly expensive, and its many stop-overs give a great return to the sponsors. It would be my first real immersion in French pro sailing. In my first race with Gael le'Cleach, a teacher at the Figaro training school, we were taken apart by the rest of the fleet—a real baptism of fire and a shocking reminder of just how much I still had to learn. In the few days I spent at the training camp, I realized just how different my life was compared with these other sailors. They focused each day on their physical ability, weather strategy, and sailing skills; and though my training was more spread out geographically, I was impressed by the thoroughness of their approach. I felt quite uncomfortable there, even nervous. In their world, I was an outsider. And their culture was completely at odds with the crazy life I was leading, literally running from event to meeting. While I was in France, I had the chance to think and take stock of where I was. Sitting around the dinner table each evening talking about the courses or race tactics, I knew that I could not drop into a life like theirs, but I could also see the real benefits of focus and studying in one place.

Mark decided that he also wanted to compete. He had all but given up his own sailing to project-manage the Vendée campaign, and it must have been tough seeing me out there on the water. He chartered a boat he named *Offshore Challenges*—the racing took no account of office hours, so we struggled to keep up to speed with the "Project," as our pursuit of the Vendée had become known. He had raced Figaros before, but he too failed to find a winning formula, although I have to say he finished ahead of us!

Perhaps the most obviously vital part of the training programme was the offshore racing. This was to culminate at the end of 1999 with the Transat Jacques Vabre from Le Havre, France, to Cartagena, Colombia. There was no way the new *Kingfisher* would be even remotely ready for this, so I needed to find another boat. We decided to approach Yves Parlier, who had raced the spacecraft-like boat, *Aquitaine Innovations*, that had made such an impression on me at the start of the last Vendée Globe. Rig and rudder problems had forced him out of the race, and then soon afterwards he had a serious accident while flying a paraglider and badly damaged his legs. Though still struggling on crutches, and with one final operation to go, he was well on the road to recovery—although a question mark still hung over his foot, in which he had lost feeling.

Mark and I went to Bordeaux to visit Yves with some trepidation. I was aware he was a rather headstrong character but knew little about him beyond that. Our saving grace was that Yves had followed the Route du Rhum closely and was aware of my result there. In the end, though, I think the strongest bond between us came from the discovery, much later, that we had both grown up far from the sea and had spent our early years dreaming about it. Yves was tall and thin, with short-cropped grey hair—it seemed to have been that colour since he was in his twenties. He comes across as one of life's great thinkers, his background in engineering leading to an almost scientific but always creative approach to problem-solving. Yves had an incredible track record: he'd competed in two Vendée Globes, had won the Mini Transat in 1985, and won the

Transat Jacques Vabre in 1997 with French sailing legend Eric Tabarly.
Kingfisher would part-sponsor his boat for the race that autumn, and
we discussed the programme in great detail. Far from just competing in
the Transat Jacques Vabre, we would train together in Arcachon, where
Aquitaine was based, and I would also sail on board her in the Round Europe Race in June.

I fit in quickly with the guys aboard *Aquitaine* and soon thought of
them as family, but one of my first trips with them turned into a classic
demonstration of the pace of the life I was now leading. Sailing to Italy
for the start of the Round Europe Race, we were delayed badly by
storms. I was concerned about missing a presentation I'd agreed to make
to one of Kingfisher's operating companies in Nice. I ended up being
dropped off in a bay off Majorca, where our enormous Open 60 was circled by German and Spanish holidaymakers in pedalos. Eventually I
hitched a lift ashore in a tiny Spanish rowing boat, with a man who understood enough English to know that I had a plane to catch! I flew to
Barcelona, hired a car for a twelve-hour mind-blowing taste of the Pyre-
nees, then flew on to Nice.

Geoff Mulcahy, Kingfisher's CEO, attended the presentation and asked
what my plans were. When I told him I was returning to the UK first
thing in the morning, he asked if it would help to get back that night. This
was incredibly useful, as we were tank- and wind-tunnel-testing models
for *Kingfisher*, and as far as I was concerned, the earlier the better. A couple of hours later, I was boarding a private jet for the first time. I was so
excited that the pilot asked me if I wanted to sit in the cockpit, from
where it looked as if we were chasing the setting sun all the way home.
We landed at Luton, and Geoff's chauffeur gave me a lift to my aunt's
empty house in nearby Hertford. At about 1 A.M., I assured everyone I
would be fine and walked off into the darkness. Only after they drove off
did I realize that, while I had a key, I didn't have the code for the new burglar alarm. I tried phoning everyone who might know but got no reply.
Admitting defeat, I made a nest in the garden and went to sleep with a
smile on my face. From executive jet to sleeping in a garden—great!

I WAS SOON BACK with *Aquitaine* in Italy for the Round Europe Race. A
surf-filled first leg in which we were in our element led to an eventual
race-winning lead, but our celebrations were muted by the news that a

crewman aboard the trimaran *Biscuits la Trinitaine* had been washed overboard and killed during the strong downwind conditions that had served
us so well—devastating for the crew and his family.

Along with the Figaros and sailing with Yves, there was one further aspect to my training on the water: racing Laser dinghies with Paul Brotherton. Paul had represented Great Britain in the Barcelona Olympics
and was an incredible natural sailor. Originally from inner-city Man-
chester, he had discovered sailing almost by accident, and we hit it off
immediately. Each time I sailed with him, I realized how talented he
was. I was on a near-vertical learning curve, but we were sure that the
skills I picked up on racing dinghies could only make me more competitive offshore in an Open 60.

Paul and I had hoped to start a race together before competing in the
Laser Eurocup Regatta in Milan, but as usual, lack of time stopped us
and we were able to complete just a few training sessions on the solent
and a day in Italy. The atmosphere on Lake Como was fantastic, however; tired as we were when we drove into Gravidona, relaxed people
and warm weather kept us going. It seemed odd for me to go into a race
environment and know so few competitors—especially while Paul
couldn't walk three paces without someone spotting him.

I was completely unsure of how I was going to find the racing. It had
been a long time since I'd competed in such close quarters, and this time
there were more than seventy boats in our class! Paul was great to sail
with. There were stressful moments, and it must have been particularly
frustrating for someone as experienced and skilled as Paul to crew while
I, a novice in this kind of sailing, took the helm. We were therefore fairly
amazed at sailing into third place on the first race. And while our results
were an absolute team effort, I fear that the importance of our contributions were weighted in favour of Paul! He must have been hoarse by the
end of the regatta, as he frequently had to employ his very verbal approach to collision avoidance:

" 'kin hell, Ellen!"

THROUGHOUT THE INTENSE sailing programme I also had much to learn
ashore. Training for an event like the Vendée is nothing like training for
athletics. We have to learn everything about the function of the weather
and the boat. That ranges from being able to repair the sails to perhaps

changing hard disc drives and replacing circuit boards or relaminating broken fittings. We can have no outside assistance whatsoever with our weather routing, so we have to make all those decisions on board ourselves. It is outside the rules of the Vendée for sailors even to pick up the phone and ask what someone thinks of their ideas—which in turn puts an enormous strain on the skipper, who has not only the welfare and speed of the boat to think about, but also its position on the ocean, which is critical to its success. I completed a course on engine repair and maintenance in Oxford and was fascinated by the knowledge I was gaining on everything from changing oil to stripping down diesel-injection pumps. By the end, I was stripping down the engine and putting it back together with some aplomb. And in La Rochelle, I had two days of intense training with Jean-Yves Bernot, a French weather expert, covering a whole range of subjects from weather-fax interpretation to the use of weather-routing software. Previously, particularly on the Mini Transat, I'd felt that I lacked confidence in this aspect of my racing, so I was keen to address it. Jean-Yves also worked with me on weather training as I sailed back to Europe from New Zealand during Kingfisher's sea trials.

As crucial to success as understanding the boat and weather is looking after yourself. Fatigue is always a potentially huge problem in long-distance single-handed racing, and I started working on a sleep training project with a chronobiology expert, Dr. Claudio Stampi. This involved wearing a wrist monitor which looked like a watch and recorded when I woke and slept. I never took it off, and the data we collected about my sleep patterns would help plan a sleep strategy for the Vendée.

Immediately after finishing the Laser regatta on Lake Como, I undertook a three-day commercial first-aid course at Warsash Nautical College in Hampshire with a mixed bunch of people from all sorts of vessels. I was unique among them in that I would be sailing alone: thus, not everything was useful—mouth-to-mouth resuscitation, for example! In the past, there had been serious medical emergencies in the Vendée—from Alan Wynne-Thomas limping into New Zealand with his smashed ribcage to Bertrand de Broc, who, deep in the Southern Ocean, had to sew his tongue back on. Being independent is not just a desirable attribute for the Vendée Globe; it's essential.

It was a taxing schedule, but somehow sheer eagerness to be out there and take things on fuelled my enthusiasm and kept my wheels turning.

People would often ask me what I was up to, and when I gave them a typical sample, they were usually fairly aghast. Though I wore a brave face and would not have chosen to change what was going on, I knew deep down that I was running not far from empty. The sporadic training sessions and snatched moments on the water, or even a brief moment looking at the hills out of a train window, were just enough to keep me going. There were moments of desperation in there, though—one in particular was filmed by the French crew when I was training in a Laser with Paul. I was knackered and finding it virtually impossible to concentrate, particularly in the strong winds—it was almost as if I wasn't there.

Part of the problem was that I was beginning to feel a lack of control. I was concerned that I had not been as in-touch as I would have liked to be with the general running and design phase of the project. I was used to being the one who was around and about putting in hands-on time, but now I was away from both our office and the design office nearly all the time, often putting in my input only by phone, making a motivational call when I sensed things were at a slightly lower ebb. I began to feel more like a pawn in a far bigger system, and it seemed as though there were many aspects of my life over which I had little or no control. A couple of years before, as I had been sailing the oceans, I had made every decision for myself—but now things were different. On the grand scale of things, they were small, though, and I knew full well that I could not have done any more or been in more places. At the end of the day, I had a great team, and they were doing a great job.

I still pushed myself to try to be involved with just about every stage of the design process of *Kingfisher* and was rewarded with the most incredible feeling, almost day by day, of a dream come true. I felt part of her from the moment she was the first line on the computer screen; it was almost like watching her grow. We made a computer-generated virtual "Ellen" which we could slot into various areas of the boat, although unfortunately we had to modify some areas; when we tried to drop in a person of more normal dimensions, there were a few problems with space!

On 18 September 1999 I flew to New Zealand for a couple of days to see the first stage of *Kingfisher*'s construction. Walking into that shed for the first time and looking up at the curve of her gigantic hull, I was in awe of her beauty. The feeling of enormity was like realizing for the first time the sheer size of a whale in the wild—almost spiritual. But this being, I knew, was going to become a close friend.

We also had a scare. On our final night in New Zealand, we heard the phone ring, and a car left the drive very soon afterwards. We were staying with Steve Marten, the owner of the yard, and discovered that he had been called out due to a fire there. An oven not far from *Kingfisher* had caught fire while cooking some of her bulkheads and had set off the burglar alarm. The guy on duty at the yard had run off to check the alarm system, not knowing that it had been triggered by the oven that was on fire. The temperature sensors measured heat of up to 130°C, and the wall between two ovens had collapsed by the time the fire was extinguished. Miraculously, *Kingfisher*'s mould was completely unscathed. How a tinder-dry wooden mould could have survived so close to such an intense fire we shall never know, but in a way it proved to us from the start that she was a born survivor.

I WAS BACK IN FRANCE by the end of September to prepare for the Transat Jacques Vabre, which started on 15 October. Life continued to be hectic, but although they were no less time-consuming, I was now a little more used to the endless interviews and photo calls that accompanied the build-up to a major race.

The night before the start we all went for a meal organized primarily for Yves Parlier's sponsors, Aquitaine. There were a number of guests from the Kingfisher side of the project, too. Although it was good to catch up with sponsors and the team, it was not, perhaps, the best night for it. I left early and slept in the car before heading back to the hotel for our final night's sleep.

We left Le Havre on a hot, still afternoon; after at least fifteen hours at the helm we were in second place and already well down the track. It felt wonderful finally to be off. There had been some friction between Yves and me on shore, as he was very much the kind of person who had to run things his way, but we both knew that on the water, our primary objective was survival—and of course the race. As we crossed that start line, any differences we had ashore melted away, and we bonded well, but while our start was clement, there was a massive depression heading across the Atlantic: Hurricane Irene . . .

3a.m. Freezing, soaking, and impossible to stand. Its been a bit full
on last few hours. We're under deep reefed main, storm jib. Just got
slaughtered whildt chaanging to storm jib—THrowm up and doen
on deck, washed sideways so many times. She mght have a wide
open flat deck [forward], but it's very ecposed! Rightnoe trying to
thype, warmer than before as put survival suit on, very tired. eyes
trying [to] shut, and stinging still from salt. DeCk . . . virtually lifted
off seat here . . . slamming is bad. and40kn . . . the slower, the
worse.
xex

During the storm we broke all the rigging on the starboard side—
which essentially means every single cable holding up our mast on one
side of the boat was slowly breaking. Hour by hour the mast was leaning
more and more, and at any time the whole lot could have fallen over the
side. The fibres with which the mast was supported were quite a new development, strong and light—PBO. Though we knew that these fibres
degraded with sunlight, no one was really sure how long they would
last.

We had winds over 60 knots at one stage, and because of the rig problems, we had just a tiny piece of sail up and had to wait, agonizing, for
more than forty-eight hours before we could repair the rig. This was not
as easy as it sounds; it involved my climbing the mast several times and
completely replacing each cable, one by one. *Aquitaine* was the first of
the Open 60s to have the deck spreaders that made her look so unusual,
the objective being that they allow a large section of wing mast to ro-
tate—they were never designed with climbing comfort in mind. It was
complicated further by having to make the replacements on deck first
and use any rope we could find on board. We spent days scrambling
about on the decks, trying to remove covers from ropes and splice
them—all made difficult and dangerous by the aggressive waves and
horrific motion, and not helped by the fact that we sailed entirely in the
French language. Although by this time I could hold a conversation in
French, I lacked certain key words in the language. It was pretty hard
working out the meaning of "anneau" when hanging 50 feet up a mast. It
turned out to be "loop"! I was incredibly motivated, though, and the
morning after our diagnosis, I was out there working as soon as the first
glimmer of light appeared in the sky.

Pretty exhausted . . . Started at 4am , and still up. Feeling lucky to
be alive after hours up the rig, one of the hardest physical challenges
ever . . . . Waves after a big storm, came down in 30 knots after
dark, just after a rain squall. . . . A lot of bruises, very sore. But
lucky. It's hard to describe how it feels to hang on up there. Like
trying to grip on to an enormous shiny pole (which for me is just
too big to get my arms around properly), with someone continually
kicking you, and trying to shake you off. At least the mast is still
sitting there vertically though—the other option does not baer
thinking about.

Although we had massive problems in the storm, nearly resulting in
our losing our mast, others were far worse off than we were. We received a message that one of the multihulls, *Group André*, had capsized
and one of its two crew was missing. Later we found out that Paul Vatine
was on deck when they went over—and tragically was never seen again.
As I sat on deck in that raging storm, I thought of what his co-skipper
and family no doubt were going through—it was a dangerous life out
here, and sure as hell, one over which we have little or no control.

We finished in eighth position after twenty days of hard racing. It had
been a tough race, both tactically and psychologically—living with disappointment and frustration—but once again I knew I'd learnt a lot, not
least about the possibility of overcoming really serious problems. The
odds had been against us all the way, but we had made it to the end, and
although eighth was not first, we still felt we'd achieved something. As
we crossed the finish line in Cartagena, Mark and Yves's team jumped on
board; it was fantastic to see them all again. Aside from the knowledge
I'd gained from the situation we'd been through, the biggest gift from
that race was confidence.

IT WAS A GREAT RELIEF to head back to New Zealand after the race. It was
now summer there, the America's Cup was in full flow, and Auckland
was buzzing. By this stage we had a great team working on *Kingfisher*;
Marie and Pipo Cairo and their two kids had moved from Guadeloupe to
live in New Zealand for five months. Pipo was responsible for the deck
gear and above-deck equipment, and Marie, with her new industrial
sewing machine, was making sail covers, cockpit covers, seat covers—
and just about anything else you could imagine! Others, such as French-

man Marc Dutiloy and South African Mikey Joubert, each had their own area of expertise, be it daggerboards or rig. On the organizational side, Martin Carter, as well as being responsible for everything below decks, took over as team leader in New Zealand, ably supported by Dana Bena. Back in the UK, designer Ian McKay produced designs for *Kingfisher's* distinctive yellow bow, sweeping into her blue hull, which we all thought was beautiful. She reflected the passion and dedication of everyone involved, and there was no doubt in any of our minds that she was going to be the best Open 60 in the world. And although ultimately I would be the one who would sail her, there would be a piece of every one of them on board with me.

Whenever I walked into the yard there would be another part attached to her, or a new piece built. *Kingfisher*, because of the work and care of every person there, was coming to life, and I can only describe it as wonderful. Every day our delivery home was getting closer.

In New Zealand I made a big effort to try to get my life in order, and even though one of the best things that's ever happened to me was taking shape in the yard, I was simultaneously struggling. My life in New Zealand was a stark contrast to the frantic schedule I had become used to in Europe, and although things were very busy, there was more time for contemplation. I was concerned about my relationship with Merv. We were living away from the rest of the team, away from Auckland and the others. I don't think it helped to be apart from them, but I'd hoped that when I settled in over there with Merv, things would get better. But they didn't. I was becoming more and more frustrated with myself for feeling frustrated with Merv; the more I tried to drag myself out of it, the more distanced I felt from him. He was putting every ounce of himself into the project, which was wonderful, but he was putting too much in, and I could see that his reserves were getting dangerously low. When we grabbed a day to try to get away from the city, he would sleep in the car rather than run on the beach or play in the surf. On the few occasions we did get away, I didn't feel I was with the same man I'd known so long; I remember leaving him collapsed in the guest house while I sprinted down to the beach and flung myself into the surf to vent my frustration. I tried to talk to him and tried to be strong to help him, but often I felt as if I was talking to a wall. He had no energy, no time for anything; long gone were the days when we would talk of exciting plans for the future. We seemed to be sharing less and less. He would crash out in the evenings while I would stay up at my computer going through my weather notes or checking e-mail.

At 0515 every day I would get up and go to the gym—it was half an hour's drive from the farm where we were staying, and I would aim to get there by six. It was a great way of getting rid of that pent-up energy. I'd often be joined by Allan from the yard, a great bloke whose easy manner and sense of humour helped me relax. Sometimes, instead of going to the gym, Allan and I would thrash around in kayaks on the river. It was great to have a mate to mess around with, but it made me realize how much I missed doing this with Merv.

I desperately needed to get away and think, and when Christmas came round, knowing I wasn't going home to Derbyshire, I bought a tent and a pair of hiking boots and headed off into the bush.

Merv dropped me off at the end of a long wooded track on Christmas Eve. The road we had hoped to take was closed, so I spent the evening finding my first campsite at 2200 hours, in the dark.

The following morning, I unzipped the tent door to be greeted by a beautiful day—Christmas—and headed off up the Twin Peaks track. I managed to get a signal on my mobile and made a quick, successful attempt to wish close friends and family a happy Christmas, before switching it off for the first time in months. I had mixed feelings whilst making the call to my family—this was my first Christmas not in Derbyshire, and I couldn't have been much farther away.

The track was incredibly steep. As I clambered up some of the slopes, the gradient and the weight of my pack forced me to use my hands and feet together. By afternoon I had climbed over the top of the hill and was heading back down to the water. I was thrilled by the sight and sound of a red-crowned parakeet: I'd dreamed of green parrots in my adventures as a child, and this was the closest I'd come to seeing it become a reality. I filled my water pot from a tiny trickling stream before stumbling across one of the most beautiful campsites I could imagine: a tiny grassy glade under the trees, right by the water's edge, with a view the full length of the water. I stood watching grebes diving and herons feeding.

I pitched my tent and used my little stove to heat a Christmas dinner of chicken curry pasta and Christmas pudding. As the sun dropped slowly over the wooded slopes, I lay back in my tent, doors wide open, and drank in the atmosphere.

Next day, after a lazy morning making porridge and berry tea, reading, and paddling amongst shoals of baby fish, I packed away my "home" and by about midday headed on along the track, determined to spend my next night by the sea. At one place, I came across a patch of long, lush grass. I happily walked straight into it—it reminded me of walks with Mac as a kid, and I missed not having her with me.

As I headed up to the ridge, the views were breathtaking. I glanced down the steep sides to see gulls circling over the water hundreds of feet below. I spotted a kingfisher on a branch in the nearby woods—a good omen for the night's camping, I felt.

It was as if I'd climbed out of my skin and could take a bird's-eye look at my worries before returning revitalized to the yard and the team. But it was hard to admit to myself that in some ways I was unhappy. After all, how could I be? I was about to see the launch of *Kingfisher*, about to sail her halfway around the world. But blanking out my true feelings would not help me or Merv in the long run. He was tired, and I wanted to support him; but however hard I tried, I just didn't seem to be getting through. Maybe I just had to try harder; we had both put so much effort into the project, and I thought that perhaps once she was in the water, things would change.

I woke the following morning at 0530. As I looked through the open tent door, I saw the orange glow of the rising sun appearing behind the cliffs. I could have sworn I was in Narnia, and as the morning warmed up, the steam from the damp grass emphasized the magical atmosphere.

> *Either side the beach stretches away for miles, not a soul to be seen, just my solitary set of footprints. . . . This seems almost surreal; if this were England the beaches would be packed and noisy. Over the past three hours I've even seen an endangered species, washed in a freshwater river, and perched on a solitary log . . . all out of sight of man, and miles from the nearest house.*

I was ready to get back to *Kingfisher*.

Although the days that followed began on a more positive note, things were not getting any better with Merv. I had been kidding myself to think they would. We celebrated the millennium together in the house. After an early night, it took me hours to fall asleep. I lay there feeling sad, and I hated myself for it. These should have been the happiest times of my life. Early on New Year's Day I tiptoed outside into the fields past flocks of sheep to the edge of the river. It was peaceful there. I knew that I had to leave Merv. It might even jog him out of this insane lifestyle he had slipped into. I thought back to our first conversation on that wet day in Southampton, when he said that his boat *Maverick* had cost him a seven-year relationship. I had thought that having so much in common, things would be different for us. But I could not carry on like this; nor, I felt, could he.

SOON AFTER NEW YEAR I returned briefly to Europe, where I spent a week in London for the International Boat Show. We had organized a live webcast and a press launch for the Vendée Globe itself, trying to stimulate awareness of the Vendée in the UK. We had invited Pete Goss, Tony Bullimore, and Catherine Chabaud from France—competitors from the previous Vendée. All three spoke of their experiences, with Catherine talking of her plans to circumnavigate again in the next Vendée with her new boat, *Whirlpool*. She talked of her experiences in the last race, saying that this time she was raising her sights, putting the sport aspect above the adventure. Pete spoke of his position in the previous race, saying that he was an adventurer and not a sailor, and that rang a bell in my head. No matter how geared up for racing you are, you can never take away that aspect of the Vendée Globe. As a result of its conditions and the hardships out there, the adventure part is almost crucial. And, as Catherine said, there were a million people in Les Sables d'Olonne to see the start of the last race. Tony said that the Vendée was the ultimate in single-handed racing, and that if that's what you love, then you can't miss it. I then went up on stage with Mike Golding, whose ultimate goal with his *Team Group 4* project had always been the Vendée. He had so much more experience than I did, as well as a reliable and well-tested boat. He was one of the favourites, and I felt nervous while he spoke.

While I was in Europe I also had time, however little, to spend with friends, which made a massive difference to the state of mind I'd got into in New Zealand. Ian McKay, the graphic designer who had worked on the project since earlier in the year, as usual proved incredibly support-ive. He was a kind man who always had time for people, and all the team members looked to him when they needed someone to talk to, which is what I did in London. It was an immense relief to unload some of my worries. In New Zealand, I was close to the team but could not really talk to them about what was going on with Merv, as it wouldn't be fair for them or him. Ian was great, though, incredibly patient, and as he himself verged on being a workaholic, I think he understood Merv's predicament. I felt about a ton lighter after sharing things with him.

I didn't sleep a wink on the flight back to New Zealand, however. While I was thinking about every aspect of sailing *Kingfisher* home, my mind drifted to Merv. I was desperately trying to work things out in my head, but time was running out. If our relationship did not get any bet-ter in the first few days, then I would have to end it.

Kingfisher was in her final stages now, and it was wonderful to see her almost ready to launch. She would be in the water in less than two weeks' time. On the Friday after I arrived, we had an evening of beers for the boys, and it was great to see the team again, to see the smiles on everyone's faces, despite the final grind to the launch, and to catch up with what had been happening while I'd been away.

But the situation with Merv hadn't changed. If anything, it was worse—to the extent that I was really worried about him. I was getting up earlier and earlier; now I would sit for an hour on the beach and watch the sun rise before going to the gym. It was becoming ridiculous, and finally I decided that if I didn't call a halt, we would probably both go mad.

Several days later, when everyone else had left the yard, I went to talk to Merv. I wished I could have broken it more softly, but the truth was too painful. He was not the same man I had known twelve months be-fore. I'm sure that the break was harder because we both knew how much he was putting into the project, but this was the root of the prob-lem. I felt desperately sad, especially when Merv disappeared to spend time alone, and I could not even talk to him. I cannot imagine what must have been going through his mind during the time he was away.

At the same time, *Kingfisher*'s launch was approaching, and the pres-sure mounted accordingly. It was a difficult situation without Merv, and I was so glad that everyone else rallied round. Martin Carter took over the final organization and Mark assumed a bigger role, too. *Kingfisher* left Marten Yachts for the first time on a lorry, and at 3 A.M. on Wednesday, 9 February 2000, the gates parted for her. Mark and I followed in the car, and I stood up through the sun roof to film her enormous hull weaving in and out of the Auckland streets. It wasn't really a time for words; I think we were both struck by just what a milestone it was to see her go through the gates of the yard that had given birth to her. Five months of effort and care emerged as *Kingfisher*—a work of art. I felt so proud of everyone who had helped us get this far.

She went into the water several days later. Mum and Dad had arrived the evening before, and, counting Brest before the Mini and St.-Malo before the Route du Rhum, it was now the third time they had ventured abroad to one of our events. Merv was now back too, and I was glad he was there to see her touch her new home, the sea, for the first time. Mum poured champagne over her keel for good luck, and as *Kingfisher* was lowered into the water, I stood on her keel bulb until I was able to wash those first splashes of real seawater over her keel.

Seeing her afloat for the first time was our dream come true—now she could really show her character. Strangely, apart from the rumble of the hoist, it was a quiet moment, though incredibly intense. I think we were all close to tears. Mark spoke to a camera, saying, "I think that from the outside it's very hard for people to appreciate just how much work actually has to happen, and how much commitment goes into getting a boat like this into the water." He was absolutely right.

We were in the water for about five days before her official public launch, so we had time to test all her systems. A boat is not just about the obvious pieces such as the mast and sails. The interior network of hydraulics and electronics is incredibly sophisticated—from solar panels to computers to autopilots and two enormous hydraulic rams to cant her swinging keel, each weighing more than I did and not only holding but moving the most incredible loads. Everything has to be fitted, checked, and tested. To see the first hoisting of her enormous sails was nothing short of spectacular, and to feel her glide through the water for the first time was unbelievable. As I took her helm for those first moments, I had the strangest feeling that I had been there before, and it wasn't like a new experience. Although I struggled to describe the feeling, it felt more like a re-acquaintance with an old friend.

The launch itself was a great occasion for everyone involved with *Kingfisher* to this point. All four of her designers—including Alain Gautier, who'd flown in from France—had joined us, and I just hoped that they all felt proud of the beautiful boat they had built.

Auckland was a great place to be at this stage of the America's Cup. The Italian team Prada had made it through to the finals and was about to race against Sir Peter Blake's Team New Zealand—current holders of the cup. There were onlookers everywhere as we tied *Kingfisher* alongside the pontoon.

Just before the launch, we attached a plaque that read, "Built in New Zealand by the team at Marten Yachts." It was carved out of a piece of kauri wood estimated to be up to 800 years old. A Maori group performed a *haka* on the pontoon beside her. It was the first time I had seen this, and I think both Mark and I were overcome by the sheer power of emotion it conveyed. *Kingfisher* will always be a Kiwi to us, and it seemed appropriate to bring her into the world that way. Her naming was carried out by Lady Pippa Blake, wife of the most outstanding sailor ever—Sir Peter Blake. I stood nervously stroking my fingers over her as Pippa's words rang out powerfully and confidently over the crowds: "I name this boat *Kingfisher*. May God bless her and all who sail in her—especially Ellen."

Once the bottle smashed over her bow, I climbed over *Kingfisher*'s pulpit and kissed her bow.

CHAPTER FIFTEEN

ONE MONTH AFTER her commissioning, *Kingfisher* left New Zealand for the 12,000-mile journey home. As we sailed away from Auckland, for the first time we watched the skyline we knew so well disappear into the distance. I'd loved New Zealand. It was the longest period of time I'd spent in one place for years, and it had begun to feel like home, through both the great spirit amongst the team and the kindness and enthusiasm that the Kiwis had shown for the project. But the delivery trip would take us halfway around the world, and I was desperately looking forward to it. We decided to stage the journey in two legs: the first stage would take us to Cape Horn, with a crew of four; then I would sail home to Europe alone. I would have the chance to really get to know *Kingfisher*.

The crew for the first part of our trip was Bruno Dubois, Martin Carter, and Andrew Cape. Capey had routed me for the Route du Rhum and had sailed as navigator in numerous offshore races, including the Whitbread twice. He was a blond Australian, and although without doubt he had the characteristic Aussie sense of humour, he was outwardly quieter. He and I were going to discuss the weather in detail with a view to our Southern Ocean leg.

Bruno was from North Sails and had been working with us on our sails since the beginning of the project. We were in the process of developing a relatively new type of durable offshore sail made in one piece on a mould, which many said would never work for the Vendée. Bruno was great to have on board, having competed and been involved in a whole host of racing events, including the Whitbread many years before.

We were a happy crew, and except for the tail-end of a depression when the wind piped up to 38 knots, we were treated very kindly on the first leg. I spent many hours talking to Martin about longer-term modifications and preparations. Not only did we have the Vendée start in ten months' time, but the Europe 1 New Man Star was coming up in June, and even if all went well, we would have just a couple weeks to prepare for it once we arrived back in the UK. It was the qualifier for the Vendée Globe for most entrants, too, so being there on the start line was very much a part of every skipper's Vendée preparations.

Life on board *Kingfisher* is pretty basic, with standing room only in an area about a metre square. On the starboard side, there's a tiny sink with two manual pump taps, one for seawater and one for fresh water. Opposite the sink is a gimballed camping gas stove, designed to stay level whatever *Kingfisher* was doing. That's it as far as kitchen and hygiene are concerned, however—no toilet, no shower, and certainly no hot water. I slept on the chart-table seat for the delivery, leaving the pipe-cot bunks on each side of her cabin to the guys and especially Capey! Apart from this tiny part in which we lived, there was just storage for sails and food, and sacrificial areas which in grave circumstances could be isolated completely from the rest of the boat with watertight doors. When we think of dangers at sea, icebergs spring to mind—they are numerous in both Arctic and Antarctic waters—but there are also plenty of other floating obstacles which can bring your race to an abrupt and frightening end.

CAPE HORN WAS STUNNING, far more than just the rugged storm-swept rock one imagines. We had arranged to meet up with another boat, *Pelagic*, skippered and crewed by Hamish Laird and his wife, Kate. Mark was on board, along with Antony Lane and a friend of his, plus a French electronics engineer who we hoped would fix our temperamental satellite communications dome. It had been a while since I had seen Antony, and his calming character was wonderful in such a short-lived but potentially very stressful moment.

In the final moments of daylight, we watched the high mountains in the distance, ice-covered and sticking jaggedly out of the fjords. That night we moored in a bay named Caleta Martial and were ferried over to

Pelagic for a meal and a sleep in cushioned bunks! I was reluctant to leave *Kingfisher* but knew that before I left on my own the next day, I would need to sleep. At daybreak, I climbed *Pelagic's* companionway to be greeted by one of the most beautiful anchorages I had ever seen. The shores were a faded, weathered green and the water pure, dark, and still; *Kingfisher* lay silently just a hundred feet away, as if resting on her perfect reflection. The cold air cut through my thermals as I perched in the cockpit, pulling my legs close to my body.

I left that afternoon, sailing *Kingfisher* alone for the first time—and only just in time, too, as a storm blew through, leaving the others to battle into 60-knot headwinds as I sailed away in the last of the lighter breeze to the north. We had several real tests on that trip, but the main thing was to learn. Weather decisions are crucial to the single-handed sailor, and each day I would work out my weather strategy as if racing and e-mail my thoughts to Jean-Yves Bernot. Not being able to discuss things, particularly when you're tired, can be enormously stressful, and working with Jean-Yves helped my confidence. I was collecting weather information from the Internet, using the satellite communication equipment on board, which consisted of two satellite telephones: a Mini-M, which has a slow Internet connection speed that I used primarily for voice, and a Satcom-B satellite connection with which I could log on to the Internet at ISDN speed. Although the Internet is a big aid to navigation, so much information is available that the real art is to decide what's useful and what's not.

As *Kingfisher* and I crossed the Equator, I felt obliged to follow King Neptune's ancient initiation rite. Tradition dictates that each sailor who passes the Equator for the first time is to be tied up and tortured. Generally, this involves being dressed up, covered in disgusting food, and often having bits of hair shaved off! I made myself a cardboard crown and trident and wrapped myself in the European flag, talking to the camera as King Neptune. Then I changed roles to become the victim, mixing up an unappetizing blend of dried peas, stew, and chocolate protein compound, which I poured all over myself. I filmed it all and sent back footage. Mark and the rest of the team were sure I'd lost it!

I thought a great deal about all of them while I was out there. I had pictures of Marie, Pipo, and the kids; another from *Kingfisher's* launch, with the team standing proudly on her afterdeck; one of Mum and Dad;

and a card Mark had given me. I had a tiny model of *Foncia*, Alain Gautier's trimaran, in the centre of the chart table he'd given me when he'd flown to New Zealand for our first sail on *Kingfisher*. The hearts and souls of a great number of people were on board with me.

I developed a very special relationship with *Kingfisher* during our time alone. We learnt to rely on each other. I could feel when she was unhappy with either too little or too much sail, or when she wanted to sail as close to 100 per cent as she could. I was continually cleaning her, tidying up any mess or minor damage. I knew exactly where things were and always stowed the ropes meticulously in her cockpit, so they didn't lie on the floor. Down below we had fitted numerous storage racks on either side and underneath her side-decks, so that we could firmly attach plastic boxes containing everything from spare winch parts to circuit board spares to dried fruit. And when I practiced tacking and gybing, I'd run through the harder jobs—such as shifting these boxes from side to side to help keep her level and consequently more powerful. Physically, tacking is one of the toughest and most frustrating jobs on board. A dinghy can be tacked in seconds, but it takes about half an hour on a 60-foot racing yacht such as *Kingfisher*. From preparing everything and shifting the weight to physically tacking and then tidying up her lines afterwards, it's a mission you certainly don't just undertake for the sake of it!

I also learnt a lot about myself. I saw that sleep had a large effect on my well-being and decision-making capabilities, and I discovered natural sleep patterns which helped me recover more quickly from fatigue. I was happy on board, and felt very much at home with *Kingfisher*. I had learnt about her, and I knew more about my own tolerances and weaknesses. I had a funny feeling that that information would be useful in the year to come—and I was right.

My first landfall was the Île de Groix, just off the French coast, and there I met up with some of the shore team to go through the jobs list and discuss the work that needed to be done before reaching UK shores.

Kingfisher looked immaculate as we made our way through the Solent, and I felt intensely proud of her. We were met by a host of people, including Mum, Dad, and Gran, who waved from the Red Funnel Red Jet! Ashley Perrin was down in the main sitting area with Gran. I saw them both looking out, and then there was a third face in the window—Mac! Gran even came on board when we had finally tied up alongside in

m and Dad at home in Derbyshire

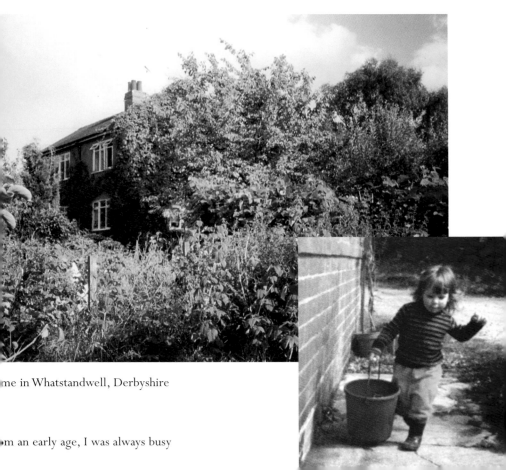

me in Whatstandwell, Derbyshire

m an early age, I was always busy

4 (*above*) On the beach with my
   sailing cap and telescope

5 (*right*) I went to farm sales with
   my dad, who could never resist a
   "bargain" . . .

6 With Lewis, my
   younger brother
   Fergus, Gran and Nan

7 Family expeditions
   were frequent

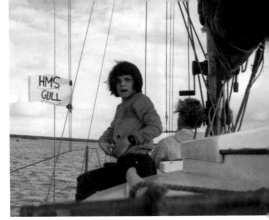

9 Sailing aboard *Cabaret*

ntie Thea's boat, *Cabaret*, under sail

10 In the garden with Mac in my first boat

11 (*left*) Sailing *Kestrel*

12 (*above*) On board *Cabaret* with David King and Auntie Thea

13 Sailing with *Alert* out of the David King
Nautical School

14 With Sir Robin Knox-Johnston, on the
day I won the BT/YSA Young Sailor of
the Year award

15 Home aboard *Iduna*

y plan of *Iduna*, drawn in preparation for sailing round Britain

ying goodbye before setting sail round Britain

18 (*above*) "Let out at last"
    in *Iduna*

19 (*right*) *Iduna* at sea

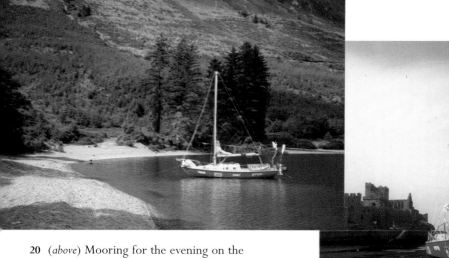

20 (*above*) Mooring for the evening on the
    Caledonian Canal

21 (*right*) *Iduna* dried up in Peel, on the Isle of Man

22 (*above*) Choppy weather off the West Coast

23 (*left*) Congratulations from Nan on finishing the sail round Britain

24 (*above*) Alan Wynne-Thomas's *Elan Sifo*, which I prepared for his transatlantic race

25 (*left*) The Sea Cadets' TS *Royalist*

26 Alan Wynne-Thomas

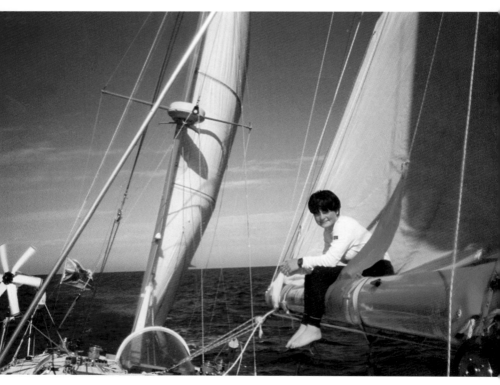

27 My first transatlantic crossing
   with Alan aboard *Elan Sifo*

28 Vittorio Mallingri aboard
   Anicaflash during my first transatlantic race. The badly designed
   tiller caused endless problems

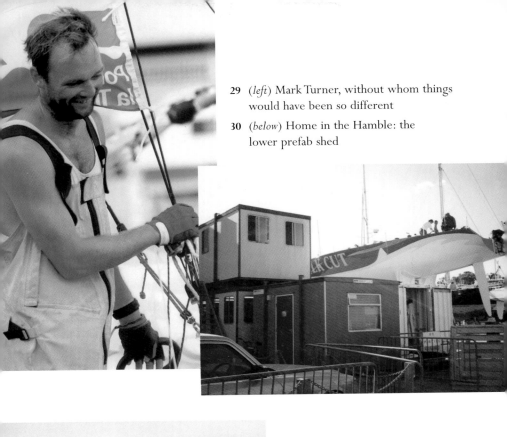

29 (*left*) Mark Turner, without whom things would have been so different

30 (*below*) Home in the Hamble: the lower prefab shed

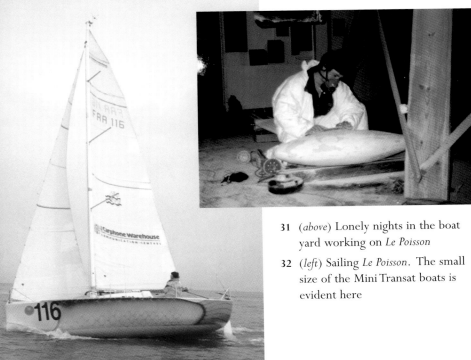

31 (*above*) Lonely nights in the boat yard working on *Le Poisson*

32 (*left*) Sailing *Le Poisson*. The small size of the Mini Transat boats is evident here

33 (*above*) Saying "Thank you" to *Le Poisson* at the end of the Mini Transat

34 (*right*) Exhausted after the Mini Transat

35 (*above*) Sunset aboard *Great Circle* . . .

36 (*right*) . . . and the storm

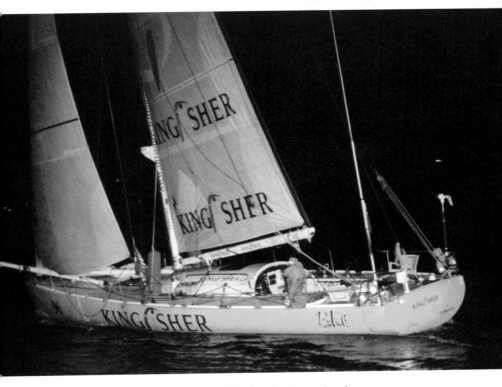

37 Pete Goss's *Aqua Quorum*, renamed *Kingfisher* for the Route du Rhum

38 (*above*) Very sunburnt and tired at the end of the 1998 Route du Rhum

39 (*left*) With Merv, working on the design of *Kingfisher*

40 (*right*) *Kingfisher* takes shape in New Zealand

41 (*below*) Sailing *Aquitaine Innovations* with Yves Parlier

42 (*above right*) Walking with Dad and Mac in Scotland during a short break

43 (*above*) A dream come true: *Kingfisher* is launched

44 (*right*) *Kingfisher* in her element. The swing keel is clearly visible

45 (*left*) If you look hard, you can just spot me in the cockpit

46 (*below*) Ducking waves in the North Atlantic

47 (*left*) Just after winning the 1 New Man Star transatlantic race—notice the cut on my forehead

ingfisher

high-tech sails

O Fibre Rigging

rbon Winch Pedestal

tellite Dome

cape Hatch & Liferafts

to Pilots

sic Galley

ter Ballast

nk

v Station & Table

ving Keel

ymmetric Boards

il Storage

atertight Bulkheads

adsails on Furlers

ashbox

mballed Radar

rbon Mast & Boom

rbon Headfoils

wsprit

Kingfisher Open 60

Length	60′	18.2m
Beam (max)	17.22′	5.3m
Draft	14.85′	4.5m
Weight	<8,600kg	
Construction	Pre-preg Carbon and Nomex	
Design	Kingfisher Design Team	
	Owen Clarke Design Group,	
	Rob Humphreys, Alain Gautier,	
	Giovani Belgrano	
Builder	Marten Yachts, New Zealand	
Management	Build – Owen Clarke Design Goup	
	Project – Offshore Challenges	

IMAGE BY KER ASSOCIATES

49 (top) Philippe Jeantot and the Vend[
skippers the day before the official

50 (above) The Vendée Globe fleet at Le
Sables d'Olonne before the race

51 (above left) The Kingfisher team.
From left to right, back row: Dana
Bena, Mark Turner, Tanguy de Lam
Martin Carter; front row: Amanda
Carter, Marie Cairo, me, Pipo Cair[

52 (above) With Mum and Dad before the
Vendée start

53 (right) Saying goodbye to Mathilde

Leaving Les Sables d'Olonne on the way to the Vendée start. Ian is on board with the video camera filming the event

Racing the Vendée

56 (*left*) Asleep in *Kingfisher*'s cabin

57 (*below*) Home! *Kingfisher*'s chart table

58 (*left*) An unexpected guest on board

59 Mending broken shelves during the Vendée Hot work!

60 (*above*) The monitor that recorded my sleep patterns during the Vendée

61 (*right*) Mending a block during a frenzied day of equatorial repairs

A wave rolls down the deck. The last picture the camera ever took!

Preparing to climb the mast

64 (*top*) Halfway up the mast, removing
the broken batten

65 (*above*) The side effects of a trip up
the mast

66 Inside the iceberg zone. The big one I saw—the size of an island

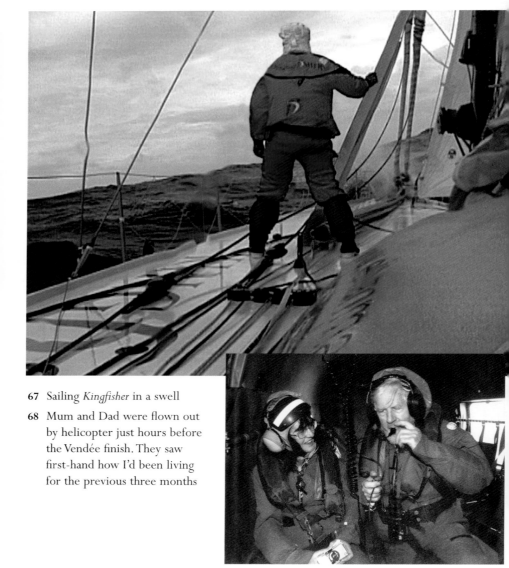

67 Sailing *Kingfisher* in a swell

68 Mum and Dad were flown out by helicopter just hours before the Vendée finish. They saw first-hand how I'd been living for the previous three months

69 The finish line

70 (*below*) Celebration

(*above, both photos*) Saying goodbye for the last time

(*right*) And all alone just minutes later

73 The first interview in
Les Sables d'Olonne

74 Mark and I share a post-
Vendée interview—a very
emotional occasion

75 Backstage at the Vendée
prize-giving. In the
foreground is Michel
Desjoyeaux, the winner

76 (*above*) With Ian, Mum, and Brian Pilcher, an incredible six years after my sail round Britain

77 (*left*) Yves Parlier, whose Vendée story was amongst the most extraordinary of all

78 With Alain Gautier, a great friend and sailing companion in 2001

79 (*right*) Back on the water—aboard *Kingfisher Foncia*

80 (*below*) *Kingfisher Foncia* doing what she does best

81 At the EDS prize-giving. The first time I raced *Kingfisher* with a crew—an incredible team

82 Euphoria: celebrating with the *Kingfisher Foncia* crew after winn the Challenge Mondial

83 With David Beckham, Sir Alex
Ferguson, and Michael Owen at
the BBC Sports Personality of
the Year award ceremony

84 (*above left*) Accepting an honorary degree from
the University of Derby, where Nan finally
completed a degree at the age of eighty-three
—an incredible achievement!

85 (*above*) At Buckingham Palace to receive my
MBE with Mum, Dad, and Gran

86 (*left*) Nan's graduation

Southampton. It was a very strange feeling having sailed halfway around the world, and odd to think that the last time *Kingfisher* had been tied up alongside a dock was in Auckland. Our good friend Erik Lindkvist the cameraman jumped aboard. Everyone loves Erik—people with personality like his really make others smile. Still, as he filmed, some of the first words I spoke were, "I don't want to get off."

PLYMOUTH WILL ALWAYS remind me of my Round Britain trip, and during our final week of preparation for the Europe 1 New Man Star across the Atlantic, we were moored in the marina right next to the Royal Western Yacht Club, where *Iduna* and *Elan Sifo* had berthed. I was acutely conscious that we were on display and nervous about how we would compete against the others. This was the first time *Kingfisher* had even been seen by her rivals, and she was very much an unknown quantity. I hoped she would be fast, but the truth was I had no idea how she would fare. Above all, though, I had no idea how *I* would fare. From weather tactics to sleep management, we had the whole lot on our shoulders. I knew that I would be out there against the best skippers in the world, and that the pace of the race would be fast. And although the Vendée Globe was fast approaching, and all would want to make it to the start line, these weren't the kind of people who would just take it easy in the interests of self-preservation, whatever they might say to the contrary.

There were twenty-five boats in Class 1, and well over half of those were monohulls. There were ten boats in our class capable of winning. In successive interviews, I was asked about my hopes for the race. I always replied that if I could finish in the top ten, I would be happy, but deep down in my heart, I knew that my goal was very definitely to finish in the top three. I ran through plans in my head. What could we do to finish in the top three? What might help me get there? There were no easy conclusions. I knew we had a fantastic shore team—the best. After all, they'd turned *Kingfisher* round in less than two weeks after she'd sailed halfway round the world, which was amazing. Although there were definitely gaps in our knowledge, we accepted that and just forged ahead. I also knew that as soon as the ten-minute gun went, it was down to me— I would be on my own then.

On the morning of the start, I felt sick with nervousness, and though I tried to put on a brave face, I knew I was struggling. Burdened by the pressure of performing well, I did not feel myself at all. We now had everything we needed, and I was competing on equal terms with every other skipper—failure would fall on my shoulders now. I had a bad pain in my right knee that had been there since I ran along the dock on return from New Zealand, and though not too agonizing, it was still a concern, as I could not put all my weight on the knee when it was bent. I said goodbye to Mum and Dad, but I wasn't fully there; they must have felt like they were hugging someone who had already left. Dad was interviewed once I'd gone; later, when I saw a recording of the interview, I could see from his face that he was worried, but his words showed that he'd reassured himself: "It's a superb moment, because this time she has a really fantastic boat to attempt this race in. It's wonderful."

At the ten-minute gun, the team jumped off. I headed away from the line, then tacked, building up speed to power across the start. *Kingfisher* and I were off. As soon as I was clear of the support boats, I put her on autopilot and grabbed my mobile. I sent a text message to everyone in the shore team to say thanks. My eyes filled with tears of joy as I typed before switching it off:

> It's great to be back at sea, it's where we belong, KINGFISHER and me. I'm relieved to have got away from the start line cleanly and she feels great. It's always an emotional moment—in particular the moment when the shore team got off—thanks guys, fantastic team effort to get us here. A DONF!

At the Eddystone Lighthouse, the only mark of the course before America, *PRB* edged ahead of *Kingfisher* to take the lead. At that point the fleet started to split, some choosing to head immediately inshore to get out of the worst of the adverse tide.

I have never felt as nervous in a race as I did in the 1 Star. Each time I grabbed twenty minutes' sleep, I would wake with the most profound knot in my stomach. I could never relax with the weather, continually worrying whether I had chosen the right option, and whether the others had picked the same route. Every few hours we would receive the position reports and would know whether we had gained or lost miles on the others. . . . Our lives on board revolved completely around these figures, and our hearts almost beat to their pace. If you lost miles for whatever reason, you couldn't allow yourself to be demoralized by it. It's as much a mental battle as a physical one, and there's a fine line between watching too closely what the others are doing and calling your own shots.

Initially we had a light breeze as we sailed along the South Coast of the UK to head out to the Atlantic, and we dropped to sixth or seventh place. I fought on, though, pushing hard and changing sails hourly at one stage to make it around the Lizard headland.

By the second day, we had retaken the lead—an incredible feeling. *Kingfisher* was holding her own. But I knew that we had a very long way to sail. I kept telling myself, just hang in there, don't do anything stupid, and don't make mistakes. Leading brings its own problems, and I had never led a fleet before. I felt the pressure mount massively. You are the "tester" of the fleet; the others sit behind you and watch your every move—and those closest are perfectly poised to sail around you if you enter a windless zone or make a bad call.

We were soon into the Atlantic depression systems, as we had been with the Route du Rhum, and life on board got tougher, not only physically but also tactically. The wind changed direction quickly with the passage of the fronts, and if we weren't to lose miles we had to tack in response immediately. Every tack meant twenty-five minutes of hard manual work, commencing with the shifting of the boxes, then the sails in the forepeak. Each weighed not much less than I did and was twice my size, so it was a bit like trying to roll an unwilling body uphill in an earthquake.

> It's blowing a *&**?& right now. 35 knots almost consistent. hAHve spent a good hor on deck checking and re-checking to c if all is OK. Found a few small probs, but nothing too serious. life on board os incredibly testing, the motion is horrnedous, and the wind and seas seem to grow not only in size3 and strength, but also in their unpredictable nature! Felt hungry so made a mushroomn pate, cheese and tomatoe sauce sanwich. FElt bizarre balancing the bread in my soaked knees, trying to pur the tom suce so it didn't get thrown everywhere as anything else looose in the cabin would be. I've spent a while sitting in thee cuddy in the past days . . . though know it feels like a fairground log-flume. Ploughing into waves, with green water darkeneing the hiding hole every few minuters . . .

though unlike the log flume, the fun [of] the spray has passed. . . . It's
impossible to see out of the windows, continously under water, be it
rain, sporay or solid waves. there is a rattle in the riggin of the
halyrds . . . I have minimised it by tyimng them back tight to the
mast, glad mikey put those covers on at the spreaders. . . .
Everything down below much drier since our mini-refit. greeat
work guys.

My knee is quite painful too, though has been the least of my
worries over the past days. . . .

Hanging in here, quite literally,

Exx

Three boats were dismasted in that first storm, including two race
favourites, Thomas Coville on *Sodebo* and Yves Parlier, and I was shocked
to hear the news. Yves had just fitted a new mast after our problems the
previous autumn. He must have been spitting fire.

Eight days in, we sailed through a vicious front. I was still struggling
to sleep. We were down to three reefs and the storm jib, and her motion
was violent, but to leeward I could see a sail with a red square, which I
recognized as belonging to Bilou (Roland Jourdain). His *Sill* was the first
boat I had seen since we cleared the Channel, and I tried to imagine
what might be happening on board, whether he was sleeping or nervous
too. There is always a strong bond among single-handed sailors, and I felt
it more strongly than ever on that stormy evening. And while I would do
anything in my power to finish ahead of him, I really liked the guy. A
funny, chilled-out character, Bilou was also incredibly good at what he
did best—race. I could see from the weather pictures that the winds
were likely to change quickly on the other side of the depression, and I
knew I could not sleep until they had. I dozed in the cockpit, freezing
cold but just waiting for a tack which, when the wind did change, took
more than forty minutes. Afterwards I collapsed in the cockpit, feeling
cold, tired, and a bit desperate. I pulled myself out of it by deciding to
strip off, dry off, and refuel—I knew I needed to try to switch off. Finally I climbed into the bunk on the leeward side, as it was safest, and
had a cup of Horlicks. As I lay there, deafening sounds echoed through
poor *Kingfisher* as she sailed on through 40-knot winds. I reached above
me to touch her deck, saying gently, "Hang in there, lass," and tried to
sleep.

With my eyes closed I still could not sleep; I thought of black places and counted sheep lying in a field of grass, but nothing would send me off. I think the general perception of sleep on board a boat is far from the truth. Many people ask, "How do you wake up?" but for us the question is "How do you sleep?" When a boat is travelling at speed—or often, even worse, when there is little or no wind—it's virtually impossible to grab sleep. Waking up is the easy bit. It's trying to get yourself divorced enough from your circumstances to sleep, or even relax, that's hard.

In the morning, the wind dropped away; after studying the latest weather fax, I realized we were in the centre of a secondary low-pressure system. I gambled on sailing at 90 degrees to the route, to where I calculated the breeze should be. Little by little the wind kicked in, and within hours we were sailing at 10, then 15, knots. When the evening position report came through, I was 75 miles ahead of Bilou. I was over the moon, though things would soon go downhill fast. A dispatch from Offshore Challenges relayed the news:

POSITIONS IN MONOHULL fleet at 1038 GMT WEDNESDAY

1. KINGFISHER 871
2. SILL +5
3. WHIRLPOOL +71
4. TG4 +86

The past 24 hours saw a change of fortune for Ellen MacArthur, now hanging on to a very slender 5-mile lead over SILL (Roland Jourdain). A lot can happen in 24 hours at sea . . .

Yesterday afternoon, Ellen was awoken by the Raytheon radar alarm. Unsure of whether it was a ship or not, she quickly went on deck, only to find herself in thick fog. With KINGFISHER steaming along at 12 to 13 knots at the time, this was a fairly nerve-racking moment! Then, fortunately, the fog began to clear, and there was the object the radar had pinged—a "beautiful" iceberg. She even managed to photograph it whilst hand-steering around its windward side (less chance of "growlers," the small lumps that fall off the main berg and are in many ways more dangerous).

A couple of hours later as she went to go down the fore-hatch to get the kite up as the wind freed, she slipped and went crashing down the hatch, hitting her hand, leg and head on the way. So now we've got icebergs around, it's just above freezing, the boat is charging along, blood on the spinnaker (which she wants to get up) and a bit of pain happening! Undeterred she got the kite up, sorted the boat out, and got back to the cabin to assess her injuries. Looks like a potentially broken finger, gash and big swelling on her head (seem to remember this one from the Route du Rhum as well!), and the other leg to the one that already hurt a bit swollen as well. Her "good news" in her call in to us was—"at least I didn't faint!" She's OK, but a little bit bashed about.

In amongst all this, the wind is moving all over the place, and Ellen struggles to get a grip on the weather situation, albeit with a lack of information to support her. The fleet heads further south, and Ellen puts some distance to the north—turns out to be the wrong choice and coupled with SILL's apparent performance advantage off the breeze, her lead is now down to zero . . . the match race begins again.

After a very busy twenty-four hours, we were just hanging onto our lead, and the following night I had the spinnaker up and was trying to relax.

Suddenly there was a bang and to my horror on deck I saw the kite collapse and fall into the water signalling a 3-hour fight to recover it. I had to sail backwards, blow all the lines and then really struggled as it wrapped itself around the keel. I'm totally drained now, going to have to sleep. My body feels like its been through a mincing machine. I've no idea how I got it back on, once it was in the water the load was enormous so we're on course again at 11 knots. No idea how many miles I've lost though.

I was lucky that Bilou had problems of his own. The following morning I found that rather than dropping into second place, I had actually increased my lead. I was exhausted but overjoyed. We were just days away and had broken free into the light upwind conditions. I collapsed on the chart-table seat and slept more soundly than at any time before on the trip.

The nervousness refused to go away, though, and even on the final day out there, when the wind stayed strong enough to help us in across the shallows and towards Newport, I was still uneasy. For the first time in any race, I knew I wanted to finish. I was exhausted and had spent every day of the race with a tension knot in my stomach that had little to do with sailing but everything to do with what was riding on the race. I had pushed myself hard, and *Kingfisher* had shown her true colours. But she was tired, too—we'd sailed more than 16,000 miles in three months, and we both needed a rest.

It was the quietest of mornings as the first signs of life slipped into view, framed by a foggy grey sky; a damp, chilly breeze blew. I thought back to my first-ever transatlantic with Alan, when we left Newport exactly four years earlier. Those four years could have been ten for all that had happened. It took a while for reality to sink in that morning, as suddenly but briefly the weight which had been on my shoulders for two weeks lifted. I thrust my fist in the air to the crack of a gun.

We had crossed the line in first place—after fourteen days, twenty-three hours, and one minute at sea.

19th June 2000—SHE DID IT!

Ellen MacArthur breaks record in Europe 1 New Man Star victory . . .

In the early hours here in Newport, USA, Ellen MacArthur crossed the line to take victory in the Europe 1 New Man single-handed transatlantic race. After a tortuous final 36 hours in light and variable winds, the 23-year-old slid into Newport, Rhode Island, at 1021 GMT this morning, to become the youngest winner of the race since its inception in 1960.

I was just about ready to drop after this race—I had been full on for more than three months, and most of that was at sea alone. When I read the results from the sleep study we had carried out, I learned that my average sleep per day over the previous fourteen days had been 4.2 hours—no wonder I felt completely drained. It's a difficult situation when you finish a race, as you know you need to download as much information as you can to your team. When they are revving up, you are clapping out!

I returned to the UK, where I gave more interviews—some in Derbyshire, which gave me a day there to catch up with the family, then more in London. I spent a day in Cowes and took a two-day trip to a place near Chamonix where Mark had once lived and where he returned as often as possible. With a guide, Michel, we set straight off to climb in the Alps, each of us making our first attempts at ice climbing, which I revelled in. We spent the night high up in a hut roughly five hours' trek from the head of the cable car. Even though I rallied to do this, I remember feeling completely exhausted. I had pushed myself hard, and I knew that my will to "go for it" often concealed my fatigue.

Immediately after this I was back in Newport, where I spent my birthday for the second time. Then I set off with Martin Carter and Erik, our awesome Swedish cameraman, to bring *Kingfisher* home after her refit over there. By this time, I was looking forward to getting out of the harbour and just being at sea again. Although I had hoped the trip would be a respite, I was wrong. I developed a cough the day we left the States and failed to shake it off all the way across. It would be wrong to say that we didn't have a smile from time to time, especially as Erik took an instant dislike to the provisions we had on board and had an entertaining way of showing it. I think he found it hard to understand why we were eating freeze-dried food. He's quite a good cook, and on Martin's birthday he separated the peas, other vegetables, and meat from one of the foil-packed dried meals and cooked each separately for a special treat. I warmed immensely to Erik during that trip, and we talked a great deal. He had a kind heart, and though he could be exasperating as he asked you to "climb the mast just one more time" for another camera angle, he always did it with a persuasive smile that could have had a prime minister standing on his hands. Erik was an absolute perfectionist and a brilliant cameraman—the images he collected from that trip were stunning.

We were now in our final dash towards the Vendée start, with just two months before I sailed *Kingfisher* to Les Sables d'Olonne, and my schedule reflected it. Interviews, corporate sailing days, and meetings filled the diary. I went to the South of France to take part in a catamaran regatta, visited Pierre Lasnier, a meteorologist in Nice, for additional weather training, then travelled throughout France and Belgium giving presentations about my life and the Vendée Globe. But although my life felt like a sleighride as I was carried along by the momentum of the project, I was put firmly back in my place by another trip to France.

Shortly after returning from America, I travelled to Brest to sail with a group of kids in an event which had been partly organized by Marine Crenn's brother, Antoine. At a young age, Antoine had suffered from leukemia and now worked with a charity called À Chacun Son Cap (Everybody Has a Goal), which had started to bring kids suffering from the disease together with kids who had recovered, and take them out on the water. It allowed them to talk to each other about their situations— which must be impossible for the majority of people to understand—but it also enabled them to forget their illness, albeit for just a few days. It was one of the best days of sailing I'd ever had. We laughed so much we had tears in our eyes, and the kids were just incredible. They were not interested in being treated differently in any way, and they were unbelievably keen and competitive on board. I joined them on the second day, and it was staggering to see just how much they had bonded already. They made me feel like a novice on board! I was very sad to leave them—the experience hammered home to me how incredibly lucky I was.

It was a hard summer that year for all of us; the pressure was increasing not only for me but also for the rest of the team. Mark's workload, in particular, was immense, and we called each other constantly to check that all was OK. For a while, when *Kingfisher* was in Cowes, we actually managed to spend some time together. Ian McKay was around, too, and as the demand grew for promotional material for the Vendée, so did the time he had to spend producing it. Ever since I opened up to him in London, we had remained very close friends. He understood the pressures we were all feeling, and it was a godsend to be able to talk to someone who was coming at all of this from a different angle. Ian treated me as an equal, and it felt like a long time since I'd had such a good mate. Except for my early days with Merv, I'd relied pretty much solely on Mark.

Mark and I had virtually lived together for four years—trying to build the project, taking things forward day by day. But though I did not realize it then, the circumstances of our coming together had shaped what followed. Mark had devoted his life to the project. We had known each other since I had been little more than an eighteen-year-old kid, and though my future had been determined before the end of my first year with Mark, and I had done a massive amount of growing up, I sometimes felt that our partnership had not moved on to reflect it. I knew that Mark respected me, but I also felt he could sometimes still see that eighteen-year-old who had first spoken to him. Things had changed, and the reality was that I had become a highly independent twenty-four-year-old professional sailor. It was a difficult transition to make, and though at times it was hard, in many ways it was Mark's nurture and support that enabled me to realize my ambitions. The reality was that it was a big step in the right direction; working like this, we could make the sponsorship work, as it enabled me to have the time to go and train on the water, and give presentations when necessary. Leading a team, being its public face, and competing for that same team was a huge responsibility. In just two years, we had gone from struggling to find enough money to get a document printed to winning a high-profile transatlantic race against the best in the world. I didn't allow myself to dwell on what we had achieved. None of us, myself especially, could afford the tiniest trace of complacency. Mark and I needed each other, thriving on each other's determination and passion to get things right.

At this stage, making a success of the project meant ignoring how tired we were. The diary was overflowing with appointments, so we had to keep going, both giving as much as, or even more than, we were capable of. With the race just weeks away, it was taking its toll.

We missed out on the family holiday that year. Mum and Dad bailed out of going to Scotland, having decided that I would be better off just spending three days at home—and they were right. But it was difficult to relax. There were always people to visit, and people who visited whenever there was word that I was at home. However well meant, this added its own pressure, along with plans to make and a race now looming startlingly close on the horizon.

My final sail alone before we based *Kingfisher* in Les Sables d'Olonne was to be the delivery from La Trinité, where we'd been filming with the BBC. Alain Gautier was going to join me on board for the first part of this. We sailed out into the Bay of Biscay, and even though we would have only twenty-four hours together, it was wonderful to share, however briefly, his experiences in the Vendée. At thirty-nine, Alain's experience was extensive, from the Figaro fleet to the Open 60 trimaran fleet to three round-the-world trips on Open 60 monohulls, including two Vendée Globes, the second of which he had won. Having Alain as part of the team had been Mark's suggestion, and it had worked well. He was someone with whom I could identify completely, and he was open and generous with his advice. Somehow, he gave me a quiet confidence. I stayed out for one day longer after I had dropped off Alain outside Lorient, but with a forecast of little to no wind, I decided to enter Les Sables early and try to get some rest.

Early on in our time there, I got together with the team for a wild night out. Marie, Pipo, and the kids had moved to the town once we returned from New Zealand, so they knew the lay of the land extremely well. We had a fantastic time; everyone relaxed and made complete fools of themselves, and we danced the night away until close to dawn. We profited from the last of the summer celebrations with a few drinks in an almost-Caribbean-style beach bar, and then finished the evening in a nightclub. None of us realized then how impossible it would be in only a few months' time to relive that kind of evening.

Before the final countdown to the race, I took a brief trip back to the UK during which Ian dragged me away for a couple of days to try to help me unwind. He'd been on a holiday on the Norfolk Broads some time before, and he suggested we spend a few days messing about on a boat with no pressure, anonymously and without fuss. Although it was not long enough, we had a wonderful time, leaving Horning on our first morning bright and early, with mist lingering over the water and amongst the foliage. We had hired the smallest sailing boat we could find so we would not be restricted about where we went, and it also happened to be the oldest available. Those three days reminded me very much of my time on Cabaret as a kid. We had visited the Norfolk Broads then, and even now, more than ten years later, I felt the same excitement at the promise of adventure.

At the end of the trip, I had to head home to Derbyshire to go through my Vendée medical kit with Uncle Glyn. Running through the list of drugs was mind-boggling. Taking each one out of its packet and labelling it with its potency was a sobering reminder of what I was about to undertake. There were drugs for serious infections to be injected three times a day, powerful painkillers, do-it-yourself kits for setting broken bones, and pre-threaded needles for sewing yourself up. I thought again of what Alan Wynne-Thomas had been through, and it hit home sharply that I would have to be completely self-sufficient out there. I even tested myself by injecting saline solution into the muscle of my leg. Once Glyn showed me on himself what to do, I couldn't back out, but at least the two of us weren't caught as we stood there with our trousers round our ankles and syringes in our hands. I knew that if I had to repair myself thousands of miles from a hospital, as others had done before, I needed to be prepared—whether that meant coping with hypothermia or sewing something back on. There was also another possibility of which all skippers are aware—the responsibility of having to treat someone we may have to rescue. As Pete Goss had shown in picking up Raphael Dinelli, we were going to places where we could rely only on one another; there was no one else out there.

While in Derbyshire, I went to say my final goodbyes to Gran, who we knew was not going to come to France to see the race start. She had never been abroad, and she felt it would be impossible for her to go out in a boat to watch us all leave. I could sense her worry at saying goodbye, but she's a strong lady, and I knew she believed I would get around safely.

BACK IN LES SABLES, the change in just the week or so I'd been away was extreme. The whole town had been completely consumed by the Vendée Globe; as I drove past shops, there were posters on the walls and pictures in the windows. The Cap Ouest restaurant had adopted the *Kingfisher* team and was already decked out in blue and yellow. The compound by the pontoons was a totally different place, with giant tents covering hundreds of square yards of ground. The most significant change was on the pontoons themselves—twenty-four of the world's most technologically advanced Open race boats were lined up there.

This was it. This was really it.

We were one of the lucky teams. Our boat was almost ready and raring to go. Other competitors were less fortunate; we saw boats with question marks on their hulls looking for sponsors, and others were still undergoing major work. The diversity of the fleet highlighted the fact that the Vendée is a unique race. There were some 50-footers among the

60s, and although their skippers were out there to race, they would leave the dockside without a realistic chance of winning. One was *Aqua Quorum*, the boat I'd raced in the Route du Rhum; ironically, she was skippered by Patrice Carpentier, now fifty, who had raced Robert Nickerson's *Panic Major* in the first Vendée. *Elan Sifo*, raced by Catherine Chabaud last time, was there once again, now sailed by Joe Seeten; it seemed a lifetime since I had docked on this very pontoon with her four years before. There was the Russian Fedor Konioukhov, the ultimate adventurer. Starting with Everest, he had climbed the world's eight highest peaks. His boat bore the number 8848, the height in metres to which he had climbed. In 1990–91, he had sailed non-stop around the world alone, and now he was going to race around it. He was a shaggy-haired and bearded man, deceptively slight, with an unassuming personality. He spoke halting English, but with even less French, it was hard for him to communicate with the majority of the fleet. I warmed to the spirit of this man who quietly goes out and just does things without fanfare. People like him underlined that the Vendée Globe was still an occasion for adventure. We'd be passing through some of the most isolated and untouched areas of the world—this really was the Everest of sailing.

There was concern in the air, though; the Vendée, a race historically known for its pioneering spirit, was now more competitive than ever. There were twenty-four boats in this fourth Vendée—more than the total number who had managed to complete the race since its inception in 1989–90. At least half the boats sitting on the start line had the potential to win. There was speculation around the pontoons about the pace of the race, whether we would be tempted to push ourselves and our boats too far . . . the tension was growing each day. There were some incredibly experienced guys here, many of whom I had raced either with or against: Yves Parlier was now setting off for his third Vendée Globe; Marc Thiercelin, who had finished second in the previous Vendée and second in the Around Alone, was here with a new boat; Catherine Chabaud, who had a new Open 60 for this edition, had finished sixth in the previous race; and of course there was Michel Desjoyeaux, dubbed "The Professor," who had twice won the Figaro, and the AG2R transatlantic once, and had already raced around the world in the Whitbread. In my own mind before the start, he, along with Mike Golding in *Team Group 4* and Bilou, with whom I'd sparred during the Europe 1 New

Man Star, would likely be my biggest rivals. I also knew that the Southern Ocean would be a different ball game to what I'd encountered before, a big unknown. . . . We all had to sail safely, but judging from the
noises being made before the start, it didn't sound as though any of us
had any plans to be hanging around down there.

Time was in short supply in the weeks before the start, and I spent a
large part of October 2000 in Les Sables d'Olonne—partly because I
wanted to be with the boat and remain aware of what was happening on
board, and partly because it was less hassle to stay in the same place, because so much needed to be done to prepare for being at sea for three
months. There was not only the weather planning and the technical side
of the boat to sort out—obviously the major things—but everything
else as well, from which kind of soap would work best in salt water to
the number of tubes of toothpaste or sunblock to take. We even vacuum-
packed my thermals and underwear so there was no chance of their getting wet before they were needed.

As the days to the start counted down, the number of visitors increased. I found I couldn't walk anywhere without being stopped and
asked for an autograph, and it was humbling to see people's excitement
when they spotted me in the street or when they walked past the boats.
People travelled hundreds of miles to immerse themselves in the atmosphere at the start of this incredible race.

"Home" in Les Sables was an apartment block just across the water
from the boats; we had taken several rooms on one floor to house most
of the team. It was fairly basic summer-holiday-type lodgings when we
moved in there, with folding beds that also served as the sofa. I put up a
few posters on the walls, spread my charts on the table, and filled the
cupboards with my bags. Everyone was busy in Les Sables, and once
again it made a real difference having Ian around. We got on better than
best friends, and I felt I had an incredible understanding with him.

The pressure was immense, and I was ill twice in the final three
weeks. Both times, I was sick and felt exhausted. I began to be concerned about how physically prepared I was. During the summer, I had
tried to use the gym, and had managed a few runs, but against what I
would have liked to achieve, I had done very little—there had not been
time. Now I was worried about living with the repercussions on the
boat. I had still not completely shaken off the cough I'd picked up during

our delivery back from America, and I was annoyed that after all we had been through, I was not A1 for the start. I even had a massage—my first—and the masseur told me that he did not think I was stressed, which was a bonus of sorts.

Castorama, one of Kingfisher's store chains, had run a competition inspired by the charity À Chacun Son Cap. They had provided ten hospitals around France with models of *Kingfisher*, and the kids had designed and painted them. A small group from each hospital had come to Les Sables for the announcement of the competition results, and I had the chance to present the prizes and show the children around *Kingfisher*. Although I felt like death warmed over, it was a very inspiring day in the blur of nerves before the start, a moment which made me forget my superficial illness and think even harder about how lucky I was to be about to set out to achieve what I'd always dreamed of . . . those kids would be with me on board.

Satellite trucks and TV cameras from all over mainland Europe flooded in, although, apart from some loyal regional TV stations, the Brits were conspicuous by their absence. The nights were the easiest time to be around the boat, when the majority of the public had gone home and I could get on with things without being stopped too much. Although the support was incredible, it could be tiring signing autographs during the day—I learnt quickly that you have to do it in short bursts or you can't really "give" to those you meet. It was always painfully hard to draw myself away, and I often relied on Mark, Dana, or Ian to help me.

Each skipper followed the weather like a hawk. We all knew that in previous races, one of the hardest obstacles to cross was the Bay of Biscay; in the past, many boats had been dismasted and forced to turn back within the first few days. The forecast for start day was horrendous—we were due to be hit with 60-knot winds on our first night—and it did not improve. On the day before the start, we all headed to the skippers' meeting. We went through the process of the start procedure and the problematic towing situation on the morning of the start, and as the meeting drew to a close, the English voice of Richard Tolkien piped up, asking whether, with such a forecast, we should actually start the race. There was a deathly silence, then much discussion, after which the decision was made to postpone the start. With the atrocious conditions forecast, we knew that it would now be nigh impossible to leave for at least two days, which was one of the safety issues: anyone who had a problem would not be able to get back in. The storm would make the entrance to Les Sables virtually impassable to the competitors, quite apart from the danger caused by the hundreds of spectator craft which would be likely to try to see us off regardless of safety considerations.

Like everyone else, I was psyched up to leave, but there was a sense of relief when the start was delayed. An odd mixture of deflation and anticipation marked the two days that followed, but they passed frighteningly quickly, and they did give us the chance to spend a bit more time with our families. I felt sad, however, for the thousands of people who had descended on Les Sables for the start weekend. It must have been very disappointing for them.

With the race delayed, Mum and Dad had departed on their original ferry booking with Glyn and his wife, Steph, Fergus, Lewis and his friend Pete, and Mum and Dad's friend Wendy. I was sad that they couldn't stay to see us all leave, but as the day progressed and the wind worsened, I was glad they were not around to see the storm. That night I went bowling with the rest of the team, although after a few throws I found it hard to concentrate. It was wonderful to see everyone smile so much—in many ways, their jobs were done now—but when everyone else went out for a meal afterwards, I headed down to the boats with Ian to check that all was well.

Outside, the storm was howling, and as we walked down to the marina, the wind was deafening as it ripped through the swaying masts and rigging. We wandered past the pontoons, shifting a few fenders on boats in danger of damaging themselves and tweaking a few mooring lines. The rain absolutely lashed down and the boats suddenly looked very vulnerable. As the spray splashed our faces, I could not help but think what it must be like out at sea in this.

As we stood, two solitary wet figures next to *Kingfisher*, we realized that we were going to be together for a long time. I held Ian's hand tightly as we stood in *Kingfisher*'s cockpit, thinking about the three months to come. What we had was a deep friendship, and the bond between us was a strong one. The time we had spent together during the year had been special. I had begun to rely on him in many ways, and despite the fact that I had been away at sea for much of the time, he was always there to encourage me, whether by phone, in person, or by e-mail. Ian shared my joy that I was competing in the Vendée. He wanted me to go and he wanted me to do well, and when he told me that he would not worry while I was out there, I knew he meant it.

The day before the start, the storm assaulted Les Sables. Waves broke so high over the harbour wall that the lighthouse at the end of the breakwater disappeared under them. When I went to the base of the breakwater to film with the BBC crew, I was amazed at how battered the waves made the place look. The banners carefully attached all along the breakwater were like rags in the breeze. The wind whipped up the spray under the dark sky with an intimidating wildness. I was glad I could go back to my room, warm up, make a cup of tea, and study the weather in peace.

I gathered up my clothes and placed them in my bags. Then I laid out what I would wear on the start day and put that in a separate pile. I had bought a tiny waterproof case in which I placed a photo of Mum and Dad, my passport, mobile phone, and two credit cards; I hoped I wouldn't be needing any of those, except the photo, until I was back in France again. I rechecked my bags, then my cupboard—that was everything. I took a final look through the latest weather fax that had come through, then crawled into bed beside Ian. My mind was full of a million things, but I felt calm here. His hand reached over and stroked my head, and though I said nothing, I felt a tear run onto the pillow. This was the last night I would be able to close my eyes and sleep soundly until dawn. As I drifted to sleep, I comforted myself with the thought of the sleep in a warm bed that would be waiting for me when I finished.

CHAPTER SIXTEEN

DANA HAD BEEN FANTASTIC and organized everything. In the end, Mum
and Dad flew out to Les Sables d'Olonne to see me off, even though we
had already said our goodbyes days earlier. I knew it would mean so
much to them to see us leave. Soon after waking on the morning of the
start, 9 November 2000, I went to see them for a final chat. They were
in the apartment at the end of the corridor, and as I walked along it my
footsteps echoed. I knocked, and Mum opened the door; both she and
Dad smiled, but I could see the expectant expressions on their faces as
they waited to see first how I would react. As I walked in, I could not
help but feel that they looked lost and almost vulnerable. Their clothes
were all packed away as if they'd been waiting, ready to be granted their
five minutes. When you are concentrating so hard on what you're doing,
it's easy to forget what the consequences are for those around you. Despite their inevitable anxiety, I knew that the last thing Mum and Dad
wanted to do was hold me back; they were confident that I had it inside
me to do it and were aware of how much I had dreamed of the moment
about to arrive.

I wanted to say goodbye properly before we were on the pontoons,
and as I hugged each of them I held up a brave face, assuring them that
we really were ready. I thought it would be great just to skip this goodbye bit and go, as it would be less painful for everyone. I kept telling myself that I wasn't saying goodbye but just "See you soon"—and somehow
the tears stayed back.

As I climbed on board *Kingfisher* that morning, the atmosphere was subdued. There were visitors everywhere, but no noise—almost an acknowledgment of what lay ahead, a kind of reverential feeling for those twenty-four boats. I wanted to see each skipper in turn to wish them a safe voyage, and Mark had suggested I give out stress balls, each of which I signed along with a message to each skipper. I just knew I had to make contact with all of them before we left. There was a heavy drizzle as I either dodged along the pontoons or ferried around from boat to boat in the RIB. I almost missed Catherine Chabaud, with whom I had a particularly strong connection, and when she spotted me just as her boat *Whirlpool* was heading away from the pontoons, she yelled at one of the harbour guys to pick me up in the Zodiac. We hugged and wished each other the best for the months ahead, before I was whisked back to the melee on the pontoons. There was a special goodbye from the guys on *Aquitaine Innovations*, and Yves, with his stress ball in one hand, looked me squarely in the eye and raised his index finger to emphasize his words: "If I don't win, you have to win, and if you don't win, I have to win." We kissed and I left.

When I handed his stress ball to the fifty-nine-year-old Pasquale de Gregorio, he smiled. I said, "See you when you get back." "I doubt you'll be around," he replied, believing I'd be long gone by the time he finished. But I knew that I would do everything in my power to see every skipper as they arrived back in Les Sables d'Olonne. I wanted to be there for each of them.

The emotion in the air was physical, but the reactions among the skippers were different; although everyone was outwardly calm, each of us wished we were already out there. As Mark and I walked along the pontoon with our arms round each other, I have no recollection of what we said to each other. His eyes were red and sore, but like everyone, he was keeping his emotions in check—the finish would be the time to let them go. He held me tight beneath his arm, his head pressed against mine. We had been through so much together, just so much—and now we had reached that moment and felt numbed by its intensity. I knew as we walked that although we would be apart for the next three months, Mark would live every second of the race with me. His mobile would never be switched off, and he would never take a night's sleep without thinking about how I was out there. I think he had the worst of it just waiting for that phone to ring, waiting for the voice on the other end, wondering whether it would be happy, worried, frightened, or exhausted. At worst, there might be no voice at all. The waiting game would be a harsh one to play.

Marie and Pipo were there waiting by the boat with Mathilde and her little brother, Pilou, and as I reached down to kiss Mathilde, I realized she knew what I was about to embark on. She grasped her Barbie doll tight in her right hand, and a little tear ran down her face as she hugged me.

"A bientôt, Mathilde," I said. "See you soon . . . "

Without a doubt the most openly emotional goodbye was with Erik, our cameraman. He hugged me harder than I think I had ever been hugged before, and sobbed into my shoulder. I tried calmly to tell him that everything would be all right, knowing but not saying that none of us knew for sure, and trying to reassure him nearly sent me over the edge. It was a stark manifestation of how close to the surface people's feelings were that morning.

I climbed back on board *Kingfisher* and looked round, but there was no sign of Mum and Dad. Although we had said our goodbyes, I hoped they would come down. I wanted them to know that I was OK and ready to leave. I popped below, scanning the cabin to check that all was well and that we were ready to go. Then I stripped off my wet jeans and put on my thermals. I passed the jeans to Ian, who promised he'd wash them for when I got back. He pushed a hard-boiled egg and an apple into my hand; I hadn't wanted any breakfast that morning, and he knew I wouldn't have eaten anything since then. As I took it and popped it into my pocket, I noted that the egg was still warm. I wished it would stay that way until I saw him again.

Martin Carter stuck his head round the cabin door and said that Mum and Dad were there. I'd been sure that they would come and that they would have waited until the last minute so they did not get in the way. I hugged Mum first, wrapping my arms round her and losing myself momentarily as I buried my face in her long black hair. Dad then hugged me firmly, giving me a firm pat on the back, as he always did. I looked up at his face and could see that he was proud, but I could also see the pain and the worry. I had done well thus far not getting emotional, but as he kissed me on my forehead, I knew it had to be for the last time. I gave

him a firm squeeze and turned away. As I looked back to give them a final wave, they had their backs to me. My heart went out to them—they
were being so brave. I felt so proud of them, too.

Things felt easier as soon as we slipped our lines from the dock and
headed slowly down the long channel to the sea. Most of the team were
still on board or alongside in the RIB. As we were towed along, the walls
were packed with people cheering "Ell-en; Ell-en; Ell-en"—I could only
hope that it would be a great race for them, too. Ian was on deck with a
video camera in his hands; he did not look up, and I knew that his way of
handling the situation was to keep himself busy. It was an unreal experience, anyway. I felt that the crowds were there not just to celebrate our
departure but to share in it, also. It was their race, too. There was a fasci-
nation with what we were about to do, as if we were astronauts or ex-
plorers, but in the Vendée there was a subtle difference—we were going
out into the unknown to race.

As I steered *Kingfisher* towards the harbour entrance, my mind was on
getting out to sea . . . and safely. I'm not sure I allowed myself to think
too hard about what we were setting off to do. With Mark, Ian, and the
guys still on board, it was easy to pretend otherwise. I suppressed the
thought that in an hour's time they would all be gone.

It became more peaceful once we edged our way out to the start
zone. The cheering drifted away on the wind, and we could hear our
own voices once more. Perversely, I was less focused then than for the
single-handed transatlantic or any other start—perhaps concentrating
too much on spending the last few precious minutes in people's company had taken my mind off it. I gave Ian a massive hug and a kiss, which
Mark captured on the boat's digital camera. It was a picture I looked at
many times during the following months. The moment didn't last,
though, as we were soon joined by the fleet of boats which had come out
to see us off. The water was getting hectic, churned into a confused
mess, and we had to take care hoisting the mainsail and stowing the lines
away. As we did so, the RIB drew alongside; it was time for the guys to
go. Only Pipo, Martin, Mark, and Ian were still on board, and as they
walked in turn to climb over the rails for the last time, I hugged them
tightly and felt the nerves really kick in. I think that the hour that followed their departure was probably the loneliest of the race. They were
all still close and I could see them, but I couldn't touch them and I knew

there wouldn't be another chance to do so until we returned.

I just wished that they would disappear in a flash, so I'd never have to look into their eyes or wave for that final time.

AS THE START GUN FIRED, I was angry with myself. We had not put up the code 5, as I had suggested earlier, before being encouraged to calm down, and it would have been the perfect sail for heading off to our first mark. Michel Desjoyeaux led the fleet out of the start zone by heading north up the coast. I worked hard over the following minutes, hoisting the code 5, and sailed around our first mark. It was incredible—we had 23,000 miles to race and were already fighting for position as if we were just racing along the coast. As the last waves and shouts came from the team, I was already thinking of rounding Finisterre . . .

That first night was a tough one, sailing in light airs yet still with the horrible swell from the storm. I don't think any of the skippers slept much that night, whether it was from the noises coming off the snatching ropes or the mixture of anticipation and apprehension at heading out into the open ocean for three months. During the night, as I was working on the computer, it finally hit me: This is it, I'm doing the Vendée Globe. Better get on with it, I thought!

There was sobering news in the morning as I called in to the first chat session with race HQ. Mike Golding, undoubtedly one of the race favourites, had been towed back into Les Sables. Late that night, he had just changed sails and was standing in his hatchway looking up when suddenly there was a loud crack and his mast came tumbling down. When I heard the news, I felt numb. Mike had been preparing for this race since I was working on the 50-footer in Cherbourg, when Merv had played such a big part in his early preparations. He must have been absolutely devastated—he had been out there to win.

Kingfisher and I came out of the first night in thirteenth position, which disappointed me, but positions change quickly in these situations, particularly if you're rounding a corner, as we were. I was astonished to learn that Bilou (Roland Jourdain) had also been forced to turn back. He had broken the halyard that held up the gennaker and at the same time smashed a tooth. He had returned for a middle-of-the-night pit stop with a dentist and a halyard maker! By 5 A.M., he was out again and on a mission! My only problem had been squashing my finger beneath one of the ballast valve handles as I leaned my whole weight on it to push it down. It throbbed like mad and instantly began to turn black—stupid.

On our first day at sea, I thought a lot about the team. I knew that on the evening of the start, they all would have been out to celebrate making it through stage 1—a successful start. A few days later, though, by the time I was around Cape Finisterre, they would all scatter, returning to their different lives. Martin and his wife, Amanda would return to New Zealand, Mum and Dad would fly home, Mark would go off to the French Alps. I hated the thought of their splitting up after all we'd been through together, but life had to go on. Anyway, I thought, I would soon be closer to Martin and Amanda in New Zealand.

Martin had given me the Maori charm he always wore around his neck. He had never taken it off since Amanda gave it to him before they were married; now it was around my neck and was going to stay there until we crossed the finish line. Marie had given me a tiny metal pulley which she had worn around her neck for more than ten years, and I'd promised her I would bring it back as fast as I could.

I was having one of those mornings—as I opened my log book, I found a long message from Merv. There was so much of him in *Kingfisher*. I just hoped that for his sake, and that of the entire design team, I could do justice to their efforts. His message ended:

> In the background or the foreground I'm always there.
> Keep safe and come back to all of us who love you. Sail
> fast, sail hard, sail safe
> Your best mate—always
> Love
> Merv xx
> PS. And for f***'s sake clip on!

I knew that I was in no way alone on this venture. There were many hearts and souls with me, following each day. Things were going to be OK out there . . .

10/11/00 (ellenmacarthur.com/day2)
Position 44° 51.8N 006° 48.1W
Heading/speed 264 0
Wind from 219 at 13.1 knots

Pressure of 1016
Sea temperature 10
Sail configuration is Full main Genoa
Percentage performance 90

Tonight the moon is out, the sky close to clear—glazing the deck
with moonlight. We're close hauled on Port tack, and with a wind
shift in our favour we're now heading towards finisterre.

All is well on board, I feel very relaxed, happy in my daily chores
and dofeel glad to be out here ondce again, even if this is for the big
one.

Spoke to Uncle Glyn today, to ask him if I should stick a burning
hot wire through my fingernail to release a bit of pressure as it was
black after I trapped it last night. The answer was yes—although he
did point out that someone would normally do it for you . . . oh
well—not the first time! He was right though, although a little sore
it didn't hurt much—and the blood spurted out, leaving a still sore,
but less painfullly hrobbing finger. THis morning I was alongside
WHIRLPOOL, GARTMORE and SOLIDAIRES. It's been a day of
tactical sailing—tacking on the shifts, and watching the wind
direction minute by minute. Our positions are changing on an
hourly basisright now—so I'm just concentrating on the best speed
in the best direction . . . II've slept well today, and some tonight
already. THough an hour period with 4 or 5 dozes would be classed
as a great sleep!

Looking forward to the sunrise tomorrow, and hoping that the
dolphins come past as they did when the sun set . . .

This is it kiddo.

a donf!

ellenx

I surprised myself that after the first difficult day I really did feel OK
out there. I did not have that desperate feeling I'd had through the 1 Star,
and I felt on top of the decisions that were being taken by the rest of the
fleet. Yves and Mich had taken an early lead which did not surprise me,
but after our magical night, the position report came in to show that I
was in third place. This was good news, but I knew the boats that were
farther offshore would begin to catch up quickly. It began to dawn on
me as we prepared to turn left for the first time how long we would be

out there, but I was excited—it was a massive challenge, and I honestly felt I was as ready for the race as I ever had been, and was just looking forward to putting into practice all the skills I had learnt. I sent a short e-mail to Mark to reassure him, and I thanked goodness that I felt better than in the 1 Star.

But as the fleet rounded Finisterre, we got a good old hammering. The breeze increased violently as the front came through, and the conditions were tough, with a freezing wind, and a fine rain which felt like pins sticking in your eyes as you tried to squint into the breeze. There was also a lot of shipping, which was always a background worry, and as I clung to the foredeck changing down to Kingfisher's storm jib, my world shrank to what was illuminated in the pool of light from my head torch. Several times I was hurled into the air so violently that I landed on deck, grabbing the rails. I made sure I was clipped on, though, and was glad I weighed 9 stone, rather than 12!

I tried to doze in the cuddy waiting for the wind shift that would allow us to plough on towards the south, but I was damp and cold, my only comfort being a pair of mittens I wore to keep the chill from them. When the wind eventually changed, and just before it reached 50 knots, I had problems fighting with the daggerboards, as with the hammering into the waves the down-haul line had jammed, which meant I had to go forward with a screwdriver to force it back into its conduit. When eventually we were able to tack, I breathed a sigh of relief, but we were sailing incredibly uncomfortably into the swell—and fast. If ever there was a break-boat situation because of sea conditions, this was it. The motion with the new wind direction was atrocious, as we literally fell off each wave, and I felt sick inside as I heard one of the sets of shelves below give way beneath the weight of the boxes stacked on it. I picked up the upturned boxes, took a quick look at the damage, and saw immediately that it was going to be a nasty repair. Sorry, Kingfisher, I thought. Cape Finisterre was certainly living up to its tough reputation.

14/11/00 02:49Z (ellenmacarthur.com/day6)
Well it's uite beutiful out here, though the wind is quite variable.
The moon orse at the begginning if the evening—making the first
our of darkness very black. THere are several cargo ships around,
one just passed behind me—heading out into the midst of the

Atlantic. Funny as he headed west I felt a little surge of excitiement for him, that he was off once agaoin on another passage.

The wind despite it's variability in strength has come round once more to the NW which I am pleased with. My course is much better, and my hesitation to put up the spinnaker was right. Just ahd the longest sleep of the race, feel a bit sleepy, but I think after the ahammering off finisterre my body needs to recover a little. My eyes are still sore, and my body aches, but inside I feel fine—just want to keep on trucking! Dissappointed at slipping back in the position reports, and after the light patch I just wen through I fear I shall have slipped back some more—though yesterday evenig things were looking much better—I was in 5th . . .

Oh well—time to send this, hope you are all well back at home. Funny it seems for a while now that time has stopped. It's wonderful to be here at the chart table litening to the water passing under her hull. The little red glow from her instruments, and a bit earlier, dare I say it. I had a 20 minute session of TOm Jones! Fantastic . . .

X

Conditions stabilized well once the seas had calmed down, and we began our gybing match down to the Canaries. Though we had to pass to the north of several points in the Southern Ocean, the Canaries were our only waypoint until we were in those freezing conditions. It was an opportunity to concentrate on the weather in that area. Behind the islands is a renowned patch of ocean—along with intense heat from Africa, you can find yourself starved of winds closer inshore. Things were still looking good, though—we were powering along, holding 5th place—but then the unthinkable happened. I was dozing in the cuddy for 20 minutes, and during that time a squall came over. I woke to feel *Kingfisher* accelerate, then broach, and our world fell on its side. I blew the mainsheet and the code 5 sheet whilst trying to bear away, but the code 5 sheet burnt off its cover and jammed on the winch—and as I reached a second time to free it, the sail blew out. I could have cried with anger and frustration. Seven days into the race—and already we had lost a sail. Without sails we go nowhere, and as they are so specialized these days, we can be hammered in certain conditions without one. I fought to get its skeleton down, cursing myself for having let this happen and at the same time thanking God I had a backup. Any self-pity soon disappeared with the news that Belgian skipper Patrick de Radigues had been knocked unconscious during a gybe, and he woke as his boat hit a beach on the Portuguese coast. Miraculously, he'd managed to hit the only beach for miles along a rocky coast, but his dream for the Vendée was shattered.

15/11/00 22:58Z (ellenmacarthur.com/day7)
Position 28° 19.6N 016° 04.4W
Heading/speed 276 12.43
Wind from 52 at 15.5 knots
Pressure of 1014
Sea temperature 16.3
Sail configuration is Full main Code 5
Percentage performance 98.6

Well it seemed a bit strange to sail once again pst the canary islands. the lsat time I was here it was just over 3 years gao, and I was with my Mini Transat boat, about to turn into port. And now—once again to see those lights, butthis time to carry on. An incredible and exciting feeling.

I didn't excpect to be in 3rd either, especially after the previous nights problems with the code 5—amazing what you have to sacrifice for a couple of places! The guys in the motor boat patrolling the waypoint zone were superb, They said so many wonderful things, and almost sounded more excited than I at my position! Wonderful . . .

Tactically I think I was lucky to get ahead of Marc T Hercelin, I would have favoured the offshore option too at the beginning, but seeing the barometer fluctuate wass good news, and did indicate that I wasn't about to be becalmed with the hot African air!

Anyway—dont want to spend too much time below—as there are a number of baots around. I just want to be away from the land again!
night,
ex

There was more good news by this stage, though. Mike Golding had been able to have his spare mast shipped over from the UK and had restarted the race. I thought a great deal about Mike during the following days. For him the race was about winning. He had already sailed around the world three times and it took real guts to do what he did, to sail back out of a quiet Les Sables and an empty channel to restart a week later—I respected him enormously for it.

On board, the winds were getting stronger as we sailed into the trade winds. Living on board became markedly more stressful, as with each wave you flew down, you held your breath. We broke a batten in the mainsail during the night—though I don't know how it happened. The only remedy was to drop the sail completely and repair it. My to-do list was getting longer.

16/11/00 22:17Z (ellenmacarthur.com/day8)
Position 23° 39.0N 020° 02.2W
Heading/speed 224 15
Wind from 78 at 24.3 knots
Pressure of 1016 Rough
Sea temperature 12.8
Sail configuration is 1st reef Code 5
Percentage performance 94.2

Hi—what a day!
Well the kettles on, and there's that gentle hissing of the gas burning away . . . Sounds tranquil if it weren't for the violent motion, and screaming surfs!
Today has been a sleigh ride . . . Non stop surfing, averag ing speeds of over 15 knots, and surfs (even on the autopilot) at over 22!!
I was glad to be away from the Canaries and into open Ocean. It's funny how confined you feel when close to land . . . RIght now it is dark once more, and there is that constant "shaking" motion as we hurtle down, across and through the waves.
I spent atleast 4 hours helming today. Not only as it's faster, bt actually an amazing feeling. AS you ride up to the top of the wave and look over the next ti's like being pushed off the top of a hill on a brake-less bike . . . There's simply no stopping you. KINGFISHER is handling fantastically, the autopilot struggles in the waves, but we're doing Ok. As I came down below I saw a avigation light on my port side. I believe it was Marc Thercelin, in ACTIVE WEAR. He

overtook last night aftert the islands, so if it is him, it's a great
feeling to be back up there. It's both exhilerating and frightening
(JUST SURFED AT 23.3knots!!) I have my legs jammed under the
chart table to hold my self in, the whole boat feels like she is one of
those fairground rides which show you a picture of a ski slope and
shake you around—though here it's pitch black—there's a fire
hydrant on you, and it's not over in 3 minutes! THinking very Much
of Mike Golding and his problems right now. It seemed just so unfair
. . . Losing your mast on the first night, Time to go—paella should
be rehydrated by now—might be time for a damp nap in the cuddy!
night,
ex

Except for negotiating the Cape Verdes about 500 miles west of Sene-
gal, we were pretty much now on the direct route for the Equator, but I
still wanted to make more progress to the west. Although the Equator is
a fickle place, one rule of thumb generally works: the farther west you
cross it, the more consistent the breeze will be. While approaching the
islands, I decided to go for a more westerly option. Although the final
position report of the day showed that no one had gone for it, I held my
breath and gybed onto a course which was not far off 90 degrees to the
route. News had come that day that Bernard Stamm, the Swiss skipper,
had retired, forced to pull into the Cape Verdes after breaking his tiller.
We were experiencing testing conditions on the way south, and although many feel that it is easier to go downwind, it is actually more
dangerous. Although you sail faster, you are also closer to the edge—and
the Southern Ocean could be the classic example of this.

I knew that the following morning, the results would be painful, but
at the end of the day, I had already dropped to eighth position. Whereas
the others had gone for speed and sailed higher, I had tried to stay as
deep as possible to keep to the west. The wind intensified during the
night, and I hand-steered for a while, keeping up the code 5 to sail
deeper and faster to the west. My worries were confirmed, though:
when the positions came in, we were sitting fourteenth. Now we were
just going to have to sail for our lives.

The sea temperature was up to over 20 degrees, and life on board was
getting fairly uncomfortable. Frustratingly, however, our gybe had
shown that there was a 6-degree difference in the readings from the two

temperature sensors—a bit of a problem, as I knew how important sea temperature would be once we plunged into the south. It's not much fun sitting down below sweating, especially when you charge the batteries for a couple of hours. The cabin turns into a sauna, and you can't even open the hatches because of the risk of waves coming into the boat. . . . Rather unexpectedly, despite being alone at sea, I was also living with the danger of being smacked in the chops! We were now well into flying-fish territory, and the frightened little things would leap out of the water—sometimes hitting the boat, sometimes passing over. I'm afraid it is instant death for a number of them, and you find the odd eye which has popped out staring at you from the cockpit floor. But the majority land relatively unscathed on the decks and make the most terrible racket as they desperately flap their wings and slap their tails in search of water. I'm a sucker for wildlife, though—every time I heard one flapping on deck, whether at night or by day, I would always lift the poor thing back into the water; I could not bear to hear them struggling. Many skippers actually ate them; having tried them myself, I knew they were good eating, but I couldn't bring myself to do it. Even though I knew I had to eat, my appetite was never that great!

19/11/00 01:54Z (ellenmacarthur.com/day10)
Position 15° 03.0N 026° 54.5W
Heading/speed 223 13.47
Wind from 79 at 17.8 knots
Pressure of 1012 Moderate
Sea temperature 15.4
Sail configuration is Full main Code 5
Percentage performance 104

Well we seem to be doing OK . . . I don't think we could be sailing any fast er in this direction anyway! THe wind seems to have shifted more into the east for the night, but progress is very good, and like this we will not be losing grond to the west. If in the morning our course is too westward we can reach back to the east—but once ground is lost to the west it's gybng to get back down there, and gybing is slow . . .

Spirit's are up, as word from the others is of there problems to get further west. They are in a NEl'y flow of air, and will have to gybe down through it to get out to their west. Maybe my severe drop in the classement was not so bad after all. 4th to 10th could be getting better—touch wood. (IN fact I have several pieces of wood inside KINGFISHER. There is the piece of [Kauri] wood engraved with "Built in New Zealand by the team at Marten Yachts" (thanks guys!!) and piece of oak tree from my gran's field which Dad has made into a pencil holder fo me, with a hundered year old threp'ny bit embedded in it—which was the name of my first ever boat . . .)

The approach to the Equator is looking a little complicated—though never a simple zone to cross. The HP of the Azores and the HP of Saint Helena are both weak (the main N ans S hemisphere HP systems)—which leaves the Doldrums as a less concentrated band, with several tropical waves rolling through, and large disturbing cloud masses.

The game is to cross it at it's narrowest point—easy to say, but harder to carry out, as this windless band is drifting daily.

On board things are generally well. THe code 5 came down for a couple of hours and I went into Genoa mode shortly after sailing through the lee of the Cape Verde's. Now though it's back to code 5—whick—excluding this two hours has been flying since the disaster with the other.

I feel well, thoguh my hands are covered in tiny, but incredibly sore little salt sores . . . . Nothing seems to be able to get rid of them once they're there, and the hotter weather is not helping . . . They need to stay dry and cool—two impossible factors on a 60 foot baking oven! THese boats (and it's begiinning now) do get incredibly hot arunnd the equator . . . THe hot sun above us bakes down onteh deck, heating our airtight living pods like a greenhouse . . .

ANyway—time to go and trim those sails—I sense a wee change in the wind.
More later.
love
ellenxx

I made the most of the relatively stable conditions during the day to attempt the repair of the shelving unit, though it was one of the most miserable jobs imaginable. With no ventilation in the cabin, the heat was sweltering. Merv had prepared a special repair kit, but sanding and cutting carbon, with dust sticking to my sweat, was itchy and uncomfortable. And it took hours to complete. I was so black and sweaty afterwards that I looked like a coal miner. I would have preferred to attempt it at night, but with the frequent thunder and lightning clouds we were now seeing, it would be too dangerous. The only bonus was that it took my mind off worrying about race positions. We were playing a lottery with the winds here in the Doldrums, and as I'm not a practiced gambler, the strain was taking its toll. I cleaned up after fixing the shelf and rewarded myself by putting on a brand-new vacuum-packed T-shirt, and though I'm certainly not fussy about luxuries, it felt great! I also thought I should try to do something about the sores on my hands; having spent five hours wearing tight rubber gloves had left them more swollen than ever. I called Uncle Glyn to ask for his advice, and he suggested I scrub them with pure alcohol and a toothbrush. As I scrubbed, the skin split apart, draining the fluid which had built up inside. It stung like mad, but it certainly seemed to relieve the soreness afterwards.

We were approaching the zone with little wind now, and I was aware that in reality there was little we could do other than try to get south as fast as possible. We had picked our longitude to cross and were beginning to pull up to the rest of the fleet.

> 22/11/00 01:49Z (ellenmacarthur.com/day14)
> Position 05° 18.5N 026° 24.5W
> Heading/speed 175 1.43
> Wind from 113 at 4.5 knots
> Pressure of 1018
> Sea temperature 16.7
> Sail configuration is Full main Genoa
> Percentage performance 25.6

Well—another still night, but this time thw horribleist swell, and a struggling 2 knots. Just seen the mst astonishing thing . . . a satellite I guess—coming hurtling sown to earth. It lit up the clouds like lightning —before heading into the water—seemingly becoming more and more orangy. Extraordinary—I thought I was dreaming!

I have slept a wee bit tonight though Ithink I shall have a few more 10 minuters . . . THe engine's on charging, and I don't really want to stay in the cabin. Feeling very relaxed—even despite several

hours on the deck tonight trying to get the girl going. Looking
forward to finding these SE trads . . . and pleased that however
briefly, we've moved up the fleet to 3rd. I can't think that anyone has
sailed more slpwly than us in the last 6 hours!
night night,
a donf! Ellenx

By morning the wind had lightened, and we really were heading into
the Doldrums. Although it was imperative to sail through there as fast as
we could, I also knew it was a good opportunity to make repairs if the
wind dried up completely—there wouldn't be many more chances before we entered the Southern Ocean. As if on cue, once I had organized
all the tools for the jobs that needed doing, it rained, and the wind vanished. Go for it, I thought, and lowered the mainsail. I worked frantically,
scurrying across *Kingfisher*'s decks, dashing below for bits and pieces.
With the tiny blowtorch, I melted three extra holes in the sail around her
third reef, so that in storms water could run off rather than sit and collect
there. I replaced the batten and put some extra patches on the sail where
it touched the spreader, and the second I had finished, I set about the ten
minutes it took to rehoist her sail. Onto the winch it was! Once I had finished, I was elated at having completed everything on the mainsail. I then
set about working on her mainsheet and jib sheets, changing a block over
and protecting others, then putting Spectra covers on the working parts
of the ropes, where wear would be the greatest. It was a wonderful feeling to complete the entire task list, and I gave *Kingfisher* a great pat on her
coach-roof as I packed away all our tools.

Now we were ready to head south, and she seemed pleased. A few
minutes after I finished up, the wind increased, and we sailed from beneath that enormous rain cloud towards the Equator, crossing the line
the following night. It was a special feeling charging along in a T-shirt
and shorts in the middle of the night, the moon shining bright above us. I
switched on the floodlight in her cockpit and talked to the camera. I had
four tiny bottles of champagne on board for such occasions—one for
the Equator on the way south, one for the Cape of Good Hope, one for
Cape Horn, and one for the Equator on the way north. I opened the first
bottle, and as I tipped a little over the side for Neptune, a little on *Kingfisher*'s deck for her, and drank a little myself, I spoke to the camera:

"First of all, thanks, Neptune, for letting us safely cross once again; thanks, *Kingfisher*, for bringing us this far and looking after me; and here's to every other boat in the fleet coming safely across this line going to the south and coming back from the south. . . ."

But while we were going well, the second half of my wish had not been granted—the following day I received news of yet another retirement. Eric Dumont, who had finished fourth in the previous Vendée Globe, had serious rudder damage and had not managed to find a way to repair it. The fleet was already thinning out.

> 26/11/00 03:20Z (ellenmacarthur.com/day18)
> Position 08° 13.6S 029° 44.2W
> Heading/speed 194 11.33
> Wind from 117 at 13.2 knots
> Pressure of 1017
> Air temperature
> Sea temperature 16
> Sail configuration is Full main Genoa
> Percentage performance 99.5

> I've changed the way I sail KINGFISHER today—trying some thing different. THings feel a bit better on board, mand my moral is a bit better than the last couple of days. Not that I've been too gloomy— but things do seem to be looking up. Hopefully in the mornign position report we'll at least be holing or own. . . . TIme will tell.
> The sunset tonight was stunning—bright orange—masked by a quite cloudy horizon—the clouds almost becoming silhouettes . . .
> Tonight—for the first time my salt sores are getting better, and I've had a couple of good hour long sleeps . . . THere are ship's around though, adn I'm only 300 miles from the coast of Brazil—so I'm keeping an alarmed and physical eye out!
> night night for the rest of it!
> ex

We were now pretty much on the upwind motorway and would be on the same tack for almost 2,000 miles. . . . I was hoping that *Kingfisher* would excel in these conditions, as she had been competitive in the Europe 1 New Man Star against the others. I was lying in fifth position, with Catherine Chabaud ahead and Bilou just having taken third place. Behind me was a little more space, though—there was a clear 60 miles before Thierry Dubois, Thomas Coville, Marc Thiercelin, and Dominique Wavre, who were all, incredibly, within just a few miles of each other. Tactics had been very interesting crossing the Equator: Catherine had passed the farthest east and encountered few problems, which surprised me. Theoretically, now through the equatorial zone and with it to her east, she was in a great position to take miles from us all—it just depended how close she would end up sailing to the centre of the St. Helena high-pressure system. It looked like it had been a good decision.

27/11/00 09:02Z (ellenmacarthur.com/day19)
Position 11° 58.1S 029° 56.8W
Heading/speed 208 13.79
Wind from 107 at 15 knots
Pressure of 1018
Sea temperature 16
Sail configuration is Full main Genoa
Percentage performance 104.9

Well it's been a very noisy and windy night. The wind picked up to 23 knots yesterday evening—so at least if nothing else we're sailing quickly, and are looking in good shape for entry into the Southern Ocean . . .
    Spent the whole day just about yesterday studying the weather—reading more about he HP, the Southern Ocean Lows etc . . . etc . . . The weather was very stable yewsterday, and I went for a different combination with Genoa and one reef in the main. She seemed much more balanced, and I was pleased with my determination to keep changing things. Yesterday it seemed to pay. In the position reports last nihgt I seem to have closed in on Bilou's latitude—so I'm feeling fiarly pleased . . .
    This moorning the wind seems to be dying a little—but I shall come up in prder to passst o the east of the Isle of Trinidade.
    Will work more on the weather again today, and try to get some sleep. IT's already getting cooler down below, which is a godsend, and makes everything on board much easier to do. Better make the most of it though! Soon there will be little chance of getting a tan!
exx

Although we were still several thousand miles from the Southern Ocean, it's incredible how much of my focus was on it. These days were the last we would have for more than fifty in anything like clement weather, with a relatively steady breeze. In the trade winds, there are squalls and sail changes, but on the whole, things are more settled. It's essential to rest as much as possible before entering the south. I was already adjusting to it, finding I was sleeping in longer bursts. It seemed to be a subconscious preparation for a phase of the race I knew was going to be harder than I could imagine. The south can be an incredibly beautiful place, with amazing long swells and surfing conditions, but no one should ever go there without total respect for it. Although those I have met who have been there say it is the most incredible place, I have also known people who have not, and nearly not, come back from it.

There is no room for error. Those who come out first will be the ones who can best handle its harsh environment. But there will always be that element of risk. No one can stop a freak wave from turning a boat over, no matter how well it was prepared for the race. I wrote in my daily log:

> *This race shall be won by the most reliable boat ... that which*
> *can push enough, for long enough—but keep things together ...*

We had already covered more than a fifth of the race, but the pace at which we were running was hellish. We were not just pushing, but pushing hard. Just how long could we keep it up? I was critically aware that now was the chance to go over *Kingfisher* from top to bottom with a fine-toothed comb, to make sure everything was as OK as possible for the south. Each day I would do general checks, but soon that in itself would be more dangerous. I did a lot of work during these days on the autopilot, which had already let me down on a couple of occasions by simply cutting out, and although I tried various options to fix it, it was still a mystery. I was all too conscious of the fact that with a single-handed race, the autopilot is everything, and losing it is one of the biggest fears. Likewise, with no power you have no pilot, and without it you simply cannot carry on. On modern race boats you cannot just lash the helm; they need computers to control them, especially since we sail at such high speeds.

There was also the rig check to do, scaling the mast to look for any signs of wear or problems. It was not the easiest job, but the sea was relatively flat, so I grabbed the opportunity. It's not easy to do it alone, as the boat never wants to sit still, and there's no one to winch you up or ease you down, so just getting up and down is tricky. Like climbers, we use jumars, hand-held brakes that can be slid up a rope but grip tight when pulled down. These enabled me to climb while always attached, but they had their disadvantages—they made getting down incredibly difficult. Not losing your grip on the mast is one of the hardest of tasks, but holding onto the mast as well as lowering a jumar is tough to say the least!

On my first attempt I discovered a problem with the genoa stay, which meant I had to go back up. As I was already tired from the first ascent, this was frustrating, but things got worse when the wind rose while I was at the top and *Kingfisher* heeled—any more wind and I could have walked down her mainsail! Once on the deck, I furled the genoa, unfurled the solent, and prepared my tools for the second ascent. All was well and *Kingfisher* was much more stable, so I climbed up once more and attacked the job. The problem came when I was ready to go down and realized that I had forgotten the second jumar, so I had to climb down from three-quarters of the way up the 90-foot mast completely unattached. I berated myself for being so stupid. I just could not afford that kind of carelessness.

I guess it was no different from what the old clipper crews did, day in and day out, but at least there were other guys around to scrape them up off the deck if they fell. My body went into overdrive, my hands clenched white-fisted around the rigging. It was a huge relief to make it back down, and even more so five minutes later when the pilot cut out and I was right there to grab the helm—thank God it hadn't happened ten minutes earlier. . . .

02/12/00 07:33Z (ellenmacarthur.com/day24)
Position 32° 11.7S 017° 44.0W
Heading/speed 200 9.84
Wind from 339 at 11 knots
Pressure of 1017
Sea temperature 12
Sail configuration is Full main Spinnaker
Percentage performance 98.9

Well the sun is rising once again, and unlike the leading boats in the fleet we seem to have escaped for the moment the front which is lying across the southern Atlantic Ocean. A night with two gybes, though I am a little concerned I have not gained enough to the south . . . we shall see shortly.

The front is in the stages of dissipating as a new low forms to the west. Yesterday we had the beginnings of a huge swell, which is asure sign that wind is on it's way. The sea has changed once again—to a darker inkier blue, the stars are progressively more and more the stars of the SOuthern Hemisphere, and as if a symbol for our entry into the SOuth the moon is back, each night showing more and more it's beauty. Last night the silvery flickers on the water were so incredibly gentle, such a dusting of beauty on a sea which looks so desceptively peaceful . . . like nothing could disturb its steady motion.

Yesterday was a day of work again. Several tactical gybes on the wind shifts to try to edge our way into the South—adn more checks. I checked all the compartments for water and dried out the sail stowage area. Bypassed part of the pilot system to try to solve our niggling problem (so far good news!). I also cheked cabling for chafe—and stowed away my second bag of rubbish! Yesterday was a day of good spirits, with a few naps and a bit of dancing to a Santana CD. Only days now before the thought of dancing as the sun sets seems a long way away.

Soon we shall cross this dissipating area, and plunge down into the south . . . where we shal stay for roughly 50 days. THe sleigh-ride round the South Pole shall not be easy. Extreme care is needed to avoid icebergs; and managing the storms as they hurl themselves over us will be a 24 hr job. I am looking forward to the South, though I am exrremely wary, and reespectful of it's danger. In my mind the SOuth is almost the start of the race. IT's the "entrance" to home—and from here we're off—we all hope—for Cape Horn. Till tomorrow . . .

exx

Although I knew that I would never stop learning, I had already learnt so much. The previous night, when I had gained miles on the rest of the fleet by choosing my gybing time carefully, I really felt that I had a handle on what I was doing. I was watching the satellite pictures like a hawk.

When the model came through at 0000Z (midnight), I knew what to do—it was a wonderful feeling, I just hoped that I could keep up the good decisions. Although conditions here were still relatively stable, we were sailing with our spinnaker, so I always slept or dozed with my eyes half open. When I woke, I would instantly jump up to check that the spinnaker was OK and that we didn't have a wrap around the forestay. The spinnaker is not the easiest sail to handle or get down in a hurry when alone, so I had to be really careful, never sleeping far from its sheets.

That morning I was startled by the flapping of sailcloth; with my heart in my mouth I ran to the bow to investigate. It was obvious what had happened. The metal ring in the corner of the sail had worked through the webbing straps which secured it, and the sail was now flying in the air held only by two corners, looking pathetic—like a sheet hung out to dry in the breeze. I changed it as fast as I could. We'd climbed into fourth place that morning, and I sure as hell was not going to let those miles slip away. I took down the wounded spinnaker, then put up the code 5 and unfurled it, relieved to feel *Kingfisher* pull away once more. I then began a tiring six hours of sewing on the foredeck, finding new webbing and sewing it into the corner of the sail. The cloth was so thick in the corners that I had to push an awl through the sail first to prevent the needle from breaking as I pushed it through. I sang to myself and tried to keep myself happy as I worked away, the occasional droplet of blood dripping onto the deck as my finger was punctured by the needle. I had to do a good job on this one—the loads on the corners of those sails are immense, and I couldn't afford to do a half-baked repair which would break again. As soon as the repair was done I changed sails and returned below.

Tactically it was complex now, too. We were all, or so it appeared, trying to move towards the southeast, but it was a question of negotiating the best route between the systems, with the central aim of getting south into the westerlies first. There was definitely the possibility for some big position changes, and although Yves had stretched away a little, a lot could happen over the next days. In just a day and a half near the centre of the St. Helena high-pressure system, Mich took over 100 miles from Yves. It was as though we were all in the slip lanes of a motorway, and although there was not much room to overtake as we came

into the slow lane, there was always someone who managed to accelerate out into the fast lane and make a gain.

Sadly, I received news of more problems in the fleet. Raphael Dinelli
hit an unidentified object and damaged his keel badly. The Southern
Ocean is the last place to be with suspect equipment, and Raphael
knew this better than most of us; in the previous Vendée, his boat rolled
and sank slowly in a horrendous storm—literally beneath his feet. He
was saved by a life raft dropped from an Australian Orion patrol plane
and by Pete Goss, who turned back in that same storm to find him and
pick him up.

I really felt for Raphael. In the last race, he'd been pretty much as
close to death as you can get, and now, having found the courage to try
again, his race had been ended again. I hoped that he would make it
round, whether in or out of the race. Mike Golding had now passed the
Equator, and though just under 2,000 miles behind, he was going strong.
It must have been so frustrating for him, as he was not in remotely the
same weather system, but I knew that he would give it all he had. Fedor
Konioukhov, too, was now a long way behind—though still a few hundred miles ahead of Mike—and as I plotted his position on my chart, I
hoped he was enjoying his race.

Now almost in the Roaring Forties, we had a welcome reminder that
we were heading down into the unknown—one of its inhabitants . . . the
albatross.

4/12/00 12:20Z (ellenmacarthur.com/day26)
As I sit at the chart table I feel far from alone . . . For above me
hovers a friend . . . Wings outstretched almost as if resting, as he
circles around and around . . . Inquisitive as I enter the cockpit he
comes closer—but almost as if wishing to be invisible to camera he
backs away as I try to film.

  Af few hours ago we gybed . . . A gybe heading amost due south
. . . THe gybe on which to enter the real Southern Ocean. As the
front passed this morning the sky cleared for a while, the sun
lighting the waves in what felt strangely like a rare fashion, so
quickly the feel of this sea has changed. Right now it is colder, the air
and the water. The waves are growing almost hourly, physicaly
picking KINGFISHER up and releasing her down the next slope . . .

like pushing a toboggan at the top of a hill. Incredible to thing that this
is merely the beginning . . . we have not yet passed the 40th parallel.

This morning I felt worse than I ever recall feeling. My body
ached all over—my head felt tired as KINGFISHER violently surfed
endlessley down the waves . . .

Yesterday evening I had been preparing her for the South. Re-
stowing all the boxes, checking coentents, etc. I was under the
cockpit floor happily stowing when iheard a fluttering and felt the
boat slow. Scared that my hand stitching had parted form the kite, I
beat on deck to find that the cloth of the sail had "peeled" it's way
out of the edges of the sail, with about 30 metres of cloth [trailing]
in the water. THen recuperation of the sail took the best part of an
hour—which involved retreiveing the halyard, cutting the sheets
off, hanging over the side with a boathook, and eventually, once the
sail had streamed out away from the boat, pulling the whole shabang
on board—not an easy task as most of it then decided to take off and
fly off in a skyward direction . . . Exhausted, I changed for the
gennaker, then an hour later the genoa . . . I slumped on the chart
table seat—and woke 2 hours later . . .
Exx

05/12/00 01:06Z (ellenmacarthur.com/day27)
Position 40° 05.9S 008° 17.9W
Heading/speed 175 13.9
Wind from 303 at 18.3 knots
Pressure of 1001
Sea temperature 18
Sail configuration is Full main Code 5
Percentage performance 98.6

well, our first nihgt in the 40s . . .

Now in the Roaring Forties, our next objective as far as the rules were
concerned was basically to leave Antarctica to starboard, and the various
waypoints which are placed to keep us from straying too far into the ice.
Over five days, the sea temperature had dropped 13 degrees, and I piled
on extra layers of thermal clothing. The Southern Ocean was upon us,
and whilst we had not yet had a particularly bad storm, I was to be the

first in the fleet to witness the other threat the Southern Ocean has to offer. It was the morning of 8 December, and after an uneasy night of concern I had managed to sleep for a while at daybreak. The wind had been getting progressively stronger over the previous twenty-four hours—it was now at 30 knots. *Kingfisher* needed constant monitoring, as we were not past the centre of the depression, and I was expecting a further increase in the wind strength.

I had been watching the sea temperature, and although the sensor was misreading, I believed it to be about 4–5 degrees. I had put on the radar with an alarm for the night, just as a backup to sticking my head out of the hatch as often as I could—though, to be honest, in the dark you'd be pushed to see anything anyway.

I was glad when morning came; on waking, I stuck my head up to peer ahead out of the windows. I could see little, as they were covered in condensation, so I decided to wipe them. As I foraged for a piece of kitchen roll, I saw that the radar was clear. The shock came as I wiped the cloth across the final window—rather than a grey sky, there was a tint of blue. . . .

"Ice!"

With a surge of adrenalin, I was out of the hatch. As I swung to look around, I saw a very melted but still-40-foot-high berg slide past us. It had missed us by feet, quite literally, and luckily we had passed on its windward side, where there were no growlers (the smaller chunks that have separated from the main berg). I felt quite sick and shaken inside, and for hours I seemed to be waiting for the splitting, thudding sound as we drove into yet more ice. We were surfing regularly at more than 20 knots, and a collision at that speed did not bear thinking about. Although we were OK, we had been just a breath away from having our world disappear. There had been no freezing water flooding into our home, nor the splintering sound of carbon . . . for the moment we were safe. From then on, rather than rely on the sea temperature indicators in the hull, I collected a bucket of water and placed my watch in it in the cockpit; it had a temperature sensor on it, and its system seemed far more accurate—I was relieved.

During the morning the wind shifted and we were able to sneak back farther north. Yves had been maintaining a 100-mile lead on Mich and Bilou, who were farther north than I, though Yves was as far south as 52 degrees. There was no doubt that he was sailing a shorter distance down there, but what he didn't realize was that he was about to become isolated from the rest of the fleet, becalmed in the Southern Ocean. Catherine had fallen back in her more northerly position, sailing a greater distance—and on the other extreme—with slightly less wind. There are all sorts of things to get your head around in the Southern Ocean, though—obviously the meteorological and ice hazards, but also the magnetic anomalies, which can result in more than 40 degrees of variation in the reading on a magnetic compass. But the barometer was still dropping, and as it fell from more than 1,000 mb to 988, I realized it was going to be a big one. Time to go surfing!

> 10/12/00 09:53Z (ellenmacarthur.com/day32)
> Position 45° 46.1S 027° 59.0E
> Heading/speed 149 17.75
> Wind from 279 at 31.6 knots
> Pressure of 988
> Sea temperature 4.3
> Sail configuration is 2nd reef Solent
> Percentage performance 109.1

> That's better! Ex

> 10/12/00 10:48Z
> Position 45° 53.1S 028° 18.8E
> Heading/speed 149 18.24
> Wind from 280 at 34.7 knots
> Pressure of 989
> Sea temperature 4
> Sail configuration is 2nd reef Solent
> Percentage performance 111.5

> Ohhhh shit!

> 10/12/00 12:58Z
> I'm not worried about positions, and told myself that this morning. I knoew I would be further behind. It's part of the cgame. Look at Yves! ANyway—had a mammoth camera sort this am, after seeing two whales 30 feet away! Now have the little BBC one working—I

feel so damn lucky to be given all this fancy equipment toplay with—
KINGFISHER herslef the cream on the cake! Better go—wind rising
agian up to 38 kn. Bloody hell we're surfing, hit 29.3 earlier . . .
More later, Ex.

By this stage we had two reefs in the main, the staysail up, and were
hitting speeds of more than 30 knots . . . wow! It was amazing, as we just
picked up a wave and accelerated, getting faster and faster with a speed
that seemed to just keep on going. The motion was violent and the noise
overpowering as we shuddered to a stop after ploughing into the wave in
front. You could feel the pressure from the weight of water as it piled
across the deck. I couldn't leave the cabin even for a second without being fully dressed for the weather.

I had one pretty intense moment during that night when both autopilots failed, meaning I ended up on the helm doing 25 knots down a
wave, unable to leave my station. I had to wait, find a good wave, get her
on a surf, then dive below to reset the instrument system so it could
kick back in. Pretty stressful, but we still were powering along.

I wasn't the only boat that was smoking, though: Dominique Wavre,
with his boat *UBP*, had just smashed the twenty-four-hour record, which
in fact Yves had set on entering the Southern Ocean. Dominique's
record was incredible—a run of 430 miles in twenty-four hours, which
worked out at an average of 17.75 knots.

By this stage it really was freezing, and I thought I'd be lucky if I ever
managed to defrost my feet. The freeze-dried meals were a godsend,
though—no matter what the variety, they slid down my cold salty throat
like nectar. But I was glad when the winds began to abate slightly, as this
gave my heartbeat a chance to slow down!

We were approaching a pair of islands about 1,200 miles south of
South Africa—the Prince Edward and Marion Islands. Pulling out my
Antarctic pilot, I was quite excited to read that both had been South
African nature reserves since 1995. As usual—and suffering from what
seems to be a physical attraction between me and any mass of rock
which could remotely be called an island—we passed very close.
Though tactically it was far from being easy, I would not have changed it
for the world. I had not even an image in my mind of what the islands
might look like, and when Marion Island appeared before us as a grey

outline, it took my breath away. As we got nearer, I was amazed by the sheer volume of wildlife which surrounded it—petrels and albatrosses—and above all marvelled at its snow-capped mountains. Its slopes were green, and though the vegetation was far from lush, I was overwhelmed by its beauty. Only a handful of people live on Marion Island, in a tiny research station, and as one of the few people who have actually seen it, I felt incredibly privileged. Even more incredible than the island were its feathered inhabitants, which followed us for days and nights afterwards, never failing to be there in the morning as it got light. We were heading for the French Îles de Crozet, just under 1,000 miles directly east, and I wondered if the birds were perhaps simply commuting from one set of islands to the next.

13/12/00 18:09Z (ellenmacarthur.com/day35)
Position 47° 57.5S 048° 54.6E
Heading/speed 166 11.84
Wind from 305 at 14.2 knots
Pressure of 978 Calm
Sea temperature –1.2
Sail configuration is Full main Spinnaker
Percentage performance 102.3
Well it's very strange when you're 1000's of miles away from
anywhere to suudenly see another boat. Yesterday morning, as the
first light drew itself from under the cloud, there was Thomas
[Coville] alongside. He's been there all day, and I have to admit that
I'd rather be physically alone. It seems funny to look over to the
South each time I leave the hatch, to have someone looking at me.
It's different when it's the albatrosses. WHen it's the whales or
dolphins for sure they're not racing against me—and if so for fun
. . . Well it's a start . . . Feeling stressed—so will try more later . . .
sorry ex

I am sure that many skippers in the race would have been over the moon to see another boat, and I still don't completely understand my reaction. I am sure it sounds ridiculous, but I felt cramped by it. Thomas called on the satellite phone, too, as it had suddenly begun to work here once more. So strange to hear his voice . . . I sensed that he was keen to talk and heard from his messages back to HQ press centre that Mark passed on that he was obviously really pleased to see another competitor. Funny, really—Mark in the Mini with Thomas alongside him, then me in the Vendée. During that day, we sailed within sight of each other, though in gradually changeable conditions. As soon as I saw Thomas on the horizon, I could see which sail he had up. The wind was dying, and I quickly decided it was time to change my own. Before long, I had switched through gennaker to code 5, then to my spare spinnaker, which I was very glad I had packed up in the sock after our disaster session earlier. I was so determined not to be passed by Thomas that it was difficult to sleep, and with a new depression in the air, sailing was testing, as I knew that I needed to sail deeper and lower than he was, staying more to the north. I took bearings of him with my compass to see whether I was making on him or slipping back. As the day drew on, we sailed towards, then below, the Îles de Crozet. Birds in the air and seaweed in the water provided visual evidence of our nearing land. Seeing the weed reminded me of sailing close to the Falkland Islands on our delivery trip from New Zealand and having enormous chunks of it caught on our keel. I'd actually prepared myself to dive in to remove it, though luckily, just as I was coming to terms with how cold the water was going to be, it miraculously slipped off. We had fitted *Kingfisher* with an endoscope, which allowed me to look under the water and see her keel to be sure there was nothing caught round it or her rudder. There is nothing worse than thinking something is there but not knowing. The procedure for removing the weed or object is not so simple either, especially when you are sailing with the spinnaker or the code 5. You must either furl the sail or sock the spinnaker, then turn head to wind and try to sail backwards long enough for the culprit to come off. Frustrating to say the least, and not ideal, as often it could be quite windy, with a risk of sail breakage—you use more sail area when sailing away from the wind than against it, so when you turn against with full sail and a good breeze, you always need to be cautious. While within sight of Thomas, I had to sail backwards twice, but once I got back on track and was sailing at full speed again, this almost made up for the feeling of frustration.

14/12/00 04:09Z (ellenmacarthur.com/day36)
Position 47° 26.7S 051° 41.4E
Heading/speed 116/9.96

Wind from 33 at 9.3 knots
Pressure of 979
Sea temperature 5
Sail configuration is Full main Genoa
Percentage performance 95.1

Oh bugger!
    This mornings not one of the best of the race. It's not
KINGFISHER, the weather nor technical problems—but the skipper
who's causing the upset this morning. From being in a very strong
position yesterday morning we have slipped back—letting at least
one boat through ahead—and almost certainly losing rapidly the lead
we had. The option to be in the north was certainly the best.
Yesterday morning the weather info showed that the wind would
switch to the west more quickkly and for longer, giving us more of a
chance to make ground to the north. But once we were trapped
below the islands it wa too late—and whether it was me tying my
brains in knots or not, we basically didn't gybe when we should have,
concentrating on sailing lower and faster than Thomas. So this
morning the wind has gone light. It has turned as I thought it was due
to earlier yesterday, and despite sailign roughly in the right direction
at 10 knots I knorw that those further north will be sailing downwind
in 25 . . . It's a real shame . . . I feel quite deflated ans frustrated at
having been so stupid . . .
    Despite all this life on board os good—the moon last night was
so so bright, and seemed to shne as strong as the sun as it rose . . .
Beautiful. There are hundred's of birs around us once more, and as I
took off the code 5 from the bow this morning, the tiny petrels were
just meters from me. CHeeky little things, they love to fly above the
mainsail, playing dare devils with the updraught . . .
    Sorry everyone—I feel right now I've let you all down . . . I
promise we'll try our best to mae up the miles . . . starting with
trimming the sails right now!
later,
ellen

It was a stressful night of staring at the satellite pictures, just waiting
to see if there would be a slim chance we might make it to the north of
the depression. I could see that the front was long and pronounced, but

we simply had to get into the downwind conditions again. A tiring eighteen hours followed—upwind for the most part and near the front in 35 to 40 knots. We held onto the staysail, but there were so many sail changes, and during the approach of the front, I only managed to get down cereal bars and some dried fruit. We made it through the front, which was a godsend, and although we were in the downwind conditions, during the first hours the going was tough, as we were sailing fast into the old wave pattern—head-on to the waves. On top of this, we developed a new problem: the Satcom C and B seemed to have stopped working. Although the C was receiving messages, it seemed unable to send them, while the B, which is the only form of telephone that works in the "deep south," had begun to lose its signal. The C's power supply also seemed to be malfunctioning. For some reason, it was turning itself on, then resetting itself, meaning that for most of the time, it couldn't receive anyway. We had tried to prepare for all eventualities, but it was a massive concern not being able to get onto the Internet via the B to pick up more detailed weather information. It was a huge advantage to know where the centre of the depression was and to be able to see how a front lay. In a race situation, equipment like this is not only a means of communicating with shore but also a vital tactical aid. I knew that if I could not manage to get it working, I would be out of communication with land until Cape Horn—at least forty days away.

It's not much good if you can receive on the Satcom C but are unable to let anyone know that you have done so. Eventually I got to the bottom of the problems—both had been caused by the reception in the area we were now sailing into—and got both systems working. While I was relieved to have them back, I was annoyed that it highlighted a stupid hole in my preparations—I should have known to which station, or area, the settings needed changing.

But there was more stress, much worse than the issues with the antenna. During the passing of the depression, I had really screwed it, and gybed too late. I should have gone much earlier, but I waited, and thus lost out, dropping myself into sixth position. Fourth had been better than that! It was incredible to think that after thirty-seven days of racing, four of us had just 14 miles between us. Mich and Bilou were out there as the leaders—by this stage a good 300 miles in front. Yves was lying third but had been on a course that took him dramatically south; now, on his way back north, he had lost his lead but was moving again and was easily holding third position.

We were sailing in an intensifying depression, and I had completely messed up. For the first time in the race, I climbed into my bunk and, gritting my teeth in anger, I felt my eyes beginning to fill with tears. The Southern Ocean was starting to wear me down. I knew I was tired, and that probably had led to my mistake in going too far north. After an hour's rest I felt stronger, which was just as well, as the depression was deepening on top of us.

The following day I was in better form and decided I would make the fastest progress I possibly could. I held the genoa up to 40 knots of breeze but hand-steered to keep it full. The wind felt incredibly powerful, and *Kingfisher* just seemed to rally, sailing faster and faster and surfing for longer and longer as the waves built around her. It was magic sailing; the sun was out and the blue water seemed to shine as its crests began to break in a starkly contrasting white. *Kingfisher* felt alive as I held her helm in my hand, and we both were loving every minute of it. Our speed went up—15 knots . . . 20 knots . . . 25 knots—incredible, almost like slalom skiing through the waves. I grinned from ear to ear— this was the best sailing anyone could imagine. This was what we had come down here to see: the enormous breaking waves, the wildlife, and the feeling of being in the largest open space on earth. I closed my eyes as we surfed down the massive waves, trying to feel *Kingfisher*'s position. The wind was cold and fresh on the side of my face, but through it I could still feel the sun. I could hear the humming as her keel flew through the water, probably with a piece of weed on it. After a few hours, I changed down to her solent, then went below to check the weather and sleep a little.

Below, every sensation of speed seemed amplified, and the sounds were deafening as she screamed down the waves. I found myself repeatedly holding my breath as we took off over the crests of the waves, and with the power in her sails and her lightness, we accelerated faster and faster. I braced myself against the violent motion by jamming my knees beneath the chart table, and as we became airborne I gripped the edge of it, hoping to goodness that the pilot would not let go. If we gybed in this, we'd be in desperate trouble.

We were approaching the Kerguelen Islands at about 50 degrees south and midway between South Africa and Australia. I was trying to cross as far to the north as I could. There is a massive patch of shallow water just to the north of the islands, so the sea was building. Shallow water means breaking waves—and big ones if it's blowing 45 to 50 knots. If at all possible I wanted to avoid gybing in this; with this wind, I risked breaking battens in the mainsail. I decided to change sails to allow me to stay deeper, using a system we'd developed whereby we could attach the tack of the staysail out to a pad eye on *Kingfisher*'s gunwale. Worth a try, I thought, and battled forward to set the sail.

> 17/12/00 09:47Z (ellenmacarthur.com/day39)
> Position 47° 50.1S 077° 19.3E
> Heading/speed 158 14.87
> Wind from 295 at 19.3 knots (remember 50 degrees W varn.)
> Pressure of 1002
> Sea temperature 3.1
> Sail configuration is Full main Code 5
> Percentage performance 95

As I sit here now I feel worse than I have ever felt in my lofe before. Physically i am totally exhausted, and mentally—not so far off. My whole body aches, and feels drained. My mind feels like it's been frozen, and is trying to wake. Yesterday was the hardest challnege of my life, though funnily this morning feels 10 times owrse. It started when the tack of the staysail blew off. THe sail had been set to windward, as teh wind waswell over 40 knots. THe day had been fantastic—surfing at over 30 knots, and really feeling we were catching the others, amter our stupid course to the north. I am learning so much—sailing the boat one of those things—and only yesterday did we seem to have got it roght in strong downwind conditions. AS the sail felw into he air I bore away quickly to hide it behind the mainsail. I dropped the halyard immediately and went on to the foredeck to sort out the mess, not easy in 45 knots, but we were slower without the sail—I just had to holsd my breath as the waves plughed overthe bow. It was then theat she started to go—to gybe, and before I could make it back to the cockpit her deck was vertical, and we were lying helplessley on our side. In itslef this is a fairly bad situation to be in—but what was to come was far worse. As she lay on her side the mainsail lay crookedly on the runners—I fought to get the other runner on to release her from this agnizing position—bt it was dfficult climbing up the deck. We did it—tthen gybed over—but had to go back as the runners were caught around the top battens . . . By this stage one of the battens had broken—in fact the car it travels on too—and alhtough annoyed I know this does happen—a nd is not so bad to fix . . . or so I thought. On further inspection, and about 20 mins to srt out the mess I realized that I couldn't get the mainsail down to fix the problem. IN fact the broken batten had slid out forward over the second spreader—and neither love, money nor the best will in the world was going to let me lower that sail with out going up there to remove the batten. GOing up the rig is generally the solo sailor's worst night mare—but going up in 40 knots plus just doesn't bare thinking about. I knew I had to do it. I kew that if the wind rose further I would be unable to get the sail down. In my mind I had no option—I just went into autopilot, put on my harness, rigegd up a taut halyard and climbed. It was bitterly cold, the biting wind cutting into the bare skin on my hands and face, the first [part] to the forst spreader was OK—not too much movement, and I still had engy—but the second part to the second spreader was 10 times harder with each inch I climbd . . . I was beginning to get tired—as each wavae we surfed on (which were about 10 meters high) was trying to throw me off the mast. As I got to the second spreader I had just two feet to go, but it felt those were the hardes towo feet of my life. I struggled to inch my way up, adn hung there a while banging away at the mast, trying to recover. I found the energy from I don't know where—and made it on to the spreader. THe batten was in front of me, and if I timed it on the sufrs I could pull it out. Relieved it would come, I dropped it to the deck.

I was now quite cold, and shaking with the effort, you'd think getting down is the easy bit—but in fact it took me forther to the edge than I wished to go. I had to take each jumar in turn and lower it, taking the weight of the owrking one to [sit] on the lazy one. Eash few inches I descended I had to take my weight with my hands—or legs—which proved exhausting still . . . I arrived at one point with a slack jumar and an unattatched one, with all my weight on my right wrist in one of the webbing loops n the sail. I hung tere—banging into the mast—trying desperaltely, and unsuccessfuly to get my foot thruogh the gap between the sail and the mst. I started to hurt badly—still no joy. GOodness knows how I managed to get thtat other jumar on—but i think that the hospital kids had a fair lot to do with it, and the want to get back home again. It took over an hour to get down—just 15 metres . . . a painful hour. Once on the deck I

was shaking but overjoyed and set about fixing the issues . . . The
batten I changed—anothter I thgihtened and sewed a part of a
spreader patch on. I barely had the energy to put the sail back up
again, then cllapsed in the cockpit. A I dashed about the deck
working my vision went funny—I was seeing stars permanelntly, as
if I was about to black out. Bizarre—i didn't but wonder if it's
something to do with adrenalin or haiing been close to the edge . . .
or then again maybe I was just frozen. I was so glad to have made the
repair, but till this morning really didn't realize how much it had
taken out of me. THis morning was worse . . . I saw a rip in the
genoa . . . along the foot. I tried to sleep last night—but was
worried about it—so at forst light tried to fix it. It was impossible
—even with the sail sheeted hard [behind] the main it flapped and
flicked in my face, and ripped the stitching out that I was trying to
put in. Hence this morning is one of the owrst. I cannot sail at full
potential . . . the sail I need is out of action . . . SO frustrating. And
now—to top it all—after putting up the gennaker in 17 knots of
wind—it's now blowing 29 and on the limit. After trying to fix that
sail I was at my lowest point tin the race. I cried out loud to the
heavens . . . just sometimes you have those moments—and that was
one of them . . . After almost killing myself yesterday to keep going
and fix the problems whilst hanging in with the flleet, today I am
losing miles, because of a stupid tear in a sail. So frustrating, I cna't
sleep, or switch off. Something else I guess I have to learn. THe good
news is though the sun has come out. Maybe I'll get a chance to dry
out that sail . . . Thanks so much for following me, everyone. THe
support e-mails are fantastic. They really change my days, and give
me more than just a reason to be ot here. SHaring this challenge is
one of the most important things for me. Second to, though I have
to say—making it back home to France!
till tomorrow. . .
exx

Oh Mark. I just want to thank you with all my heart . . . I could not
or would not ever wnat anyone else there as my number 1. You're
the best, I have tears in my eyes as I wrie because I am so glad you're
there. I really have been close to the edge—and I want you to know
that you played a very big part in carrying me back.
Love ex

That evening as I charged my batteries I fired up the Satcom C to find two messages—one from Mark and one from the race organizers. They were flagged Urgent; something had happened to Yves. I felt a sickness in my stomach.

The French message required me to divert my course to Yves's position, confirmed that his speed had dropped to less than 5 knots, and said that there had been no contact. I checked his position—we were less than 100 miles apart. My heart raced as I switched on the breaker to activate the Satcom B. Thankfully, it was working again, although it still seemed like an eternity as I waited for it to connect to a satellite and find a signal. All sorts of things went through my mind. Had Yves fallen off his boat? Had he been dismasted? Was he injured? Still I waited for a connection. I dialled Mark's number. He always answered. His voice sounded surprisingly calm, and he had more news—Yves had sent a short message to say that he had been dismasted but was OK—that was it. I threw my head back in relief. Thank God.

I had still been requested by the race organizers to continue to his position, so I changed sails to remain on a more northerly heading. Mark and I arranged for a rendezvous call when I was 20 miles away, so I switched off the B—it was just before midnight when I called back. Mark told me that my diversion had been called off. I felt for Yves—his third Vendée Globe, in a boat he knew so well. His last had been halted by a broken forestay and rudder, now by a broken mast. But I did think back to his words before the race: "If I don't win, you have to win, and if you don't win, I have to win." I felt determined. The race was on.

The following day Mark sent on Yves's statement about his problems as a result of what had happened out there in the storm. We knew from his speeds that he had been pushing very hard, and after he'd dropped to third due to his too-southerly weather option, he'd been really going for it.

> Everything happened very quickly. The wind climbed very fast, and very strongly under a storm cloud. My boat took off, gybed uncontrollably and wiped out on its side. As she came back up, the shock loads were so big that the boat gybed a second time and I was thrown across the cockpit. The boat took off again on a surf, but nose-dived with the water coming right up to the mast—and it was

that that brought the mast down. Now all is well, and I confirm that
I do not require assistance.

Yves surprised everyone the following day with the news that he
would not abandon the race. As he had 6 to 8 metres of his 25-metre
mast remaining, he intended to continue under the jury rig, permitting
him to sail with a fourth reef in his mainsail, and he believed he might be
able to attach the broken mast for the remaining part of the Southern
and Atlantic Oceans. He would have to find a quiet spot from which to
work—not easy, as he was miles from anywhere, but this said a great
deal about Yves—his determination and his nickname: the Extra Terres-
trial! It took him fifteen days to sail on to a beautiful, remote, natural
harbour in Stewart Island, New Zealand. Vendée Globe rules allow the
sailors to stop to repair their boats if they need to, but only by anchoring
the boat—touching any part of the land above the high-water mark is
not allowed. He spent two weeks in the bay repairing and rebuilding his
mast, using lightbulbs to build a makeshift oven in which he could "bake"
the carbon. Having rerigged his sails, he was able to continue his circumnavigation with his extraordinary jury rig. Throughout his amazing experience, one of the biggest issues was food. He had only bargained for
100 days. So while making repairs he'd eaten shellfish plucked from below the waterline, and he then had to collect and dry seaweed for his
long trip home. His repair job was incredible, and although he no longer
had a chance of winning the race, his spirit was intact. Awesome.

18/12/00 16:23Z (ellenmacarthur.com/day40)
FOund the tinkling noise . . . it was the pin from the hinge on the
two doors into the back storagea area. Today I've re-spliced the
vang, whipped around a few ropes. FIxed the genoa, re-fixed the
camera housing. fixed the car on port side outobard, found wheree
the carbon piece came froem . . . it was the winch on mast . . .
smething caught arouund the tailer, and damaged it . . . It's useable
though. Have refixed the piece inside the tailer, and seems OK . . .
gennaker went up on it—no probs . . . even had a nap!
    I'm sorry the last few days were so hard, I know it's as bad at
your end too. Maybe give you a call later . . . not looking foraward
to those lost miles . . . though looking at the last few reports—
miricles can happen!
later, ex

I was sitting in fourth position by this stage and was intensely frustrated that I was not sailing faster than Thomas, who was ahead of me at the time in third. I was farther south than he was, though, which for the time being was good news, as I was sailing a relatively shorter course. There was one issue, though. The depression to the south of us was slowing and had virtually stopped; I had a choice between two headings: either just south of the direct route (by far the fastest) or farther north and away from the ice and the Antarctic convergence zone. I was tired, but still having to make these crucial decisions. We were out of the ice zone for the time being but were approaching it, and while I wanted to keep away from the bergs, I also desperately needed to stay out of the centre of the lingering depression. We had 25 to 30 knots where we were, but those to the north had 40 to 45 knots. To the south, though, there was even less, then nothing.

> I grit my teeth as I open the fore-hatch, as the frezing handles seem
> to "bite" my cold, hard hands. Feeling stupid, I use my feet, frustrted
> at myself for making an unhealed knuckle bleed once more. For this
> is not the Atlantic, here it is cold and remote—the nights movng
> in—with a feeling that the icy Antartic winds slowly place their
> arms around you . . . the cold seeping through to your bones.
>   The days at the moment are better—the sun rises and sets—
> which seems extrardinary for the south. I always imagines an endless
> grey—but it has proved to me that it has many faces, many moods
> and many seasons. It is unpredictable and as I sit here there is a
> massive band of dark clouud to windward. As always it approaches
> us slowly but surely—with the rain clearly visible as it pelts down to
> the sea below.
> Ex

The hardest part out there is assessing the weather, especially when you're cold and tired. The pressure never goes away, and each time I made a decision, I felt an apprehension, followed by painful hours of worrying whether or not it would pay off. The sheer exhaustion just seeps into your bones, and miles gained or lost against rivals become the core of each day. Win miles and morale soars. Lose them and you have to try to harness that frustration to fuel further decisions.

On day 44 of the race there was fantastic news: we had leapt into third position—our southern route had paid off. We were down below 55 south, but with the most fantastic reaching winds coming up, we had made a spot-on decision. That day things really seemed to be going our way.

The night came in and the winds were no stronger than 20 to 25 knots. The sailing was fast and the waves were building. I helmed that evening, enjoying the feeling of *Kingfisher* just sliding over the waves; I was comforted by the feeling of being in control, knowing when she would turn as I gently pushed and pulled her helm—a feeling I missed when the autopilot steered her in its own impersonal way.

As we sailed, I thought of Thomas. If we just sailed fast and safely, we could keep him there. Then, with an agonizing silence and cruel lack of drama, the code 5 sail came away from the top of the mast and floated down into the water. *Kingfisher* slowed, and I instantly ran to drop the main halyard to stop her completely so I might have some chance of re-covering the sail. Shit! My fingers worked overtime—opening clutches, loosening sheets. I looked up to see, swinging from the top of the mast, a metre of halyard; the rest had come away with the sail. I just couldn't be-lieve it—we'd lost our third sail.

An hour later I felt wretched. My knee burnt from being dragged down the deck as I struggled to hold onto the sail. My clothes were wet and cold as, hanging on the end of the bowsprit, I was repeatedly plunged into the freezing water as we wallowed without power.

I couldn't believe we'd lost another sail—not here, not now. Things seemed so bleak. I was forced to cut the sheets to stop the sail from act-ing as an anchor under the water, then I left myself with no choice but to drag the sail out from the sea by hand. It took all my strength to get just an inch or so over her guard wires, and often I would lose five minutes of work as an unusually large wave swept over the boat and mercilessly dragged the sail back with it. As I edged it up over the guard wire, I prayed that there would be no damage, but my heart sank as I saw a mas-sive rip, then another. The sail was well and truly destroyed.

I was relieved that the wind was increasing, though. At least we were able to sail with the genoa and not feel that we were painfully undercan-vased. That night I lay on the chart-table seat with my head back on my fleecy pillow and called Mum and Dad to let them know what had hap-pened—this was something I had begun to do after each disaster, so at least they would know that I was OK. The last thing I wanted was for

Mum and Dad to hear a story on the news which worried them. At least this way, no matter how bad it was, they would hear my voice first to know that I really was OK.

When I had dried out I felt better, but I knew what was to come. It was blowing 30 knots, and I was going to have to climb the mast to replace the halyard. I called Mark to tell him of all that had happened, and I felt some relief to have described it to someone. I said on the phone, "I will guard that gennaker with my life!"

I climbed the mast on Christmas Eve, and though I had time to get ready, it was the hardest climb to date. I had worked through the night preparing for it, making sure I had all the tools, mouse lines, and bits I might need. I had agonized for hours over the way to prepare the halyard so it would stream out easily below me and not get caught as I climbed.

When it got light I decided the time was right. I put on my middle-layer clothes, as I didn't want to wear so much that I wouldn't be able to move freely up there. The most dangerous thing, apart from falling off, is to be thrown against the mast, and though I would be wearing a helmet, it would not be difficult to break bones up there.

I called Mark. It was evening in France where he was living in the mountains, and he was just about to sleep. I told him not to worry if he tried to contact me and I did not reply as I would be up the mast for the next couple of hours. Though his words were reassuring I could sense his concern.

I laid out the new halyard on deck, flaking it neatly so there were no twists. As I took the mast in my hands and began to climb, I felt almost as if I was stepping onto the moon—a world over which I had no control. You can't ease the sheets or take a reef, nor can you alter the settings for the autopilot. If something goes wrong, you are not there to attend to it. You are a passive observer looking down at your boat some 90 feet below. After climbing just a couple of metres I realized how hard it was going to be. I couldn't feel my fingers—I'd need gloves, despite the loss in dexterity. I climbed down, getting soaked as we ploughed into a wave—the decks around my feet were awash. I unclipped my jumar from the halyard and put on a pair of sailing gloves. There would be no second climb on this one—I knew that I would not have the energy.

As I climbed, my hands were more comfortable, and initially progress was positive. But it got harder and harder, as I was not only pulling my

own weight up as I climbed but also the increasingly heavy halyard—
nearly 200 feet of rope by the time I made it to the top. The physical
drain came far less from the climbing than from the clinging. The hardest
thing is just to hang on as the mast slices erratically through the air.
There would be the odd massive wave which I could feel us surf down,
knowing we would pile into the wave in front. I would wrap my arms
around the mast and press my face against its cold and slippery carbon
surface, waiting for the shuddering slowdown. Eyes closed and teeth
gritted, I hung on tight, wrists clenched together, and hoped. Occasionally on the smaller waves I would be thrown before I could hold on
tight, and my body and the tools I carried were thrown away from the
mast; I'd be hanging on by just one arm, trying to stop myself from
smacking back into the rig.

By the third spreader I was exhausted; the halyard was heavier and the
motion more violent. I held onto her spreader base and hung there,
holding tight to breathe more deeply and conjure up more energy. But I
realized that the halyard was taut; it had caught on something. Damn! I
knew that if I went down to free it I would not have the energy to climb
up again. I tugged and tugged on the rope—the frustration was unreal.
It had to come, quite simply, the rope had to come free. Luckily, with all
the pulling I managed to create enough slack to make it to the top, but
now I was even more exhausted. I squinted at the grey sky and watched
the masthead whip across the clouds. The wind whistled past, made visible by the snow that had begun to fall. Below, the sea stretched out forever, the size and length of the waves emphasized by this new aerial
view. This is what it must look like to the albatross.

I rallied once more and left the safety of the final spreader for my last
hike to the top. The motion was worse than ever, and as I climbed, I
thought to myself, not far now, kiddo, come on, just keep moving. . . . As
the masthead came within reach there was a brief moment of relief; at
least there was no giving up now that I had made it. Whatever happened
now, I had the whole mast to climb down. I fumbled at the top of the rig,
feeding in one end of the halyard and connecting the other end to the
top of *Kingfisher*'s mast. The job only took about half an hour—then I began my descent. This was by far the most dangerous part, and my heart
was in my mouth. No time for complacency now, I thought, not till you
reach the deck, kiddo. It's far from over. . . .

It was almost four hours before I called Mark back, and I shook with exhaustion as we spoke. We had been surfing at well more than 20 knots while I was up there. My limbs were bruised and my head was spinning, but I felt like a million dollars as I spoke on the phone. Santa had called on *Kingfisher* early, and we had the best present ever—a new halyard.

MERRY XMAS!!
Well it seems incredible to think that just 12 months ago we were not so far fro the Southern Ocean . . . It's also inredible to think that since then KINGFISHER has been finished—launched, delivered—double-transated and now globe-ing it! Once again a Christmas alone—though last time it was up in the [Waitakaruru] Mountain Rnge in New Zealand. I don't really kow why I chose to be aloe last year too. I guess it was subconcious preparation for now. I was sitting in the cuddy the other day thinking . . . thinking about how much time KINGFISHER and I have spent together . . . Well we've sailed over 35 thousadn miles—and providing all goes well and I finish the Vendée we'll have spent over 6 months at sea in th past 12. That shocked me when I though it! THe past six years seems to have come into focus over the past weeks. In a weeks time we'll be about half way round, again, incredible to think that the trip is passing so quickly. Because the Vendée is quickening its pace I think we're finding time is flying by—though there are still those days where it seems like home is a long, long way away (which it is!) About 8 thousand 200 miles as the crow flies from here. It would have to be a very brave crow though—because settingoff a journey from 50 degrees south could be a chilly affair—he would certainly need additional fuel tanks and a very warm scarf! Navigation though would be easy, as there are plenty of seabirds to ask diections from!
    I pause to find something warmer to wear as I type, and I can't help thinkigng that if I dry out this jacket one more time I shall have a salt-crystal garden hanging from each of the sleeves!
    This whole project has been one of the best experiaences of my life. I have learn't more than I ever believed possible—worked with the best team I could ever imagine, and have travelled the world—much of which under sail.
    In a way that makes this all sound very easy . . . but in fact it's been the hardest thing I've ever done—[partly being] out here, because for the forst time i my life I feel I've found [my] limit, [and

partly] the decision-making and [the] sheer number of jobs we had
to get through to be here right now. I have to thank the team for
basically dedicating their lives to the project. An awesome effort.

So we're here—thanks to everyone, and it's my turn to get
round quickly and safely. I a m finding the race to be the most
inredible experience. It's dificult but rewarding. Hte pace of this
race is like no other. THough we have a long way to go, we are
racing liek a transatlantic. Incredible pace, crazy speeds and—with
every one of us a will to get to the finish—a difficult jobto balance.
The hardest thing of all is the constnat decision-amaking, the
relentless movement . . . It's not like we get a chance to relax.
Tactically a small mistake can cost us hundreds of miles . . . Errors
just can't be made . . . It would be a very diffierent situation of it
were not a race out here!!

Finally; like to wish every one of you out htere a happy
Christmas. It shall feel strange opening my presents alone, and as my
heater's broken there's little chance of Santa popping down the
chimney—the exhaust's got a bung in it now anyway! Thank you all
so much for your thousands of messages. I cannot thaknk you
enough—I just hope you can feel what a difference they make to life
out here. WHen things are tough I really feel like I'm not alone—
and your energy and support shines through every time . . .
thankyou. I just hope that we can hang in here, and catch those
others up before we get home! Now that would be the prefect gift
for Xmas.
Take care, Merry Christmas,
love ellen

It was odd being so far away from the rest of the world on Christmas
Day, but I did my best to do things properly. I was lucky with the
weather. The wind stayed reasonably steady, and we were able to sail all
day without major sail changes. I had everything from a miniature
Christmas tree to tinsel and plastic farm animals, and even a tiny lantern
with a small supply of candles which I hung from the cabin roof at night.
It brought tears to my eyes to see the kindness and amount of thought
that each person had put into the gifts that I'd stowed away on board before the start. But the best thing that happened on Christmas Day was a
conference call Mark organized for all my friends and family to call in. It
was an odd feeling having people drop in and out of the conversation,

coming and going as if they were literally dropping in for a chat! It was only after twenty minutes that I discovered Mum and Dad had been there the whole time but had just not said anything! Ian was there too, and contributed his usual funny comments and dry wit, and the team from the office joined in. Although I could not have been physically much farther away from them all, I felt very close to everyone that day. A real Christmas.

I scattered the tinsel in the chilly cabin and put the tree above the chart table. I heated Gran's Christmas pudding, which I had on board as pretty much my only weight concession, then sprinkled the tiny bottle of rum I'd been given onto it. Dad had even included a sprig of Derbyshire holly in the parcel, and I lit it, just as he did each Christmas. . . . I blew up a balloon and wrote on it in indelible pen, "Happy Xmas everyone, luv you all xx," then threw it over the side into the Southern Ocean.

I sat down to reply to some of the festive e-mails that I'd received, including one from gardener Alan Titchmarsh. He'd been following the project and we'd become friends. I needed his advice!

Dear Alan . . .
Hello there—and thanks for your Xmas e-mail. Xmas here was a little strange—though I was lucky with the weather, and got a bit of a break. I neded it after my Xmas Eve nightmare of the mast ascent. Above all the rum custard and Gran's Xmas pudding warmed the cockles—which since our 3 hour airobatic's session were still a little chilly! Today is a great day . . . we are in 3rd (though you probably know)—and now—just 36 miles behind Bilou. I am so pleased, and just hope that we can hang in here without getting into trouble . . .
Now back to Xmas . . . I recieved a whole host of small and light presents which ranged form crochet dog hair charms to spare pants from Mum (as always), the good old chocolate penny, a few glo in the dark dolphins, and a tiny candle lantern which hangs in the cabin, to remind me of sailing when I was a kid with the paraffin lamp. THere was one present though—one which would interest you the most.
It's a tiny pot-your-own bonsai tree from Helen (who you breify met at the ferry terminal before we sailed in Cowes). Now Helen is very keen on nature, and has a degree in Environmental Science—so

very apt on her part, and great to be able to rekindle those
memories of harvesting and planting runner beans in the old Ski
yoghurt pots with Dad when we were kids.

So, being the forst person to spring to mind, I'm writing to ask
you for asdvice on the finer matters of seed cultivation! I though the
wee plant might be a little confused if I plant him in the summer—
in the Southern Hemisphere—and a little bemused as he fries as we
cross the Equator . . . Will he have a sense of where he belongs—or
will he—for the sake of argument remain a bit of a wanderer—like
myself—who lives his life dashing from season to season? Might it
be that I will be obliged to travel the word with this tree . . . ?

The instructions say to moisten the compost with water. Now I
have only water-maker water—mineral-less I guess, and wondered
if this would make a big difference to his growth—should I dissolve
a vitamin tablet in his compost. . . ?

Mmmm . . .

I guess that it must seem a little strange being asked for
gardening advice from a boat about as far away from soil as you can
get . . . Well there you go, funnier things have happened!

Hope this message finds you well, and that you've had a great
Xmas, and all the best for 2001.
Best Wishes!
ellen
(and samuel the Carob seed, obviously, as a bonsai with small aims in
life)

28/12/00 05:13Z (ellenmacarthur.com/day50)
Position 53° 36.9S 167° 48.5E
Heading/speed 66 15.52
Wind from 290 at 25.6 knots
Pressure of 976
Sea temperature 7.3
Sail configuration is 1st reef Gennaker
Percentage performance 93.3

Again I sit . . . THe wind has dropped after a alrge cloud. already I
have taken the reef i and out of the mainsail 6 times. t's frustrating,
as after 20 minutes had passed the wind always seems to pick up . . .
thogh you never know. The sun shines between the squalls around
us, and the seabirds play, swoop and swim as we chundle past. It's

been a good morning for progress—though frustrating as always with the squalls. I've never seen squalls quite so violent as here . . . Going from 15–30 knts in one hit. I' afraid for the gennaker, and it's our last! THough there is no option but to fly it if we are to make progress. . . .

It's great to be a little ahead right now, and I feel more than before now I am away from the others that I am sailing my own race . . . No longer in quite the same weather as those ahead—or behind, I feel—for the want of a better phrase—a little freer!

We are just sailing under the most western part of New Zealand as I type, and in just over 24 hours time we shall be on the same longituse as Auckland. I thik KINGFISHER is feeling she's close to home right now, though we've had a talk, and I've told her that we might stop off the NEXT time round.

The wind continues to die . . . just 14 knots now . . . CAn it be that the wind will stay so light, maybe I'll wait another 10 minutes . . . yes 10 minutes. THen shake out the reef. It's a hard one to take in and out is the frst, as I have to pull up the whole sail. Frustrting, long—but rewarding as we speed off after.

There we go . . . 24 knots of wind. I knew it was worth waiting! Today I have checked for oil in the generator—pumped out water that was kicking around in the forepeak. Changed the rubbish bag (always a great one!) and generally checked around down below. Oh yes—I've wired the Sat C into the 24V transformer to see if I can kick it into life. So far—i seems to be working better anyway.

I'm a bit worried about a depression which is due to form ahead of us. I don't feel like getttiing trapped beneath it as it streaks to the SE—but it looks like it'sll be hard to stay to it's north. It seems to be developing earlier than we think which is good news though—so maybe it'll drop south ahead of us.

Better pop up and ease out the sails a little.

ellen

xx

We were approaching the International Dateline where we would en-joy 29 December twice! We were sailing between the Bishop and Clerk Islands, which lie several hundred miles to the south of New Zealand, and it was here that I saw my first boat since Thomas—a massive Australian fishing vessel named *Austral Leader*. She called up on the radio, and it was fantastic to chat with the lads on board. They seemed quite fascinated by what I was up to—so much so that they came over for a look. There were thirty-two guys on board, all off for a three-month trip. But somehow, while it was exciting to see land and another vessel on the same day, there was also the same familiar feeling of claustrophobia—so it felt good to leave those final islands behind us en route for Chile.

The leading boats were sailing into the most remote waters of the world—the South Pacific Ocean. The next land we all hoped to see would be Cape Horn itself—still well over two weeks away. We were lying third, and I was over the moon about our position. We were catching Bilou fast—and Mich was being reeled in bit by bit. . . .

Farther back, Mike Golding, who was slowly creeping up through the fleet, got caught in 58-knot winds. He lost one of the battens in his mainsail and eventually decided just to go below and sit it out while the autopilot steered his boat. The deck is a dangerous place during a Southern Ocean storm.

There was news that Frenchman Thierry Dubois was to pull out of the race due to a complete electrical failure. Thierry had also been one of the casualties of the last Vendée, and he had incredible strength of character to return to race in those same waters. He had built his boat largely himself and had been a friend since those early years in La Trinité.

29/12/00 07:20Z (ellenmacarthur.com/day51)
Position 54° 25.2S 178° 30.2E
Heading/speed 64 14.58
Wind from 312 at 19.5 knots
Pressure of 981
Sea temperature 7.9
Sail configuration is Full main Genoa
Percentage performance 103.5

Well we're flying right now . . . great wind angle, and eay sailing. A bit frustratinig at times as the little gusts come, and we fall over a bit, but all in all we're going well now. Today has been a day of sleeping, weather study and spilicing. The weather study reveals that there is one mother of a dpression heading over us around the 31st—Happy New Year! For KINGFISHER it will be the worst yet—so I'm trying to position myself for it in the best place. Difficult—as the weather information here is not so accurate. Had a good splicing session, and repaired the old gennaker halyard to re-use if ever the new one breaks. It was a long job, and a very difficult and tight vectran splice . . . Lots of pulling and squeezing, feeding and fiddling! after an hour and a hlaf the job was done—so pleased I was at cracking it I went straight on to make a new spare jib sheet . . . again—in case. I was quite chuffed at havigng completed the whole job in the cuddy withought a oilies on—I just dodged the torrents of water as they sluiced over KINGFISHER.

During tonight we're lined up to cross the Date Line—so roll on once more the 29th of december. Very strange—though it helps keeping theboatsclocs in GMT. At least we don't completely lose the plot. We've passed under Auckland now—so we're more in known territory, it feels a little comforting to know KF has sailed this bit before, though I am quite sure that the Pacific will not be wearing the same face for us this time. Prudence is the key word.

I heard yesterrday that Marc Thierecelin is saying that hee "is fed up with sailing behind the little ellen" . . . well I could throw that one back by saying that I'm missing sailing with Bilou. So I'm hurrying along to enjoy some company!

Take care everyone. Ellen

I always felt much better for having repaired things, finding it an al-most therapeutic way of taking my mind off the immense stress of the decisions. It was something that was always burning away inside me; looking after *Kingfisher*, making sure she was always repaired as soon as possible, and ready to face whatever was coming next. This involved not only repairs but scores of checks—from the oil in the engine to the amount of food I was consuming, to each fixing on *Kingfisher*'s deck and the lashings on her rigging. It was easy to tire yourself out, but at the end of the day, you had to do what you had to do. It was now approaching New Year, and there were yet more difficult decisions to make. Spirits were high once again; I had caught up to just over 100 miles behind Mich . . . we were on a roll. But all was not straightforward; there was an enormous depression roaring up behind us, and for Bilou, still less than 50 miles away, and me it was looking as though we would not make it to the north of it. . . .

31/12/00 07:41Z (ellenmacarthur.com/day53)
Position 55° 15.7S 165° 30.5W
Heading/speed 106 10.3
Wind from 46 at 23.6 knots
Pressure of 972
Sea temperature 19.5
Sail configuration is 2nd reef Solent
Percentage performance 86.7

I feel quite low roght now—akin to the weather system which has moved on top of us. I am very tired, and can't sleep. The motion of KF is horrible—nothing i seem to be able to do makes her feel more comfortable. we are between two wind ranges—where she'd be better off wiht the Solent—but i daredn't risk brreaking the sail—so we bounce and pound along with 2 reefs and staysail.

There are clearly two weather options . . . this morning I was hoping to stay with that of the north—t o pick up the westerlies and fire east—but the wind has turned earlier, and now we are heading to the south of SE—in a wind which is basically east. I am not sure if my chouice is th4e right one. the wind is fluctuating, and my emotions rn from laughter to crying as the wind swings, [and the] rain pours . . .

We stand to losee a gret dealif I am worong. we could get trapped in the south, not make the waypoint, and have to sail some stupid course 90 defgrees to the route to get there. I am very worried, northing ai can do makes m emfeel better inside, nothing relaxes me,—I ahevne't even managed a proper meal today.

This is hte harsdest part—it's harder than the breakages, and the problems. It's putting us in the right place. we wroked hard to get bac up the fleet, and now we stand to lose what we ahve gained, and that is eating away at me right now likke it wantsto engulf me. I find it impossible to put into words the anguish inside. The worry, the constant [fraying]—the hors and hours staring at a computer screen analysing and reanalysing till your blue in the face, and after all your work could easily convince yourself that either opteion is the oene to go forl. I guess hta' what I lack—the experience. The expxeriece of standing by a decision, and understanding it in a way different to I do now.

This for me is the hardest part.

At this point I was at my most tired in the race. Never had I pushed myself so hard before, and never had I felt so desperate. I had never before forced myself beyond what I thought were my limits, and now that I was there it was the hardest thing ever to come back from. Reasoning was virtually impossible, the constant danger and stress of the race were taking an immense toll, and the sapping effect of living on the edge for more than fifty days was for the first time becoming startlingly obvious. We were being pushed to the south, with no option as far as the race was concerned to head any way other than towards the ice. It's almost as if I had lost control of myself; when you reach this place you feel completely in despair, as though things will never get better. It's hard to see anything but the dark side, and as you're physically thrown about, and desperately cold, you frustrate yourself more by going way below despair. *Kingfisher* was not happy—she was uncomfortable in the waves, and it was transmitted through to me like a signal ringing warnings in my brain. There was nothing I could do; we were sailing slowly in a direction in which we did not want to go, and the sea was horrendous. I slumped down in the cockpit onto my knees, banging my fists against my legs. I hurled my head back and yelled, screaming so loud that my throat was sore.

"Why? Why us? Please, just please give us a chance!"

But the dark sky wasn't listening, and the torrential rain trickled down my neck, slowly sapping yet more of those precious reserves of heat from my body. Images of Mich sailing away downwind flashed through my head. I was angry and frustrated and felt that I was letting people down. We were losing miles to Mich, and losing them fast. It was more than just physical exhaustion, it was causing more pain inside than I had ever felt before. I clenched my teeth and threw my head down against the hard, wet floor and wept. I cried like a baby till I was so numb with the cold that the pain was dulled. Shivering and weak, I crawled into the cabin and slept in my waterproofs, curled up in a ball in the footwell by the engine.

On waking again, in a distraught and washed-up state, I called Ian. In the past, he'd had an uncanny knack of picking me up and making me smile when I thought I couldn't, and I needed a hug right now. Mark had already said that I was lucky not to be in the same position as some of the other Vendée skippers who'd had to stop to repair their boats, but I felt he had totally lost patience with me. I couldn't shake off the feeling that I had made the wrong decisions in the last days and thus had let people down. In my weakened state I doubted my decision-making skills, but Ian let me talk; I unloaded my worries and insecurities, and everything just flowed down the phone. He knew I needed to be snapped out of this destructive slump, and at the end of the conversation he reported something that really shocked me. He said he had been told never to tell me this, but he felt right then that he had to do it. After finishing an interview before the Vendée, Mich reportedly made an off-the-cuff comment in which he claimed that various skippers believed that I had received banned outside assistance when winning the Europe 1 Star. Ian reasoned that comments like this would not be made unless I was doing something right. It was the biggest kick-start I could have had. I was furious—no one cheats, and I sure as hell never had, and Mich would have known the impact of even suggesting it. The anger rose inside me, and, fuelled by it, I refused to accept my position in this race. We still had 10,000 miles to sail, and I was going to give my all.

LESS THAN A DAY LATER we were heading straight into an iceberg field. The water temperature cooled, and I knew it was just a matter of time before we encountered the first ice. As morning broke I spotted the first berg looming out of the greyness of the sea and sky. I was in a state of expectant nervousness, laced with a thrill from the potential danger. You are fully aware that more than ever you are living on the edge, that you cannot fall asleep, and that profound dread of a splitting, crunching, gut-wrenching halt to your journey is ever-present. You try not to think about the "what ifs" of a collision with an iceberg weighing thousands of tons; you mustn't imagine how *Kingfisher* would react to an impact at 15 knots with a cliff of solid ice any more than you would think of a car crash each time you went for a drive. But you know damn well inside that it's not just the race that could end, but everything. The only other boat in the iceberg zone was Bilou's, and his sobering remark was that this was not a place for a father.

02/01/01 18:28Z (ellenmacarthur.com/day55)
F****** close and nothing on radar. Not exactly small or melted either. I'll be glad to gybe to the North! I saw it on the beam again
. . . Bollocks. Deep breaths and relaxing req'd. x

I sent an e-mail to race headquarters with the positions and sizes of the first bergs I saw, stating that the second was half a mile long! I finished by saying that I hoped that was enough for one day . . . it's freezing here!

> 6 iceberg seperate mais pas petite (500M par 200M approx) sur une ligne 58 24.8S 143.03W et 58 07S 145 07W . . . Une a 58 35.85 143 19.3W (enorme—une demi mille en longeur) Une a 58 32 28S 143 15W (avec beaucoup de growlers sou le vent) Une petite a 58 09.5S 142. 41.5S Une grande a 57 44.5S 142 00.1W . . .
> Voilà, j'espère c'est sufficement pour une journée! Ca Caille ici!
> ellen

I felt completely trapped by the ice; each time a berg slipped behind us into the grey gloom, I would make out another before us. There seemed no easy way through—even though there were gaps between the bergs, they were strewn with growlers, often still the size of cars or even houses. Most of the larger bergs looked like sections taken from the cliffs of Dover, hundreds of feet high and jagged with crevasses. Even sheltered from the icy wind outside, the cabin felt like a freezer. It was only after the seventh berg that I felt it was safe to gybe out of the zone to the north. Gybing is a long job on an Open 60—swapping the sides of all the boxes below, preparing the runners, rolling up the gennaker— then that horrible moment where the mainsail flicks over and poor *Kingfisher* is pushed way over onto her side as the wind fills in on the new side of the sail. It's a fantastic feeling easing the mainsheet and feeling her accelerate away before unfurling her gennaker, bringing up her swing keel, and tidying away all the lines scattered throughout her cockpit.

After the gybe I saw a further three bergs, the first quite small but the second gigantic. From a distance, it looked like an island, long and sloping gently into the ocean. Its sheer mass became more evident when it seemed to take hours before we felt any nearer. I took pictures and a video of it, in complete and utter awe at the beauty of this massive block. I could see families of birds on top of it as we drew closer, and I could clearly see and hear the waves breaking around its base, as on a rocky shore in a storm. The wind was up to 30 knots by now, a rise of 5, which was pushing us closer and closer to the side of the berg; though we made it safely round, we passed it well within a mile. As we rounded its northernmost point, I was stunned to see two enormous ice caves, perfectly arch-like in shape and sinking away to darkness deep within the berg it-self. Each was large enough to sail *Kingfisher* into—a trip, though, from which there would be no coming back. Its sides were tinted aqua-blue, and it looked so white against the inky-grey sea and darkening sky. There was an aura around this berg, a feeling of complete and utter isolation. I knew that it was highly unlikely that human eyes had ever seen it before.

The next and final berg, though, posed the greatest problem. It only became visible a couple of miles ahead as dusk was approaching—I had no option other than to go below it, past its leeward face—the danger-ous side. Growlers are guaranteed on the downwind side of these bergs, and though I had seen a few scattered around, they had been car-size and visible. But ahead of me, I could see more growlers, and though I sailed as low as I could to miss the berg, and was more than a mile from its po-sition, there seemed no way to avoid what was ahead. The dark sea was strewn with ice, almost like ice-cubes floating in a glass. Shit.

I punched OFF on the autopilot and grabbed *Kingfisher*'s helm, lifting it so I could steer standing up to see over her bow. I found myself slalom-ing between these lumps, just hoping that there would not be a cluster close together.

That evening I dozed in the cuddy and made hot coffee to keep myself awake. I never normally drink coffee, so its effects at sea are more dra-matic, and it did the trick this time, warming me too. It was even colder at night, and I used the discomfort this caused as another aid to keeping myself awake. I pulled a pair of mittens firmly onto my numb hands to try to protect them from the cold so they would work if I needed to use them in a hurry. The wind was strong now, between 28 and 30 knots; with the driving rain I knew it would be almost impossible to see a berg even if it were only a few hundred feet in front of us. The dark clouds scared me a few times, fooling me into thinking that there was a berg looming before us, but as my heart raced, I decided that for at least the next ten minutes we would be OK. I felt strong during that time in the ice fields; it was a wake-up call, something to focus my concentration and take my mind off the pressures. I joked at the camera and spoke to it with obvious concern but amazement on my face. That was one of my strengths—just digging in when the going got tough—but then, as often as not, suffering later the consequences of overdoing it.

I had been in touch with Mark several times that day, keeping him up to date with what was going on. He had been having dinner with friends in Chamonix during my day, and now—my evening being the early hours of his morning—we were talking as he lay in his bed. We'll never know if it was just worry, but Mark was violently ill throughout that night as he lay awake waiting for the next phone-call, waiting to be reassured that all was OK.

ALTHOUGH I DID NOT KNOW it at the time, I was not the only one who had had a bad start to the New Year. There had been tough times on all of the top three boats. Mich had broken the starter motor on his engine and, unable to charge his batteries, was in trouble. It's always a judgement call to decide how many spares you should have on board—how many backups to backups—and part of the learning process is knowing what to take. So far I felt we had been lucky, except for the broken halyards and the loss of our sails, but Mich was definitely facing a major setback. If not resolved it would have a massive impact on his result in the race. Bilou, too, was in a desperate situation; a section of track had ripped off his mast, which meant he could put up his mainsail only with two reefs in. Not being able to increase sail was of crucial importance—especially in light airs. When Mark told me the news, I could not stop thinking about Bilou all day—he is the nicest guy you'll ever meet. He had had this problem since entering the Southern Ocean but had chosen to keep it quiet till now. It's a very different type of emotion when you are exhausted and thousands of miles away from anywhere . . . you are not driven to cry because you are feeling upset, but you are simply driven to your instincts; there is nothing inside you to fight with any longer, no reserve left to draw from.

I was encouraged enormously by contact with others. Ten or so e-mails would be filtered through to me each day from the thousands which were flooding into the website. The correspondents ranged from families in Germany, to classes of kids in schools all over France, to the Swallows and Amazons group at the Alverstoke Junior School. There were always messages which stood out, though—some cheered me up, some made me realize how lucky I was. One of the most memorable was about a young girl named Chiara.

Dear Ellen,

Our daughter Chiara is five years old. She came home from hospital this afternoon. Her treatment for leukaemia has produced new side effects and, once again, given us a real scare.

Still, Chiara amazes us a little more each day with her sense of humour, her ability to laugh at her condition and at her mother and me when she senses our concern. Her remarkable courage and perseverance give her great beauty and radiance.

The reason for my writing to you today is that I know that you support sick children, and this has moved me greatly, especially as the long journey that you have undertaken alone in the Vendée Globe bears some resemblance to Chiara's own journey. You are crossing areas which you alone can explore but which you allow us to glimpse. You alone can win your race. Dear Ellen, I wish you to win this Vendée Globe. Your victory would send a fantastic message of hope to our daughter Chiara as she too hopes to transform her solitude into victory, with all the strength and perseverance that she is able to muster.

If the whims of the ocean were to frustrate your efforts before you reach the Sables d'Olonne, we would remain extremely grateful and attached to you for the exceptional journey which you have been sharing with us over the last two months and for the beauty that emanates from you.

05/01/01 22:35Z (ellenmacarthur.com/day58)
Oh Bilou

I saw your news this morning. I am very sad for you. I've been thinking a lot during to day . . . I hope that you will find all the energy to repair it. It must be hard, but we are with you . . . be careful up there, I've been up several times, and it's not easy—the best is on deck AT THE END! You must come back, I'm missing you! We must stay together till the end . . . Wish I could help . . .
Kisses,
Soon Ellen.

Sent: Sunday, January 07, 2001 04:08Z
Subject: Thank you
Thank you so much for your message Ellen.
I'ts not easy at the moment . . . On top of everything I broke my gennaker halyard attatchment yesterday, I'm sailing with two reefs

and the genoa half unfurled! I't been hard since the 16th December to have this mainsail 2 reefs from the top, without being able to do anything, but well, that's racing.

Your are racing a great race, and I too find it superb to be once more in contact with you. I wish you all the best for the next stage, continue how you know you should.

Kisses Bilou

Shortly after our communication with Bilou, we passed ahead of him into second place. I now had Mich in my sights but still had a lead of around 400 miles to overhaul. When Bilou and I had been pushed south of the weather system, Mich had jumped into the next one, and he had a lead which was extending day by day as he surfed along within the next system. When a boat ahead is in a different system, it can have a concertina effect—they can get into better and better weather and just eat away the miles while you're stuck in the light airs between two systems.

06/01/01 08:09Z (ellenmacarthur.com/day59)
Position 53° 42.7S 118° 34.8W
Heading/speed 59 10.28
Wind from 279 at 12.9 knots
Pressure of 995
Sea temperature 4.4
Sail configuration is Full main Spinnaker
Percentage performance 95.7

Wel all I can manage to say right now is Wow. . . .
As I type there is less movement in KINGFISHER than we have had for a long time. She slides gracefully along under spinnaker in a lght downwind breeze. The moon is out, and is getting close to being full, and there are stars filling the sky—a site that I have rarely seen down here. An cloudless sky, and a very thin mist filling the air—giving the world tonight outside my little hatchway appear alost magical . . . Spirit's are high on board after a constructive day, and again a reaonable amount of god recuperative sleep . . .

The pressure was on during our crossing of the South Pacific, and I was pulling out a clear lead over Bilou as the days passed. He was sailing wounded without his full main—and now, above all, his gennaker. Poor

Bilou needed at least 30 knots of wind before he had a hope of sailing his boat in the way she wanted to be sailed. Having attempted a mast climb once to replace the halyard, he had been forced to give up—it was too dangerous. I recalled the days in the Transat Jacques Vabre with Yves when I spent the best part of three days up a similar rig—his boat, like Bilou's, had a wing mast, and hanging onto it was a nightmare. This had certainly been one of the deciding factors for us in fitting a classic, smaller-section mast. But I was in second place, and though 500 miles was a long way behind Mich, we still had a long way to go. I now was running my race looking ahead more than behind. It would have to be a fairly flash move to gain all those miles, but I felt nothing was impossible.

The stress and anxiety of the last few weeks had eaten away at both Mark and me, however, and things had definitely frayed around the edges. Like Mark, I had a tremendous amount of respect for Mich, but I felt that Mark considered Mich unbeatable. I had to believe he could be beaten, but I didn't feel that Mark shared this view with quite the same conviction. I felt so strongly that it wasn't over till it was over. Mark was exhausted, too, but at the time when I was at my lowest ebb, I needed to be able to turn to him without worrying about how I'd be received. It had to be an uncomplicated relationship, and I vented my frustration in an e-mail.

> I'm not goning to beat about the bush—but you're really upsetting me at the moment.
>
> I hat hearing you so down. I know you've been, and you're tired and exhausted> please try to get some f*****g rest.
>
> When I'm stressed and tired and worroied I know you are too—so please appreciate that it works both ways!
>
> I feel awful right now. I feel shit, and all I can think of is haveing upset—or upsetting you. Don't tell me it's stupid, and to get on with the race because I can't—because I'm ellen—and I need to know you're OK—in a tone of voice that really means it. And if you're not OK then TELL ME—beaciauae I can see that, and I haven't just been born!
>
> Now please GO TO F******G BED, and be better tomorrow because I need you more than you realize, I need to talk bullshit on the pohone, and explaiun things you really don't want to hear,

because we're sailing this race together—and I need you with me till the very end.

After I wrote to Mark I sat on the bow and watched the water swish past for at least half an hour. I was worried about what I'd said, and I knew he would reply that same night. We'd cleared the air, but I still felt I needed to emphasize one thing.

> Michel Desoyeaux is NOT the best in the world. He simply isn't he's not perfect, and I refuse to believe he is. Yes he has more expereince, but i refuse to be phased by him. The best in the world is that little kid CHiara in hospital. ANd if she wants me to win—then I'll do everything in my power to do that for her, even if it nearly kills me, because Christ, i'm achieving very little compared to her . . . When Iread her e-mail I cried, because I know that I can beat Michel—and I have to. Please understand that. I will not let him cross that line first—I WILL NOT!
>
> And yes there will be tears, I know that, it's not easy. But I want to beat Mich more than anything else in the world right now. ANd I dont' want to win this race for me. Far from it. I honestly and truthfully want to win the race for everyone that's fololowing this project—for all those kids, and for you lot. Mark, that's how I get my energy. . .
>
> I know I've said it before, but the thought of ringing you when I got down from that mast was one of the things that really pushed me on. I'm not joking. I was so glad to hear your voice, because I know you understand, and when you said to me "Don't worry you'll be fine" I knew that you were pretty much shitting yourself as much as I was—beacuse we both knew it was going to be far from fine . . .
>
> My final word is that i've changed my keyboard, and am amazingly impressed by it's ease of typing . . . I can almost touch type now.

I knew Mark would notice and appreciate my switching straight back to business. No nonsense. I hoped it would raise a smile.

08/01/01 05:48Z (ellenmacarthur.com/day61)
Position 53° 23.0S 103° 43.0W
Heading/speed 63 12.95

Wind from 170 at 15.4 knots
Pressure of 994
Sea temperature 6.3
Sail configuration is Full main Genoa
Percentage performance 97.1

It's been a quiet, and a busy day really. THis morning we were gybing under gennaker in a wind which came predominantly from the NW, and then now—to be sailing in a wind basically southerly—as the front of the small depression which has formedto our South passes. The wind had been very inconsistent in strength, and patches of clesr sky have been mixed with several hours of a kind of gentle but squally drizzle.

Even as I write the wind has risen to 20 knots . . . the sun has set, and there is a very delicate light shimmering arornd the skies before the world around us is hushed into that almost-darkness by the strengthening evening breeze of the Southern Ocean. A solitary albatross flickers through the air, as if trying to hide before the clouds, as he glides away from his silent visit to our little world.

Cape Horn beckons, nd as the hours pass we become closer and closer to htis ancient amaritime monument. How diferent it feels to be approaching this time—very much in the middle of an adventure, as oppose to our last passage—very much the beginning. I remeber vividly the feelings which flowed through me as we rounded the horn last April. THe emotion of "turning the corner home" with the most beautiful Open 60 I could imagine in the world. THe tears of thanks shed for everyone who had helped—an whatever way for this dream to become reality.

And now, once again to be nearing this point . . . Who Knows what emotions will flow. ut one thing is for certain, and that's that we'lll be heading home. Each mile bringing us closer to that finish line. I promise you all that I shall sail this next chapter of the race with all theskill and energy I have, and can muster. Its not long now, and we're going to do our level best through and past that final mile . . .

AsI finish this message something catches my attention through the window abave. The moon is beaming it's prescence through the tiny openings in the clouds . . . Round and beautiful—it's not often I have seen it down here . . . A gentle reminder that it's that very same moon that you can all see in your hours of darkness . . .

exx

Things were going well on the race front, and although Mich was 540 miles ahead by this stage, with a repaired engine, I was now maintaining a 100-mile lead over Bilou, and Marc Thiercelin on *Active Wear*. It was a lead I was having to fight for, though, as the leech of our gennaker had split quite badly, and this being our last furlable sail, I was scared the damage might get worse. Reluctantly I decided I would have to take it down to make repairs. The wind was not too strong, but the motion of the boat was horrible as she wallowed in the massive swell of the approaching storm. Having lowered the furled sail to the deck, I tried to unfurl it by hand, but it was more than 80 feet long and contorted on a 60-foot deck. The more I unfurled, the harder it became to work each twist all the way down the sail to the bow. I knew I was sailing slowly, and I was desperately frustrated. "Come on, kiddo," I kept urging, "come on." But after an hour my patience finally snapped when I slipped as a wave threw us sideways and I smashed my face, causing a streaming nose-bleed. Wiping away the blood, I swore at the camera. Once again I knew that I was teetering on the edge of my limits, but finishing the job of unfurling and repairing the sail was a proper tonic. Once it was up again, I made myself turkey and chestnut, one of my favourite freeze-dried meals, to celebrate. There was a very fine line between joy and despair: it was only afterwards that things felt good on board again. Conditions were fractionally more stable, and for the first time in days, the weather situation remained fairly predictable, so at least I was able to get some sleep. But by the following evening, the wind had filled in and the new depression was well and truly in contact with us. . . . We were back to the unpredictable winds of the south.

09/01/01 09:30Z (ellenmacarthur.com/day62)
As I sit here and type I am cold and wet—wet with my oown chilled sweat. It was a busy day once again . . . weather study, and many many sail changes as the wind slowly turned, and fluctuated in int's normal Southern Ocean way. By suset I had the gennaker, and was asailing in about 15-29 knots of breeze. There were squall clouds around, and as I had the gennaker up I was worrled that if I slept inside for a while I may be to slow to get to the [autopilot], so iI piled on the lyers of clothes, and as best as I could tried to keep warm and dose in the cuddy. I put a spare oilskin over me to try to keep warm, te water temerpture here is warmer, so it wasn't as cold as it has been. Iwas just drifting through a plethora (is this the right

word?) of dreams, when the heart-stopping slowing of the boat happenned, and the grim realisastion that we had once again blown the halyard . . . no [squall], nothing—just a chafed through halyard. The gennaker—our only gennaker was lying over the waters surface, I immediately blew the main halyard, and her driving sail came slithering down into an unarranged heap on the boom. I had to work out the best plan to save the sail in the water—at least when we were stopped we bought ourselves some time. KINGFISHER wallowed around over the waves, and as I stumbled back across her rolling deck, seeing her sails down I could not help but feel she resembled a wounded bird, I felt for her. An hour later the sail was on the deck—a fight and a half as it's covered in a film which is like trying to drag a plastic sheet which is tugging away at you. As I gingerly but forcefully dragged it over the guard wire my worse fears were realized as I swa the leech was damaged, and on further hauling huge rips were present . . . Myu hear t sank, I hope to god we can fix it . . . Again up the mast, and a repair which I'm not even sure is possible. Tha hardest part of all I think was [getting] the sail through the forehath—it's not quite the same when i'ts' rolled up. It took all the energy I had left to jump on it till it wast rhough—it tikk at least 20 minutes, and everything at that stage ached. [Only] got the mainsal to get back up now I thought to myself . . .

It was yet again a gut-wrenching situation. I felt once more like my world had crumbled around me. Why, oh why did this have to happen again? The sail was badly ripped, but I knew that I would simply have to repair it. It was going to be a hellish job—and one that I would have to do as soon as possible. I would also have to climb the mast once again. I drew small consolation from the fact that at least I'd repaired the broken halyard and it was ready to go. With up to 35 to 40 knots of breeze and just over 500 miles from the Horn, I was not ready to climb it. Plus, with the wind we would see between now and the "corner," it was not worth risking a change now. We shouldn't need it till we were round.

But the frustration and disappointment were fuelled by other news: Mich had just rounded the Horn with a 536-mile lead.

11/01/01 04:32Z (ellenmacarthur.com/day64)
Just trying to think of everything whilst I try to sit here yawning . . .
Shit am I tired. Wind alll over the place, and despite getting tinto sleep bag—can't sleep. Back in oilies once again. Wind now coming

from 070 at 27–30 kn. motion horrid—I am at 45 apparrent and am trying to leave forward ballast out so as not to load up mainsail too much. Speed is down to 11 kn, as I try to keep N-ish. Hard going. Will be along wait for front, as it runs NE–SW. Big risk that I'll not even make it above centre, and willbe easten by it as it moves SE. F****** hope not. Scat [scatterometer] show that the wind behind front is maybe less than 29 kn. We're in deep shit if this is the case, as cannot sail [down] enough to make Horn. It will be a frustrating shambles. Wish I cold stop yawning. Not lookingforwatd to all the media stuff. Really don't feel like it this time. It's hard with so many worries! talk later, WIll try tonight—time for 3rd reef.
bye e

The rounding of Cape Horn was not to be the way I had imagined it in the build-up to the race. As I began to write out my thoughts on the computer before we arrived, I knew that it would not be the silent rounding we had wished for. I could not stop thinking of the other competitors, and I hoped that they, too, would make it safely round the corner. Of the twenty-four starters, seven were already out of the race and another five had either had to anchor to repair or had serious problems. There was Pasquale de Gregorio, the Italian, in his 50-footer *Wind*. With his long grey curly hair, cigar, and small round spectacles, he was a real character. Since the descent of the Atlantic he'd been sailing with three reefs, as he had broken a vital piece of rigging. For Fedor Konioukhov, things were looking very bleak. He was more than 8,000 miles behind *Kingfisher* and not only was suffering massive sail damage but also had a serious kidney infection. I felt sad for the shy Russian who had already climbed just about every peak in the world. As I spoke to him on the morning of the start he had had an almost childlike enthusiasm for the race. His eyes had sparkled, and he spoke of rounding the Horn in daylight, but his dream was not to come true. Fedor would not make the Horn on this trip; instead, he was forced to sail hundreds of miles north to Australia for urgent medical attention.

12/01/01 17:46Z (ellenmacarthur.com/day65)
Well I feel quite overwhelmed reallyu. The stress and difficulties of the last few days seem to be melting into emotion as I approach the horn. The second time for KINGFISHER aND I TOGETHER . . . it's

a great symbol for the two of us personally, as the very frost time i
was ever alone on here, was just a few miles form this famous rock. I
cannot helpl but feel moved deep inside. THe thoughts of the past
storms and struggles off this point. This race has been hard, but
when I think of those here huindreds of years ago I feel very humble
sitting here. For then, the corner was literally life or death, and my
heart goes out to all those who have struggled, survived and died
on this piece of water. . . Those memories shall never be forgotten
here . . .

The weather is misty, I strain my eyes to see, but I must wait till
I'm a little nearer . . . ECH TIME i think of where we are, and where
we've been I find my eyes welling with tears. It's been a long haul
since the launch in NZ, and the most incredible adventure of my
life. Not one just of the story of A GIRL ALONE ON THE SAEA,
BUT FAR MORE THATN THAT. foR ME IT's a stiry of teamwork,
friendship and love, the story of so many people working towards a
goal, and if not working—willing us on . . . I feel there are so many
others with me on board, i've never been lonely—far from it—even
in times of stress. I've been haoopy here with my friend
KINGFISHER, and am now looking forward to the atlantic trip.
Firstly so we can be on our way home, ands secondly so we can get
our repairs done in warmer condioitns. I cannot help but feel wer
are "wounded" rght now, and need the warmer weather to repair and
get our strtength back . . .

I was right about our rounding, which ended up being almost like
keeping to an itinerary. I was glad I had had time to contemplate what an
incredible place this was just hours before, and even more pleased to
have actually stopped there a year previously. From filming it to doing
live radio interviews about it, to being filmed by another boat, to talking
with the guys on the rock itself was far from being the peaceful moment
Fedor had imagined; in fact it was a very stressful time. At one point I
had a camera in my hand, a call on the mini M phone, one on the Satcom
B, and a French voice screaming over the VHF radio trying to ask more
questions. It was odd seeing the faces of people on the yacht which was
filming us, something for which I don't think I was really prepared. It
was 1845 GMT on 12 January 2001; we were now in a similar time zone
to Europe. And I was still two days behind Michel Desjoyeaux.

Within about an hour of rounding Cape Horn, the wind died and we found ourselves in almost flat water sailing close-hauled. I grabbed the opportunity the calm presented, shinning straight up the mast to repair the halyard. In these conditions I had it done in less than thirty minutes—incredible to think that a few weeks before the job had taken me three and a half brutal hours.

15/01/01 13:18Z (ellenmacarthur.com/day68)
Position 47° 52.0S 056° 16.7W
Heading/speed 55 14.48
Wind from 318 at 25.8 knots
Pressure of 999
Sea temperature 5.1
Sail configuration is 2nd reef Solent
Percentage performance 99.6

STOP PRESS
ONe of the seeds has sprouted!! exx

Life after the Horn changed dramatically as we headed north; from wind speed to temperature, everything switches in an instant. The sky suddenly becomes blue, and the water takes on a green tint you never seem to see in the south. You remember what it's like to be able to sleep at the chart table without shivering and to look at the weather without constantly searching through the information for the next depression that is going to run up behind you and bite you. Five weeks is an awful long time to be down in those conditions, and the relief is certainly proportionate as you start the trek north toward home.

Our first obstacle was fairly substantial, as we had to negotiate the Falkland Islands. I remembered from the delivery from New Zealand that there would be a terrific amount of kelp in the water, so I was not keen to take a route inside the islands. Each time I had looked at the weather I felt that the western option was best, though generally every weather book said it was best to stay outside to the east. The weather was up to its usual tricks, however, changing in speed and direction and making me really work to make progress to the north. I was still tired and again felt the enormous pressure of making that vital decision: whether to go east or west.

I finally sheeted in the sails, and rather than go for the faster-reaching

conditions to head to the east, I slowed down and stayed west. My plan
was to get the new breeze more quickly and then have a better angle for
approaching the Equator. As we had seen on our way down in this ocean,
it paid to be in the west, and that was my plan. I had to do something
very different from Michel. With upwind conditions, things were more
stable for a while, though I had to be very careful of fishing boats heading
out from Stanley. After the islands, though, the wind freed and built a
little, and at last I had a chance to rest.

16/1/01/ 01:43Z (ellenmacarthur.com/day69)
Position 45° 51.4S 053° 04.9W
Heading/speed 44 14.86
Wind from 310 at 23.4 knots
Pressure of 1001
Sea temperature 5.6
Sail configuration is 2nd reef Solent
Percentage performance 105.4

Well all is well n board, it's great to be eating away the miles, though
hte situation ahead is lookking les than straight forward.
KINNGFISHER is fluying along, she seems [to like] the pooint of
sailoing . . . The motion though is quie violent—the waves now
building, and a NW swell meean we're pounding, and it's a fragile
balance between sped and saffety. This evening the wind has
strengthened once again, though less than consistent . . . it's gusting
from 19 to 25 knots, so difficut to set the tight smount of sail. Glad
to seethat one by one the fleet are rounding the horn, i don't know
about the others but iyt'll be a relief for me when everyone is safely
round. Its a wonderful place, but one in whih to be very cautious.
Everything on board is quite hard with this motion . . . it's ecen less
predicatable that tnhe Southern Ocean surfs . . . The god news is I've
had a good while to study the wearthertoday, and have nhad large
amounts of much needeed sleep both early this morning, and during
the day. Feeliong much better of it, and really feeliong ready to wrk
hard tillthe finish. It's easy tp relax after the horn as the weather
warms, but it's just the astart of the journey home. . . . With just
under 6,000 miles to go, we're far from round the corner . . .
everyone in media centre hot on story of gaining miles on michel. i
said that I waould sail kf how she wnts to be sailed till the end, and

not push her to 120 percent to ctch mich.\if we gain miles it[s
greatl, if not hat's life as we are not in the same weather conditions
. . . talk later ex

The seas were generally pretty horrible, and we were really thrown
around in those conditions. We were right at the wind limit for the solent, too, which meant going forward for constant checks. If it came to
it, it was a big step down to the staysail, and we'd really stop moving. I
lost count of the number of times I dashed up to the foredeck to check
that the solent was still OK. Each time I went, there was the little challenge of seeing if I could get up there and back without being dumped
on by a wave. It was hard even to walk along the side-deck with conditions like that, let alone get there and back quickly. I would get as far as
the daggerboard standing upright through the deck, wrap my arms
around it, and hang on for grim death. It was pretty full on but reassuring that we were OK!

Already, just a few days into our new regime and with the water temperature rising quickly, I was feeling the massive pressure of closing
miles on Michel.

17/01/01 07:25Z (ellenmacarthur.com/day70)
Well it's been a very frustrating night . . . Nothing i seem to have
done will make KINGFISHER go! It's been a struggle. I just hope
that oour apparrent lack of speed is a pure illusision, and the
position reports show this, though with the others in a different
weather system now it's doubtful it will eb a gfood indication.
   I've changed from 2 reefs and solent to fulll main and genoa. I've
had ballast in and out, i've even lifted up and down the daggerboard
to check there was nothing caught on it . . . THings seema little
better now, but it's been a long an dtiring period of darknes. Not
helped by the fat that i'm sailing in thick fog—so despite it not
raining, the seond you venture outside you become soaked with a thin
but penetrating mist of chill! THe high point of the night so far has
been the dolphin which came too join us for a short while, his smalll
dark body leaping from the waves in the misty darkness . . . It still
amazes me each time one of these creatures comes over to visit . . .
   Quite a contrast to yesterday as we had close reaching and blue
skies for the most part of the day, though yesterday too started with

fickle conditions as we had 30+ knots on the nose for a while. THe
forecasts are subtley changinf daily, and it's our job to be able to spot
each subtelytly as it subtley shows itself!
bye for now, ellen x

But despite the problems we were having with the wind speed and
wave patterns, we were making good progress. Mich was now less than
200 miles ahead, stuck doing just 7 knots in the high-pressure zone of
St. Helena. We were fairly clear from behind, too, as Marc Thiercelin
was more than 200 miles behind us. I was still being spurred on by anger
at Mich's remarks, and it was the biggest motivation ever to be gaining
miles on him—and above all to see that it would be some time before he
could get away to the west. He was sailing north to the centre of the St.
Helena high-pressure system, and as I got closer, the system drifted to
the east. He needed to catch the wind shift to get out to the north, but
that shift was just not coming for him. There was no question of being
happy with the position I was in until that line was crossed; I had a fire
inside me which was pushing me on, and with each day, as we closed on
our ultimate destination, it was getting hotter and hotter.

There was interesting news from Bilou, though—he had anchored
the boat in the little anchorage we had stopped in on our return from
New Zealand and climbed and repaired his mast. He was celebrating the
fact that he could put up his whole mainsail. It had been four weeks since
he'd been able to do this, and he was hot on Marc's tail. For every skipper in the race, it seemed it was far from over. Even Yves was off once
again from his adventure, rebuilding his rig in New Zealand.

21/01/01 (ellenmacarthur.com/day74)
Position 28° 47.9S 030° 31.1W
Heading/speed 67 11.75
Wind from 357 at 16.1 knots
Pressure of 1013
Sea temperature 21.1
Sail configuration is 1st reef Solent
Percentage performance 101.1

What a night . . .

This mornign the sky looks like a picture postcard—deep
pastel-like clouds against a lighteneing blue sky. The night however
was not so clement! A couple fo hours after sunset it started, the
clouds grew, and suddenly we were surrounded by a group iof
particularly ugly ones . . . 6 hours later it was sunriuse and we were
out the other side—but what a battle. As the clouds grew nearer the
wind increased—it turned through 90 degrees from one cloud to
another—the wind went from 17 to 35 knts, and twice in between I
had to unfurl the genoa just to keep us moving. I dozed in the
cockpit—but many times jumped up like i was on fire as the wind
blew like mad—as if from nowhere. Each cloud had it's own
charachter—each cloud its own wind. Yesterday we had the same—
but it seems different in the day time. THough being sucked under
those clouds makes it often feel like dusk. The sky darkens—the
horizon is lost in the rain—and the wind blows, and blows . . . The
rain so hard that the waves are flattened, so hard you have to squint
to see. Often the way is to bear away, adn KINGFISHER takes off
like there is air between her and the water . . . the waves flow away
from her bow—almost like they're unattaached . . . Incredible.

Manging to stay in front of the fornt . . . just hoping the wind
turns back a wee bit into the west. . . . ellen xx

It was hard work just waiting for the weather front to come over. We
had been sailing in grey, foggy conditions, but as the front approached, I
could see the sky once again—and not only the clouds around it, but
also the mass of grey behind us as the front in the distance crept nearer.
Although the front was fairly ominous in its appearance, it was a blessing
in disguise—the longer we stayed ahead of it, the longer we stayed in a
good breeze. Nonetheless, I was looking forward to its passing, as we
would then be in lighter airs and, more important, dry weather. I was
still worried about the gennaker I'd been unable to fix; it would be crucial for our crossing of the Equator. I had tried just after Cape Horn, but
I failed because it wasn't hot enough to burn off the moisture from its
surface, making it impossible to work on. The passing of the front was as
ugly as ever, with changing winds, lightning, and just about every other
condition you could imagine thrown in, but basically the weather was
improving. I was now wearing just a single layer of thermals and even
enjoying bare feet—a stark contrast to the Southern Ocean.

This morning feels like a new start, it's incredible . . . I had a great
sleep last night, and at about 0100 set about checking KINGFISHER
all over from head to toe . . . we've had littel wind—and now, thank
goodness—the wind has turned—and it looks like—if 24 hours
eraly we might be able to tack . . .The wind is unsteady—but erring
on the side of northerly . . . During the night I busied around below
emptying water out of all her compartments (only a few bucket-
fulls) right up before her watertight bulkheads, 1 and 2! The motion
of KINGFISHER is more silent than ever before . . . the sky was as
open as ever shrouded by a delicate veil of glittering stars. Despite
littel wind we never stoipped once, and she gently trod across the
smooth ocean surface. THis morning as the sun rose the sky went
pink in the west, and in the easy the striking orange glow looked like
it hid a million treasures as it peeked out from behind the scattered
clouds. Teh clouds themselves suspended almost as if pre-arranged in
the sky . . . There were layers and layers of them, adn I could not
help but gfeel that there were towns ande villages hidden among
them . . . It really is so very beautiful . . . As I stood in the cockpit I
watched in wonder . . . My eyes began to fill with tears as I
marvelled at this intense beauty, an intense beaauty—which at that
second in time, had only I along wtith that rising sun as onlookers.
ex

I made the most of the more stable conditions finally to carry out the
gennaker repair. I dragged it up through the tiny forehatch—it weighed
almost 50 kilos—and only then did I realize for the first time the full extent of the damage. There were rips up to 8 yards long, and threads
which had broken and pulled out of the fabric, fraying the edges like an
ugly wound. It took me well over an hour to clean them up, carefully
leaving enough fabric to be able to match the edges together, and to remove the hair-like fibres that would keep both halves from sticking to
each other. I painstakingly dried each side of each tear and began the
long process of patching the two sides together—first with "stitches" of
adhesive-backed cloth, then with larger pieces. The sun beat down during that day, making work uncomfortable, but I was determined to finish
it before the wind increased and became too high to keep the sail on the
deck, so I put every bit of energy I had into it. Thirteen hours later, as
the evening dew was just beginning to settle on the deck, I was finished.
I bore away from the wind, hoisted the sail, and furled it.

The final part of the repair had been a large white patch on the leech at the bottom corner of the sail, and the words I had scrawled in capital letters on the fabric were still visible in the twilight: "North Sails—Born to survive." I smiled—we'd done it.

25/01/01 09:28Z (ellenmacarthur.com/day78)
Another hard night . . . the trades with the lack of consistency of the high pressure are fickle and frustrating, though I'm not complaiinig as it's great to have wind! As I type the wind is blowing from 13 to 17 knots—and though that doesn't sound much—it's the difference between being OK or not for the genoa—so there's little peace! The wind over the past 12 hours has swung iregularly through 50 degrees . . . it really is a full time job to keep her moving well . . . On the other hand it's a lovely mornign—the massive zones of storm clouds have mnelted away in the morning heat . . . Maybe today will be abetter for some sleep . . .
X

26/01/01 04:14Z (ellenmacarthur.com/day79)
Well the wind has died right off tonight . . . we sail along at 9–10 knot's . . . it's frustrating, but I'm hoping it won't last for too long . . . maybe the temperature change has brought this on . . . Im not sure. Today has been a day of varied winds, and again—many sail changes, the temperature has increased forther, and sleeping— especially during the day is difficult. It's hard work pulling out and putting in the reefs . . . The 1str reef especauilly as it has the most friction, and incolves lifting the weight of the whole mainsal . . . it's a big reef—the biggest of the three—so takes the wind out of you every time . . . Not made esasier by the heat. It really is a grind, and if the boat isn't bouncing to ease the reefing ennanats through it's almost achieved by half-turns with the pedestal . . . Despite the exhaustion iin this heat of atually shaking out the reef—it becomes well worth while as KINGFISHER once agiain begins her mission across the waves at her full potential . . . a great feeling which makes the breeze flow across her—taking away some of that continuous heat . . .

It was hard work making progress in the fickle winds, and trying to sleep in the heat was almost impossible. I covered myself in cream to protect myself from the sun, but once below, I would sweat so much I'd end up kneeling in a pool of milky perspiration. My appetite disappeared as well, and though I am usually quite good at feeding myself, all I could eat in the heat was a bowl of lukewarm couscous. With a seawater temperature of 25 degrees, even the water from the desalinator was already warm. I was tired, and as the Doldrums were coming up I was going to need every ounce of energy.

Tactics were not so complicated here, though, as basically the farther west you are, the more quickly you get through the zone. In the satellite images the way looked clear; I was 40 miles to the west of Mich, so things were looking fairly good. If ever we had a chance to pass him, it was now. I made a conscious decision to hold onto my position to the west and keep those 40 miles between us. Unfortunately, someone else had different ideas. Two nights before entering the Doldrums I was sailing with the repaired gennaker and full main. We were making great progress and trucking along to the north. The issue was that the nights were strewn with squalls—and with our delicate gennaker, one of these could destroy our repair. I felt nervous and found it very difficult to sleep. But things went wrong for us in a big way that night. The wind instruments at the top of the mast started to malfunction. This meant that I could not use the autopilots to sail on an "apparent wind angle" but only on a fixed compass heading. It was a nightmare, as it meant we weren't at all responsive to changes in the wind direction. If ever the gennaker was going to break, it would be by being hit by a squall before I could make it to the helm. I tried using the spare instruments that were on a pole on the back of the boat, but they were not sensitive enough for these light, changeable winds. I would have to steer by hand.

I spent most of the night hand-steering and watching out for the demon clouds which bring strong breezes with them, and preparing for yet another climb up the mast—to the top once again, this time to replace the wind wand that held her anemometer.

26/1/01 16:15Z (ellenmacarthur.com/day79)
What better to take your mind off a race than a bit of early morning DIY [do-it-yourself]? . . . Yes that sounds great, but what will it involve? Mmm. Now a bit of sanding, and quite a lot of drilling—oh yes, and a bit of wiring. Fantastic—when can I start . . . Straight away, but unfortunately your workdshop is at 27 meters!

Yes ellen was once again up the mast this morning—will she ever shake this habit! During the night I expereinced problems with the wind instruments, the boat [tacked] herself due to a lack of wind data, and I quickly deduced that the anemometer was tired . . . It's amazing how imperative that wind data is to us . . . Things have meoved on from looking at the wooly telltales and the clouds— wind speeds and angles are imperative to fast sailing, and sail limits—so it was change over the anemeoeter time . . . As usualk a beautiful calm sunrise turned into a gusty bit of sea once I'd reached half way . . . I nmust have looked fairly silly as I had a long wand strapped to my back, and a massive bag of tools . . . (it's a bit far to come down if you've forgotton something!) It went OK other than the violent motion, and the amount of sanding needed to fit the wand. THe most frustrating part was the first time I fitted it—just to see how far it went in—and I couldn't get it out again! Once fitted I had to drill out for the retaining pin—quite a task juggling drill [bits] and drills at 27m! THe painful part was the slamming in the waves, causing the bag with drill in poking into my leg . . . the beautiful part was taking just a second to galnce out over that orange sea scape as the sun rose . . . The waters surface so delicate as the waves texture it . . . Just stunning . . .

Well its nice to be becak down again, and despit a few holes and brusies we're on good form. Well Mark did say it's about time I went back up the meast again . . . Thanks mark!

love ellen

I was overjoyed to have new instruments, and I had a great day with the gennaker. But the worst was far from over. Just as I was looking forward to my last real opportunity to sleep in the cool of the night before the Doldrums, the instruments failed again. I was distraught, and sick inside. This time it was not going to be so easy to see the lighter side. I spent another tiring night hand-steering with the gennaker up, forcing myself to keep my eyes open in that hot breeze, with the intermittent stars lighting our decks as the squall clouds passed. Several times we were completely surrounded by clouds, the wind dying and then hurling back at us. The thunder, lightning, and cool rain helped enormously to keep me alert. It is a strange feeling in those battles through the rain storms. It's almost as though you are transported to another world with the rain powering down on the water—the lightning and darkness and the hot and the cold gusts of wind that pelt the rain at you. Then, sud-denly, nothing—just the sounds of the water running off the decks; no rain, just an agitated silence . . . till that next crack of thunder.

At first light the following morning I undertook yet another mast climb. This time it should have been easier: before starting up the mast I exchanged the broken circuit board in the wind vane I'd replaced the previous day. Then I prepared my tools, furled the gennaker, and set off again on that journey taking me to the farthest point I'd reach from *Kingfisher*'s deck in eighty days.

The climb went well and the vane changeover was relatively straight-forward. But as I worked away I noticed a squall cloud heading towards us. The wind increased and *Kingfisher* heeled over, her side-decks echoing with the sounds of the sea pounding along them. I had no option—I had to finish the job and get down. The rain began, and I tried my best to keep the water from the wires I was joining, but it was virtually impos-sible. The stronger wind didn't cause undue problems, though; what really sent my heart racing were the light airs that immediately followed the squall. The less sensitive instruments on the back of the boat that were now steering us couldn't pick up the soft breeze and, confused, forced us to gybe. The mainsail swung across the boat, jamming my legs between the runners and the sail. I forced the sail back over with my feet, but each time it would gybe back again, trapping my legs. My mind went into overdrive. Although we had only a few knots of wind, I knew that at any moment the wind would come back strongly. But I also knew that I had no control over the situation; more than 90 feet above the deck, I could do nothing except just try to finish the job. The adrenalin was rush-ing through me, causing my arms to tremble as I fumbled to connect the wires. I tried to ignore the pain in my legs. If the wind came back now I would be in real danger—20 knots of wind from the wrong direction would mean that the top of the mast would be pushed down to the water, and, though it didn't really bear thinking about, I would be underneath it.

I think that was the moment during the entire race when I felt the most scared, because my fate was entirely out of my own hands. Even in the Southern Ocean when I was hanging from the rig with one hand, I was in control—either I let go or I didn't, but I still had a choice. Here I had none.

When I eventually got back to the deck I was shaking from head to toe, and black and blue as a result of two successive mornings thrashing around up there. I called Mark to let him know what had happened, then slept, almost comatose, for an hour or so before pulling out the gennaker once more.

As WE APPROACHED the Equator I was catching up on Michel literally hour by hour, and watching the position reports eagerly. But while up the mast the day before and later recovering sleep, I had lost the 40 miles of longitude I'd had in the bag and was downright angry with myself for that. Why did we have those problems now? Just a couple of days later and the outcome of the Vendée Globe could have been very different.

On 28 January I was just 26 miles behind Mich and closing the gap. We crossed the Equator at 0907, and in light winds beneath an overcast sky, I made my offering. I threw my second-to-last packet of ginger nuts over the side and thanked Neptune for letting us pass safely, finishing off my thanks with "Thank you for putting Mich in a windless hole; I know that's not nice; but thanks."

That afternoon the wind died again and we began a forty-eight-hour fight to extract ourselves from the Doldrums. It was hot, frustrating sailing, and I knew that I was absolutely worn out. I spoke to Mark.

> It's so fluky. It's scary. I just want the wind to steady, it won't stay still for more than 3 minutes . . . oh @£!$%$ . . . the wind has switched, the genoa is flapping. I've got to tack again I think . . .
> [several minutes later] This is so hard. I'm going 3 knots. When the wind changes the boat can't easily steer around it, even hand-steering, it's impossible. It's not easy. . . . It's really not easy. There is no real weather information, we're just fighting for each mile, and hoping the Doldrums will move and let us through. You feel if you see the genoa flap one more time you're going to pull your hair out. The problem is we don't have any breeze to get anywhere, we've made our choice . . . the wind has swung again . . . unbelievable . . . it's been like this all night . . .

The following morning, and after what was probably the worst night, I took the lead in the race. Not knowing the news, I called Mark for the radio schedule that morning. I was curled up on the chart-table seat, and when he told me, I managed to smile, but I was so tired I could barely speak. I knew that I was slightly farther to the east than Mich and that it would be a miracle if I popped out first, which was a real damper on the news. My comment to Mark was, "Sorry—you're going to have a busy day, aren't you?" Then the wind shifted, and it was time to tack once more. When we left the Doldrums Mich had already pulled out a 40-mile lead on us, so *Kingfisher* and I made a pact together that we would sail just that bit faster and draw a couple of miles closer each day. As long as the race was not over, neither was our hope.

WE HAD MADE OUR BED but we were not happy to be lying in it and now was the time just to get on with it, I kept telling myself. We were going to give it all we had to catch the white boat in front. Spirits were up, mentally I had thrown down the gauntlet and was pleased to be taking on the race again—it was as if we had just restarted it.

We were pushing on, desperate to make up the miles to Mich, but now, since popping into the lead, however briefly, the phone was ringing off the wall with requests for interviews and video chats via satellite. Mainstream UK had woken to the race but we had not crossed the finish line yet—could we please get on?

We were making a reasonable fight of chasing Mich, and *Kingfisher* was fit and revelling in the breezes away from the Doldrums. I took a moment in the cuddy to rest as the sun went down. Then my head was smashed violently against the bulkhead, and the peaceful evening air was ripped by a horrific splitting sound. We had hit something hard—probably a container lost off a cargo ship—and stopped dead in the water.

Looking behind from the cockpit, I saw the tip of the rudder and the daggerboard floating away. My first reaction was fuelled by pure adrenalin, and I tore through the boat checking every compartment to be sure no water was flooding in. I could hear my heart beating so loud that it was not even worth swearing to vent my fears. A quick check showed that no water was coming in. I grabbed the endoscope, fumbling to get it out of the box and then through the valve in the bottom of the boat. I pressed my eye to its rim—I could see no damage, thank goodness, and the keel looked OK. My mind switched from pure survival back towards racing. I could see one side of the daggerboard swaying pathetically from side to side below us, and I knew I would have to get it out; it was slowing us down badly as it dragged through the water. I returned to the cockpit and tacked over, leaving the water ballast on the wrong side so I could check *Kingfisher*'s rudder. She heeled over erratically as her keel was to leeward, but I got a good look at the rudder—the tip was broken, but otherwise it seemed OK. As I tacked back, I slipped on a book full of photos of Derbyshire I'd been given for Christmas. Just a few minutes earlier I'd been reading—transported to a very different world. I couldn't retrieve the last of the daggerboard—it seemed stuck—so I tacked back and called Mark to tell him what had happened and to get the designers together in a conference call to discuss the best plan. I was worried for the rudder more than anything else. We had a spare, but it would not be easy to change, and I wanted to hear the guys say that they thought it would be OK. It was a massive problem, as we had several days of sailing upwind to the Azores high; although I felt hopeful that *Kingfisher*'s hull and structure were still sound, we were definitely going to be without one of our daggerboards. Without it protruding vertically below the hull to stabilize us, we would slide steadily sideways, losing miles on Mich. And if things were really against us, the others would get through on our inside. I was beyond frustration. I just had to deal with it.

The first task after we'd established that all should be OK was to get the damaged board out of its case. We were sailing a third slower than we should have been, which I had to stop as soon as possible. The problem was that each time I tacked over, I was sailing at 90 degrees to the route I wanted to take, and I would be losing miles to Mich just as much as if I was standing still. When I tacked again to do the job, I was on a mission! It took more than an hour to remove the board, as the impact had rammed it back into its case, and by the time I had solved that, I had sworn more than during the whole race put together! After rigging a pulley on the front of the boat, I passed a rope around the daggerboard with a boathook beneath her. This allowed me to winch the board forward, but annoyingly, the rope cut into the damaged carbon and became almost impossible to move. Bit by bit, I winched the rope out of the board and started again . . . we had to do this, there really was no option. Finally, after breaking the up-haul rope and attaching a halyard directly to the top of the board, I had loosened it enough to remove it from its case. I left it in there for the time being, but at least it was out of the water.

After tacking back, it was already dark, and after a further chat with Merv, I prepared my tools and set about trying to get some sleep. I was still exhausted from the Doldrums, and I had to have my wits about me to do the next part of the job.

At first light, I began the task of refeeding the broken ropes in the strut which is used to lift and drop the board. It wasn't easy poking fishing line and weights down a tube so as to feed the line on the correct side of a pulley, as it was blowing 25 knots and waves were washing down the deck—but I managed it. By far the hardest part, though, was removing the board from the starboard side and finding the emergency pulleys which were hidden in its structure. They had been designed so they could go into the other case, but being asymmetric, they would have to go in upside down. It was going to be a very nasty job, but even so, little did I know how much it was going to take out of me.

I struggled for three hours, trying to get the board from its case; each time I tried winching on the halyard, it jammed just millimetres from coming out. I jiggled it and winched, and tried attaching blocks to the mast—but I only succeeded in destroying the bracket for the radar and driving myself mad! Each time, I climbed 20 or so feet up the mast to shift the block or move the bracket. Conditions were horrible, and I was tired.

All this was taking my nerves well beyond where they wanted to go. The board wasn't shifting, and I had the feeling I was continually taking backwards steps. I punched it, kicked it, and shouted at it—finally, after at least five hours' work, it popped out, spinning and whacking me on the side of the head in the process.

The next step was to lay the board on the deck to find the pulleys, but even that was easier said than done, as it was covered in a graphite compound which made it slide hopelessly everywhere; if it fell over the side, I really would be in trouble. I lashed it hastily to the deck in a way which certainly would not have won me any prizes, then set about trying to shield the drill from the waves to find the pulleys. The two board ends were not exactly the same shape, and in re-fairing them, I had lost the small imprints showing the internal tubes. Drilling holes in the boards would undoubtedly weaken their structure, so I was only going to get one shot at this. Each time *Kingfisher* went over a big wave and hammered down into the trough, I withdrew the drill for fear of breaking the bit; it was a long and frustrating task, as it seemed to take forever to find the holes. Once I'd found the pulley, I had to file away the remaining carbon; it felt like sacrilege just hacking away at this perfect and functional board. Meanwhile, the damaged daggerboard was lying on the foredeck where I had laid it, and I could hear it begin to wear away at everything around it.

I must have looked like a coal miner at this stage, as I was covered in carbon dust and cuts, and my eyes stung, raw from the fibres that had blown into them. As I worked away, I was hurting, suffering acutely each time I saw what a mess *Kingfisher* was in and how helpless she seemed. That helplessness was reflected by me, too—I was shedding tears of frustration, and physically there was little left inside me. I was fighting with a 12-foot board which weighs more than an average man and which refused to stay still while we were crashing through 20- to 25-knot waves. I was struggling.

Finally, by sunset, the starboard daggerboard was in the port case and we were moving along once again. The cockpit seats were covered with the drill (now taped into a plastic bag), files, hammers, and tape. Poor *Kingfisher*—after all we had been through, she didn't deserve this. She had looked after me so well, and then this happened. For the first time in the race we were faced with something we had no chance of fixing out at sea. It's amazing what can be fixed, but this was a solid piece of her which was smashed to bits, and we were going to have to finish the race like that. I felt as if I had let her down. I couldn't repair her. We had worked so hard to look after each other, and we'd arrived at this point where nothing I could do would really help.

As for our distance from Mich, I was livid. We were now 76 miles behind . . .

I feel very sad to see the damage. It breaks my heart, I've tried so hard to look after her, and to win the race. The rudder, there is nothing I can do about, its out of sight and out of mind really. But lying on the foredeck is a very broken dagger board, and there are black marks all over the deck where the board was crashing around when I was trying to move it. I know the board which is down now isn't working 100 per cent because it is the wrong way, and that's pretty hard . . . you have to try to

put it out of your mind and race like before but . . . it never
really goes away. Something like that will never leave for the
rest of your life. To hit something so hard. After all the energy
we have put in, it's just pretty frustrating . . .

   I will just try to do the best that I can. I promised that . . .
can I still catch **PRB***? Big question. I don't think there's much*
chance of hitting something. Anything can happen, absolutely
anything can happen. For sure with the problems we've had
there is a loss of performance, but very much in my own mind,
the race is still on. I'm looking ahead at Mich and at the guys
behind, and I promised myself I wouldn't give up until we
passed that finish line . . . am I allowed to swear?!!

I was glad that we were in the trade winds now, to give me some
chance to catch up on sleep and try to prepare myself for the breeze we
would have after the high. Things were relatively simple tactically: we
had to sail into the Azores high-pressure system, then out onto the sleigh
ride back to France. During our repairs, we had lost 25 miles to Mich,
and it was frustrating to see wild speculation flying around as to why we
had lost the miles on Mich. We had simply decided not to make our collision public until I knew that the repair was achievable and completed.

01/02/01 03:34Z (ellenmacarthur.com/day85)
It has been a bit of a 24 hours, and as I sit here I'm glad that it's over.
Today was one of the hardest in the race for me, fighting—when
you're struggling to find what's in you to fight. The good news is that
the starboard board is [now] in the port side, after a nightmare 9
hours of battles with pulleys, lines, drills and files! The board weighs
more than I do, and shifting it around in 20 knots upwind wasn't
easy—nor dry!
   Oh Mark, as I reached the end of your mail I had tears in my
eyes. The last 4 years have been the most incredible adventure I
could ever have wished to expereice. When I thihnnk how much I
have learned I feel so very grateful to you . . . THinking back to the
first time we really talked in your office seems like a lifetime away
. . . it's incredible . . .
   Thanks so much for supporting me over the past 2 days. Solving
that problem was I think the hardest challenge so far in the race. And

above all striking at a time when we were below par, and trying to recover. Thank you for being there, thank you for organizing everything so clearly and coolly—when your head was probably in as much of a spin as mine.

I know it's not long till the finish, and I know that we'll have to dig deeper still and push harder, but also, and we've known this from the first time we worked together—that it will be more than worth it, and our blood, sweat and tears (and those of the team) have been some of the best spent ever—I just hope that everyone will feel this, even partially as strongly as we do.

As far as Mich is concerned I know it's far from over. We shall see—I may be ide of the mark. I shall not try to do anything other than my own race. What shall happen will happen, and I'm not giving up . . . I'm not ready to gover up till I've crossed that line. We've all worked to hard for giving up.

What ever happens I do know that the project has been a success, that we havve touched millions. For the forst time in my life the media thing sc ares me. TO have some privacy is important to me, but I know it will be OK, and in a way the baord probalem was a godsend because it took my mind off worrying about the finish.

Though I know, that the moment you hug me, that you will look after me, and Mark—that is one of the biggest comforts I have right now. Thank you for everything, for ebing the best friend and companion . . . Never doubt yourself Mark, you're f****** awesome too . . . And don't doubt that I am in a very qualified position to say that. I'm looking forward very much to being with you, laughing with you and almost above all working with you once again. We make the best team Mark.

always exx

It was quite obvious from the vibes I was getting via Mark, and the interviews that I was already doing, that things ashore were changing fairly dramatically. In France any finish of a Vendée Globe is big news, and I was half prepared for that, but I was increasingly aware of how the story was developing in the UK, and internationally too. Now, less than ten days from the finish, it was hard to prepare for it mentally. The e-mails coming in could not have been more diverse, and the encouragement people were offering was just second to none. I was completely and utterly bowled over. It was a strange position to be in, because although I knew damn well that life would be turned on its head in a few days' time, I still had to put 100 per cent of my efforts into getting to that line as fast as possible. The race was still winnable.

One of the few e-mails I received from home came towards the end of the race.

Sent: Friday, 2 February 2001 17:35
Subject: Home

Hope all is well there and you have managed to recoup some sleep to build up some energy. Had a strange experience today. There was a knock on the door and I thought it might be another reporter wanting photographs so I had my words ready. Standing on the doorstep was a "lifelong sailor" wanting to show his admiration for what you are doing and gave me some flowers. I had to prize a name out of him which I have found in the directory. Tonight I will ring him and thank him again and send him one of your posters. There is a feeling of tension, excitement and expectation here. Take care—I can't express my feelings right now—I'm a bit full. Love as always—will you thank the team for cushioning me from the truth.
Mum

04/02/01 07:29Z (ellenmacarthur.com/day88)
I had the weirdest experience yesterday evening—a sand storm! Suddenly it was raining sand, the whole deck was brown. It was on the sails, the ropes, everything. Africa feels a long way away, but I guess this came from Morocco.

I have been working quite hard on a long jobs list, making sure everything is done before we attack the area of light winds ahead. I've re-spliced the spinnaker sheets, re-stitched a few strops and even cleaned the deck. I wish I could get the black marks out though, I hate it when she's not looking perfect.

Had the best night's sleep for a long time last night. Lots of 70-minute naps, with a few 20-minute ones as well. Fantastic! The wind was quite steady, on a clear night, with stars everywhere.

This next 48 hours is going to be decisive—the last chance for anyone to pass I think. We seem to have been keeping our distance on Bilou though he's been climbing slightly on both of us, but thats probably due to a better wind angle out in the west. [Trying to] get a bit of separation from Mich by sailing a bit closer to the wind—at least I'm not just following his tracks. We'll see whether it makes any difference—this shouldn't be as bad as the Doldrums, but in every unstable wind mass there are always chances.

As we approached the Azores high-pressure system, there was more morale-boosting news. Once again the number of miles between us and Mich was shrinking. At the time he tacked to clear the system, we were just 15 miles behind—and although once again he was going to get away first, the gap was now smaller. We just had to hang in there and sail the best possible race. In the light winds, I swapped the broken daggerboard from one side of the boat to the other, an almost military procedure which took a fifth of the time in the flat sea and with the knowledge I had gained. I then dropped the broken board into its old socket so the decks were once again clear; with most of the damage out of sight and in some ways out of mind, it felt a lot better to see *Kingfisher* looking more normal once again. I would need to switch the boards again in the reaching conditions heading out of the Azores high, but in the meantime, I was going to profit from the light airs to try to sleep and tidy *Kingfisher* so that she looked as smart as she could for the finish.

The following afternoon, she was sailing beautifully in a very light northeasterly breeze. I spent an hour or so trying to remove the black marks from her deck and cleaning the marks from around her exhaust pipe. I put electrical tape around her broken board to protect myself from its serrated edges and tidied any fraying rope ends. Each time I thought about her broken board, I felt my stomach turn. At least we should not be needing it between now and the finish.

That afternoon I sat in the bow beneath the most beautiful blue sky and talked to the video camera, thanking everyone for all they had done to get us out there for the race. I talked about the situation at the finish and the fact that I did not know what to expect. I said that I wished the race did not have to finish, and that it had been the most incredible experience of my life. There was an unbelievable quietness and tranquillity about that whole moment—no breeze, not even wind blowing on the camera microphone—my words spoken softly but clearly to the lens.

Just twenty-four hours later we had left the high-pressure system; the wind was already increasing with the approach of the storm which was

about to propel us to the finish. Now, within a week of the finish, communications were more often by phone than by e-mail.

07/02/09 09:22Z (ellenmacarthur.com/day91)
I had the first good sleep for a while last night. Yesterday was once of
my worst days, I was so tired, and I couldn't pull myself out of it.
Every small thing became a big problem in my head. But last night I
reduced sail a bit, the sea state forced us to do that anyway, and
sailed all night with two reefs and the small staysail. And managed to
sleep a number of hours in total, although I woke every thirty
minutes or so to check everything was OK.

The really good news is that I am on to a new chart—and it
shows the finish and even the Shetland Islands! Even better, I'm
nearly a third of the way up the chart towards Les Sables now. In my
mind, we are on the last stretch now, but it's still 1,000 miles. I
don't think they are going to be easy ones either.

I've had from 17 to 33 knots during the night, which makes for
some pretty exciting and nerve-racking moments as the wind picks
up and the boat just goes in to turbo-mode surfing, almost out of
control at up to 25 knots. There is water crashing everywhere, and
the noise is deafening.

Got to go—looks like my lashing on the radar, broken during
the dagger-board removal exercise, has come loose . . . the radar is
hanging down . . . got to try to save it.
ex

It was physically hard going with the changing winds—and the ever-
increasing pressure of Mich being ahead of us. It almost seemed that
with each day as we neared the finish, life on board got harder. But the
strong winds were in many ways good news, as I found myself absorbed
in looking after *Kingfisher*, spending a lot of time on deck to make sure
no problems were developing. In the rough weather, it's very easy to sit
below in the warmth of the cabin and let your boat hammer along in the
waves, but I could never let myself do this. If *Kingfisher* began to feel uncomfortable, then so did I, and I would be out like a flash either to reef
her down or change her angle to the waves a little to see if it made a difference. Often I would find myself giving her a pat on her coach-roof or
crying out, "Go, girl! You can do it!" as she took off across the waves. We
were on a mission, sailing as fast as we could—Mich was 122 miles

ahead—but we still had more than 1,000 miles to go. The race was far from over and we were far from giving up.

THE OUTSIDE WORLD was unaware of what was going on when at 1722 on Wednesday, 7 February, *Kingfisher*'s genoa forestay broke—one of two fixed cables which stop the mast from falling backwards, and crucial to its rigidity. Though less dramatic than the collision, it was actually the biggest threat so far to our completion of the race. Not finishing at all became an appalling possibility, and I was as wounded by the damage as *Kingfisher* was physically. This was about the worst thing that had happened, as it removed the mast's structural integrity. It had not fallen down, but it would remain a risk we would have to live with until we finished the race. The strength of the lashings on the sail held the stay in place, but the 90-foot carbon mast had lost one-third of its forward lateral support, and we would be unable to use one of our most important sails or sail at 100 per cent again.

I was completely devastated. The ominous bang as the stay broke signalled the end of our chances of beating Mich in the Vendée Globe. Unless something unbearable happened to him, we now had no choice but to limp across the finish line, preserving *Kingfisher*'s crippled rig in the hope that we could stay ahead of Bilou. But if the mast tumbled, we would lose virtually all hope of hanging onto our second place in the Vendée Globe or of finishing the race at all. It felt as though someone had taken my feet out from under me.

Those final four days of the race were among the most draining mentally. For more than twenty-four hours I sailed with two reefs in the main and the solent, with half the sail area we should have had up. We were sailing no faster than a boat of half *Kingfisher*'s size, as she wallowed in the waves she should have been surfing down. It was killing me.

I knew that it would be a risk to set more sail and that if we unfurled the power of the gennaker, each gust could pose a fatal threat to the mast, but I just couldn't handle it any longer.

There was little rationale in my decision to go for the gennaker. The new depression was on its way, which would take us into the finish line, but I was determined to be as close as possible behind Michel. After a final call to the mast manufacturer, I climbed up on deck and unfurled the sail; as I sheeted it in to harness the wind, *Kingfisher* took off through the water. I sighed and yelled out loud with relief and delight as she leapt forward again.

Those final days blended fairly much into one—powering downwind past Finisterre and into the Bay of Biscay. There were ships around, too, a welcome sight, briefly reminding me of my days up in Hull on the River Humber. There was also a plane, which flew over to take pictures, a weird experience as we hurtled down the waves towards the finish. When its wings dipped as it flew over for the final time, I realized it had been a long time since I'd seen a gesture by another person.

During the final days, I received a long and touching e-mail from Catherine Chabaud. She was lying in seventh position and had said that she felt the pace of this race was extreme, but she was glad to have been out there again. Later on, she too broke a stay on her mast. In a cruel irony, she was instantly dismasted; even though she was just a few hundred miles from the finish line, she was unable to finish the race. A pointed reminder of what could have happened to us.

I felt excited, but at the same time more and more claustrophobic as we neared the French shore. Inside of me was a pain that was hurting more and more; mentally I was washed out, physically I was spent. And in a few hours' time, Michel Desjoyeaux would cross the finish line, taking first place in the 2000–2001 Vendée Globe Race. Soon there would be only one winner of the race around which my life had revolved for the last four years, and no matter how hard we tried, it was not to be us. I spoke to Mark about the arrangements, but we both pretty much avoided talking about Mich's finish—it was imminent, but it just seemed something that mustn't matter any more. When I called Ian later, however, I could no longer hold back my emotions. I began angrily blaming myself for all that had gone wrong, wishing we could wind back time and start again from our position a few hundred miles south of the Equator. If only I could relive those moments with the benefit of hindsight! For the first time in the race, Ian just didn't seem to understand me. We couldn't connect, and as I ranted down the phone, I heard the fireworks going off for Mich's arrival. I knew that it was not just I who had lost the race—we all had. Ian's despair, though, put me back on an even keel, because this time I realized *he* needed *my* support.

Somehow the pain disappeared once Mich had finished the race. I was 243 miles behind him, and now I was glad to have those miles. Suddenly

I felt all the richer for still being out there on this beautiful, wild ocean. Our battle was over, we just had to sail home. There were no tactical decisions to make, nor was there any competition close on our heels. Bilou was 400 miles behind us, after a difficult crossing of the Azores high. We now had a light breeze coming in from the north, and a strikingly flat sea. I walked along *Kingfisher*'s deck, checking everything, and noticed that the starboard bow light was not working. I went below and dug out a bulb, taking the screwdriver with me to remove the waterproof cover. I wanted her to look her best for the finish. I was sitting on her pulpit when I heard that familiar clicking sound, and I looked down into the water to see the glowing shapes of a pair of dolphins. I squeaked with excitement and laughed out loud as they played magnificently beneath *Kingfisher*'s bow.

As I sat there soaking in what was around me, I looked up at a beautiful starlit sky, a gigantic blanketed dome that was somehow protecting us—as it had for the previous ninety-three days. I was sure I could see more stars than ever before in my life, and as I watched *Kingfisher*'s tall mast glide beneath them, I leaned forward and laid my cheek against the cool, damp fabric of her furled genoa, swaying unnaturally on its stay. If ever there was a moment which got close to summing up what we had been through, this was it.

Trying to stop the tears, I hung my head over her pulpit to watch the dolphins, but before their streamlined shapes appeared again I saw only the reflection of the most beautiful boat in the world. She felt more like home to me than any place I had lived during the previous seven years; of the past twelve months, I had spent well more than six at sea with her. I gave up trying to resist and cried with sheer pleasure, watching my tears fall to the water's surface. If ever there was a heaven, then surely I must be there.

CHAPTER SEVENTEEN

MY FEET BARELY TOUCHED the pontoon as we headed towards the crowds. I was packed in amongst hundreds of journalists, many of whom I knew, but the faces were too blurred to identify. I could see several large guys around me wearing Kingfisher jackets. I figured they must be the bodyguards I'd been forewarned about, though it seemed odd that I didn't even know their names. One of them was by my side and had his arm around me; he began to speak to me, and although I don't remember his words, which were drowned in the madness, they were kind and, considering the situation, seemed remarkably friendly. I could sense the tension in his voice, however, and realized that he was shaking. I turned to look at his face and saw the stressed expression in his eyes, which managed a brief glance at me before returning to their job. He held me so tightly that I could barely breathe as we were squeezed along those few hundred yards of pontoon. I had never been under close protection before.

As we hurried along I was acutely conscious that *Kingfisher* was behind me. When my hand slipped away from her cool, damp, rounded gunwale, I knew it was all over. We had made it, but it was over.

I was suddenly immersed in a world which had clearly been racing along during my three-month absence, but which I had grown away from. I saw *Iduna* tied up alongside and tried to stop, but this exodus of people was something I could not control. Within seconds, I was whisked away once again. As we stepped onto dry ground for the first time, to be honest I did not even notice—my feet were hardly touching the ground as it was. We passed the gangways up towards the Vendée Globe village, and I heard, then saw, the crowds of people collected along the railings. I was conscious that my eyes were still quite red, but I was comforted by the fact that I could still see *Kingfisher*. There were a few people around her, but most had left. I felt so sad that she was down there—how could I abandon her like that? She was alone.

As we walked to the stage, people were shouting and screaming. Then the crowd went wild as I was directed up the steps. All I could do was wave and smile—I felt completely out of place and quite lost as the microphone was passed to me. *Kingfisher* was not there with me. I could not hold a part of her, nor climb inside her for security. Here on the stage, waiting to be interviewed, I felt truly alone too.

The lights shining on me were so bright that I couldn't clearly see the 250,000 people before me. A video wall behind me showed an image of my face, which must have been ten times my height; my every emotion was there for all to see. As the questions began I thought about the welcome I had enjoyed. I felt indebted to everyone there, to every single person who had come to see me that night. We started in French, then I was asked if I'd like to say a word to the many English people present. As I talked I glanced at *Kingfisher*. I could see the tiny strobe light flashing on top of her mast, as if she was trying to tell me she was OK. My eyes filled with tears and my voice began to break. I smiled to the crowd, waved my thanks, then turned away back down the steps.

I now had my first chance to see my family, but we were behind schedule, and the press conference was waiting. It seemed bizarre to be spending so little time with those I loved after so long away, but although it was precious, it also seemed unreal. I realized how apart from theirs my life had grown over the previous three months. I stood there in my thermals, boots, and oilskin trousers—with no wallet, money, or mobile phone. My hands still had sores on them, and I had not really washed for three months. Mum gave me a letter from Gran which took me straight back to Derbyshire as I read it.

> As I write this letter I do not know the winner of the Vendée Globe Race. In my heart there is only one winner—you, dearest Ellen. Your determination and courage

have touched the hearts of the public worldwide. Sorry I
cannot be with you on this memorable occasion. I will be
with you in spirit and look forward to our hug and kiss
later.

Just before leaving, I received a phone call from Prime Minister Tony
Blair. Everything and nothing seemed odd at this stage; I felt like I was
living in a bubble looking out at all that was passing before me. I was
waiting for Mark to tell me when I had to be where; having no idea of
what was going on, a stark contrast to just hours ago, I felt helplessly re-
liant on others. On the way to the press conference I asked if I could go
to the toilet. I remember sitting down, putting my head on my knees,
and taking several deep breaths. I sighed with relief at the momentary
quiet I had found, and I smiled at the alarming comfort; it was the first
time I'd sat on a toilet seat for three months.

Two days later I witnessed my first-ever Vendée arrival when several
of us went out in our RIB. Bilou was storming towards the finish line,
having just broken the single-handed twenty-four-hour speed record. I
shall never forget seeing his tiny sail appearing over the horizon—then,
as he neared, the look of pure joy on his face. There were boats everywhere to see him in, and the sound of Breton pipes blew out across the
water. As he entered the channel in broad daylight, we could see the
sheer number of people lining the walls and cheering him on. He stood
on the bow of his bright red boat with his son, each of them holding a
flare. In the RIB with us was a French journalist, Yves Pelissier, who had
done that first "A donf" interview in Plymouth. He turned to me and
said, "You must look after Mark, too." At the time, I'm not sure his remark really registered, but in hindsight I know that he knew how things
were—he'd covered every Vendée.

Just before Bilou reached the pontoon, we picked up my family from
the shore and pulled alongside his boat. Dad called to him, and he came
over to the side of the boat. Bilou leaned over to shake Dad's hand, and
Dad reached up and hugged him as if he had known him all his life. I'm
not even sure they had spoken before. Roland Jourdain is a very special
man. Mich, an old friend of Bilou's, was there too, and as *Sill* crept along
the channel we boarded her together and lifted Bilou high onto our
shoulders.

Since the finish, Mich and I had spoken several times. His words at his press conference when he was asked what he thought of the "petite Ellen" were very touching, as he pondered aloud that he was not sure what he "had been doing for the past ten years." The anger I had channelled towards him during the race was gone. And later in the year he approached me and apologized for adding fuel to the rumours that I'd had outside assistance. It meant a lot to hear it, although Ian had told me the shock was probably the saving of me. It had eaten away at me, and I was glad to be able to put it to rest.

With the end of the Vendée, more lives than mine had been altered. The day after the finish two scathing and groundless articles about Mark appeared in the French press. The headlines implied that I was the innocent Ellen, who was basically being "managed" by the "monsters." It hurt us all to read those words; and the pain in Mark's tired eyes at a time when he should have been euphoric was tragic. Throughout the entire race and the years running up to it, we had looked forward to the months after the Vendée when we could celebrate, laugh, and have fun together without the stress of the race around us. But now that time had come, Mark and I were not able to share in the success. Although for me this feeling was numbed by the constant stream of engagements and travelling, I hadn't had time to stop to think what the repercussions would be. I was fire-fighting, and for the time being far from pro-active in my thoughts or actions. For Mark, though, this was an unmistakably raw deal. His Vendée Globe had been taken away, and he had been faced with an impossible mission: trying to take care of everyone, trying to do the right thing when the demands on us were twice what we could physically achieve. In addition, the public relations demands were such that Mark was speaking nearly all the time and having to switch constantly between English and French—and all this when, like me, he was totally and utterly exhausted.

I was amazed by the things which occurred during those few days of media frenzy—we desperately wanted the world to know what was going on, but that undoubtedly came at a price. I recall a rare occasion when I was out walking with Mark—for the third time he was trying to tell a film crew that they could not follow me round for the day. It was two days after my finish, and I had still spent no more than an hour with my family. The photographers seemed not to understand that I needed time in private with my family; surely that would go without saying? Suddenly I had the impression that my life (and increasingly the lives of those around me) was beginning to be at the beck and call of others. As of this moment, life had well and truly changed.

OUR ARRIVAL back in the UK with *Kingfisher* was a complete shock to my system. I had imagined a few boats might be there to meet us, but I was aghast as chartered ferries, choppers, and tugs came out to see us in. As we headed up Southampton Water, the guys at the oil terminal sounded the sirens and waved from the jetties as we passed; I was really touched by that and gave them the biggest wave I could. "Welcome home, lass," I said, and patted *Kingfisher*'s bow.

The sides of the marina were lined with people, many of them waving little Kingfisher flags. I stood on the foredeck and, as I had done in Les Sables, I lit a flare to say a thousand thanks to all who had come. There were many familiar faces, all smiling and cheering, and one of them I could not miss—it was Brian Pilcher, whose enthusiasm had made such an impression when I first presented my plans to sail round Britain. I jumped from the boat and ran straight into his arms. He was there with his daughter and three-year-old granddaughter, who, despite the excitement on offer, was unimpressed by anything but my weathered yellow *salopettes*. Her only comment: "Nice dungarees"!

DURING THE NEXT FEW DAYS I was exhausted, fit to drop—a state I would spend most of the year in. I was living off adrenalin to fuel the smiles and the energy for the interviews. Somehow I managed to carry on, functioning on little sleep and delivering my thoughts to cameras from Germany to the United States. Ian was brilliant, travelling round with me and giving Mark a chance to try to cope with the immense pressures we were under to meet the demands on us.

Although I should have grabbed this time to take a holiday, I found it impossible to tear myself away. Every few days Vendée boats were finishing, and I had promised myself to be there to see in as many of them as I could. Ian and I took more flights between Nantes and London than most people would take in a lifetime—it was madness. We saw a triumphant Mike Golding finish an incredible seventh after all he had been through—sailing up to the fleet and overtaking shortly before two other

60s. There was Yves Parlier, who finished thirteenth with his impressive-looking repaired mast. As I climbed on board to sail up the channel with him, his family, and his team, he let me taste some of the seaweed he had dried for his trip back. It wasn't that bad—but the texture was awful. An incredible story!

Each time I dropped into the office I would find another enormous pile of press clippings. The media was going crazy with the story, but we also got an unbelievable number of letters. The requests from individuals and companies as well as the media were flooding in, as was news of everything from beer to mountains being named after me—even a sweet pea, which reminded me of my granddad, who had taken such pride in his own sweet peas. All sorts of articles appeared in newspapers—from "Ellen to be millionaire" to a surreal piece claiming I had been stalked by a man who had swum around the globe after me! I was asked repeatedly about Ian and my family, and Mum and Dad had to get used to having journalists calling the house and turning up on the doorstep. They were very brave about it all, but my intention had never been to involve them in this, nor to become famous myself. The attention was mind-boggling. I am just very much in love with my sport, and I still want desperately to be better at it.

One afternoon I managed a quick trip to an editing studio to see a rough cut of the documentary being made by the BBC about my participation in the Vendée Globe. There was silence as they ran through the first version of the edit, and I sat cross-legged on the chair staring at the screen. For the first time I heard what the others had said as I left, and I saw the expressions on their faces. I saw the moment when I hugged Mum and Dad goodbye—even though we'd been surrounded by cameras, I had no recollection that they had been there. There was the all-telling glance between them as I walked away—Dad briefly looking down, then turning to Mum for strength. She gave him a supportive smile, but it was far from a happy one. I was almost traumatized by seeing the effect I'd had on everyone by sailing off in such a colossal race. A quote from Dad was dropped over the footage at that moment: "You can't prepare for whatever your daughter might do. . . . You might disagree with it, you might support her, you might go along with it, but at the end of the day you can't prepare for it."

I felt an overwhelming gratitude to Mum and Dad for encouraging me to go off and follow my dreams. It would have been far easier for them early on just to have said no.

Then, as I watched *Kingfisher* slip away from the dock, Mark was asked, "What would be your goal for her in this race?"

"Come back; safely, finish. . . ." I saw his eyes fill with tears as he looked away from the camera. "Ellen belongs at sea, and the boat belongs at sea. The sooner they're out there, the better, and I have a lot of confidence in that combination when they're out there."

IN MAY 2001, only a few weeks after Pasquale, the last competitor, finished after 158 days at sea, we returned to Les Sables d'Olonne for the official Vendée Globe prize ceremony. I hadn't expected a big event, nor one that attracted such crowds. As I turned up to do my first TV interview, I cast my eyes over the beach and saw lights and speakers suspended from two enormous cranes, and a big stage on stilts. If you hadn't known otherwise, you would have thought it was all for an outdoor concert.

After dinner that evening we were summoned outside to the beach for the presentation. It was almost dark, and the set looked incredibly impressive. Thousands upon thousands of people were packed along the beach, though in the dark it was impossible to see just how many were there. Forty-foot-high video images were projected onto two massive screens flanking the stage. The atmosphere was electric. As I stood looking up to watch the video, my knees began to shake. Pipo, Mathilde, and Pilou were there and came to say hello—Pilou grasping his football, which must have been at least half his size, and Mathilde looking proud and happy. As I was ushered towards the stage, I kissed Ian and headed down to the beach. The crowds were behind barriers, reaching out towards us. A man thrust at me a photograph taken just after the finish. I tucked it into the inside pocket of my jacket and read it later: "Ellen, thank you for helping us dream."

All the skippers were asked to walk onto the stage together. The video continued to show images of each of us which we had taken during the race. I had only seen a few of these, and it shocked me to hear the others' voices—so happy or so sad, so loud and overpowering. Sixty thousand onlookers were transfixed. As the video stopped, the music began to play and the lights dimmed. Every second person in that audience turned on a torch and gently waved it before us. The MC told us, "That is for you, they're doing it for you." It was a beautiful way to show their appreciation.

The most wonderful feeling—which I know was shared by all twenty-four of us—was that we were all there to tell the tale. However long or short the journey, we had made it, every one of us, safe and sound. As we lit flares and held them above our heads, the music crescendoed. Each skipper, whether finished or abandoned, first or last, held strong memories of an extraordinary race. I was sad that I had not made it back to see every one of them in. I had missed Joe, Patrice in the renamed *Aqua Quorum*, Didier, Marc, and Bernard in *Voilà*. I had also missed Raphael Dinelli and Thierry Dubois, both of whom had completed the course but weren't classed. Looking round those faces that last time on stage, I realized there was another arrival I had missed, one which I could not have tried harder to see. As the last of the fireworks burst and showered above us, with the powerful sound track pumping out of the speakers, I turned away from the cameras, overcome with emotion for the first time that evening. I shall always remember missing and always regret missing one arrival—that of the man sitting right next to me, Michel Desjoyeaux.

I FOUND IT DIFFICULT to cope with the recognition that followed the Vendée. I was particularly alarmed that people would ask, "How are you going to stay in the limelight?" However well intentioned, they just didn't get it—I had never done this to be famous, that was never the objective; I had just wanted to race around the world. Friends stopped phoning—under the impression that their calls would no longer be welcome—then seemed genuinely bowled over when I rang them to say "hi." I felt very strongly that it was not I who had changed, but everyone else.

At no point did I feel like reversing what had happened, though. I just knew that I needed to learn to adapt, and to have people around me who understand how hard it sometimes can be. Few people realize just how difficult it is to keep smiling and looking happy when you're tired and exhausted, and how intimidating it feels to go into a room knowing that it's filled with people who want to talk to you. I had seen at sea that state of mind is critical to the way we perform—now I seemed to be struggling just to be me.

The hardest part was coping with the loss of freedom to act as I wished. After such a big race, I wanted nothing more than to slide away and collapse, but I was on duty. When I had crossed the finish line of the Vendée Globe, I felt it didn't matter if I didn't sleep for a month, because the job was done—but the job was far from finished, and in many ways it had only just begun. During the summer of 2001, I was being pulled in every direction, but I forced myself to carry on. I must have been hell to live with as I beat myself up, angry and unable to relax because I had so much to do and no time to do it. We'd put aside thirty-four days to write this book, which became one of the biggest causes for my frustration. I had wanted to write since I was a child, but now the task just seemed to loom over my head. It became startlingly obvious that I hadn't allocated enough time. A possible solution was to have the book ghost-written, but I couldn't do that—in my own mind, it had never been an option. Nan would have turned in her grave at the thought!

Everything was getting too much. I desperately needed to take a day away but found the thought of not using any spare time to write even more stressful. I needed to get back in control and be in a position where a day away from writing was not a reason for self-torture. One night at Ian's, I snapped—so distressed that I began punching the stairs and crying in sheer frustration. My life was out of control, and at that moment there seemed to be absolutely nothing I could do about it. I knew that Ian, after spending so much time with me, knew how serious things were and had been waiting for me to break. He, too, felt helpless, as his warnings to others seemed to be lost with the constant pressure. He let me blow my top, but eventually I just felt I had to disappear; I left to walk the streets of London.

At the same time, with each presentation or interview, recounting my experiences, I was digging deep emotionally. And while I found myself becoming more and more protective of some things, no matter how I looked at it, one thing remained clear—it had been my choice to be out there. I'd been lucky, but now I found myself in a dilemma—I wanted desperately to share what I had been through, but as I tried to do so I was beginning to suspect that soon there would be nothing left inside to give. So many people wanted a slice, and to deal with that, I knew I needed to regrow. Only the core was left—the slices were gone.

Matters progressively worsened with Mark, too. As our lives became more reactive than pro-active, the constant pressure under which we both had lived for almost five years was for the first time revealing itself. Despite our tiredness, things had been easy before the Vendée; we had had a common goal which had allowed us to put aside whatever tensions developed, but our relationship had essentially remained the one we first formed five years earlier. Now things were going to have to change in some way between us, and we were about to find out that the transformation would be a painful one when Mark left for a life-saving and long-overdue holiday with Dana.

Although Ian and I had always hoped to go away at the same time, it simply wasn't possible. Writing the book was not something I could just pick up and put down again, and though I was desperate for a break, I had committed to it and opted to stay at Ian's house in London. It was the first time I had stayed put in one place for as long as I could remember.

Everyone *said* they understood, but still the pace didn't let up, nor did my physical and mental state improve. I was trying to recover not only from five years of hard grind but also from three months of the most profound fatigue imaginable. But it proved impossible to get away. Requests were pouring in each day—from interviews to prize-givings to TV programmes to endorsements—and with each I wanted to give my best. Everybody stressed that they just needed an hour or two, and that they'd do all they could to make it as painless as possible. But if you are asked to do ten things on the same day, and each thing takes just a few hours, you simply cease to function. The hardest thing for everyone involved was to say "no" because it went against our philosophy.

One evening I even took my entire family to an informal evening event in the hope of spending some time with them. As soon as the meal was finished I was ushered into a corner and signed autographs for two hours. In the end, my only escape was to go and sit in the toilet for ten minutes—at least there I was alone. The whole situation made me feel so dependent on others, which just wasn't me, as I'd always been so independent.

I knew that I could not continue regarding every interview and event with the same positive outlook. It frustrated me immensely that I couldn't be in ten places at once, nor say "yes" to all the opportunities which came my way. I wished I had all the time in the world—I could have filled it!

More than anything, I needed to get back on the water.

LUCKILY, several long-planned races were approaching.

Months ago, in fact the week before the start of the Vendée, Alain Gautier had come to Les Sables d'Olonne. We'd grabbed a meal together and he and I had agreed to race the Transat Jacques Vabre aboard his 60-foot trimaran *Foncia*—it was the same race I'd done with Yves Parlier less than two years earlier. I had a tremendous amount of respect for Alain; he'd already played a massive part in the *Kingfisher* project, and it was great to have a goal for the year. Things weren't going to be quiet on the *Kingfisher* front, either, with a programme that culminated with the EDS Atlantic Challenge, a five-leg race which included two transatlantics.

First of all, though, came the Challenge Mondial with Alain on *Foncia*. This was an amazing event—my first truly competitive offshore race on a 60-foot trimaran. Alain had a great team and a boat he knew inside out, which bode well for the spirit among the five of us on board. Trimarans are very different from monohulls, relying on their beam for stability and power and on their lightness for speed. They are just over half the weight of a boat such as *Kingfisher* but have a wing mast several metres higher, so it doesn't take an expert to work out that they are blisteringly fast. Life on board was very different, with the waves screaming over the decks as we fired our way through them, whilst living in an almost survival-like capsule in the central hull. Their concept originally came through the pursuit of a multihull design that could be sailed single-handed, and despite their massive increases in performance, they are still sailed single-handed in some races. The experience racing aboard *Foncia* was one I will remember forever—sailing at unbelievable speeds, with all of us aboard grinning with pleasure.

It was the closest finish imaginable as we sailed towards the line off the Spanish coast. *Belgacom*, the leading trimaran, was a mile ahead, but by sailing a little faster and lower we managed to pull off something a bit different; with one tack, we crossed the line just minutes before they did. The feeling on *Foncia* was euphoric—the value and power of sailing on a team really hit home. I shall be forever indebted to those guys. If I'd been asked straight after the Vendée whether I preferred sailing alone or with a team, I undoubtedly would have said alone, but just a few months later, my view had changed—sailing with the *Foncia* crew had been one of the best experiences of my life, and I was hungry for more.

At one precise moment in the race, as I sat alone on the windward hull looking at the arid shores of the Mediterranean, I realized that I wanted to sail more in multihulls. The decision was to be a mental turning-point. For the first time since I had finished the Vendée, I felt I was exercising some control over my life. I could feel that passion inside me again, and I smiled broadly into space. I remembered what my dad had said during an interview: "Ellen wants to compete, she's always wanted to compete—she will fight to finish the race. . . ."

He was right. The race was far from over.

On returning from Spain, I decided that it would be impossible to finish the book in 2001. I was angry with myself for not having come to the realization earlier, but it was a massive relief not to have it hanging over me. It didn't mean I was comfortable with the decision, though.

With the journey to France for the start of the EDS came another major turning-point—both the end and the beginning of my relationship with Mark. During the crossing, we'd decided to spend an hour or so going through various things that needed discussing. We'd had little time together during the previous months, and the ferry seemed to offer a good opportunity. We sat in the dim four-berth cabin and waded through the printed sheets and notes that we each had made. Already tired, I knew I was at my wits' end. I felt I just could not manage any more. The schedule was still frantic, and after giving up on the book, I felt like a failure. The comments people made after I had delayed made me more angry—I had never tried to write a book before, and it became clear that others thought I'd undertaken an impossible mission. It was pretty hard to swallow after I'd just worked myself into the ground trying to complete it. I'd always said I was OK when anyone asked, but with hindsight, I wish that people could have realized just how bad things were for me inside. By the stage when I actually admitted that things were bad, it was too late. I'd reached a breaking-point and did not know how to articulate it. That night on the ferry, though, the full force of the anger came out. Never before in my life had I hit anyone, but I snapped and laid into Mark as if I were trying to kill him. I think it was the only way I had left to communicate. He did not retaliate, just tried to protect himself, until eventually, feeling as though my insides had been turned upside down, I ran out of the cabin. I spent the rest of the night either outside huddled in a corner on the cold deck, watching England disappear, or curled up in a ball beneath the seats in the lounge area. Wherever I was, though, my eyes remained firmly open. I felt more mixed up than ever before. I was searching for the way out, trying to find something to grab onto.

The following morning, I met Mark at the car in silence. We spoke very little on that short drive, but as we pulled into the car park by *King-fisher*, he said, "I don't know what you'll choose to do, but I'll be there for you, even if it's just to be the punch-bag." I forced a grin, which he returned. Then he opened the door and left. Though I had felt suffocated in the aftermath of the Vendée Globe, I could now see just how much Mark was suffering, too.

I took off in the car straight away and parked up on the cliffs overlooking the sea. Just five years before, as a twenty-year-old, I had raced into St.-Malo after my first transatlantic race, passing the very headland on which I was sitting. I had passed it again in the Route du Rhum, when it was covered with a couple hundred thousand people shouting and encouraging us. As I sat there, I began to draw up mental plans for the future, and though I knew then that I was pretty much as low as I'd ever been, that passion was still very much inside me, and I was going to do my damnedest to let it out.

I loved the sea, I was drawn by the sea, and my job and motivation were to race on the sea. My career was only just starting, yet here I was feeling as though I was at the end of the line. I tried to be pragmatic, and I thought through my options again and again. After several hours, I finally began to drift off, so I locked the car doors and slept.

I THINK IT WAS DURING this next race, aboard *Kingfisher* with a crew for the EDS Atlantic Challenge, that I set out on the road to recovery. Initially, it was tough. The first leg to Germany from France was the hardest for me; I felt trapped on board, feeling that I just did not fit in with the guys. But we had 45 knots on the second leg, which was a great settler-in, and things improved after that. Nick Moloney, an Australian, was on board. He'd looked after *Kingfisher* during the spring while I was writing, and though few things had changed, it took a while for me to get to know her once again. It had been hard letting her go at all, but Nick was a great guy and a good friend—he'd even raced Le Poisson in the 1999 Mini Transat. It was still hard being on a boat and having others doing things, when I was used to doing everything myself. Having an extra four crew putting things in unexpected places, and having to stow everyone's gear, took some adjustment. But we still pulled off a second in both those legs, our good friend Bilou taking first!

One particularly notable crew member was Mark, who had returned to the water with a vengeance. I think Mark began to appreciate the change in me as he watched me take on the responsibility of skipper during this race. It was as good for him to get back on the water as it was for me, and the race undoubtedly marked the beginning of the rebuilding of our relationship.

A COUPLE OF MONTHS before the Jacques Vabre, I eventually escaped for a holiday with Mum and Dad. They had rented a little cottage on the Isle of Skye. It sat next to a loch with an island just a mile or so from the sea. Watching the countryside spread out before my eyes felt little short of a miracle, and seeing the speed at which Mac's tail wagged when I climbed off the ferry had me smiling immediately. We were to have a wonderful few days together, discovering our family's past as we researched in the local Portree library, and we found the circular remains of Dad's great-grandfather's croft. We discovered that on Dad's side of the family, the MacArthurs' trade was fishing—at last I'd found a family link with the sea!

> *Looking out of the window here as I write I am amazed at the*
> *sheer beauty of the Scottish countryside. I see the golden*
> *greens, and waving branches, the depth of the landscape. As I*
> *walk across the grass I feel a spring in my step.*

I'd felt recently that I was becoming myself again, and Scotland hastened this. I would go running there, pushing myself as hard as I could. Life had changed for sure, but I was now looking ahead again, and it energized me. The summer of 2001 had been atrocious in lots of ways. Mark and I had hated each other and lost the understanding we'd had, but time on Skye gave me the chance to write up the next five years. It had been taking shape in my mind for a while, but at this point I hadn't discussed any of it with Mark. For me, the first real step into the future would be when we sat down together and decided whether we would run with it. I needed to be sure, and I needed to know that Mark was with me.

THE MULTIHULLS had challenged me enormously. Sailing with Alain was already proving to be the most incredible learning curve, and I revelled in it. I wanted to learn more and test myself. I somehow knew that the Jacques Vabre would show the way ahead. Racing single-handed in a trimaran pushes human endurance to its limits. I was desperate to tackle the Route du Rhum in one of these incredible machines. But the next Rhum was in just twelve months' time, and I knew that although I could be on the start line, I wouldn't be ready for it. To give myself time to gain the experience I needed and build the right boat, I would go for the 2006 edition, while racing the 2002 edition in *Kingfisher*. This felt perfect, and I was glad it would present us with the ideal opportunity to race together once again. The Vendée finish now felt like a long way away.

And that was, of course, the next big question—the Vendée Globe. It seemed the entire world was trying to encourage me to cross that start line again. I knew that I wanted to return to the south and to sail in the Southern Ocean, but I was not sure that the next Vendée was the best way. Although it was a race in which I felt there was unfinished business, my gut reaction was that the next Vendée, in 2004, was too soon. I had come back from the previous race wanting to attempt it again, but if I completed the 2006 Rhum in a trimaran, the next Vendée would be two years away, and I would still be only thirty. The Vendée in 2008 was looking like the one. In the meantime, I would have to find another way to sail south.

Ever since winning the Young Sailor of the Year award back in 1995, I had been fascinated by Sir Peter Blake and Sir Robin Knox-Johnston's Jules Verne record. In a catamaran named *Enza*, they had made it non-stop round the world in just over seventy-six days. In 1996, that record was beaten by Olivier de Kersauson, and it stood at just over seventy-one days. I had seen the footage of these incredible boats—so powerful, monstrous, and quick, crewed by about ten people; this kind of sailing was a very different ball game from soloing a monohull. I was beginning to understand the multihull way now, and for the first time, I felt ready to take a team of people around the world. I'd made my decision. The Jules Verne was going to take me back to the Southern Ocean!

I typed in a frenzied state to get these thoughts into the computer, hammering away as the words seemed just to flow from my fingertips. It was a wonderful feeling to be planning something concrete once again, and though unsure of what Mark's reaction would be, I was excited at the thought of sharing it with him. I heard a rustling behind me from Mac, who lay on her pouf by my feet. There was barely a foot and a half behind my chair, but she had slotted herself in without making the slightest fuss. I reached down to stroke her and she looked up, her muzzle against my arm. Always there for me, through good and bad.

When I left Scotland, I knew I was ready to share my plans with Mark. There had been times since the Vendée finish that I just wanted to crawl away and hide, but now I felt revitalized. And, quite frankly, I couldn't wait.

We sat in a little French café at the ferry terminal in Southampton. Mark was almost speechless as I handed over the sheet outlining the plan for the Jules Verne and the trimaran, but quickly that wry smile turned to excitement, and his eyes began to beam at the prospect of getting involved again. All things considered, I thought he took the news rather well!

A few months later, I received a card from Mark containing two photographs—one taken before the Mini Transat and the other after the Vendée Globe. The note read:

> Two very different pictures. . . . A world between the two
> and another once since. . . . I wouldn't swap the last 4 years
> with you for anything—and I hope that I can say it again in
> 4 years time.
> Mxx

ON COMING BACK from Scotland, I felt like a different person and was simply desperate to get on board the trimaran for the Jacques Vabre. It was going to be a massive challenge, and I was raring to get out there and just go for it again. We would be racing against the best in the world,

and it would be awesome. At just over four years old, *Foncia* was not a
new boat compared to some, but she was reliable, and Alain knew her
inside out—so I think we were quietly optimistic. The most worrying
aspect of trimarans compared with monohulls is that there is just no
room for error. Just two years before, when Alain had been racing the
same boat with none other than Michel Desjoyeaux, they had capsized
just six hours into the race. Unlike monohulls, 60-foot trimarans will
never right themselves: they are more stable upside down than right side
up. The dangers out there are real.

Each time I arrived at the docks in Le Havre and saw the magnificent
row of fourteen of the most powerful 60-foot multihulls in the world, I
felt very privileged, and I felt so grateful to Alain for asking me to race
with him. Since he'd won the Vendée, I was sure he understood what I
had been through: he had known how vital it was just to get back out on
the water.

The Transat Jacques Vabre was without doubt the climax of my season
after the Vendée. It offered a fantastic chance to learn. The route would
take us to Salvador da Bahia in Brazil and, for the multis, via Ascension
Island in the South Atlantic. But before heading south to the Equator, we
would first have to tackle the sail out of the English Channel, with its
busy shipping, and the ominous headlands of Ushant and Finisterre.
Again I would tune myself into the ocean, and develop once more that
awareness of all that was going on around me. Your instincts change on a
multihull—they are centred even more on survival.

E-MAIL UPDATE FROM ELLEN ON BOARD KINGFISHER
FONCIA
06/11/2001
What a night . . . it's been incredible, feeling like you are balancing
on a tight rope with the wind howling past every part of you. Well
we're past finisterre, and though 200 miles off it, we knew it. I shall
never forget the feeling as i rounded in the Vendée—45-50 knots on
the nose, though this time it was behind us . . . it was incredibly dark
at the beginning of the night . . . The clouds seemed to come down
touching the water, and its blanket covered over everything but the
wind. FONCIA became harder and harder to steer, as we continued
in 25-30 knots with gennaker and full main . . . bit by bit though we
reduced sail—till this morning we were flying along at 22-28 knots

under 1 reef and trinquete. The wave crests become your guide, as they are the only thing you can make out at speed . . . Thank goodness that after a few hours of the long night the moon rose—though behind clouds it was a godsend. . . . As you grip the side of the seat with your free hand, and the tip of the tiller with the other, you think of little but protecting that person who is sleeping below. it is your watch, and you are in control of this mighty machine which is eating up the miles towards the south . . . each wave taken and passed there is a sigh of relief, and each squall brings a newly held breath as you hope that as the leeward bow digs in it wills lowly lift and free itself from its dark descent into the waves.

There was something quite strange this am, a bright red sky at three am in the north, with a shimmering light coming up from behind the clouds. Never have i seen that before, it could neither have been sunrise or sun set—they were hours away . . . You can't help but cast a thought to those who are sleeping, and how much they are missing. The night time is a special time.

After 3 hours on the helm your arms feel like they will never bend again, and your concentration is spent . . . You never feel like sleeping though—the adrenalin of keeping things together stops any hint of wearyness . . . we have tried different lenghts of watches and with this motion, it's almost impossible to sleep at all, and takes at least half an hour to dry off and drop off. Solid water has been breaking up through the trampoene as we ride over breaking crests and the spray flying off the windward foil continuosly flies into the air like a tornado . . .

On my last off watch i curled up in a ball pulling a sleeping bag over my front. It's still quite cold, especially at night, and when the water botttles fly off the shelf above your head onto your face, you know you must have planted quite hard into a wave . . .

Time to go, it'll soon be my steer—funnily enough, im actually looking forward to it!

e&ax

As we sailed down towards the Equator, we were in first position, then Mich, sailing with Jean Luc Nelias, overtook us in *Belgacom*. But in picking a point to cross farther east, we managed to creep ahead. Tactically, it was incredibly stressful—particularly as you're sailing in a big area of unknown. But the feeling on board was fantastic once we had crept through and headed south. We were in first position once again, all was well on board, and furthermore we had a lead of more than 30 miles. But as Mich sailed farther west, a boat named *Groupama* had sailed farther east and managed to find wind there and take more than 100 miles from us.

Despite their proximity, we held off *Groupama* until twenty-four hours before the finish of the race. In virtually the worst run of bad luck you can imagine, we not only broke the bowsprit but also found several hours later that we had a malfunctioning hydraulic ram. Our night was spent switching the 8-foot-long rams, which hold the mast up, from one side of the boat to the other. We were covered in hydraulic oil, sad, and exhausted.

Overall we did have a great race, though, and on that final night, once *Groupama* had finished, Alain and I sat in the cockpit eating pasta, coming to terms with the fact that we had not won. We both felt that there was little more we could have done, and that we'd had a great race regardless of our position. Alain and I knew that we had unfinished business, so we vowed that we would race in the Jacques Vabre together two years later. I felt more motivated than ever before.

THOUGH WE HAD NOT WON, our result in the Jacques Vabre marked the end of a very successful two years of sailing. As a result, on our return to Paris I was summoned to attend the FICO Lacoste Offshore World Championship prize-giving. Over the previous two years I had accumulated a sum of points from offshore events which led to my winning the title. I could remember being at the presentation only two years earlier, just months before *Kingfisher* went into the water. I could not believe what had happened to me over such a short period—it had been an incredible two years. For me, the winning of that world championship represented the hard work of an awful lot of people both on and off the water. As I spoke on the stage with the trophy in my hands, I wished that a whole host of names could have been marked on it.

But the reception of the award was not the usual affair I had seen in previous years. This time the atmosphere was almost one of reverence—just days before, we had lost a friend and quite probably the most highly respected sailor this world shall ever see. Tragically, Sir Peter Blake was killed on 6 December 2001 while on his boat, *Seamaster*, in Brazil. He

TAKING ON THE WORLD 333

was the man I had seen on the big screen when I was eighteen years old, winning the Yachtsman of the Year award with Robin Knox-Johnston. He was a driven man and an inspirational leader, and at the same time he had the most gentle character imaginable. He'd won every title, from the Whitbread to the Jules Verne to twice winning the America's Cup. But his second America's Cup win for New Zealand was not enough. He undertook an expedition to sail to each corner of the world on a mission to open the world's eyes to the state of its oceans; in brief, he wanted as many people as possible to fall in love with the environment. While in the depths of Antarctica, on the expedition which cost him his life, he wrote this log, which had been e-mailed to me during the Vendée.

> Today is a perfect day.
> The written part of the Log is brief—because I want to sit on deck and take it all in. I want to kayak to some of the ice floes and watch the seals; I want to see the penguins still heading for home— to their hungry families ashore; I want to get close to a large iceberg that is heading our way on the current—a berg whose design Disney would have been proud of. It is great that we have time—time to look, time to take it all in, time to indelibly etch the scene on one's memory—because no camera can do it justice.
>
> 2000 hrs: The sun is still blazing out of a clear blue sky—but it is about to disappear down behind the knife-edged peaks just astern. There is a chill in the air that probably heralds a very cold night.
>
> This is Antarctica!

As Nan said, "Life holds a lot of treasure." I've made a promise to my-self never to forget that.

EPILOGUE

ON A COLD MORNING in January 2002, Ian and I drove north. We'd be visiting home and also Derby University. I'd had several offers of honorary degrees since finishing the Vendée, but in Nan's memory I chose Derby, the university at which she had graduated just four years earlier. In her will, she had set up a small trust fund to make an annual award of a few hundred pounds to a student who had also had to struggle to attain a degree. An important part of the day was to hand over the first of these awards. I felt very nervous about this speech and discussed it at length with Ian in the car. I was always nervous when I had to speak to a crowd, and that morning was certainly no exception. I figure that the day the nerves stop, things will have ceased to matter, and that will be the day when I should stop.

As we pulled into the car park next to the playhouse where the ceremony was to take place, we were stopped by the gatekeeper to ensure we had the correct pass. As he looked in through the window, he smiled, recognizing me. Then, in a broad Derbyshire accent, he said in a particularly touching way that he was "reet proud" of what I'd done. It was great to be back here. The last time I'd been to the playhouse was when Mum had taken me to see *Button Moon* at the age of four to try to take my mind off the disappointment of not going sailing with Auntie Thea!

On our arrival, there was little time to spare, as the ceremony was about to start, so after a quick cup of tea I donned my cap and gown and was whisked away with the university senate to take our seats on the stage. Everyone was so friendly, and even during those minutes when I was waiting to go into the hall, there were many mentions of Mrs. Lewis—my Nan.

I am often aware of people looking at me as I walk from place to place, but when I headed to the stage at the front of that room, I felt I did not see a single set of eyes. The cloaks and gowns were like a forest, and I just looked to the stage at the front where I would be sitting. I knew as soon as I walked into the hall that Nan was there with me.

I sat through the first part of the ceremony with emotions so high that I could not tell if I was trying to hold back the tears or stop myself from grinning. When I thought of Nan in her long gown with her cap that wouldn't stay on I wanted to smile, but that made me think of her more, which was painful. Mum, Dad, and Ian were sitting in the front row, and I found it hard to look in their direction. I tried to see the sea of faces as the water and to concentrate on what I was going to say. I wanted this to be a good speech—for Nan.

My name was soon called, and I was invited to stand and listen to a speech of introduction. I was OK to start with, but as the speech went on, I could feel myself swallowing hard. It was a thoughtful speech, which triggered feelings from within me. The speaker finished by talking of Nan and of the time she had spent at the university. My mind began to focus on her, and as it did, I could feel my emotions going through overload. I could think of little else than how much courage she must have had to fight the pain to achieve her goal after all she'd been through.

Just as I wished I could be sitting in a room alone, it was time for me to speak. I was standing before several thousand graduates and their families sitting in complete silence. I knew at that point that I would not be able to finish the speech; already I was choking and could feel the tears welling. Never before had I failed to complete a speech, but this time, after I'd said that I had come here primarily because of my Nan, I felt myself choking, and I knew there was little more I could say. I could barely manage the words, "It was her wish," before handing over the envelope.

I stepped backwards into my seat, and as the weight came off my feet, I felt almost dizzy. As I sat down, all I could do was think of Nan's face in the photograph taken on the day of her graduation; from then on, I could do little but smile with her. Her face was beaming, her eyes were sparkling, and her skin was glowing. Nan had proved that she'd been quite literally living for that moment; she had achieved the goal which throughout her whole life she had refused to let out of her sight.

I realized then what an incredible inspiration she had been and always would be to me.

Thank you, Nan.

Love always,

Ellenxx

Appendix

VENDÉE GLOBE 2000–2001
FINAL POSITIONS

Position	Skipper	Country	Boat
1	Michel Desjoyeaux	France	*PRB*
2	Ellen MacArthur	Great Britain	*Kingfisher*
3	Roland Jourdain	France	*Sill*
4	Marc Thiercelin	France	*Active Wear*
5	Dominique Wavre	France	*UBP*
6	Thomas Coville	France	*Sodebo*
7	Mike Golding	Great Britain	*Team Group 4*
8	Bernard Gallay	France	*Voilà*
9	Josh Hall	Great Britain	*Gartmore*
10	Joe Seeten	France	*Nord Pas de Calais*
11	Patrice Carpentier	France	*VM Matériaux*
12	Simone Bianchetti	Italy	*Aquarelle*
13	Yves Parlier	France	*Aquitaine Innovations*
14	Didier Munduteguy	France	*DDP 6oième Sud*
15	Pasquale de Gregorio	Italy	*Wind*
16	Catherine Chabaud	France	*Whirlpool*
17	Thierry Dubois	France	*Solidaires*
18	Raphael Dinelli	France	*Sogal-Extenso*
19	Fedor Konioukhov	Russia	*Modern University for the Humanities*
20	Javier Sanso	Spain	*Old Spice*
21	Richard Tolkien	Great Britain	*This Time*
22	Eric Dumont	France	*Euroka Un univers de Services*
23	Bernard Stamm	Switzerland	*Armor Lux Foie Gras Bizac*
24	Patrick de Radigues	Belgium	*Libre Belgique*

Days	Time	Speed	Hours	Deficit (hours)	Comment
93	03:57:32	11.95	2,235	0	
94	04:00:25	11.95	2,260	25	
96	01:02:33	11.58	2,305	70	
102	20:37:49	10.82	2,468	233	
105	02:47:12	10.82	2,522	287	
105	07:24:00	10.59	2,527	292	
110	16:22:00	10.05	2,656	421	
111	16:07:11	9.96	2,680	445	
111	19:48:02	9.95	2,683	448	
115	16:46:50	9.62	2,776	541	
116	00:32:48	9.59	2,784	549	
121	01:28:00	9.19	2,905	670	
126	23:36:00	8.76	3,047	812	Completed race under jury rig
135	15:17:00	8.20	3,255	1,020	
158	02:37:25	7.04	3,794	1,559	
					Retired; dismasted
					Retired with electrical problems
					Retired because of collision damage
					Retired with illness
					Retired with rudder damage
					Retired with rig damage
					Retired with rudder damage
					Retired with steering damage
					Retired; ran ashore

ELLEN AT SEA

Year	Event	Rank	Details	Boat	Crew
1995	Round Britain	n/a	5 ½-month solo circumnavigation of England, Scotland, and Wales	*Iduna*	Ellen MacArthu
1996	Québec-St.-Malo Race	3rd in class	1st transatlantic race	*Anicaflash*	Ellen MacArthu and Vittorio Malingri
1997	Mini Transat Race	1st in class, 17th overall	Brest, France, to Martinique	*Financial Dynamics* (formerly *Le Poisson*)	Ellen MacArthu
1998	Round Britain and Ireland Race	1st in class		*Jusqu'au Bout du Monde*	Ellen MacArthu and David Rowen
1998	Route du Rhum	1st in class	St.-Malo, France, to Guadeloupe	*Kingfisher* (formerly *Aqua Quorum*)	Ellen MacArthur
1999	Round Europe Race	1st in class		*Kingfisher*	Ellen MacArthu and Yves Parlie
1999	Transat Jacques Vabre	6th monohull	Le Havre, France, to Cartagena, Colombia	*Aquitaine Innovations*	Ellen MacArthu and Yves Parlie
2000	Europe 1 New Man Star	1st monohull	Plymouth, U.K., to Newport, Rhode Island	*Kingfisher*	Ellen MacArthu
2000–2001	Vendée Globe	2nd overall	solo nonstop round-the-world race starting and ending in Les Sables d'Olonne, France	*Kingfisher*	Ellen MacArthu
2001	Challenge Mondial Assistance	1st overall	Cherbourg, France, to Tarragona, Spain	*Foncia-Kingfisher* (trimaran)	Ellen MacArthu Alain Gautier, and crew
2001	EDS Atlantic Challenge	1st overall	5-leg race from St.-Malo, France, including two transatlantics	*Kingfisher*	Ellen MacArthu Nick Moloney, and crew
2001	Transat Jacques Vabre	2nd in class	Le Havre, France, to Bahia, Brazil	*Foncia-Kingfisher* (trimaran)	Ellen MacArthu and Alain Gauti(
2002	Route du Rhum	1st in class	St.-Malo, France, to Guadeloupe	*Kingfisher* (monohull)	Ellen MacArthu

Offshore Challenges

It DOESN'T HAVE TO STOP HERE. . . . When Ellen and her team are out racing, her company Offshore Challenges—in collaboration with her title sponsors, European Retailer Kingfisher PLC—transmit her daily logs to thousands of people by e-mail.

If you would like to receive these e-mails from Ellen, please sign up at www.kingfisherchallenges.com or e-mail to updates@kingfisherchallenges.com with your request. Include your name, full e-mail address, country, and frequency required.

You can request updates daily, weekly, or just when there is major news.

You can also receive a short text message update—daily during a race, weekly during a race, or just when there is a major newsflash. E-mail smsupdates@kingfisherchallenges.com with your name, mobile number including country code, and frequency required.

Offshore Challenges
Whitegates
Arctic Road
Cowes PO31 7PG
Isle of Wight
United Kingdom
www.offshorechallenges.com

NAUTICAL TERMS

abeam. Perpendicular to the side of the boat.

bilge. The part of the hull that's below the waterline. It collects any water that has entered the boat.

block. A pulley.

boom. The spar that extends backwards from the mast to which the foot of the mainsail is attached.

bow. The front of the boat.

bowsprit. A spar that extends forward from the bow.

broach. A potentially dangerous situation when the boat spins out of control and lies on its side across the waves and wind.

buoy. A float that acts as a navigational aid.

cabin. Living area below deck level.

cans. Buoys.

catamaran. A twin-hulled boat.

cockpit. The area of the boat where the steering is done. Most of the control of the boat originates here.

code 5. A cross between a spinnaker and a gennaker. A furling sail, thus safer to drop.

cuddy. The small roof-like shelter over the cockpit.

daggerboard. A retractable fin that extends vertically downward from the hull to prevent leeward drift when upwind.

deck spreader. A massive boom-like spreader which can hold the rigging far enough from the mast to allow the resultant airfoil-shaped mast to twist.

Force 1, Force 2, . . . Force 12. Levels of wind speed correlated with wave heights and other conditions as defined by the Beaufort Wind Scale.

forestay. A metal rod supporting the mast from the bow. *Kingfisher* had three.

furl. To roll up a sail around its stay, rather like a window shade that's vertical rather than horizontal.

gennaker. A large sail that is a cross between a spinnaker and a genoa.

genoa. A large jib sail that sets on a stay in front of the mast but extends aft of the mast.

gunwale. The upper edge of the boat's side at deck level.

gybe. To change direction so that the stern passes through the direction of the wind.

halyard. A rope used for raising and lowering sails.

hank. Metal clips used for attaching a sail to a stay. To *hank* is to make fast.

heel. The leaning of the boat away from horizontal because of the action of the wind.

jib. A triangular sail in front of the mast.

jumar. An ascending device that grips a rope so it can be climbed.

jury rig. A temporary, improvised repair to a broken rig.

keel. A vertical fin that extends downward from the bottom of the boat. Ballast (weight) in the keel helps keep the boat upright.

kite. See *spinnaker.*

knot. One nautical mile per hour.

leech. The trailing edge of a sail.

leeward. Downwind.

line. A rope.

luff. The leading edge of a sail.

mainsail. A large triangular sail between the mast and the boom.

mainsheet. The rope used to control the mainsail.

pad eye. A U-shaped bolt attached through the deck as a strong fixing point.

pontoon. A flat-bottomed float.

port. The left side of the boat when facing the bow.

pulpit. The metal guard rail at the bow of the boat.

pushpit. The metal guard rail around the stern of the boat.

reach. A point of sail with the wind perpendicular to the side of the boat.

reef. Reducing the area of the sail in high winds by partially lowering it. Also, the reduction itself.

RIB. A rigid inflatable boat. A powerboat with a rigid hull and inflatable tubes around the top edges.

rig. The arrangement of the mast, shrouds, and sails.

RNLI. Royal National Lifeboat Institution.

rudder. A vertical steering fin at the stern of the boat.

runner. The running or shifting inner forestays.

RWYC. Royal Western Yacht Club.

scat. C-band scatterometer; a reading taken by satellite of the water's surface conditions.

sheet. A line (rope) used to control a sail.

shrouds. Wires, rods, or man-made fibres supporting the mast.

sole. The floor of the boat.

solent. The intermediate jib sail, between the staysail and the genoa.

spinnaker. A very large, light balloon-like sail used when sailing downwind. Sometimes referred to as a *kite*.

spreader. A long horizontal fitting holding the shrouds away from the mast and creating a framework of strength.

stanchion. A post around the edge of the deck that supports the guard wires (fore and aft deck lines intended to keep people from falling overboard).

starboard. The right side of the boat when facing the bow.

staysail. A triangular sail similar to, but smaller than, the jib.

stern. The rear of the boat.

storm jib. A very small, strong sail used in rough conditions.

swing keel. A hydraulic- or pulley-controlled keel which swings from side to side to stabilize the boat.

tack. The direction the boat is sailing in relation to the wind; or, to change the direction of the boat so the bow passes through the direction of the wind.

tiller. An arm attached to the rudder and used for steering the boat.

trampolene. Netting hung between the hulls of catamarans or trimarans.

transom. The flat part of the hull at the stern of the boat.

trim. To adjust the sails in relation to the wind.

trimaran. A three-hulled boat.

trinquete. A staysail.

windward. Upwind.

ACKNOWLEDGMENTS

FIRST OF ALL, to all those people I have not included in this list, a massive *thank you*. This was a difficult task!

Mum and Dad for never trying to stop me from doing what I had burning in my heart. Lewis for inventing cool things, and Fergus for being patient with me in your youth! Mac for your happiness and never-ending tail-wagging—wish I could see you more often! Auntie Thea for introducing me to the water, and for sharing so many thoughts and ideas. The rest of the family for providing such wonderful support, and putting up with me. Sarah and Ben for being such fantastic and understanding friends. Everyone else at school who became friends during those years. Karl Stanley for making me just grit my teeth and get on with things. John Manning for donating so much of your time to teaching young people sailing. The girl who befriended me on the dinghy course at Rutland, thank you! Malcolm Stanton for commenting about my writing to Mum and Dad when I was sixteen. Simon Ashton for putting up with, and caring for, an over-enthusiastic seventeen-year-old. Mr. Law for giving up your time to take us sailing on Friday evenings. Simon Reeve for being such a great friend and giving me a weekend outlet for my energy—and being so generous with your pork pie! David for giving so much, and Maureen for providing Tunnock's and moral support, and of course for thinking to enter me for that eye-opening competition. Robert Nickerson—what can I say, Robert? Thanks for giving me the helm! Joe Sempik for taking me sailing on *Knippa*, buying me beers, and talking boats. John Duckett for bringing friendship and food to my life at the nautical school! Darren, Mick, Pete, Mike, and all at Hull Marina for taking such an interest. Dave Anderson for your field, Dave's mate who towed *Iduna* over the bridge. The Infamous Steve and Shamus for your amusing stories and generosity. Alan Brooks for being as far from the ogre examiner as you can imagine! The *Yachting* journalists who voted for me back in 1995 for the YSOY Award. Karl Kanti for your stainless-steel work. Don Hayes for believing in me, then letting me spread my wings. Graham Percy for being the driving force behind my first press dossier. Brian Pilcher—what more can I say but thank you for being simply Brian. Keith, Nigel, and all at Musto for your continuing support, and for keeping me dry! James Flynn and Navico for taking the helm for such a large proportion of the trip! John Hurry and Yamaha—without you, I think I'd still be sailing around Britain! Howard Anguish and Hull Marina for allowing me to sanely prepare *Iduna*. Cosalt for supplying those items that I hoped I would not be using! Paul Mills and all at Marinecall for giving me a 24-hour weather service to tap into. John Goode and James Stevens for giving me the chance to prove myself. Tony, his dog, and everyone from Scarborough—great pie and peas! The crew of *Royalist*, Paul, JB, Howy, Dave, JP, and Joe, for their acceptance of me and non-stop laughter! Mr. S. Skene, St. Abbs, for the *Olsen's Fisherman's Nautical Almanack* and advice. Harry the harbourmaster from Montrose for all your help and the tea-shed key! Hamish McDonald and family for your words and the most incredible welcome. Ross Buchan and his friends for making me so welcome in Whitehills. (Thanks for the shackles, and hope you got your placement and your engineering is going well!) The harbourmaster at Whitehills for those five fantastically fresh haddock! Keith, Ben, and the team from RAF Lossiemouth for a great night out, and my first-ever official flypast—awesome! Sebastian Naaslund for being another crazy person with different ideas, and for teaching me that other languages are not impossible to learn. Barry Mercer and the crew of *Sakhr-El-Bahr*—who'd have thought it, Kentallen Bay! John Fitzgerald for letting me use your mooring and running me across to Oban so early—hope you've managed to get your Folkboat finished! Bernard on *Dulas Dragon* for buying *Iduna*'s stove and then supplying a meal on it! The fantastic company I had in Loch Feochan, and our night out to the pub. *Fulmoral* and her crew for sharing stories in the most beautiful anchorage. The family in Ardrishaig for their cruising guides, tea, and oatcakes. Frank McAllum and partner for a short break from a stormbound journey. Gordon Azzur and his friends for having a laugh and showing me round *Excalibur*. Roddie Leech for his active welcome in Girvan—escorted by bicycle! The crew of *Dream Twister*, Timmy, Jeremy, Mum and Dad, and little sister—thanks for the help and the late-night but very welcome Portishead curry! *Dream Twister*, *Kittiwake*,

Camelina (thanks for the flag), *Scatha*, and *Balandra* all for collecting £22 in that brown envelope marked "BEST OF LUCK WITH THE REMAINDER OF YOUR VOYAGE!" The crew of *Morning Roll* for inviting me on board and introducing me to squirty custard! Gemma and the crew from *Lady of Penpole* for inviting me out. Iain Rennie for a great night of conversation—hope you're still designing bike bits! Jeremy from the island opposite Croabh Haven—your lifestyle still inspires me now. The harbourmaster in Peel for the tyres, and the welcoming lot from the yacht club! Also the Girvan harbourmaster. Marc Lawler for a great interview with a great photo—I still have the clipping! Dave Morton and crew for the bacon and eggs that morning! Derek and Carol Jones for their company and the most wonderful photo I have of *Iduna* (it's in the book!). Bill McGill in the harbour office in Pwllheli for advice on heading down the coast. Sion Edwards from Aberystwyth, thanks for all your help and for keeping in contact. The crews of *Hi-Jinks*, *Mac-y-Sol*, *Fly*, *Fidget*, *Sea Horse*, the RNLI inshore lifeboat, and *The Squib*, which all sailed out of Fishguard to come to welcome us in! John and Margaret Richards for giving me the best night's sleep ever, making me feel completely at home, and introducing me to so many fantastic people like Emlyn! Paul Camen and family for the cider and mackerel, and the lifeboat crew from Fishguard for an insight into chart plotters, a tour of the engine room, and a quick spin! The Sea Cadets for showing me around their base and taking me on board TS *Appelby*. Richard Davies for my first trip to Ireland and a new experience travelling on the bridge of a "sea cat" (wonder if that inflatable crocodile is still out there!). Ian Tite for the very early morning rescue, and the subsequent bed! Marcus from *Shebeen* for so many stories, and baking that wonderful loaf of bread! The crew of the boat I was alongside in Milford Lock—I couldn't find your letters! The lift in Newlyn to the petrol station—it was a long way, I'd have been in a fix! John Lewis from the RWYC for making me feel so welcome in the club during the Round Britain and for hosting so many fantastic short-handed races! Sam Brewster for showing me round *Heath Insured II*, and checking *Iduna* out! The crew of the *Corribee Rubicon* for the race out of Plymouth Harbour! Col Brooks and all at ICC for a berth alongside *Egremont* with such great atmosphere! Carol Newman and her father from *Skycatcher* for coming over to say "hi." Jonathan and Jennifer Blain for their meals and company. Chris and Shirley from the SCOD *Aderyn*—shame we didn't meet up again in Poole. Steve Belasco for letting me go to work on your furling system, and the photos! Ruth Macai and family from Portland, thanks for having me to dinner! Norman Meech for sharing his passion and building such a beautiful boat in Arish Mell. John

Bolter for the free berth, the chat, and that fantastic bacon sarnie! The BMIF and everyone from the organizers' office at the boat shows—you made me feel so welcome, both then and now; I shall never forget my first official show! MDL—free berthing in Ocean Village. You made it possible for us to stay for the show. Everyone at the Southampton Boat Show who helped us out in any way at all! Merfyn Owen for sharing everything, and for encouraging me to the ends of the earth. Jock Smith and crew for a wonderful meal out and keeping in touch ever since. (Who knows, maybe pigeons will come back in as a form of communication!) Adam Allan and the Sea Cadets for a fantastic week's sailing from Gosport. VTS *Humber*—your voices were so fantastic to hear after four and a half months! Charles Boot for bringing Mum, Dad, and family out to see me in at the end of the trip. Any port who gave us free berthing—financially, it would have been impossible without you all. I just hope there will be an occasion in the future to come back and visit! Finally, all those who helped me out on the way around Britain, I am sure I have missed so many of you, but that doesn't mean that your help, kindness and friendship did not make all the difference to that adventure.

James Grazebrook and Halyard Marine for your support at the 1996 London Boat Show. The guys from ISIS mouldings who took me under their wing in London that year! The man from the Citroën garage who let me change the brake pipe. Dick Saint, Kay, and the boys at HYS—especially Jim, who went out of his way to help! Led Pritchard—you were one of the few people in Hamble who gave me confidence. The guy from Hamble who talked to me in the pub. Trog, for that fantastic sail from Brighton to the Solent, and for being so funny! Nick Butt for being my crew for that delivery to Guernsey and for chatting in Hamble. Darren Wills for your help on *Elan Sifo*. Alex and Darren for a mad Irish Sea trip! Wolfgang Quix. Alan Wynne-Thomas for having the guts to take me on, and for sharing so many of your Vendée experiences. You gave me so much confidence in those months. Bob and Carole for going out there and doing it, and housing us after the 1 Star. Will from Portway for taking out Mum and Dad. Mike Golding for commissioning me to do that painting. Vittorio and the boys for inviting me along, becoming such great friends, and showing me the North Atlantic and her icebergs for the first time. Giovanni Soldini, Andrea Tarlarini, and Enrico for a fantastic trip to Italy on the 50. The crew of the *Matthew*, in particular James, Luke, Richard, David, and John the Bowman—for tales and malt loaf!

Ashley for the hours spent discussing projects; for your meals and floors in several countries; and of course, more than all those, for your friendship.

Martin and Steve from Bowman Yachts for being such great friends in a tough year. Len the dog and his owners! Ed Gorman for my first-ever national newspaper interview. Nigel Irens for your deep love of the sea, inspiring boats, and for being such a solid and wonderful person. Nigel from Hampshire Trailers for bringing a little sanity to a crazy situation! Mark Orr for lending part of that crucial money which allowed me to buy *Le Poisson*. The Silk Cut Boys for your friendship and kindness. Dick and Steve at Airwaves, especially for burning the midnight oil on our sponsorship video, and taking Reima and me off in Martinique just to see a little of the island. Thierry Fangent at AMCO, the Guru of Minis, the master of roll-ups, teacher of French, and all our suppliers and friends in La Trinité sur Mer (not forgetting Louise, the dog). Thierry Martinez for sharing your house with us for so long, the perfect place to be! Nic LeMarchand, our first, and dedicated, preparateur. Richard Vass of Burland Solutions, you made a massive difference. Charles Dunstone and Carphone Warehouse, our first major sponsors for the Mini Transat in 1997. But not forgetting the many other players in that project. Royal Solent Yacht Club, IOW Council. G. Askew, Musto, SP Systems, UKSA, Simpson Lawrence, Mel Sharp, Nautix, Autohelm, Regis Electronics, Suunto, Ian Terry Engineering, Spinlock, Andrew Bishop, Marlow Ropes, Whale, Westaway Sails, Relling Sails, Tony Bertram and Bainbridge, Riggarna, Tim Dean and Formula Spars, Ocean Safety, Ratsey and Lapthorn, Navico, DG Wroath, Simon and Reb Rogers, Johnny Caulcutt, Vix, my mum and dad, Mark's mum and dad. Hugh and Financial Dynamics for making the difference to Mark's chances. The Foundation for Sports and the Arts for sending the letter of support that transformed 1997! It couldn't have arrived at a better time. The Honda salesman who gave me a lift to Portsmouth. Woolfie for coming over to fit that pilot for free just days before the start. David Gown, Jim Doxey, and Peter Halliwell for their help in the run-up to the Mini. Peter Bentley for getting stuck in helping me to leave with "some" clothes! And to the organizers and skippers in the Mini Transat for the most passionate race with the closest-knit community among skippers I have known.

Our 1998 Route du Rhum campaign was supported by a number of suppliers and individuals. Without them, that project could never have succeeded. There are many personal supporters, friends, and workers who make up the team to get a single-handed racer to a start and finish line.

Skandia Life, Peter Nicholson, John Caulcutt for inspiring everyone else to contribute as well; Royal Southampton Yacht Club (for a bed in their launch!), Royal Southern Yacht Club, Hardwick Press and Publicity, Acorn

Maintenance Systems, PC Maritime, A. McIrvine, A. Chilvers, N. Hodkin, D. Moore, S. Hobday, R. Parker, Jock Wishart, S. Gordon—you all made the impossible seem possible.

Christian Stimson, our first office space, and one of the Rhum voluntary preparateurs. Nick our first student employee, and Marine our first real one! Hugh Morrison for your boundless energy and unwavering enthusiasm for the project; we would not be here without you, Hugh. Liam and Chris, your energy, jokes, and patience got us to the Rhum in 1998. Bitzy and Cannon Ball for being the kindest and friendliest faces in a foreign port. Herb for your life-saving weather information as we were crossing the Atlantic. Stuart and Angela in Plymouth for looking after us, feeding us, and entertaining us! (Not forgetting that incredible home-made ketchup and Paddy's visits.)

Mike Hingston, the master of all-night working, and the real driver of *Kingfisher*'s sponsorship in the early days, supported by Jo Bootle, dedication beyond the call of duty! Geoff, for putting your faith in us, against the odds as others would see it. Jean, George, Lydia, Andrew, Gwen, Jerry, Graham, Patrick, Arvind, and everyone at Kingfisher PLC since 1998, and in the operating companies around the globe, who have supported me for every single mile. It's been a pleasure working with you all!

In addition to our primary sponsor Kingfisher, and our supporting sponsor Big Blue (Colin Campbell from National Boat Shows), we were actively supported by: TMI Atlantic Foundation, Marlow Ropes, Airx by Bainbridge International, Osen Sails of Plymouth, Botalo Shoes, McMurdo Ocean Sentry (radar target enhancer), Pains Wessex Safety Systems, Nautix Antifouling, Anne Whitlock, PR Works, David Zorab, Spinlock, TT Designs, North Sails (UK), Northern Star Insurance, Aura Fabric Engineering. And many others who gave their time and energy to support us, including the committed shore crew of Liam, Jude, Sam, Emma, Jim, Nic, Christian, Marine, Tanguy De Lamotte, Capey, and Andy from Goss Challenges, who prepared the 50 in record time, and many voluntarily! James Boyd for being dedicated to his sport. And Ed Gorman again—that front page was timed perfectly! And all the other journalists from France, the UK, and all over the world—without you no one would ever have heard of these incredible races. Tony Banks for being such an avid supporter, and momentarily taking your mind off football!

The Kingfisher Vendée preparation and shore team of Martin, Amanda, Pipo, Marie (Pilou & Mathilde), Mikey, Tanya (Matthew), Marc, and Tanguy. A dedicated team, and a very special and emotional time. Wonderful job, guys. You were the best! The Kingfisher Design Team of Merv and Allen at

Owen Clarke Design, Rob and Nick at Humphrey's Design, Giovanni Belgrano, and Alain Gautier. For designing the most beautiful open 60 ever. You brought her alive from that first sketch. Thank you. The BMF for your support and your counterparts in France and New Zealand. Yves Parlier, an important teacher for me, and his great team at Aquitaine Innovations of Stephane, Michel, Romaric, Agathe, and Co. Mick and Keep Safe Self Storage for staying late to let me in on my whirlwind missions! Paul Brotherton for being so patient in teaching me everything I needed to keep dry! Gael le' Cleach for a patient introduction to a different type of sailing. The Bourgnon brothers for an unforgettable Fastnet experience, Pierre Lasnier and Jean-Yves Bernot for teaching me so much about the weather of the world. Audrey, James, Mary, Dana, and the team back at home in Cowes, thank you for everything. Bruce Guthrie from 3M New Zealand—you went completely out of your way to help! Steve Marten, Allan, and the great team of guys at Marten Yachts, Auckland, NZ. Moët Chandon, Bruno Trouble, Marcus, Maria Ryan, and the team at the Louis Vuitton Cup Media Centre, Auckland—it was a dream come true to even launch *Kingfisher*. Lady Pippa Blake, your blessing of the boat and even me has brought immense luck. Sir Peter Blake, tragically lost in 2001, the best professional sailor the world has ever seen and a great leader who was an inspiration on and off the water both personally and for the team at Offshore Challenges. Pat Ashworth for "true grit," Darren from York for your great news, Dennis Skillicorne for those fantastic minidisks of your favourite radio programmes! The kids from À Chacun Son Cap, Sargent and the hospitals in France I visited, your smiles, gifts, and incredible energy—if anyone has been a hero to me, it is you guys!

As well as a great team of suppliers, our Partners for the Vendée Globe project: Kim and the team at BT (communication services)—it seems a long time since we first met back in 1995! W. S. Atkins (R&D using Computational Fluid Dynamics), Raymarine (autopilot technology and radar), Bainbridge (Titan winch handles, Tylaska snaps, Sailmaking kits, and all canvas work material), B&G performance instrument system, Volvo Cars UK, Red Funnel, EP Barrus (Yanmar engine), Marlow Ropes, Musto (technical clothing), Future Fibres, Stratos, Wolfson Unit, Oceanair Marine (blinds), Pains Wessex McMurdo (marine safety equipment), Nautix antifoul, Harken winches, Bruno and his team at North Sails France, and Bill at 3DL—"born to survive," Ocean Yacht Systems (standing rigging), Bananas and Southern Spars, Suunto wrist top computers, TBS, Will and T&G, Facnor, Titan Australia Pty, TMI, UKSA, Team McLube, Richard Butcher, Travelwell, Debbie@Global Travel, Peters & May, Diverse, and TOC Scotland.

The thousands of people who came to Les Sables d'Olonne, who made the atmosphere what it was and showed such incredible warmth towards the team and myself. Philippe Hutcheon for the work Castorama did with the Castokids Programme. Steve, Llion, Hugh, Tim, Gwynfor, and the team at BBC Wales Extreme Lives. Howard and Pete for being such skilled RIB drivers with a sense of humour! The team on shore during the Vendée that helped us share the story with millions, including Andrew, Richard, Erik, Lou and the team at APP, Rick, Jacques, Thierry M, Green Design, Gwenola, Marie, Ian, Windreport, Claudio Stampi thanks for sweeter dreams, Jean, Rachel and the team in London. Mark, Helen, Josie, Dana, Rosie, and the team in the office in Cowes, you guys lived and breathed that race with me—quite literally. There was not a moment in any day when I did not feel you were with me. It was "your" race and your success—awesome! Björk for taking on a mission cleaning after us lot! Sue, Wendy and Debs, Matt, Munners, Rhidian, Bob, Nobby, Max and the others, for your contributions in all sorts of diverse areas—awesome job, thank you. Philippe Jeantot and his team in Les Sables and Paris—thank you for such a great race. Dana's parents for building shelves and housing so much of our equipment! Every skipper who took part in the Vendée Globe, for your spirit, friendship and passion. Thanks also to the previous skippers of the Vendée, those who returned and, tragically, those who did not but shall never be forgotten. The 52,500 people who have e-mailed during the Vendée and other races, I only wish I could reply personally to you all! You have always kept me going—don't stop! Ian for your unwavering support. Paul Peggs, Brian Meerloo, and Rice and Cole's Yard—for taking the time to bring *Iduna* back to life for my homecoming. Mrs. Gration for being such a good friend to Nan and for your dishcloths and news!

Alain Gautier in particular for understanding and helping me through 2001. Loick, Ewan, Nico, Florent, P-Peche, Kiki, Xavier, Kinou, Mammouth, Frank, and Mick for some of the best times and best sailing ever! *Ça part de là les gars!!* Nick Moloney for being such a great friend, sharing everything with us and being such a motivated guy. Hendo, Adrienne, Brian, Antony, and Mark for being the best guys ever to sail with anywhere—that EDS was a very, very special race. Ayy! Daphne, Steve, Jonny the Wylester, Adrian, Breeny, Nobbers, and Little Richard for your care and time spent looking after, preparing, sailing, and improving "The Fish." Every single person who voted for me in the Sports Personality of the Year Award! Mark, Helen, Josie, Jonny, Kate, Lou, Mike, Charles, Kristie, Nick, Little Richard, Ant and Hendo. Wow, looking forward to the next one with you all! Natasha

Fairweather at A.P. Watt, Clare Pollock at Penguin, and Helen Campbell in Mallaig for being so patient. Rowland—well, what can I say! This is your book, too—I cannot speak highly enough of your patience and dedication. Thank you for making this experience not just bearable but enjoyable. Once again the team at Kingfisher PLC, and Offshore Challenges Ltd. For the experiences behind us—and those before us. Thank you from the bottom of my heart. To *Kingfisher* for looking after me for every moment of those ninety-four days. I could not imagine ever having that same relationship with another boat. We grew up together. Finally, Mark Turner. There are few on this list whose names you do not know, Mark; we really have shared so much. The future is always beckoning. . . . Let's never let that go . . .